BEN WATSON

C# 4.0

HOW-TO

SAMS | 800 East 96th Street, Indianapolis, Indiana 46240 USA

C# 4.0 How-To

ISBN-13: 978-0-672-33063-6
ISBN-10: 0-672-33063-6

Library of Congress Cataloging-in-Publication Data

Watson, Ben, 1980–
C# 4.0 how-to / Ben Watson.
p. cm.
Includes index.
ISBN 978-0-672-33063-6 (pbk. : alk. paper) 1. C# (Computer program language) I. Title.
QA76.73.C154W38 2010
005.13'3—dc22
2010002735

Printed in the United States of America

First Printing March 2010

Trademarks

Warning and Disclaimer

Bulk Sales

Sams Publishing offers excellent discounts on this book when ordered in quantity for bulk purchases or special sales. For more information, please contact

U.S. Corporate and Government Sales
1-800-382-3419
corpsales@pearsontechgroup.com

For sales outside of the U.S., please contact

International Sales
international@pearson.com

Editor-in-Chief
Karen Gettman

Executive Editor
Neil Rowe

Acquisitions Editor
Brook Farling

Development Editor
Mark Renfrow

Managing Editor
Kristy Hart

Project Editor
Lori Lyons

Copy Editor
Bart Reed

Indexer
Brad Herriman

Proofreader
Sheri Cain

Technical Editor
Mark Strawmyer

Publishing Coordinator
Cindy Teeters

Designer
Gary Adair

Compositor
Nonie Ratcliff

Contents at a Glance

Table of Contents

Part III: User Interaction

About the Author

Ben Watson has been developing in .Net since its release. Before joining Microsoft, he worked as a lead developer for satellite imaging firm GeoEye, where he developed nautical communication systems in .Net. More recently, he has been working on the Query Pipeline team for Bing, where he helps design and implement massively scalable distributed systems and other internals of the search engine.

Dedication

To my parents, Michael and Dianna Watson, who, on at least two occasions during my teenage years, humored me when I wrote up a proposal for them to buy me C++ compiler software, and who did everything possible to foster my talents and interests. I would not be a success without their example, love, and guidance.

To my wonderful wife, Leticia, who showed great patience and love as I took on this new and daunting project amidst all the other changes in our life.

Acknowledgments

I am very grateful to the people who have gone out of their way to help with this book.

To Brook Farling, the editor who found me and gave me this opportunity, for all his coordinating work, patience, and drive to get the product done.

To Mark Strawmyer, technical editor, who went through a lot of code and text to ensure the quality of what is contained in here.

To the publishing team at Sams: Mark Renfrow, Lori Lyons, Bart Reed, Nonie Ratcliff, Sheri Cain.

We Want to Hear from You!

As the reader of this book, *you* are our most important critic and commentator. We value your opinion and want to know what we're doing right, what we could do better, what areas you'd like to see us publish in, and any other words of wisdom you're willing to pass our way.

You can email or write me directly to let me know what you did or didn't like about this book—as well as what we can do to make our books stronger.

Please note that I cannot help you with technical problems related to the topic of this book, and that due to the high volume of mail I receive, I might not be able to reply to every message.

When you write, please be sure to include this book's title and author as well as your name and phone or email address. I will carefully review your comments and share them with the author and editors who worked on the book.

Email: feedback@samspublishing.com

Mail: Neil Rowe
Executive Editor
Sams Publishing
800 East 96th Street
Indianapolis, IN 46240 USA

Reader Services

Visit our website and register this book at informit.com/register for convenient access to any updates, downloads, or errata that might be available for this book.

INTRODUCTION

Overview of *C# 4.0 How-To*

This book is very different from a typical "bible" approach to a topic. By structuring the book as a "how-to," it presents the material by scenario in steps that are easily followed. Throughout, I have tried to keep the explanatory text to the minimum necessary and keep the focus on the code itself. Often, you will find comments embedded in the code to explain non-obvious bits.

This book is not strictly a language/library book. Besides covering the language features themselves, it dives into practical examples of application patterns, useful algorithms, and handy tips that are applicable in many situations.

Developers, both beginner and advanced, will find hundreds of useful topics in this book. Whether it's a section on lesser-known C# operators, how to sort strings that contain numbers in them, or how to implement Undo, this book contains recipes that are useful in a wide variety of situations, regardless of skill level.

In short, this is the book I wish I had on my desk when I was first learning programming and C# as well as now, whenever I need a quick reference or reminder about how to do something.

How-To Benefit from This Book

We designed this book to be easy to read from cover to cover. The goal is to gain a full understanding of C# 4.0. The subject matter is divided into four parts with easy-to-navigate and easy-to-use chapters.

Part I, "C# Fundamentals," covers the common C# functionality that you will use in every type of programming. While it may seem basic, there are a lot of tips to help you get the most of these fundamental topics.

- Chapter 1, "Type Fundamentals"
- Chapter 2, "Creating Versatile Types"
- Chapter 3, "General Coding"
- Chapter 4, "Exceptions"
- Chapter 5, "Numbers"

- Chapter 6, "Enumerations"
- Chapter 7, "Strings"
- Chapter 8, "Regular Expressions"
- Chapter 9, "Generics"

Part II, "Handling Data," discusses how to store and manipulate data, including Internet-based data.

- Chapter 10, "Collections"
- Chapter 11, "Files and Serialization"
- Chapter 12, "Networking and the Web"
- Chapter 13, "Databases"
- Chapter 14, "XML"

Part III "User Interaction," covers the most popular user interface paradigms in .Net, whether you work on the desktop, the Web, or both.

- Chapter 15, "Delegates, Events, and Anonymous Methods"
- Chapter 16, "Windows Forms"
- Chapter 17, "Graphics with Windows Forms and GDI+"
- Chapter 18, "WPF"
- Chapter 19, "ASP.NET"
- Chapter 20, "Silverlight"

Part IV, "Advanced C#," has the advanced stuff to really take your applications to the next level in terms of performance, design patterns, useful algorithms, and more.

- Chapter 21, "LINQ"
- Chapter 22, "Memory Management"
- Chapter 23, "Threads, Asynchronous, and Parallel Programming"
- Chapter 24, "Reflection and Creating Plugins"
- Chapter 25, "Application Patterns and Tips"
- Chapter 26, "Interacting with the OS and Hardware"
- Chapter 27, "Fun Stuff and Loose Ends"
- Appendix A, "Essential Tools"

All of the code was developed using prerelease versions of Visual Studio 2010, but you can use earlier versions in many cases, especially for code that does not require .NET 4. If you do not have Visual Studio, you can download the Express edition from www.microsoft.com/express/default.aspx. This version will enable you to build nearly all the code samples in this book.

You can access the code samples used in this book by registering on the book's website at **informit.com/register**. Go to this URL, sign in, and enter the ISBN to register (free site registration required). After you register, look on your Account page, under Registered Products, for a link to Access Bonus Content.

How-To Continue Expanding Your Knowledge

No book can completely cover C#, the .NET Framework, or probably even hope to cover a small topic within that world. And if there were, you probably couldn't lift it, let alone read it in your lifetime.

Once you've mastered the essentials, there are plenty of resources to get your questions answered and dive deeply into .NET.

Thankfully, the MSDN documentation for .NET (located at http://msdn.microsoft.com/en-us/library/aa139615.aspx) is top-notch. Most topics have code samples and an explanation use. An added bonus is the ability at the bottom of every topic for anyone to add useful content. There are many good tips found here from other .NET developers.

The .NET Development forums (http://social.msdn.microsoft.com/Forums/en-US/category/netdevelopment) are an excellent place to get your questions answered by the experts, who, in many cases, were involved in the development and testing of .NET.

I have also found StackOverflow.com a good place to get questions answered.

The best advice I can give on how to continue expanding your knowledge is to just write software. Keep at it, think of new projects, use new technologies, go beyond your abilities. This and other books are very useful, to a point. After that, you just need to dive in and start coding, using the book as a faithful reference when you don't know how to approach a topic.

Happy coding!

PART I

C# Fundamentals

IN THIS PART

CHAPTER 1

Type Fundamentals

IN THIS CHAPTER

- Create a Class
- Define Fields, Properties, and Methods
- Define Static Members
- Add a Constructor
- Initialize Properties at Construction
- Use `const` and `readonly`
- Reuse Code in Multiple Constructors
- Derive from a Class
- Call a Base Class Constructor
- Override a Base Class's Method or Property
- Create an Interface
- Implement Interfaces
- Create a Struct
- Create an Anonymous Type
- Prevent Instantiation with an Abstract Base Class
- Interface or Abstract Base Class?

This chapter explains the basics of creating types in C#. If you are already familiar with C#, much of this chapter will be a review for you.

After we cover class members such as fields, properties, and methods, you'll learn about constructors, how to create and implement interfaces, and when to use structs.

The information in this chapter is basic, but vital. Like so many things, if you don't get the fundamentals right, nothing else will work out.

Create a Class

Scenario/Problem: You need to create a class declaration.

Solution: Let's begin by declaring a simple class that will hold 3D coordinate points.

```
//default namespaces to import, that Visual Studio includes in each file
using System;
using System.Collections.Generic;
using System.Linq;
using System.Text;

namespace ClassSample
{
    //public so that it's visible outside of assembly
    public class Vertex3d
    {
    }
}
```

The class we've defined is empty so far, but we'll fill it up throughout this chapter.

The class is defined as public, which means it is visible to every other type that references its assembly. C# defines a number of accessibility modifiers, as detailed in Table 1.1.

TABLE 1.1 **Accessibility Modifiers**

Accessibility	Applicable To	Description
Public	Types, members	Accessible to everybody, even outside the assembly
Private	Types, members	Accessible to code in the same type
Internal	Types, members	Accessible to code in the same assembly
Protected	Members	Accessible to code in the same type or derived type
Protected internal	Members	Accessible to code in the same assembly or a derived class in another assembly

If the class does not specify the accessibility, it defaults to `internal`.

Define Fields, Properties, and Methods

Scenario/Problem: You need to add fields, properties, and methods to a class definition.

Solution: Let's add some usefulness to the `Vertex3d` class.

```
public class Vertex3d
{
    //fields
    private double _x;
    private double _y;
    private double _z;
    //properties
    public double X
    {
        get { return _x; }
        set { _x = value; }
    }
    public double Y
    {
        get { return _y; }
        set { _y = value; }
    }
    public double Z
    {
        get { return _z; }
        set { _z = value; }
    }
    //method
    public void SetToOrigin()
    {
        X = Y = Z = 0.0;
    }
}
```

Some notes on the preceding code:

- The fields are all declared `private`, which is good practice in general.
- The properties are declared `public`, but could also be `private`, `protected`, or `protected internal`, as desired.

- Properties can have `get`, `set`, or both.
- In properties, `value` is the implied argument (that is, in the code).

In the following example, `13.0` would be passed to `X` in the `value` argument:

```
Vertex3d v = new Vertex3d();
v.X = 13.0;
```

Use Auto-Implemented Properties

You will often see the following pattern:

```
class MyClass
{
    private int _field = 0;
    public int Field { get { return _field; } set { _field = value; } }
}
```

C# has a shorthand syntax for this:

```
class MyClass
{
    public int Field {get; set;}

    //must initialize value in constructor now
    public MyClass()
    {
        this.Field = 0;
    }
}
```

NOTE You cannot have an auto-implemented property with only a `get` (if there's no backing field, how would you set it?), but you can have a private set:

```
public int Field { get ; private set; }
```

Define Static Members

Scenario/Problem: You need to define data or methods that apply to the type, not individual instances. They are also often used for methods that operate on multiple instances of the type.

Solution: Add the modifying keyword `static`, as in the following method for adding two `Vertex3d` objects:

```
public class Vertex3d
{
    ...
    public static Vertex3d Add(Vertex3d a, Vertex3d b)
    {
        Vertex3d result = new Vertex3d();
        result.X = a.X + b.X;
        result.Y = a.Y + b.Y;
        result.Z = a.Z + b.Z;
        return result;
    }
}
```

The static method is called like in this example:

```
Vertex3d a = new Vertex3d(0,0,1);
Vertex3d b = new Vertex3d(1,0,1);
Vertex3d sum = Vertex3d.Add(a, b);
```

Add a Constructor

> **Scenario/Problem:** You need to have automatic initialization of new objects of the class.

Solution: Define a special method, called a *constructor*, with the same name as the class, with no return type. A constructor runs when a type is created—it is never called directly.

Here are two constructors for the `Vertex3d` class—one taking arguments, the other performing some default initialization.

```
class Vertex3d
{
    public Vertex3d()
    {
        _x = _y = _z = 0.0;
    }

    public Vertex3d(double x, double y, double z)
    {
        this._x =x;
        this._y = y;
        this._z = z;
    }
}
```

NOTE Constructors do not need to be public. For example, you could make a protected constructor that is only accessible from derived classes. You could even make a private constructor that prevents instantiation (for utility classes) or is accessible only from other methods in the same class (static factory methods, perhaps).

Add a Static Constructor and Initialization

Scenario/Problem: The class has static data that needs to be initialized.

Solution: Static fields can be initialized in two ways. One way is with a static constructor, which is similar to a standard constructor, but with no accessibility modifier or arguments:

```
public class Vertex3d
{
    private static int _numInstances;
    static Vertex3d()
    {
        _numInstances = 0;
    }
    ...
}
```

However, because of performance reasons, it is preferable to initialize static fields inline whenever possible, as shown here:

```
public class Vertex3d
{
    private static int _numInstances = 0;
    ...
}
```

Initialize Properties at Construction

Scenario/Problem: You want to initialize class properties when the variable is created, even if the constructor does not provide the arguments to do so.

Solution: Use object initialization syntax, as in the following example:

```
class Person
{
    public int Id { get; set; }
    public string Name { get; set; }
    public string Address { get; set; }
}

...

Person p = new Person()
               { Id = 1, Name = "Ben", Address = "Redmond, WA" };
```

Use const and readonly

Scenario/Problem: You need to specify fields that cannot be changed at runtime.

Solution: Both const and readonly are used to define data that does not change, but there are important differences: const fields must be defined at declaration. Because of this and the fact that they cannot change value, it implies that they belong to the type as static fields. On the other hand, readonly fields can be set at declaration or in the constructor, but nowhere else.

```
public class Vertex3d
{
    private const string Name = "Vertex";
    private readonly int ver;

    public Vertex3d()
    {
        ver = Config.MyVersionNumber;//Ok
    }

    public void SomeFunction()
    {
        ver = 13;//Error!
    }
}
```

Reuse Code in Multiple Constructors

Scenario/Problem: You have multiple constructors, but they have a subset of functionality that is common among them. You want to avoid duplicating code. In C++ and some previous languages, you often had the case where a class with multiple constructors needed to call common initialization code. In these cases, you usually factored out the common code into a common function that each constructor called.

```
//C++ example
class MyCppClass
{
public:
    MyCppClass() { Init(); }
    MyCppClass(int arg) { Init(); }
private:
    void Init() { /* common init here*/ };

}
```

Solution: In C#, you are allowed to call other constructors within the same class using the `this` keyword, as shown next:

```
public class Vertex3d
{
    public Vertex3d(double x, double y, double z)
    {
        this._x = x;
        this._y = y;
        this._z = z;
    }

    public Vertex3d(System.Drawing.Point point)
        :this(point.X, point.Y, 0)
    {
    }
    ...
}
```

Derive from a Class

Scenario/Problem: You need to specialize a class by adding and/or overriding behavior.

Solution: Use inheritance to reuse the base class and add new functionality.

```
public class BaseClass
{
    private int _a;
    protected int _b;
    public int _c;
}

public class DerivedClass : BaseClass
{
    public DerivedClass()
    {
        _a = 1;//not allowed! private in BaseClass
        _b = 2;//ok
        _c = 3;//ok
    }
    public void DoSomething()
    {
        _c = _b = 99;
    }
}
```

Deriving from a class gives access to a base class's public and protected members, but not private members.

Call a Base Class Constructor

Scenario/Problem: You have a child class and want its constructor to call a specific base class constructor.

Solution: Similar to calling other constructors from the constructor of a class, you can call specific constructors of a base class. If you do not specify a constructor, the base class's default constructor is called. If the base class's default constructor requires arguments, you will be required to supply them.

```
public class BaseClass
{
    public BaseClass(int x, int y, int z)
    {    ...    }
}
```

```
public class DerivedClass : BaseClass
{
    public DerivedClass()
    : base(1, 2, 3)
    {

    }
}
```

Override a Base Class's Method or Property

Scenario/Problem: You want to override a base class's behavior in your child class.

Solution: The base class's method or property must be declared `virtual` and must be accessible from the derived class. The derived class will use the `override` keyword.

```
public class Base
{
    Int32 _x;
    public virtual Int32 MyProperty
    {
        get
        {
            return _x;
        }
    }

    public virtual void DoSomething()
    {
        _x = 13;
    }
}

public class Derived : Base
{
    public override Int32 MyProperty
    {
        get
        {
            return _x * 2;
```

```
        }
    }

    public override void DoSomething()
    {
        _x = 14;
    }
}
```

Base class references can refer to instances of the base class or any class derived from it. For example, the following will print "28," not "13."

```
Base d = new Derived();
d.DoSomething();
Console.WriteLine(d.MyProperty().ToString());
```

You can also call base class functions from a derived class via the `base` keyword.

```
public class Base
{
    public virtual void DoSomething()
    {
        Console.WriteLine("Base.DoSomething");
    }
}

public class Derived
{
    public virtual void DoSomething()
    {
        base.DoSomething();
        Console.WriteLine("Derived.DoSomething");
    }
}
```

Calling `Derived.DoSomething` will print out the following:

```
Base.DoSomething
Derived.DoSomething
```

Overriding Non-`virtual` Methods and Properties

> **Scenario/Problem:** The base class's functionality was not declared with `virtual`, but you want to override it anyway. There may be cases where you need to derive a class from a third-party library and you want to override one method, but it was not declared as `virtual` in the base class.

Solution: You can still override it, but with a caveat: The override method will only be called through a reference to the derived class. To do this, use the new keyword (in a different context than you're probably used to).

```
class Base
{
    public virtual void DoSomethingVirtual()
    {
        Console.WriteLine("Base.DoSomethingVirtual");
    }

    public void DoSomethingNonVirtual()
    {
        Console.WriteLine("Base.DoSomethingNonVirtual");
    }
}
class Derived : Base
{
    public override void DoSomethingVirtual()
    {
        Console.WriteLine("Derived.DoSomethingVirtual");
    }
    public new void DoSomethingNonVirtual()
    {
        Console.WriteLine("Derived.DoSomethingNonVirtual");
    }
}
class Program
{
    static void Main(string[] args)
    {
        Console.WriteLine("Derived via Base reference:");

        Base baseRef = new Derived();
        baseRef.DoSomethingVirtual();
        baseRef.DoSomethingNonVirtual();

        Console.WriteLine();
        Console.WriteLine("Derived via Derived reference:");

        Derived derivedRef = new Derived();
        derivedRef.DoSomethingVirtual();
        derivedRef.DoSomethingNonVirtual();
    }
}
```

Here is the output of this code:

```
Derived via Base reference:
Derived.DoSomethingVirtual
Base.DoSomethingNonVirtual

Derived via Derived reference:
Derived.DoSomethingVirtual
Derived.DoSomethingNonVirtual
```

Make sure you understand why the output is the way it is.

Create an Interface

Scenario/Problem: You need an abstract set of functionality, with no defined implementation, that can be applied to many types.

Solution: Here's a sample interface for some kind of playable object—perhaps an audio or video file, or even a generic stream. An interface does not specify what something is, but rather some behavior.

```
public interface IPlayable
{
    void Play();
    void Pause();
    void Stop();
    double CurrentTime { get; }
}
```

Note that interfaces can contain methods as well as properties. (They can also contain events, which we will cover in Chapter 15, "Delegates, Events, and Anonymous Methods.") You do not specify access with interfaces' members because, by definition, they are all public.

Implement Interfaces

Scenario/Problem: You need to implement an interface's functionality in your class.

Solution: To implement an interface, you need to declare each interface method and property in your class, mark them public, and provide implementations.

```
public class AudioFile : IPlayable
{
    private IntAudioStream _stream;
    ...
    public void Play()
    {
        //implementation details
        _stream.Play();
    }
    public void Pause()
    {
        _stream.Stop();
    }
    public void Stop()
    {
        _stream.Stop();
        _stream.Reset();
    }
}
```

NOTE Visual Studio can help you out here. When you add ": IPlayable" after the class name, it will show a Smart Tag over it. Clicking the Smart Tag will give you the option to generate empty implementations of the interface in the class.

Implement Multiple Interfaces

Scenario/Problem: A single class needs to implement multiple interfaces, possibly with conflicting methods.

Solution: A class can implement multiple interfaces, separated by commas:

```
public class AudioFile : IPlayable, IRecordable
{
...
}
```

However, you may run into instances where two (or more) interfaces define the same method. In our small example, suppose both `IPlayable` and `IRecordable` have a `Stop()` method defined. In this case, one interface must be made explicit.

```
public class AudioFile : IPlayable, IRecordable
{
    void Stop()
    {
```

```
        //IPlayable interface
    }

    void IRecordable.Stop()
    {
        //IRecordable interface
    }
}
```

Here is how to call these two methods:

```
AudioFile file = new AudioFile();
file.Stop();//calls the IPlayable version
((IRecordable)file).Stop();//calls the IRecordable version
```

Note that we arbitrarily decided that `IRecordable`'s `Stop()` method needed to be explicit—you could just have easily decided to make `IPlayable`'s `Stop()` method the explicit one.

Create a Struct

Scenario/Problem: You need a type with a small amount of data, without the overhead of a class.

Unlike in C++, where structs and classes are functionally identical, in C#, there are important and fundamental differences:

- Structs are value types as opposed to reference types, meaning that they exist on the stack. They have less memory overhead and are appropriate for small data structures. They also do not have to be declared with the `new` operator.
- Structs cannot be derived from. They are inherently sealed (see Chapter 2, "Creating Versatile Types").
- Structs may not have a parameterless constructor. This already exists implicitly and initializes all fields to zeros.
- All of a struct's fields must be initialized in every constructor.
- Structs are passed by value, just like any other value-type, in method calls. Beware of large structs.

Solution: Defining a struct is similar to a class:

```
public struct Point
{
    private Int32 _x;
    private Int32 _y;
```

```
    public Int32 X
    {
        get { return _x; }
        set { _x = value; }
    }
    public Int32 Y
    {
        get { return _y; }
        set { _y = value; }
    }

    public Point(int x, int y)
    {
        _x = x;
        _y = y;
    }

    public Point() {} //Not allowed!
    //Not allowed either! You're missing _y's init
    public Point(int x) { this._x = x; }
}
```

They can be used like so:

```
Point p;//allocates, but does not initialize
p.X = 13;//ok
p.Y = 14;

Point p2 = new Point();//initializes p2
int x = p2.X;//x will be zero
```

Create an Anonymous Type

Scenario/Problem: You want to define a one-off, temporary type that does not need a name.

Solution: The `var` keyword can be used to create anonymous types that contain properties you define inline.

```
class Program
{
    static void Main(string[] args)
    {
        var part = new { ID = 1, Name = "Part01", Weight = 2.5 };
```

```
        Console.WriteLine("var Part, Weight: {0}", part.Weight);
        Console.WriteLine("var Part, ToString(): {0}", part.ToString());
        Console.WriteLine("var Part, Type: {0}", part.GetType());
    }
}
```

This program produces the following output:

```
var Part, Weight: 2.5
var Part, ToString(): { ID = 1, Name = Part01, Weight = 2.5 }
var Part, Type:
➥ <>f__AnonymousType0`3[System.Int32,System.String,System.Double]
```

See Chapter 3, "General Coding," for more information on how to use the var keyword.

NOTE var might look like it's untyped, but don't be fooled. The compiler is generating a strongly typed object for you. Examine this code sample:

```
var type1 = new { ID = 1, Name = "A" };
var type1Same = new { ID = 2, Name = "B" };

var type2 = new { ID = 3, Name = "C", Age = 13 };

type1 = type1Same; //Ok
type1 = type2; //Not ok
```

For that last line, the compiler will give this error:

```
Cannot implicitly convert type 'AnonymousType#2' to
'AnonymousType#1'
```

Prevent Instantiation with an Abstract Base Class

Scenario/Problem: You want a base class with common functionality, but you don't want to allow anyone to instantiate the base class directly.

Solution: Mark your class as abstract.

```
public abstract MyClass
{
    ...
}
```

```
public MyDerivedClass : MyClass
{
    ...
}
MyClass myClass = new MyClass(); //not allowed!
MyClass myClass = new MyDerivedClass(); //this is ok
```

You can also mark individual methods inside a class as abstract to avoid giving them any default implementation, as shown here:

```
public abstract MyClass
{
    public abstract void DoSomething();
}
MyClass myClass = new MyClass();//not allowed!
```

Interface or Abstract Base Class?

When designing class hierarchies, you often need to decide whether classes at the root of the hierarchy (the parent classes) should be abstract base classes, or whether to implement the concrete classes in terms of interfaces.

Here are some guidelines to help make this decision.

In favor of interfaces:

- Will classes need to implement multiple base classes? This isn't possible in C#, but it is possible to implement multiple interfaces.
- Have you separated concerns to the point where you understand the difference between what your class *is* and what it *does*? Interfaces are often about what the class does, whereas a base class can anchor what it is.
- Interfaces are often independent of what a class is and can be used in many situations. They can be added onto the class without concern for what it is.
- Interfaces often allow a very loosely coupled design.
- Deriving too many things from a base class can lead to it being bloated with too much functionality.

In favor of base classes:

- Is there reasonable common functionality or data for all derived types? An abstract base class may be useful.
- Implementing the same interface over many types can lead to a lot of repetition of code, whereas an abstract base class can group common code into a single implementation.

- An abstract base class can provide a default implementation.
- Abstract base classes tend to rigidly structure code. This may be desirable in some cases.

If you find yourself trying to put too much functionality into abstract base classes, another possibility is to look into componentizing the various areas of functionality.

As you gain experience, you'll come to realize what makes sense in different situations. Often, some combination of the two makes sense.

CHAPTER 2

Creating Versatile Types

IN THIS CHAPTER

- Format a Type with `ToString()`
- Make Types Equatable
- Make Types Hashable with `GetHashCode()`
- Make Types Sortable
- Give Types an Index
- Notify Clients when Changes Happen
- Overload Appropriate Operators
- Convert One Type to Another
- Prevent Inheritance
- Allow Value Type to Be Null

Whenever you create your own classes, you need to consider the circumstances under which they could be used. For example, will two instances of your `Item` struct ever be compared for equality? Will your `Person` class need to be serializable, or sortable?

NOTE Versatility means being able to do many things well. When you're creating your own types, it means outfitting your objects with enough "extra" stuff that they can easily be used in a wide variety of situations.

This chapter is all about making your own objects as useful and versatile as possible. In many cases, this means implementing the standard interfaces that .NET provides or simply overriding base class methods.

Format a Type with `ToString()`

Scenario/Problem: You need to provide a string representation of an object for output and debugging purposes.

Solution: By default, `ToString()` will display the type's name. To show your own values, you must override the method with one of your own. To illustrate this, let's continue our `Vertex3d` class example from the previous chapter.

Assume the class initially looks like this:

```
struct Vertex3d
{
    private double _x;
    private double _y;
    private double _z;

    public double X
    {
        get { return _x; }
        set { _x = value; }
    }

    public double Y
    {
        get { return _y; }
        set { _y = value; }
    }
```

```
    public double Z
    {
        get { return _z; }
        set { _z = value; }
    }

    public Vertex3d(double x, double y, double z)
    {
        this._x = x;
        this._y = y;
        this._z = z;
    }
}
```

Override `ToString()` for Simple Output

To get a simple string representation of the vertex, override `ToString()` to return a string of your choosing.

```
public override string ToString()
{
    return string.Format("({0}, {1}, {2})", X, Y, Z);
}
```

The code

```
Vertex3d v = new Vertex3d(1.0, 2.0, 3.0);
Trace.WriteLine(v.ToString());
```

produces the following output:

```
(1, 2, 3)
```

Implement Custom Formatting for Fine Control

Scenario/Problem: You need to provide consumers of your class fine-grained control over how string representations of your class look.

Solution: Although the `ToString()`implementation gets the job done, and is especially handy for debugging (Visual Studio will automatically call `ToString()` on objects in the debugger windows), it is not very flexible. By implementing `IFormattable` on your type, you can create a version of `ToString()` that is as flexible as you need.

Let's create a simple format syntax that allows us to specify which of the three values to print. To do this, we'll define the following format string:

```
"X, Y"
```

This tells `Vertex3d` to print out X and Y. The comma and space (and any other character) will be output as-is.

The struct definition will now be as follows:

```
using System;
using System.Collections.Generic;
using System.Text;

namespace VertexDemo
{
struct Vertex3d : IFormattable
{
    ...
    public string ToString(string format, IFormatProvider formatProvider)
    {
        //"G" is .Net's standard for general formatting--all
        //types should support it
        if (format == null) format = "G";

        // is the user providing their own format provider?
        if (formatProvider != null)
        {
            ICustomFormatter formatter =
                formatProvider.GetFormat(this.GetType())
                        as ICustomFormatter;
            if (formatter != null)
            {
                return formatter.Format(format, this, formatProvider);
            }
        }

        //formatting is up to us, so let's do it
        if (format == "G")
        {
            return string.Format("({0}, {1}, {2})", X, Y, Z);
        }

        StringBuilder sb = new StringBuilder();
        int sourceIndex = 0;
```

```
        while (sourceIndex < format.Length)
        {
            switch (format[sourceIndex])
            {
                case 'X':
                    sb.Append(X.ToString());
                    break;
                case 'Y':
                    sb.Append(Y.ToString());
                    break;
                case 'Z':
                    sb.Append(Z.ToString());
                    break;
                default:
                    sb.Append(format[sourceIndex]);
                    break;
            }
            sourceIndex++;
        }
        return sb.ToString();
    }
}
}
```

The `formatProvider` argument allows you to pass in a formatter that does something different from the type's own formatting (say, if you can't change the implementation of `ToString()` on `Vertex3d` for some reason, or you need to apply different formatting in specific situations). You'll see how to define a custom formatter in the next section.

Formatting with `ICustomFormatter` and `StringBuilder`

Scenario/Problem: You need a general-purpose formatter than can apply custom formats to many types of objects.

Solution: Use `ICustomFormatter` and `StringBuilder`. This example prints out type information, as well as whatever the custom format string specifies for the given types.

```
class TypeFormatter : IFormatProvider, ICustomFormatter
{
    public object GetFormat(Type formatType)
    {
```

```
        if (formatType == typeof(ICustomFormatter)) return this;
        return Thread.CurrentThread.CurrentCulture.GetFormat(formatType);
    }

    public string Format(string format, object arg, IFormatProvider
formatProvider)
    {
        string value;
        IFormattable formattable = arg as IFormattable;
        if (formattable == null)
        {
            value = arg.ToString();
        }
        else
        {
            value = formattable.ToString(format, formatProvider);
        }
        return string.Format("Type: {0}, Value: {1}", arg.GetType(),
value);
    }
}
```

The class can be used like this:

```
Vertex3d v = new Vertex3d(1.0, 2.0, 3.0);
Vertex3d v2 = new Vertex3d(4.0, 5.0, 6.0);
TypeFormatter formatter = new TypeFormatter();
StringBuilder sb = new StringBuilder();
sb.AppendFormat(formatter, "{0:(X Y)}; {1:[X, Y, Z]}", v, v2);
Console.WriteLine(sb.ToString());
```

The following output is produced:

```
Type: ch02.Vertex3d, Value: (1 2); Type: ch02.Vertex3d, Value: [4, 5, 6]
```

Make Types Equatable

Scenario/Problem: You need to determine if two objects are equal.

Solution: You should override `Object.Equals()` and also implement the `IEquatable<T>` interface.

By default, `Equals()` on a reference type checks to see if the objects refer to the same location in memory. This may be acceptable in some circumstances, but often, you'll want to provide your own behavior. With value types, the default behavior is to reflect over each field and do a bit-by-bit comparison. This can have a very negative impact on performance, and in nearly every case you should provide your own implementation of `Equals()`.

```
struct Vertex3d : IFormattable, IEquatable<Vertex3d>
{
    ...
    public override bool Equals(object obj)
    {
        if (obj == null)
            return false;
        if (obj.GetType() != this.GetType())
            return false;
        return Equals((Vertex3d)obj);
    }

    public bool Equals(Vertex3d other)
    {
        /* If Vertex3d were a reference type you would also need:
         * if ((object)other == null)
         *  return false;
         *
         * if (!base.Equals(other))
         *  return false;
         */

        return this._x == other._x
            && this._y == other._y
            && this._z == other._z;
    }
}
```

NOTE Pay special attention to the note in `Equals(Vertex3d other)`. If `Vertex3d` was a reference type and `other` was null, the type-safe version of the function would be called, not the `Object` version. You also need to call all the base classes in the hierarchy so they have an opportunity to check their own fields.

There's nothing stopping you from also implementing `IEquatable<string>` (or any other type) on your type—you can define it however you want. Use with caution, however, because this may confuse people who have to use your code.

Make Types Hashable with GetHashCode()

Scenario/Problem: You want to use your class as the key part in a collection that indexes values by unique keys. To do this, your class must be able to convert the "essence" of its values into a semi-unique integer ID.

Solution: You almost always want to override GetHashCode(), especially with value types, for performance reasons. Generating a hash value is generally done by somehow distilling the data values in your class to an integer representation that is different for every value your class can have. You should override GetHashCode() whenever you override Equals().

```
public override int GetHashCode()
{
    //note: This is just a sample hash algorithm.
    //picking a good algorithm can require some
    //research and experimentation
    return (((int)_x ^ (int)_z) << 16) |
           (((int)_y ^ (int)_z) & 0x0000FFFF);
}
```

NOTE Hash codes are not supposed to be unique for every possible set of values your type can have. This is actually impossible, as you can deduce from the previous code sample. For this reason, comparing hash values is not a good way to compute equality.

Make Types Sortable

Scenario/Problem: Objects of your type will be sorted in a collection or otherwise compared to each other.

Solution: Because you often don't know how your type will be used, making the objects sortable is highly recommended whenever possible.

In the Vector3d class example, in order to make the objects comparable, we'll add an _id field and implement the IComparable<Vertex3d> interface.

The _id field will be what determines the order (it doesn't make much sense to sort on coordinates, generally).

The sorting function is simple. It takes an object of Vertex3d and returns one of three values:

< 0	this is less than other
0	this is same as other
> 0	this is greater than other

Within the CompareTo function, you can do anything you want to arrive at those values. In our case, we can do the comparison ourself or just call the same function on the _id field.

```
struct Vertex3d : IFormattable, IEquatable<Vertex3d>,
                    IComparable<Vertex3d>
{
    private int _id;

    public int Id
    {
        get
        {
            return _id;
        }
        set
        {
            _id = value;
        }
    }

    public Vertex3d(double x, double y, double z)
    {
        _x = x;
        _y = y;
        _z = z;

        _id = 0;
    }
    ...
    public int CompareTo(Vertex3d other)
    {
        if (_id < other._id)
            return -1;
        if (_id == other._id)
            return 0;
        return 1;
        /* We could also just do this:
         * return _id.CompareTo(other._id);
```

```
        * */
    }
}
```

Give Types an Index

Scenario/Problem: Your type has data values that can be accessed by some kind of index, either numerical or string based.

Solution: You can index by any type. The most common index types are `int` and `string`.

Implement a Numerical Index

You use the array access brackets to define an index on the `this` object, like this sample:

```
public double this[int index]
{
    get
    {
        switch (index)
        {
            case 0: return _x;
            case 1: return _y;
            case 2: return _z;
            default: throw new ArgumentOutOfRangeException("index",
                "Only indexes 0-2 valid!");
        }
    }
    set
    {
        switch (index)
        {
            case 0: _x = value; break;
            case 1: _y = value; break;
            case 2: _z = value; break;
            default: throw new ArgumentOutOfRangeException("index",
                "Only indexes 0-2 valid!");
        }

    }
}
```

Implement a String Index

Unlike regular arrays, however, you are not limited to integer indices. You can use any type at all, most commonly strings, as in this example:

```
public double this[string dimension]
{
    get
    {
        switch (dimension)
        {
            case "x":
            case "X": return _x;
            case "y":
            case "Y": return _y;
            case "z":
            case "Z": return _z;
            default: throw new ArgumentOutOfRangeException("dimension",
                "Only dimensions X, Y, and Z are valid!");
        }
    }
    set
    {
        switch (dimension)
        {
            case "x":
            case "X": _x = value; break;
            case "y":
            case "Y": _y = value; break;
            case "z":
            case "Z": _z = value; break;
            default: throw new ArgumentOutOfRangeException("dimension",
                "Only dimensions X, Y, and Z are valid!");
        }
    }
}
```

Sample usage:

```
Vertex3d v = new Vertex3d(1, 2, 3);
Console.WriteLine(v[0]);
Console.WriteLine(v["Z"]);
```

Output:

```
1
3
```

Notify Clients when Changes Happen

Scenario/Problem: You want users of your class to know when data inside the class changes.

Solution: Implement the `INotifyPropertyChanged` interface (located in `System.ComponentModel`).

```
using System.ComponentModel;
...
class MyDataClass : INotifyPropertyChanged
{
    public event PropertyChangedEventHandler PropertyChanged;

    protected void OnPropertyChanged(string propertyName)
    {
        if (PropertyChanged != null)
        {
            PropertyChanged(this, new
PropertyChangedEventArgs(propertyName));
        }
    }

    private int _tag = 0;
    public int Tag
    {
        get
        { return _tag; }
        set
        {
            _tag = value;
            OnPropertyChanged("Tag");
        }
    }
}
```

The Windows Presentation Foundation (WPF) makes extensive use of this interface for data binding, but you can use it for your own purposes as well.

To consume such a class, use code similar to this:

```
void WatchObject(object obj)
{
    INotifyPropertyChanged watchableObj = obj as INotifyPropertyChanged;
```

```
    if (watchableObj != null)
    {
        watchableObj.PropertyChanged += new
                PropertyChangedEventHandler(data_PropertyChanged);
    }
}

void data_PropertyChanged(object sender, PropertyChangedEventArgs e)
{
    //do something when data changes
}
```

Overload Appropriate Operators

Scenario/Problem: You want to define what the +, *, ==, and != operators do when called on your type.

Solution: Operator overloading is like sugar: a little is sweet, but a lot will make you sick. Ensure that you only use this technique for situations that make sense.

Implement `operator +`

Notice that the method is `public static` and takes both operators as arguments.

```
public static Vertex3d operator +(Vertex3d a, Vertex3d b)
{
    return new Vertex3d(a.X + b.X, a.Y + b.Y, a.Z + b.Z);
}
```

The same principal can be applied to the -, *, /, %, &, |, <<, >>, !, ~, ++, and -- operators as well.

Implement `operator ==` and `operator !=`

These should always be implemented as a pair. Because we've already implemented a useful `Equals()` method, just call that instead.

```
public static bool operator ==(Vertex3d a, Vertex3d b)
{
    return a.Equals(b);
}

public static bool operator !=(Vertex3d a, Vertex3d b)
{
```

```
    return !(a==b);
}
```

What if the type is a reference type? In this case, you have to handle null values for both a and b, as in this example:

```
public static bool operator ==(CatalogItem a, CatalogItem b)
{
    if ((object)a == null && (object)b == null)
        return true;
    if ((object)a == null || (object)b == null)
        return false;
    return a.Equals(b);
}

public static bool operator !=(CatalogItem a, CatalogItem b)
{
    return !(a == b);
}
```

Convert One Type to Another

Scenario/Problem: You need to convert one type to another, either automatically or by requiring an explicit cast.

Solution: Implement a conversion operator. There are two types of conversion operators: `implicit` and `explicit`. To understand the difference, we'll implement a new `struct` called `Vertex3i` that is the same as `Vertex3d`, except the dimensions are integers instead of doubles.

Explicit Conversion (Loss of Precision)

Explicit conversion is encouraged when the conversion will result in a loss of precision. When you're converting from `System.Double` to `System.Int32`, for example, all of the decimal precision is lost. You don't (necessarily) want the compiler to allow this conversion automatically, so you make it explicit. This code goes in the `Vertex3d` class:

```
public static explicit operator Vertex3i(Vertex3d vertex)
{
    return new Vertex3i((Int32)vertex._x, (Int32)vertex._y,
➥                      (Int32)vertex._z);
}
```

To convert from `Vertex3d` to `Vertex3i` then, you would do the following:

```
Vertex3d vd = new Vertex3d(1.5, 2.5, 3.5);
Vertex3i vi = (Vertex3i)vd;
```

If you tried it without the cast, you would get the following:

```
//Vertex3i vi = vd;
Error: Cannot implicitly convert type 'Vertex3d' to 'Vertex3i'.
       An explicit conversion exists (are you missing a cast?)
```

Implicit Conversion (No Loss of Precision)

If there will not be any loss in precision, then the conversion can be implicit, meaning the compiler will allow you to assign the type with no explicit conversion. We can implement this type of conversion in the `Vertex3i` class because it can convert up to a double with no loss of precision.

```
public static implicit operator Vertex3d(Vertex3i vertex)
{
    return new Vertex3d(vertex._x, vertex._y, vertex._z);
}
```

Now we can assign without casting:

```
Vertex3i vi = new Vertex3i(1, 2, 3);
Vertex3d vd = vi;
```

Prevent Inheritance

Scenario/Problem: You want to prevent users of your class from inheriting from it.

Solution: Mark the class as `sealed`.

```
sealed class MyClass
{
...
}
```

Structs are inherently sealed.

Prevent Overriding of a Single Method

Scenario/Problem: You don't want to ban inheritance on your type, but you do want to prevent certain methods or properties from being overridden.

Solution: Put `sealed` as part of the method or property definition.

```
class ParentClass
{
    public virtual void MyFunc() { }
}

class ChildClass : ParentClass
{
    //seal base class function into this class
    public sealed override void MyFunc() { }
}

class GrandChildClass : ChildClass
{
    //yields compile error
    public override void MyFunc() { }
}
```

Allow Value Type to Be Null

Scenario/Problem: You need to assign null to a value type to indicate the lack of a value. This scenario often occurs when working with databases, which allow any data type to be null.

Solution: This isn't technically something you need to implement in your class. .NET 2.0 introduced the `Nullable<T>` type, which wraps any value type into something that can be null. It's useful enough that there is a special C# syntax shortcut to do this. The following two lines of code are semantically equivalent:

```
Nullable<int> _id;
int? _id;
```

Let's make the _id field in our `Vertex3d` class `Nullable<T>` to indicate the lack of a valid value. The following code snippet demonstrates how it works:

```
struct Vertex3d : IFormattable, IEquatable<Vertex3d>,
                  IComparable<Vertex3d>
{
    private int? _id;

    public int? Id
    {
        get
        {
            return _id;
        }
        set
        {
            _id = value;
        }
    }
    ...
}
...
Vertex3d vn = new Vertex3d(1, 2, 3);
vn.Id = 3;      //ok
vn.Id = null;   //ok
try
{
    Console.WriteLine("ID: {0}", vn.Id.Value);//throws
}
catch (InvalidOperationException)
{
    Console.WriteLine("Oops--you can't get a null value!");
}

if (vn.Id.HasValue)
{
    Console.WriteLine("ID: {0}", vn.Id.Value);
}
```

CHAPTER 3

General Coding

IN THIS CHAPTER

- Declare Variables
- Defer Type Checking to Runtime
- Use Dynamic Typing to Simplify COM Interop
- Declare Arrays
- Create Multidimensional Arrays
- Alias a Namespace
- Use the Conditional Operator (`?:`)
- Use the Null-Coalescing Operator (`??`)
- Add Methods to Existing Types with Extension Methods
- Call Methods with Default Parameters
- Call Methods with Named Parameters
- Defer Evaluation of a Value Until Referenced
- Enforce Code Contracts

This chapter contains essential, general C# knowledge that doesn't fit easily into other chapters: from the multitude of ways to declare variables to the different types of multidimensional arrays and some of the "unusual" operators in C#.

Declare Variables

Scenario/Problem: You need to store data in a class.

Solution: C# provides many ways to declare and define variables. We'll start with the simplest:

```
int x = 13;//declare and define at once
int y;//declare and define later
y = 13;
```

Use Type Inference (Implicit Typing)

Scenario/Problem: You want to declare a variable and assign it a value, without having to figure out the type, but still take advantage of strong typing rules.

Solution: Type inference allows you to let the compiler decide what type a local variable is (it cannot be used for class fields). It is important to realize that variables are still strongly typed—`var` is *not* equivalent to `Object`. You are merely giving the job of figuring out the type to the compiler. Once that's done, the type can't change during runtime.

```
class MyType { }

class Program
{
    static void Main(string[] args)
    {
        var x = 13;
        var myObj = new MyType();
        var myNums = new double[] { 1.0, 1.5, 2.0, 2.5, 3.0 };
        //not allowed to initialize to null
        //var myNullObj = null;
        //but setting it to null after definition is ok
        var myNullObj = new MyType();
        myNullObj = null;
```

```
        Console.WriteLine("x, Type: {0}", x.GetType());
        Console.WriteLine("myObj, Type: {0}", myObj.GetType());
        Console.WriteLine("myNums, Type: {0}", myNums.GetType());
    }
}
```

This program produces the following output:

```
x, Type: System.Int32
myObj, Type: MyType
myNums, Type: System.Double[]
```

Apart from the benefit of convenience when typing (by omitting repeating type names), implicit typing is highly useful when using LINQ (see Chapter 21, "LINQ").

NOTE There is some amount of controversy about the usage of `var`. On one hand, it is mighty convenient when you don't want to figure out and write out the type of an object you won't be using outside of a narrow scope (especially when it's long or has type parameters). On the other hand, it can definitely be overused.

My favorite place to use `var` is in `foreach`, so I don't have to figure out what the precise type in the collection is, as in the following example:

```
Dictionary<string, List<Mystruct>> dict =
    new Dictionary<string, List<Mystruct>>();
...
foreach(var elem in dict)
{
    Mystruct s = elem.Value[0];
}
```

Defer Type Checking to Runtime (Dynamic Types)

Scenario/Problem: You want to delay type resolution until runtime.

Solution: Use the `dynamic` keyword for your variables and method parameters.

This functionality is most useful in dynamic languages that require runtime binding, but it can be useful in other occasions. Here's a simple demo:

```
class Program
{
    class Person
    {
```

```
    public int Id { get; set; }
    public string Name { get; set; }
    public string Address { get; set; }
}

class Company
{
    public int Id { get; set; }
    public string Name { get; set; }
    public bool IsBig { get; set; }
}

static void Main(string[] args)
{
    //declare three types that have nothing to do with each other,
    //but all have an Id and Name property
    Person p = new Person()
           { Id = 1, Name = "Ben", Address = "Redmond, WA" };
    Company c = new Company()
           { Id = 1313, Name = "Microsoft", IsBig = true };
    var v = new { Id = 13, Name = "Widget", Silly = true };

    PrintInfo(p);
    PrintInfo(c);
    PrintInfo(v);

    try
    {
        PrintInfo(13);
    }
    catch (Exception ex)
    {
        Console.WriteLine("Oops...can't call PrintInfo(13)");
        Console.WriteLine(ex);
    }
}

static void PrintInfo(dynamic data)
{
    //will print anything that has an Id and Name property
    Console.WriteLine("ID: {0}, Name: {1}", data.Id, data.Name);
}
}
```

For other examples, see the next section and in Chapter 24, "Reflection and Creating Plugins," to see how dynamic typing can make method execution on reflected types easier.

NOTE While the dynamic keyword gives us dynamic behavior, behind the scenes, the Dynamic Language Runtime (DLR) uses compiler tricks and reflection to bind the calls involving dynamic types to standard static types.

Use Dynamic Typing to Simplify COM Interop

Scenario/Problem: You want to use objects from COM components and avoid the typical requirement of casting everything from `object`.

Solution: Use dynamic typing to have the runtime do the checking and binding for you, as in the following example, which uses the Excel 2007 COM component.

```
//add a reference to Microsoft.Office.Interop.Excel to the project
using System;
using Excel = Microsoft.Office.Interop.Excel;

namespace DynamicTypesInExcel
{
    class Program
    {
        static void Main(string[] args)
        {
            var app = new Excel.Application();
            app.Visible = true;
            app.Workbooks.Add();
            //to avoid a lot of casting, use dynamic
            dynamic sheet = app.ActiveSheet;
            sheet.Cells[1, "A"] = 13;
            sheet.Cells[2, "A"] = 13;
            sheet.Cells[3, "A"] = "=A1*A2";
            sheet.Columns[1].AutoFit();
        }
    }
}
```

Declare Arrays

Scenario/Problem: You need to declare an array of objects.

Solution: There are many variations of array declaration and definition syntax.

```
//These are all equivalent
int[] array1 = new int[4];
array1[0] = 13; array1[1] = 14; array1[2] = 15; array1[3] = 16;

int[] array2 = new int[4] { 13, 14, 15, 16 };

int[] array3 = new int[] { 13, 14, 15, 16 };

int[] array4 = { 13, 14, 15, 16 };
```

NOTE These additional ways of initializing an array actually apply to anything that implements IEnumerable (See Chapter 10, "Collections", for examples of this). This is actually just another form of object initialization, which was described in Chapter 1, "Type Fundamentals."

Create Multidimensional Arrays

Scenario/Problem: You need to declare an array with multiple dimensions, such as a 2D or 3D grid.

Solution: First decide which type of multidimensional array you need. There are two types in C#: rectangular and jagged. The difference is illustrated in Figures 3.1 and 3.2.

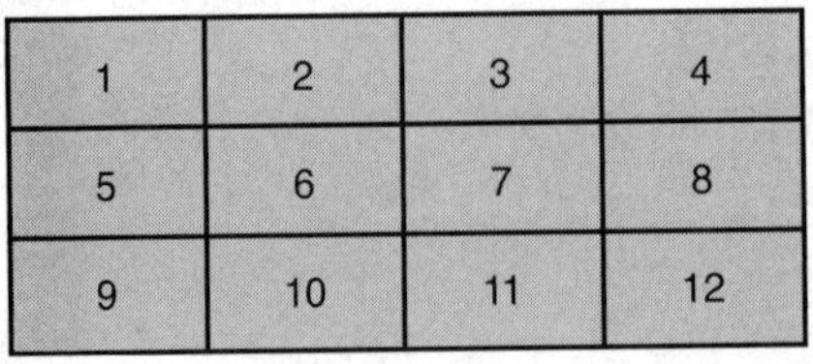

1	2	3	4
5	6	7	8
9	10	11	12

FIGURE 3.1
Rectangular arrays have same-sized rows.

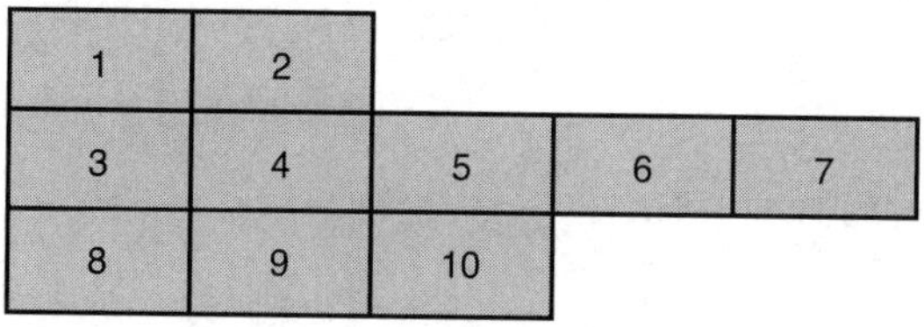

FIGURE 3.2
Jagged arrays are more like arrays of arrays.

Create Rectangular Arrays

Rectangular arrays are exactly what they sound like: every row is the same length. Here's an example:

```
int[,] mArray1 = new int[,]
{
    {1,2,3,4},
    {5,6,7,8},
    {9,10,11,12}
};
float val = mArray1[0, 1];//2
```

Create Jagged Arrays (Arrays of Arrays)

Jagged arrays are actually just arrays of arrays. Here's an example:

```
int[][] mArray2 = new int[3][];
mArray2[0] = new int[] { 1, 2, 3 };
mArray2[1] = new int[] { 4, 5, 6, 7, 8 };
mArray2[2] = new int[] { 9, 10, 11, 12 };
int val = mArray2[0][1];//2
```

Alias a Namespace

Scenario/Problem: You want to create an easy-to-use name for a namespace that conflicts with another namespace or for a namespace that is just long. For example, suppose you want to use classes from the `System.Windows.Controls` namespace as well as controls from your own namespace, `Acme.Widgets.Controls`.

Solution: Rather than importing both types and thus polluting the current context (which would crowd IntelliSense, as one bad side effect), you can alias one or both of them into something shorter for easier use.

```
using System;

using WpfControls = System.Windows.Controls;
using AcmeControls = Acme.Widgets.Controls;

namespace MyProgramNamespace
{
    class MyClass
    {
        void DoSomething()
        {
            WpfControls.Button button = new WpfControls.Button();
            AcmeControls.Dial dial = new AcmeControls.Dial();
        }
    }
}
```

NOTE The keyword *using* is also used in the context of the Dispose Pattern (see Chapter 22, "Memory Management").

Use the Conditional Operator (?:)

Scenario/Problem: You want to choose between two alternate values within a single statement.

Solution: Use the conditional operator, sometimes called the *ternary operator* (for its three arguments). For example, `(condition?a:b)` is shorthand for `if (condition) { do a } else {do b}`.

```
class Program
{
    static void Main(string[] args)
    {
        bool condition = true;

        int x = condition ? 13 : 14;
        Console.WriteLine("x is {0}", x);

        //you can also embed the condition in other statements
        Console.WriteLine("Condition is {0}",
                          condition ? "TRUE" : "FALSE");
```

```
    }
}
```

This program prints the following output:

```
x is 13
Condition is TRUE
```

NOTE This operator is not limited to just assignments. You can also use it in situations like this:

```
bool actionSucceeded = CheckIfActionSucceeded();
actionSucceeded ? ReportSucceeded() : ReportFailed();
```

Use the Null-Coalescing Operator (??)

Scenario/Problem: You want to simplify checking for null values. This is a common situation, where you need to check for a null value before you use a variable.

Solution: The null-coalescing operator can simplify the syntax a bit.

```
int? n = null;
object obj = "Hello";
int x = 13;

//short for if (n!=null) o = n; else o = -1;
int? o = n ?? -1;
object obj2 = obj ?? "ok";

//doesn't make sense since x can't be null
//int y = x ?? -1;

Console.WriteLine("o = {0}", o);
Console.WriteLine("obj2 = {0}", obj2);
```

The output is as follows:

```
o = -1
obj2 = Hello
```

Add Methods to Existing Types with Extension Methods

Scenario/Problem: You want to add a method to an existing type (for which you cannot change the source code) so that the syntax you use is `existingType.MyNewMethod()`.

Solution: Create an extension method using special syntax, as in this example:

```
//extension methods must be defined in a static class
static class IntMethods
{
    //extension methods must be static
    //the this keyword tells C# that this is an extension method
    public static bool IsPrime(this int number)
    {
        //check for evenness
        if (number % 2 == 0)
        {
            if (number == 2)
                return true;
            return false;
        }
        //don't need to check past the square root
        int max = (int)Math.Sqrt(number);
        for (int i = 3; i <= max; i += 2)
        {
            if ((number % i) == 0)
            {
                return false;
            }
        }
        return true;
    }
}

class Program
{
    static void Main(string[] args)
    {
        for (int i = 0; i < 100; ++i)
        {
            if (i.IsPrime())
```

```
            {
                Console.WriteLine(i);
            }
        }
        Console.ReadKey();
    }
}
```

A lot of extension methods are defined for you already (mostly for use in LINQ). Figure 3.3 shows how Visual Studio marks extension methods graphically.

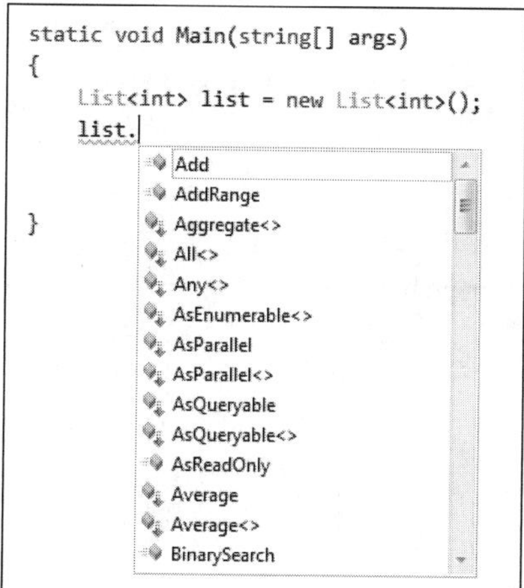

FIGURE 3.3
Visual Studio marks extension methods in IntelliSense with a down arrow to make them easy to identify. In this figure, Aggregate, All, Any, etc. are extension methods that operate on IEnumerable<T> types.

NOTE Like operator overloading (See Chapter 2, "Creating Versatile Types"), you should be careful about defining extension methods because they pollute the namespace for *all* variables of that type.

Call Methods with Default Parameters

Scenario/Problem: You want to avoid creating many overloads of a method by specifying default values for some parameters.

Solution: Use the new syntax in C# 4.0 to specify parameters with default values.

```
class Program
{
    static void Main(string[] args)
```

```
    {
        ShowFolders();
        ShowFolders(@"C:\");
        //no, you can't do this
        //ShowFolders(false);
    }

    static void ShowFolders(string root = @"C:\",
                            bool showFullPath = false)
    {
        foreach (string folder in Directory.EnumerateDirectories(root))
        {
            string output =
                   showFullPath ? folder : Path.GetFileName(folder);
            Console.WriteLine(output);
        }
    }

    //not allowed: default parameters must appear after
    //all non-default parameters
    //static void ShowFolders(string root = @"C:\", bool showFullPath )
    //{
    //}
}
```

NOTE Default parameter usage can be a contentious issue. Personally, I'd rather have more overloads than use default parameters, but the feature is now here if you want it. Make sure you don't hurt readability and maintainability with its usage.

Call Methods with Named Parameters

Scenario/Problem: You want to be able to call methods with named parameters, possibly to interface with dynamic languages.

Solution: Use the new syntax in C# 4.0 to call methods with named parameters.

Let's use the same method from the previous section:

```
//order doesn't matter when they're named
ShowFolders(showFullPath: false, root: @"C:\Windows");
```

Defer Evaluation of a Value Until Referenced

Scenario/Problem: You want to defer creation of a complex value until and unless it's needed.

Solution: Use the simple helper class Lazy<T> to wrap the value creation and pass it around as needed. Once the value is created, it is stored so that subsequent accesses use the already created value.

```
class Program
{
    static void Main(string[] args)
    {
        Lazy<ICollection<string>> processes =
                              new Lazy<ICollection<string>>(
        //anonymous delegate to do the creation of
        //the value, when needed
        () =>
        {
            List<string> processNames = new List<string>();
            foreach (var p in Process.GetProcesses())
            {
                processNames.Add(p.ProcessName);
            }
            return processNames;
        });

        PrintSystemInfo(processes, true);
        Console.ReadKey();
    }

    static void PrintSystemInfo(Lazy<ICollection<string>> processNames,
                    bool showProcesses)
    {
        Console.WriteLine("MachineName: {0}", Environment.MachineName);
        Console.WriteLine("OS version: {0}", Environment.OSVersion);
        Console.WriteLine("DBG: Is process list created? {0}",
              processNames.IsValueCreated);
        if (showProcesses)
        {
            Console.WriteLine("Processes:");
            foreach (string p in processNames.Value)
            {
```

```
                Console.WriteLine(p);
            }
        }
        Console.WriteLine("DBG: Is process list created? {0}",
            processNames.IsValueCreated);
    }
}
```

The output is similar to the following:

```
MachineName: BEN-DESKTOP
OS version: Microsoft Windows NT 6.1.7100.0
DBG: Is process list created? False
Processes:
conhost
explorer
svchost
svchost
iexplore
Idle
...many more...
DBG: Is process list created? True
```

Enforce Code Contracts

Scenario/Problem: You want methods that obey rules you specify, including invariants that must be obeyed at the beginning and end of method calls.

Solution: Use the `Contract` class to add constraints to your methods.

```
class Program
{
    static void Main(string[] args)
    {
        List<int> list = new List<int>();
        AppendNumber(list, 13);

        AppendNumber(list, -1);

        Console.ReadKey();
    }
```

```
    static void AppendNumber(List<int> list, int newNumber)
    {
        Contract.Requires(newNumber > 0, "Failed contract: negative");
        Contract.Ensures(list.Count ==
➥                  Contract.OldValue(list.Count) + 1);

        list.Add(newNumber);
    }
}
```

At first glance, these look like assertions—when you are running a debug build, they are. However, they do much more:

- When used with an external tool (called a binary rewriter), they inject code to verify the contract is obeyed, including possibly at the end of methods when needed.
- Emit metadata about the constraint that can then be analyzed by static code analysis tools.
- When run in debug mode, they throw exceptions when contracts are violated.

At the time of this writing, using Code Contracts required an extra download from Microsoft (go to http://research.microsoft.com/en-us/projects/contracts/). Once installed, Code Contracts will add a new tab in your project settings (see Figure 3.4).

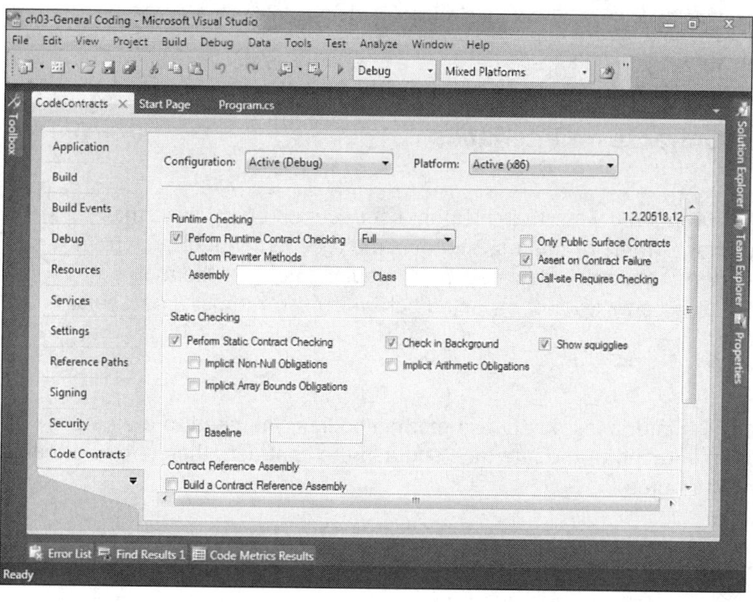

FIGURE 3.4

Code Contracts adds some new configuration settings to Visual Studio.

With the Visual Studio Team System version, you can also have a static checker that evaluates your code as you write it and notifies you of problems immediately (see Figure 3.5).

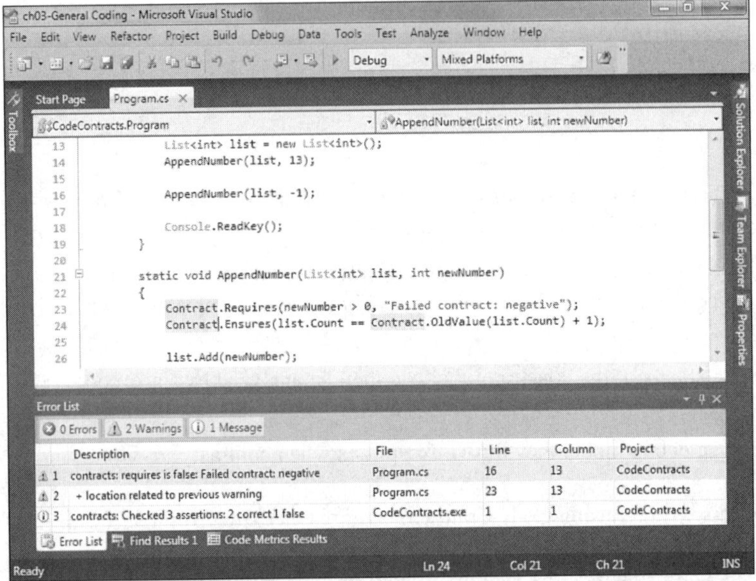

FIGURE 3.5
The static checker integrates with Visual Studio Team System to interactively notify you of contract violations in your code.

Implement Contracts on Interfaces

Scenario/Problem: You want to implement contracts on every class that implements an interface. Think of this as extending the requirements of an interface even deeper then the method declaration, by requiring not just the method signature, but also some level of expected behavior, even without a particular implementation.

Solution: Because interfaces don't have method bodies, you need to create a surrogate implementation of the interface and add the contracts there. You tie them together using attributes.

```
[ContractClass(typeof(AddContract))]
interface IAdd
{
    UInt32 Add(UInt32 a, UInt32 b);
}
```

```
[ContractClassFor(typeof(IAdd))]
class AddContract : IAdd
{
    //private and explicit interface implementation
    UInt32 IAdd.Add(UInt32 a, UInt32 b)
    {
        Contract.Requires((UInt64)a + (UInt64)b < UInt32.MaxValue);
        return a+b;
    }
}

//this class does not need to specify the contracts
class BetterAdd : IAdd
{
    public UInt32 Add(UInt32 a, UInt32 b)
    {
        return a + b;
    }
}

void SomeFunc()
{
    BetterAdd ba;
    //this will cause a contract exception
    ba.Add(UInt32.MaxValue, UInt32.MaxValue);
}
```

CHAPTER 4

Exceptions

IN THIS CHAPTER

- Throw an Exception
- Catch an Exception
- Catch Multiple Exceptions
- Rethrow an Exception
- (Almost) Guarantee Execution with `finally`
- Get Useful Information from an Exception
- Create Your Own Exception Class
- Catch Unhandled Exceptions
- Usage Guidelines

Exceptions are .NET's primary mechanism for communicating error conditions. Exceptions have great power, but with great power comes great responsibility. Like anything, exceptions can be abused, but that is no excuse to underuse them.

Compared to returning error codes, exceptions offer numerous advantages, such as being able to jump up many frames in a call stack and including as much information as you want.

Throw an Exception

Scenario/Problem: You need to indicate an unrecoverable error from an exceptional situation. In this case, unrecoverable means unrecoverable at this level in the code. It's possible something higher can handle it.

Solution: Use the `throw` syntax while creating the exception.

```
private void DoSomething(string value)
{
    if (string.IsNullOrEmpty(value))
    {
        throw new ArgumentNullException("value",
➥                                    "parameter value cannot be null");
    }
    ...
}
```

Catch an Exception

Scenario/Problem: You must handle an exception that was thrown.

Solution: Wrap the code that could potentially throw an exception inside a `try { }` followed by a `catch { }`.

```
try
{
    DoSomething(null);
}
catch (ArgumentNullException ex)
{
    Console.WriteLine("Exception: " + ex.Message);
}
```

Catch Multiple Exceptions

Scenario/Problem: You must handle many potential exceptions.

Solution: You can have multiple `catch` blocks after a `try`. .NET will go to the first `catch` block that is polymorphically compatible with the thrown exception. If you have code that throws both `ArgumentException` and `ArgumentNullException`, for example, the order of your `catch` blocks is important because `ArgumentNullException` is a child class of `ArgumentException`.

Here's an example of what *not* to do:

```
try
{
    throw new ArgumentNullException();
}
catch (ArgumentException ex)
{
    //will reach here
}
catch (ArgumentNullException ex)
{
    //will not reach here!
}
```

Because `ArgumentNullException` is a type of `ArgumentException`, and `ArgumentException` is first in the `catch` list, it will be called.

The rule is: Always order exception `catch` blocks in most-specific-first order.

```
try
{
    throw new ArgumentNullException();
}
catch (ArgumentNullException ex)
{
    //now we will reach here!
}
catch (ArgumentException ex)
{
    //catch any other ArgumentException or child
}
```

Rethrow an Exception

Scenario/Problem: You need to handle an exception at one level (logging it or changing program behavior, for example) and then pass it up for higher-level code to handle.

Solution: There are two ways to do this, and the difference is important.

The naive (that is, usually wrong) way is this:

```
try
{
    DoSomething();
}
catch (ArgumentNullException ex)
{
    LogException(ex);
    // probably wrong way to do this
    throw ex;//re throw it for higher up
}
```

What's so wrong with this? Whenever an exception is thrown, the current stack location is saved to the exception (see later in this chapter). When you rethrow like this, you replace the stack location that was originally in the exception with the one from this `catch` block—probably not what you wanted, and a stumbling block during debugging. If you want to rethrow while preserving the original stack trace call, throw without the exception variable.

```
try
{
    DoSomething();
}
catch (ArgumentNullException ex)
{
    LogException(ex);
    throw ;//re throw it for higher up, preserve the stack
}
```

Here's the difference in a sample program:

```
Stack trace from rethrow (no stack preservation):
   at Rethrow.Program.RethrowWithNoPreservation() in Program.cs:line 52
   at Rethrow.Program.Main(String[] args) in Program.cs:line 14
```

```
Stack trace from rethrow (stack preservation):
   at Rethrow.Program.DoSomething() in Program.cs:line 39
   at Rethrow.Program.RethrowWithPreservation() in Program.cs:line 65
   at Rethrow.Program.Main(String[] args) in Program.cs:line 26
```

You can see that the first stack trace has lost the original source of the problem (`DoSomething`), while the second has preserved it.

> **NOTE** Be smart about when to intercept an exception. For example, you don't usually want to log an exception and then rethrow at multiple levels, causing the same error to be logged over and over again. Often, logging should be handled at the highest level.
>
> Also, beware of the trap of habitually handling exceptions at too low of a level. If you can't do something intelligent about it, just let a higher level worry about it.

(Almost) Guarantee Execution with `finally`

> **Scenario/Problem:** You need to guarantee that resources are cleaned up, even when exceptions occur. Often when using objects that encapsulate external resources (such as database connections or files), you want to ensure that you release the resources when you're done. However, if an exception is thrown while using them, the exception will normally bypass any cleanup code you've written.

Solution: Use `finally`, which is *guaranteed* to run at the end of a `try` or a `try-catch` block. This happens whether you return, an exception is thrown, or execution continues normally to the line after the `try-finally`.

```
StreamWriter stream = null;
try
{
    stream = File.CreateText("temp.txt");
    stream.Write(null, -1, 1);
}
catch (ArgumentNullException ex)
{
    Console.WriteLine("In catch: ");
    Console.WriteLine(ex.Message);
}
finally
{
```

```
        Console.WriteLine("In finally: Closing file");
        if (stream != null)
        {
            stream.Close();
        }
}
```

The output for this program is as follows:

```
In catch:
Buffer cannot be null.
Parameter name: buffer
In finally: Closing file
```

Note that a `catch` block is not necessary when `finally` is used.

> **NOTE** Yes, `finally` is guaranteed to run—except when it's not. If your code forces an immediate process exit, the `finally` block will not run.
>
> ```
> try
> {
>     //do something
>     Environment.Exit(1);//program exits NOW
> }
> finally
> {
>     //this code will never run
> }
> ```

Get Useful Information from an Exception

Scenario/Problem: You want to extract useful information from a caught exception.

Solution: Exceptions are very rich objects—far more powerful than simple return codes. Table 4.1 lists the properties available to all exception types.

TABLE 4.1 **Exception Properties**

Property/Method	Description
`ToString()`	Prints the type of the exception, followed by `Message` and `StackTrace`.
`Message`	A brief description of error.
`Source`	The application where the exception occurred.
`StackTrace`	A list of the methods in the current stack. Helpful to retrace the path that caused the exception.
`TargetSite`	The method that threw the exception.
`InnerException`	The exception that caused the current exception. Often, exceptions are wrapped inside other, higher-level exceptions.
`HelpLink`	A link to a help file, often in the form of a URL.
`Data`	Exception-specific key-value pairs providing more information.

Here's an example:

```
static void Function()
{
    try
    {
        DivideByZero();
    }
    catch (DivideByZeroException ex)
    {
        Console.WriteLine("ToString(): " + ex.ToString());
        Console.WriteLine("Message: " + ex.Message);
        Console.WriteLine("Source: " + ex.Source);
        Console.WriteLine("HelpLink: " + ex.HelpLink);
        Console.WriteLine("TargetSite: " + ex.TargetSite);
        Console.WriteLine("Inner Exception: " + ex.InnerException);
        Console.WriteLine("Stack Trace: " + ex.StackTrace);
        Console.WriteLine("Data:");
        if (ex.Data != null)
        {
            foreach (DictionaryEntry de in ex.Data)
            {
                Console.WriteLine("\t{0}: {1}", de.Key, de.Value);
            }
        }
    }
}

private static void DivideByZero()
{
```

```
    int divisor = 0;
    Console.WriteLine("{0}", 13 / divisor);
}
```

This program produces the following output:

```
ToString(): System.DivideByZeroException: Attempted to divide by zero.
   at PrintExceptionInfo.Program.DivideByZero() in Program.cs:line 41
   at PrintExceptionInfo.Program.Main(String[] args)
➥in Program.cs:line 15
Message: Attempted to divide by zero.
Source: PrintExceptionInfo
HelpLink:
TargetSite: Void DivideByZero()
Inner Exception:
Stack Trace:    at PrintExceptionInfo.Program.DivideByZero()
➥in Program.cs:line 41
   at PrintExceptionInfo.Program.Main(String[] args)
➥in Program.cs:line 15
Data:
```

This is when the program is run in Debug mode. Note the differences when the program is run in Release mode:

```
ToString(): System.DivideByZeroException: Attempted to divide by zero.
   at PrintExceptionInfo.Program.Main(String[] args)
➥in Program.cs:line 15
Message: Attempted to divide by zero.
Source: PrintExceptionInfo
HelpLink:
TargetSite: Void Main(System.String[])
Inner Exception:
Stack Trace:    at PrintExceptionInfo.Program.Main(String[] args)
➥in Program.cs:line 15
Data:
```

There is less information in the stack trace when a program is compiled in Release mode because the binary does not contain all the information necessary to generate it.

Create Your Own Exception Class

> **Scenario/Problem:** You need a custom exception to describe errors particular to your application. When you develop a program of a nontrivial size, you will often need to create your own exception types.

Solution: Your exception can contain whatever data you desire, but there are a few guidelines to follow. In particular, you should have certain standard constructors:

- No arguments (default constructor).
- Takes a message (what is returned by the `Message` property).
- Takes a message and an inner exception.
- Takes data specific to your exception.
- Takes serialization objects. Exceptions should always be serializable and should also override `GetObjectData` (from `ISerializable`).

Here is a sample exception that implements all of these recommendations:

```
[Serializable]
public class MyException : Exception, ISerializable
{
    private double _exceptionData = 0.0;

    public double ExceptionData
    {
        get { return _exceptionData; }
    }

    public MyException()
    {
    }

    public MyException(string message)
        :base(message)
    {
    }

    public MyException(string message, Exception innerException)
        : base(message, innerException)
    {
    }

    public MyException(double exceptionData, string message)
        :base(message)
    {
        _exceptionData = exceptionData;
    }

    public MyException(double exceptionData,
                       string message,
                       Exception innerException)
        :base(message, innerException)
```

```
    {
        _exceptionData = exceptionData;
    }

    //serialization handlers

    protected MyException(SerializationInfo info,
                          StreamingContext context)
        :base(info, context)
    {
        //deserialize
        _exceptionData = info.GetDouble("MyExceptionData");
    }

    [SecurityPermission(SecurityAction.Demand,
                        SerializationFormatter = true)]
    public override void GetObjectData(SerializationInfo info,
                                       StreamingContext context)
    {
        //serialize
        base.GetObjectData(info, context);
        info.AddValue("MyExceptionData", _exceptionData);
    }
}
```

Taking the time to implement exceptions as deeply as this ensures that they are flexible enough to be used in whatever circumstances they need to be.

Catch Unhandled Exceptions

Scenario/Problem: You want a custom handler for any and all exceptions thrown by your application that are not handled by the normal `try...catch` mechanism. The exception should be logged, the program restarted, or some behavior initiated by a "catchall" handler.

Solution: A thrown exception is passed up the call stack until it finds a `catch` block that can handle it. If no handler is found, the process will be shut down.

Fortunately, there is a way to trap unhandled exceptions and execute your own code before the application terminates (or even prevent it from terminating). The way to do it depends on the type of application. The following are excerpts demonstrating the appropriate steps. See the sample code for this chapter for full working examples.

NOTE When running these sample projects under Visual Studio, the debugger will catch the unhandled exceptions before your code does. Usually, you can just tell it to continue and let your code attempt to handle it.

Catch Unhandled Exceptions in the Console

In console programs, you can listen for the UnhandledException for the current AppDomain:

```
class Program
{
    static void Main(string[] args)
    {
        //Unhandled exception handling is by application domain
        AppDomain.CurrentDomain.UnhandledException +=
   new UnhandledExceptionEventHandler(
                CurrentDomain_UnhandledException);
        throw new InvalidOperationException("Oops");
    }

    static void CurrentDomain_UnhandledException(
        object sender, UnhandledExceptionEventArgs e)
    {
        Console.WriteLine("Caught unhandled exception");
        Console.WriteLine(e.ExceptionObject.ToString());
    }
}
```

Catch Unhandled Exceptions in Windows Forms

In Windows Forms, before any other code runs, you must tell the `Application` object that you wish to handle the uncaught exceptions. Then, you can listen for a `ThreadException` on the main thread.

```
static class Program
{
    [STAThread]
    static void Main()
    {
        //this must be called before creating any UI elements
        Application.SetUnhandledExceptionMode(
                UnhandledExceptionMode.CatchException);
        Application.EnableVisualStyles();
        Application.SetCompatibleTextRenderingDefault(false);
        Application.Run(new Form1());
    }
}
```

```
public partial class Form1 : Form
{
    public Form1()
    {
        InitializeComponent();
        //handle any exceptions that occur on this thread
        Application.ThreadException +=
    new System.Threading.ThreadExceptionEventHandler(
             Application_ThreadException);
    }

    void Application_ThreadException(
        object sender, System.Threading.ThreadExceptionEventArgs e)
    {
        StringBuilder sb = new StringBuilder();
        sb.AppendLine("Trapped unhandled exception");
        sb.AppendLine(e.Exception.ToString());

        MessageBox.Show(sb.ToString());
    }

    private void button1_Click(object sender, EventArgs e)
    {
        throw new InvalidOperationException("Oops");
    }
}
```

Catch Unhandled Exceptions in WPF Applications

In WPF, you listen for unhandled exceptions on the dispatcher:

```
public partial class Window1 : Window
{
    public Window1()
    {
        InitializeComponent();
        Application.Current.DispatcherUnhandledException +=
➥new System.Windows.Threading.DispatcherUnhandledExceptionEventHandler(
➥Current_DispatcherUnhandledException);
    }

    void Current_DispatcherUnhandledException(object sender,
➥System.Windows.Threading.DispatcherUnhandledExceptionEventArgs e)
    {
```

```
        StringBuilder sb = new StringBuilder();
        sb.AppendLine("Caught unhandled exception");
        sb.AppendLine(e.Exception.ToString());

        MessageBox.Show(sb.ToString());

        e.Handled = true;//prevent exit
    }

    private void button1_Click(object sender, RoutedEventArgs e)
    {
        throw new InvalidOperationException("Oops");
    }
}
```

Catch Unhandled Exceptions in ASP.NET Applications

In ASP.NET, you can trap unhandled exceptions at either the page level or the application level. To trap errors at the page level, look at the page's `Error` event. To trap errors at the application level, you must have a global application class (often in `Global.asax`) and put your behavior in `Application_Error`, like this:

```
public class Global : System.Web.HttpApplication
{
...
    protected void Application_Error(object sender, EventArgs e)
    {
        //forward to an application-wide error page
        Server.Transfer("ErrorHandlerPage.aspx");
    }
...
}

//in the page
public partial class _Default : System.Web.UI.Page
{
    protected void Page_Load(object sender, EventArgs e)
    {
        Button1.Click += new EventHandler(Button1_Click);
        //uncomment to handle error at page-level
        //this.Error += new EventHandler(_Default_Error);
    }
```

```
    void Button1_Click(object sender, EventArgs e)
    {
        throw new ArgumentException();
    }

    //void _Default_Error(object sender, EventArgs e)
    //{
    //    this.Response.Redirect("ErrorHandlerPage.aspx");
    //}
}
```

Usage Guidelines

Here are some general guidelines on exception handling:

- The .NET Framework uses exceptions extensively for error-handling and notification. So should you.
- Nevertheless, exceptions are for *exceptional* situations, not for controlling program flow. For a simple example, if an object can be null, check for null before using it, rather than relying on an exception being thrown. The same goes for division by zero, and many other simple error conditions.
- Another reason to reserve their use for exceptional error conditions is that they have performance cost, in both speed and memory usage.
- Pack your exceptions with as much useful information as you need to diagnose problems (with caveats given in the following bullets).
- Don't show raw exceptions to users. They are for logging and for developers to use to fix the problem.
- Be careful about the information you reveal. Be aware that malicious users may use information from exceptions to gain an understanding about how the program works and any potential weaknesses.
- Don't catch the root of all exceptions: `System.Exception`. This will swallow all errors, when you should be forced to see and fix them. It is okay to catch `System.Exception`, say for the purpose of logging, as long as you rethrow it.
- Wrap low-level exceptions in your own exceptions to hide implementation-level details. For example, if you have a collection class that is implemented internally using a `List<T>`, you may want to hide `ArgumentOutOfRangeExceptions` inside a `MyComponentException`.

CHAPTER 5

Numbers

IN THIS CHAPTER

- Decide Between `Float`, `Double`, and `Decimal`
- Use Enormous Integers (`BigInteger`)
- Use Complex Numbers
- Format Numbers in a String
- Convert a String to a Number
- Convert Between Number Bases
- Convert a Number to Bytes (and Vice Versa)
- Determine if an Integer Is Even
- Determine if an Integer Is a Power of 2 (aka, A Single Bit Is Set)
- Determine if a Number Is Prime
- Count the Number of 1 Bits
- Convert Degrees and Radians
- Round Numbers
- Generate Better Random Numbers
- Generate Unique IDs

Numbers form an integral part of many applications. Although seemingly a simple topic, when you consider how the world's many cultures represent numbers, and even how computers can represent numbers, the topic is not so simple after all. This chapter covers a lot of tips that are useful in many applications.

Decide Between `Float`, `Double`, and `Decimal`

Scenario/Problem: You need to decide which floating-point type to use in a situation.

Solution: Deciding which floating-point type to use is application dependent, but here are some things to think about:

- How big do the numbers need to be? Are they on the extreme, either positive or negative?
- How much precision do you need? Is seven digits enough? Sixteen? Need more?
- Do you have memory requirements that influence which you choose?
- Are the numbers coming from a database that already specifies the size it's using? This should match what you choose so you don't lose data.

Given these questions, Table 5.1 demonstrates the differences.

TABLE 5.1 **Floating-Point Types**

Type	Range	Precision (Digits)	Largest Exact Integer	Size
`Float`	$\pm1.5\times10^{-45}$ – $\pm3.4\times10^{38}$	7	2^{24}	4 bytes
`Double`	$\pm5.0\times10^{-324}$ – $\pm1.7\times10^{308}$	15–16	2^{53}	8 bytes
`Decimal`	$\pm1.0\times10^{-28}$ – $\pm7.9\times10^{28}$	28–29	2^{113}	16 bytes

Largest exact integer means the largest integer value that can be represented without loss of precision. These values should be kept in mind when you're converting between integer and floating-point types.

NOTE For any calculation involving money or finances, the `Decimal` type should always be used. Only this type has the appropriate precision to avoid critical rounding errors.

Use Enormous Integers (BigInteger)

Scenario/Problem: You need an integer larger than can fit in a UInt64.

Solution: .NET 4 ships with the BigInteger class, located in the System.Numerics namespace (you will need to add a reference to this assembly). With it, you can do arbitrarily large integer math, such as the following:

```
BigInteger a = UInt64.MaxValue;
BigInteger b = UInt64.MaxValue;

//this is a really, really big number
BigInteger c = a * b;
```

BigInteger is immutable, which means that calling

```
BigInteger a = 1;
a++;
```

will result in the creation of a second BigInteger object, assigning it back to a. Although this is transparent to you in practice, you should be aware that it has potential performance implications.

BigInteger has many static methods, such as the typical Parse(), TryParse(), and ToString() methods (which support hex format as well) found in other integer types, as well as mathematical helpers such as Pow(), Log(), Log10(), and others.

BigInteger's ToString() method accepts the usual format specifiers ("C", "N0", and so on), plus one more: "R". With all except "R", only 50 digits of integer precision are output, with the rest replaced by zeroes. With "R", all digits are preserved, but you can't apply other formatting (such as digit separators). The difference is shown here:

```
string numberToParse =
➥"234743652378423045783479556793498547534684795672309
➥482359874390";
BigInteger bi = BigInteger.Parse(numberToParse);
Console.WriteLine("N0: {0:N0}", bi);
Console.WriteLine("R: {0:R}", bi);
```

Output:

```
N0: 234,743,652,378,423,045,783,479,556,793,498,547,534,684,
➥795,672,300,000,000,000,000
R: 234743652378423045783479556793498547534684795672309482359874390
```

Using the output of the "R" format, you could of course perform your own manual formatting.

`BigInteger` also includes some instance helper properties, such as `IsPowerOfTwo` and `IsEven`, to simplify some tasks.

Use Complex Numbers

Scenario/Problem: Many engineering and mathematical problems require the use of imaginary numbers, often represented in the form *4+3i*, where *i* is the square root of -1.

Solution: Use the `System.Numerics.Complex` class to represent imaginary numbers. `Complex` wraps both the real and imaginary parts using doubles as the underlying format.

```
Complex a = new Complex(2, 1);
Complex b = new Complex(3, 2);
Console.WriteLine("a = {0}", a);
Console.WriteLine("b = {0}", b);
Console.WriteLine("a + b = {0}", a + b);
Console.WriteLine("pow(a,2) = {0}", Complex.Pow(a,2));
Console.WriteLine("a / 0 = {0}", a / Complex.Zero);

//this will assign -1 to the real part, and 0 to the imaginary part
Complex c = -1;
Console.WriteLine("c = {0}", c);
Console.WriteLine("Sqrt(c) = {0}", Complex.Sqrt(c));
```

This has the output

```
a = (2, 1)
b = (3, 2)
a + b = (5, 3)
pow(a,2) = (3, 4)
a / 0 = (NaN, NaN)
c = (-1, 0)
Sqrt(c) = (0, 1)
```

Format a Complex Number

While *(a, b)* is a valid format for imaginary numbers, it is common to see it written *a+bi* instead. This is easily accomplished with a custom formatter (as you learned in Chapter 2, “Creating Versatile Types”).

```
class ComplexFormatter : IFormatProvider, ICustomFormatter
{
    //accepts two format specifiers: i and j
    public string Format(string format, object arg, IFormatProvider
                          formatProvider)
    {
        if (arg is Complex)
        {
            Complex c = (Complex)arg;
            if (format.Equals("i", StringComparison.OrdinalIgnoreCase))
            {
                return c.Real.ToString("N2") + " + " +
                  c.Imaginary.ToString("N2") + "i";
            }
            else if (format.Equals("j",
                        StringComparison.OrdinalIgnoreCase))
            {
                return c.Real.ToString("N2") + " + " +
                  c.Imaginary.ToString("N2") + "j";
            }
            else
            {
                return c.ToString(format, formatProvider);
            }
        }
        else
        {
            if (arg is IFormattable)
            {
                return ((IFormattable)arg).ToString(format,
                           formatProvider);
            }
            else if (arg != null)
            {
                return arg.ToString();
            }
            else
            {
                return string.Empty;
            }
        }
    }

    public object GetFormat(Type formatType)
    {
```

```
        if (formatType == typeof(ICustomFormatter))
        {
            return this;
        }
        else
        {
            return
➥System.Threading.Thread.CurrentThread.
➥CurrentCulture.GetFormat(formatType);
        }
    }
}
```

Example usage:

```
Complex c = -1;
Console.WriteLine("Sqrt(c) = {0}",
    string.Format(new ComplexFormatter(), "{0:i}", Complex.Sqrt(c)));
```

This gives the output:

```
Sqrt(c) = 0.00 + 1.00i
```

Format Numbers in a String

Scenario/Problem: You need to format a number for display purposes in the appropriate local culture, or any other type of formatting.

Solution: The .NET Framework provides a wealth of number formatting options. There are so many options that it can be confusing at first. This section highlights a few of the more interesting options, including a table summarizing many examples.

NOTE If you call `ToString()` with no arguments, the current thread's culture will be assumed. It is often in your best interest to explicitly specify the culture.

Format a Number for a Specific Culture

Culture defines how the formatted number looks. Depending on the culture, some or all of these variables could change:

- **Decimal separator**—1.5 or 1,5?
- **Digit separator**—1,000,000 or 1.000.000?

- **Digit grouping**—In some cultures (such as India), digits are not grouped by threes.
- **Currency symbol**—U.S. Dollar ($), British Pound (£), Euro (€), Japanese Yen (¥).
- **Default number of decimal places for certain formats**

`CultureInfo` implements `IFormatProvider`, so any method that takes it can accept a culture. Here are some examples:

```
double val = 1234567.89;
Console.WriteLine(val.ToString("N",
➥         CultureInfo.CreateSpecificCulture("fr-FR")));
Console.WriteLine(string.Format(
    CultureInfo.CreateSpecificCulture("hi-IN"), "{0:N}", val));
```

This code produces the following output:

```
1 234 567,89
12,34,567.89
```

> **NOTE** Use the invariant culture whenever you need to store data for the application to consume. This is vitally important because it is impossible to accurately parse numbers when the format is not known beforehand. Alternatively, use binary formats because culture information is not relevant.

Print Numbers in Hexadecimal

Note that the "0x" that is typically prepended to hexadecimal numbers must be added by you. You can also specify how many digits you want shown (they will be zero-padded).

```
Int32 number = 12345;
string hex = number.ToString("X", CultureInfo.InvariantCulture);
//to get 0x before the number, do:
string hexUsual = "0x" + number.Format("X8",
                                       CultureInfo.InvariantCulture);
Console.WriteLine(hex);
Console.WriteLine(hexBetter);
```

The output is as follows:

```
3039
0x00003039
```

Group Digits

To group digits, use the "N" format option, as shown here:

```
int number = 12345;
Console.WriteLine(number.ToString("N", CultureInfo.InvariantCulture));
```

This produces the following output:

```
12,345
```

Print Leading Zeros

You can print leading zeros with the D and X format strings. The number specifies the total number of digits to output. If this number is greater than the number of digits in the number, the output is padded with zeros; otherwise, the number is output normally. Here's an example:

```
int number = 12345;
Console.WriteLine(number.ToString("D8", CultureInfo.InvariantCulture));
```

And here's the output:

```
00012345
```

Specify Number of Decimal Places

You can specify the number of decimal places with the C, E, F, G, N, and P format strings:

```
double number = 12345.6789;
Console.WriteLine(number.ToString("F3", CultureInfo.InvariantCulture));
```

The output is as follows (note the rounding):

```
12345.679
```

Use a Custom Format String for Finer Control

> **Scenario/Problem:** If the predefined format strings do not do exactly what you need and you require finer control, you can supply custom format strings. Suppose you want to control leading zeros, decimal places, and digit grouping all at once? What if you want negative numbers to be formatted differently than positive numbers? You cannot do any of this with the built-in format strings.

Solution: Use custom format specifiers.

```
double number = 12345.6789;
CultureInfo ci = CultureInfo.InvariantCulture;
```

```
//zeroes specify placeholders that will be filled in as needed
Console.WriteLine(number.ToString("00000000.00", ci));
Console.WriteLine(number.ToString("00,000,000.00", ci));

//note that in Hindi, commas do not go every 3 digits
Console.WriteLine(number.ToString("00,000,000.00",
          CultureInfo.CreateSpecificCulture("hi-IN")));

//show different format for negative/zero numbers
double neg = number * -1;
Console.WriteLine(neg.ToString("00,000,000.00;(00000000.000)", ci));

double zero = 0.0;
Console.WriteLine(
➥    zero.ToString("00,000,000.00;(00000000.000);'nothing!'", ci));
```

Here's the output:

```
00012345.68
00,012,345.68
0,00,12,345.68
(00012345.679)
nothing!
```

Number Format Strings Summary

Table 5.2 provides a summary of number format strings.

TABLE 5.2 **Number Format Strings**

Input	Format String	Types Allowed	Culture	Output
12345.6789	G	Integer, floating-point	Invariant	12345.6789
12345.6789	G4	Integer, floating-point	Invariant	1.235E+04
12345.6789	G5	Integer, floating-point	Invariant	12346
12345.6789	F	Integer, floating-point	Invariant	12345.68
12345.6789	F6	Integer, floating-point	Invariant	12345.678900
12345.6789	e	Integer, floating-point	Invariant	1.234568e+004
12345.6789	E	Integer, floating-point	Invariant	1.234568E+004
12345.6789	E3	Integer, floating-point	Invariant	1.235E+004
12345.6789	N	Integer, floating-point	Invariant	12,345.68
12345.6789	N0	Integer, floating-point	Invariant	12,346
12345.6789	N5	Integer, floating-point	Invariant	12,345.67890
12345.6789	C	Integer, floating-point	en-US	$12,345.68

continues

TABLE 5.2 **Number Format Strings** (continued)

Input	Format String	Types Allowed	Culture	Output
12345.6789	C3	Integer, floating-point	En-GB	£12,345.679
0.12345	P	Integer, floating-point	Invariant	12.35 %
0.12345	P1	Integer, floating-point	Invariant	12.3 %
12345	D	Integer	Invariant	12345
12345	D8	Integer	Invariant	00012345
12345	X	Integer	Invariant	3039
12345	X8	Integer	Invariant	00003039
12345.6789	000000.00	Integer, floating-point	Invariant	012345.68
12345.6789	000,000.0	Integer, floating-point	Invariant	012,345.7

Convert a String to a Number

Scenario/Problem: You need to parse string input into a number.

Solution: You can choose between `Parse`, which throws an exception if anything goes wrong, or `TryParse`, which is guaranteed not to throw an exception. I think you'll find that `TryParse` makes sense in most situations because of the performance implications when using exceptions.

```
string goodStr = " -100,000,000.567 ";
double goodVal = 0;
if (double.TryParse(goodStr, out goodVal))
{
    Console.WriteLine("Parsed {0} to number {1}", goodStr, goodVal);
}
```

Note that `goodStr` has digit separators, decimal points, spaces, and a negative sign. By default, `TryParse` will accept all of these. If you know the format of the number, you can restrict the format using the `NumberStyles` enumeration.

```
string goodStr = " -100,000,000.567 ";
double goodVal = 0;
if (!double.TryParse(goodStr, NumberStyles.AllowDecimalPoint,
        CultureInfo.CurrentCulture, out goodVal))
{
    Console.WriteLine(
        "Unable to parse {0} with limited NumberStyle", goodStr);
}
```

NOTE If you don't specify a culture when you parse, the current thread's culture is assumed. To specify another culture, do this:

```
string frStr = "-100 100 100,987";
double frVal = 0;
bool success = double.TryParse(frStr, NumberStyles.Any,
 CultureInfo.CreateSpecificCulture("fr-FR"), out frVal);
```

Parse Hex Number

To parse hexadecimal number strings, you must remove any "0x" that precedes the number before calling `TryParse()`.

```
string hexStr = "0x3039";
Int32 hexVal = 0;
if (Int32.TryParse(hexStr.Replace("0x",""),
                   NumberStyles.HexNumber,
                   CultureInfo.CurrentCulture,
                   out hexVal))
{
    Console.WriteLine("Parsed {0} to value {1}", hexStr, hexVal);
}
```

The following output is produced:

```
Parsed 0x3039 to value 12345
```

Convert Between Number Bases

Scenario/Problem: You need to display a number in any arbitrary base.

Solution: You can't convert numbers, per se, to different bases. They are, after all, always represented as binary in the computer. You are merely showing a representation of that number—in other words, a string. How to do it depends on whether you want the typical "computer" bases or an arbitrary one.

Convert from Base-10 to Base-2, -8, or -16

Thankfully, if you want a standard base such as 2, 8, or 16, the functionality is already built into the Framework:

```
int sourceNum = 100;
int destBase = 16;
string destStr = Convert.ToString(sourceNum, destBase);
```

`destStr` will contain the value 64, the hexadecimal equivalent of 100 in base-10.

Convert from Base-10 to an Arbitrary Base

What if you need a really strange number base, such as 5 or 99? For that, the following code will help:

```
private string ConvertToBase(Int64 decNum, int destBase)
{
    StringBuilder sb = new StringBuilder();
    Int64 accum = decNum;
    while (accum > 0)
    {
        Int64 digit = (accum % destBase);
        string digitStr;
        if (digit <= 9)
        {
            digitStr = digit.ToString();
        }
        else
        {
            switch (digit)
            {
                case 10: digitStr = "A"; break;
                case 11: digitStr = "B"; break;
                case 12: digitStr = "C"; break;
                case 13: digitStr = "D"; break;
                case 14: digitStr = "E"; break;
                case 15: digitStr = "F"; break;
                //don't know what do after base-16
                //add letters, define your own symbols
                default: digitStr = "?"; break;
            }
        }
        sb.Append(digitStr);
        accum /= destBase;
    }
    return sb.ToString();
}
```

Note that although this can accept any destination base, you will need to define any characters for digit values up to `destBase - 1`.

Convert to Base-10

The following code converts a string representation of a number in an arbitrary base (up to 16 in this example) to base-10:

```
private Int64 ConvertFromBase(string num, int fromBase)
{
    Int64 accum = 0;
    Int64 multiplier = 1;
    for (int i = num.Length - 1; i >= 0; i—)
    {
        int digitVal;
        if (num[i] >= '0' && num[i] <= '9')
        {
            digitVal = num[i] - '0';
        }
        else
        {
            switch (num[i])
            {
                case 'A': digitVal = 10; break;
                case 'B': digitVal = 11; break;
                case 'C': digitVal = 12; break;
                case 'D': digitVal = 13; break;
                case 'E': digitVal = 14; break;
                case 'F': digitVal = 15; break;
                default: throw new FormatException("Unknown digit");
            }
        }
        accum += (digitVal * multiplier);
        multiplier *= fromBase;
    }
    return accum;
}
```

NOTE If you need to convert between two arbitrary bases, it is easier to first convert to base-10, then convert to the other base using a combination of the methods given.

Convert a Number to Bytes (and Vice Versa)

Scenario/Problem: You need to convert a number into bytes.

Solution: The handy `BitConverter` class will help you.

```
Int32 num = 13;
byte[] bytes = BitConverter.GetBytes(13);
```

Here's how to convert back:

```
Int32 num = BitConverter.ToInt32(bytes);
```

`BitConverter` can work on all number types except, oddly enough, `Decimal`. For that, you need this code:

```
static byte[] DecimalToBytes(decimal number)
{
    Int32[] bits = Decimal.GetBits(number);
    byte[] bytes = new byte[16];
    for (int i = 0; i < 4; i++)
    {
        bytes[i * 4 + 0] = (byte)(bits[i] & 0xFF);
        bytes[i * 4 + 1] = (byte)((bits[i] >> 0x8) & 0xFF);
        bytes[i * 4 + 2] = (byte)((bits[i] >> 0x10) & 0xFF);
        bytes[i * 4 + 3] = (byte)((bits[i] >> 0x18) & 0xFF);
    }
    return bytes;
}

static Decimal BytesToDecimal(byte[] bytes)
{
    Int32[] bits = new Int32[4];
    for (int i = 0; i < 4; i++)
    {
        bits[i] =  bytes[i * 4 + 0];
        bits[i] |= (bytes[i * 4 + 1] << 0x8);
        bits[i] |= (bytes[i * 4 + 2] << 0x10);
        bits[i] |= (bytes[i * 4 + 3] << 0x18);
    }
    return new Decimal(bits);
}
```

NOTE Whenever you are converting numbers to bytes (and vice versa), you need to be concerned about *endianness*, which is merely the order of the bytes in memory. Numbers are said to be little endian if they start with the least-significant byte first. Big endian values start with the most-significant byte. Most personal computers these days are little endian, but the `BitConverter` class provides a handy static property called `IsLittleEndian` that can tell you about the current hardware.

Determine if an Integer Is Even

Scenario/Problem: You need to determine if an integer is even.

Solution: An integer is even if the least-significant bit is 0.

```
public static bool IsEven(Int64 number)
{
    return ((number & 0x1)==0);
}
```

Determine if an Integer Is a Power of 2 (aka, A Single Bit Is Set)

Scenario/Problem: You need to determine if an integer is a power of 2, or if there is exactly one bit set in a number.

Solution: The solution relies on the fact that integers are twos-complement encoded and that a power of 2 has only a single 1 bit.

```
private static bool IsPowerOfTwo(Int64 number)
{
    return (number != 0) && ((number & -number) == number);
}
```

The check for 0 could be omitted if the function needed to be called a lot and you could ensure that 0 will never be passed to it.

Determine if a Number Is Prime

Scenario/Problem: You need to determine if a number is prime.

Solution: A prime number is divisible only by 1 and itself. A popular solution is this example:

```
static bool IsPrime(int number)
{
    //check for evenness
```

```
    if (number % 2 == 0)
    {
        if (number == 2)
        {
            return true;
        }
        return false;
    }
    //don't need to check past the square root
    int max = (int)Math.Sqrt(number);
    for (int i = 3; i <= max; i += 2)
    {
        if ((number % i) == 0)
        {
            return false;
        }
    }
    return true;
}
```

NOTE See Chapter 23, "Threads and Asynchronous Programming," for an example of splitting up the work `IsPrime()` is doing across multiple processors.

Count the Number of 1 Bits

Scenario/Problem: You need to count the number of 1 bits in a number. Aside from interview questions, counting the number of bits can actually have a useful application (counting the number of flags set in a bit-field, for example).

Solution: There are many solutions to this problem, but here's my favorite:

```
static Int16 CountBits(Int32 number)
{
    int accum = number;
    Int16 count = 0;
    while (accum > 0)
    {
        accum &= (accum - 1);
        count++;
```

```
    }
    return count;
}
```

This runs in time proportion to the number of 1 bits set in `number`.

Convert Degrees and Radians

Scenario/Problem: You need to convert degrees to radians or vice versa.

Solution: This code is common in many types of graphical applications, where degrees make sense to humans, but many graphics APIs handle radians. If your application uses these a lot, you might consider making them extension methods on `double`.

See the RadiansAndDegrees sample project to see this code in action in conjunction with the mouse.

```
public static double RadiansToDegrees(double radians)
{
    return radians * 360.0 / ( 2.0 * Math.PI) ;
}

public static double DegreesToRadians(double degrees)
{
    return degrees * (2.0 * Math.PI) / 360.0;
}
```

Pi, as well as other useful constants and mathematical functions, is in the `Math` class.

Round Numbers

Scenario/Problem: You need to control the type of rounding done to numbers.

Solution: The `Math` class provides a handy function that performs rounding for you. You can specify the decimal precision as well as the type of midpoint rounding (the behavior when on a middle value such as .5, .05, and so on). If no rounding type is specified, the default is `MidpointRounding.ToEven`, also known as *banker's rounding*.

TABLE 5.3 **Rounding Methods**

Value	Meaning	Example
`MidpointRounding.ToEven`	Round to nearest even number	2.5 to 2.0
`MidpointRounding.AwayFromZero`	Round to nearest number away from zero	2.5 to 3.0

Here are some examples (the sample output is from the `RoundNumbers` example in the chapter's source code).

Table 5.4 summarizes the results from calling with Math.Round() with various arguments.

TABLE 5.4 **Rounding Samples**

Code	Result
Math.Round(13.45);	13
Math.Round(13.45, 1);	13.4
Math.Round(13.45, 2);	13.45
Math.Round(13.45, MidpointRounding.AwayFromZero);	13
Math.Round(13.45, 1, MidpointRounding.AwayFromZero);	13.5
Math.Round(13.45, 2, MidpointRounding.AwayFromZero);	13.45
Math.Round(13.45, MidpointRounding.ToEven);	13
Math.Round(13.45, 1, MidpointRounding.ToEven);	13.4
Math.Round(13.45, 2, MidpointRounding.ToEven);	13.45
Math.Round(-13.45);	–13
Math.Round(-13.45, 1);	–13.4
Math.Round(-13.45, 2);	–13.45
Math.Round(-13.45, MidpointRounding.AwayFromZero);	–13
Math.Round(-13.45, 1, MidpointRounding.AwayFromZero);	–13.5
Math.Round(-13.45, 2, MidpointRounding.AwayFromZero);	–13.45
Math.Round(-13.45, MidpointRounding.ToEven);	–13
Math.Round(-13.45, 1, MidpointRounding.ToEven);	–13.4
Math.Round(-13.45, 2, MidpointRounding.ToEven);	–13.45

Round Numbers to Nearest Multiple

Scenario/Problem: In many graphical editors, a common feature is to restrict mouse positions to gridlines. This makes the user's job easier because they don't have to make ultra-precise mouse movements when editing shapes. For example, if the mouse were at (104, 96) and you wanted the values snapped to a 5-by-5 pixel grid, you could change them to (105, 95).

Solution: This is easily accomplished with the following code:

```
private static Int32 SnapInput(double input, Int32 multiple)
{
    return (((Int32)(input + (multiple / 2.0))) / multiple) * multiple;
}
```

Table 5.5 demonstrates this algorithm when rounding/snapping values to the nearest multiple of ten.

TABLE 5.5 **Snap to Multiples of 10**

Input	Output
0	0
6.7	10
13.4	10
20.1	20
26.8	30
33.5	30
40.2	40
46.9	50

See the SnapToGrid project in the code for this chapter for an example of snapping actual mouse input to a grid.

If you want to round to a floating-point value (say, the nearest 0.5), you need to massage the inputs and outputs of the preceding function slightly, as shown here:

```
private static double SnapInput(double input,
                                double multiple,
                                Int32 precision)
{
    double scalar = Math.Pow(10, precision);
    return SnapInput(scalar * input,
                     (Int32)(scalar * multiple)) / scalar;
}
```

The precision argument specifies how many decimal points your input values can contain. This is important because the multiple needs to be scaled to an integer so that the math can work correctly. Table 5.6 uses a precision of two.

TABLE 5.6 **Snap to Multiples of 0.5**

Input	Output
0	0
0.15	0
0.3	0.5
0.45	0.5
0.6	0.5
0.75	1
0.9	1
1.06	1

Generate Better Random Numbers

Scenario/Problem: You need random numbers for anything related to security.

Solution: The standard way to generate random numbers is with the `System.Random` class, which produces numbers that appear random, based on a seed value (often the current time). That usage is shown here:

```
Random rand = new Random();
Int32 randomNumber = rand.Next();
```

If you just need an arbitrary number for noncryptographic purposes, this is perfectly fine. However, if you are doing anything security related, you should never use `Random`. Instead, use `System.Security.Cryptography.RNGCryptoServiceProvider`. Here's an example:

```
System.Security.Cryptography.RNGCryptoServiceProvider cryptRand =
    new System.Security.Cryptography.RNGCryptoServiceProvider();
byte[] bytes = new byte[4];
cryptRand.GetBytes(bytes);
Int32 number = BitConverter.ToInt32(bytes, 0);
```

NOTE Both methods of generating random numbers are actually *pseudorandom* (that is, not truly random). Pseudorandom numbers are based on some seed, or known data. `System.Random` uses a seed value (often the current time), and `RNGCryptoServiceProvider` uses a combination of processor info, operating system counters, cycle counters, time, and other information to generate cryptographically secure bytes. True randomness can generally be achieved only through more complicated phenomena (static noise, mouse movement, network traffic patterns, and so on).

NOTE You may not always want or need cryptographically secure random numbers. For instance, if you just need an *arbitrary* number and there are no security considerations, using `System.Random` might be preferable for easier testing because you can reproduce the desired numbers at will by giving a known seed value.

Generate Unique IDs (GUIDs)

Scenario/Problem: You need an ID that is nearly guaranteed universally unique.

Solution: Use the `System.Guid` class to generate 128 bytes of data that has a very high probability of being unique across all computers and all networks, for all time.

```
Guid g = Guid.NewGuid();
Console.WriteLine("GUID: {0}", g);
```

produces the output:

```
GUID: ea8b716c-892a-4bed-b918-0d454c1b8474
```

GUIDs are used all over in databases and operating systems to uniquely identify records and components.

NOTE GUIDs are generated from a combination of hardware information and the current time, but the generation is one way; that is, you cannot infer any information about the hardware from a given GUID.

The `Guid` class provides `Parse()` and `TryParse()` methods to convert strings to GUID objects. There are a few common string representations of GUIDs, so there are also `ParseExact()` and `TryParseExact()` methods.

```
//parsing
var guids = new Tuple<string,string>[]
{
    Tuple.Create("d261edd3-4562-41cb-ba7e-b176157951d8", "D"),
    Tuple.Create("d261edd3456241cbba7eb176157951d8", "N"),
    Tuple.Create("{d261edd3-4562-41cb-ba7e-b176157951d8}", "B"),
    Tuple.Create("(d261edd3-4562-41cb-ba7e-b176157951d8)", "P"),
    Tuple.Create("{0xd261edd3,0x4562,0x41cb,
➥{0xba,0x7e,0xb1,0x76,0x15,0x79,0x51,0xd8}}", "X"),
};
```

```
foreach (var t in guids)
{
    Console.WriteLine("Parse {0} ==> {1}",
                      t.Item1,
                      Guid.ParseExact(t.Item1, t.Item2));
    Console.WriteLine();
}
```

This produces the output:

```
Parse d261edd3-4562-41cb-ba7e-b176157951d8 ==>
➥d261edd3-4562-41cb-ba7e-b176157951d8

Parse d261edd3456241cbba7eb176157951d8 ==>
➥d261edd3-4562-41cb-ba7e-b176157951d8

Parse {d261edd3-4562-41cb-ba7e-b176157951d8} ==>
➥d261edd3-4562-41cb-ba7e-b176157951d8

Parse (d261edd3-4562-41cb-ba7e-b176157951d8) ==>
➥d261edd3-4562-41cb-ba7e-b176157951d8

Parse {0xd261edd3,0x4562,0x41cb,
➥{0xba,0x7e,0xb1,0x76,0x15,0x79,0x51,0xd8}} ==>
➥d261edd3-4562-41cb-ba7e-b176157951d8
```

CHAPTER 6

Enumerations

IN THIS CHAPTER

- Declare an Enumeration
- Declare Flags as an Enumeration
- Determine if a Flag Is Set
- Convert an Enumeration to an Integer (and Vice Versa)
- Determine if an Enumeration Is Valid
- List Enumeration Values
- Convert a String to an Enumeration
- Attach Metadata to Enums with Extension Methods
- Enumeration Tips

Enumerations bridge the gap between numbers and objects. More than a numerical ID, less than a struct, they fill that niche where you want a well-understood name without any extra baggage. You can think of them as (mostly) type-safe constants.

Enumerations also provide type-safe functionality for flags.

Declare an Enumeration

Scenario/Problem: You need to represent a limited set of well-known, constant values. These can be a set of options, aliases for IDs, or (as we'll see later) flags.

Solution: Enumerations can be defined within namespaces or classes with this syntax:

```
enum BookBinding
{
    None,
    Hardcover,
    Paperback
};
```

This code declares a `BookBinding` enumeration containing three values. The first value is `None` and is often included to indicate the lack of a value.

You can use the enumeration like this:

```
BookBinding binding = BookBinding.Hardcover;
```

Declare an Enumeration with Explicit Values

Scenario/Problem: You need an enumeration's specific values to have specific values, perhaps to match values in a database.

Solution: Simply assign values inside the enumeration. You don't have to define every value. You can define some of them and the compiler will fill in the rest sequentially.

```
enum BookLanguage
{
    None = 0,
    English = 1,
    Spanish = 2,
```

```
    Italian = 3,
    French = 4,
    Japanese = 5,
};
```

NOTE There is nothing preventing you from assigning duplicate values to the enumeration constants. I'm not sure if there is a legitimately useful reason to do this, but it is legal.

Declare Flags as an Enumeration

Scenario/Problem: You need a set of flags, that is, values that can be combined in a single variable.

Solution: In C++, you would `#define` constants, often at a global level. In C#, you can use enumerations to achieve bit-field flag functionality in a type-safe way. You do need to explicitly set the values to multiples of two, however.

```
[Flags]
enum BookGenres
{
    None = 0,
    ScienceFiction = 0x01,
    Crime = 0x02,
    Romance = 0x04,
    History = 0x08,
    Science = 0x10,
    Mystery = 0x20,
    Fantasy = 0x40,
    Vampire = 0x80,
};
```

You can use the `BookGenres` enumeration in bit-field operations. To see what `[Flags]` does, examine the following code and its output:

```
BookBinding binding = BookBinding.Hardcover;
BookBinding doubleBinding =
    BookBinding.Hardcover | BookBinding.Paperback;

Console.WriteLine("Binding: {0}", binding);
Console.WriteLine("Double Binding: {0}", doubleBinding);
```

```
BookGenres genres =
    BookGenres.Vampire | BookGenres.Fantasy | BookGenres.Romance;
Console.WriteLine("Genres: {0}", genres);
```

Output:

```
Binding: Hardcover
Double Binding: 3
Genres: Romance, Fantasy, Vampire
```

Note that the enumeration with the `[Flags]` attribute printed out each genre correctly.

Determine if a Flag Is Set

Scenario/Problem: You need to determine if a particular flag is set on an enumeration variable.

Solution: The standard way of doing this is to use the bitwise & operator:

```
BookGenres genres = BookGenres.Vampire | BookGenres.Fantasy;
bool isVampire = ((genres & BookGenres.Vampire)!=0);
```

However, .NET 4 introduces the `HasFlag()` method, which accomplishes the same thing:

```
bool isVampire = genres.HasFlag(BookGenres.Vampire);
```

Convert an Enumeration to an Integer (and Vice Versa)

Scenario/Problem: You need to convert an enumeration to its numeric equivalent.

Solution: Enumerations cannot be implicitly converted to integers (and vice versa) like they can in C++. You need to explicitly cast the values.

```
int value = (int)BookLanguage.English;
BookLanguage lang = (BookLanguage)value;
```

When converting from integer to an enumeration, make sure you validate the result (see the next section).

Determine if an Enumeration Is Valid

Scenario/Problem: You need to determine if an arbitrary value is valid for a given enumeration type. Often, the value will come from an external, untrusted source.

Given the preceding enumeration definition, the following is still valid code:

```
BookBinding = (BookBinding)9999;
```

Therefore, you will need to validate enumeration values wherever necessary.

Solution: .NET provides the `Enum.IsDefined()` method to do this.

```
BookBinding badBinding = (BookBinding)9999;
bool isDefined = Enum.IsDefined(typeof(BookBinding), badBinding);
```

List Enumeration Values

Scenario/Problem: You want to get a list of all valid values for a given enumeration type.

Solution: To get a list of all defined values for a specific enumeration, call `Enum.GetValues()`, as shown here:

```
foreach (BookGenres genre in Enum.GetValues(typeof(BookGenres)))
{
    Console.WriteLine("\t" + Enum.GetName(typeof(BookGenres), genre));
}
```

`Enum.GetName()` returns the same string you would get if you just called `ToString()` on a value. You can also just call `Enum.GetNames()` to get all the strings back directly.

Convert a String to an Enumeration

Scenario/Problem: You need to parse a string into its equivalent enumeration value.

Solution: While `Enum` does contain a standard `Parse()` method, this can throw exceptions and requires you to cast the result to the desired enumeration type. Instead, use

`TryParse()`, which is both safe and strongly typed, using generics, as in this code example:

```
string hardcoverString = "hardcover";
BookBinding goodBinding, badBinding;
//this succeeds
bool canParse = Enum.TryParse(hardcoverString, out goodBinding);
//this fails
canParse = Enum.TryParse("garbage", out badBinding);
```

Convert a String to a Set of Flags

Scenario/Problem: You need to parse a string that contains multiple enumeration values into the flag equivalent of an enumeration.

Solution: `Enum.TryParse()` also works for flags, and it will handle duplicate values as well, as in this sample:

```
string flagString = "Vampire, Mystery, ScienceFiction, Vampire";
BookGenres flagEnum = BookGenres.None;
if (Enum.TryParse(flagString, out flagEnum))
{
    Console.WriteLine("Parsed \"{0}\" into {1}", flagString, flagEnum);
}
```

The following output is produced:

```
Parsed "Vampire, Mystery, ScienceFiction, Vampire" into
➥ScienceFiction, Mystery, Vampire
```

Attach Metadata to Enums with Extension Methods

Scenario/Problem: It's often useful to be able to associate extra data with Enum values, such as a string display value (since you can't override `ToString()`) or any other type of data you want.

Solution: Using extension methods combined with attributes (see Chapter 24, "Reflection and Creating Plugins"), you can add a method to your enumeration to access the values you attached in attributes. For this example, let's create our own attribute called `Culture`, which we'll attach to our `BookLanguage` enumeration values.

```
[AttributeUsage(AttributeTargets.All, AllowMultiple=true)]
class CultureAttribute : Attribute
{
    string _culture;

    public string Culture
    {
        get
        {
            return _culture;
        }
    }

    public CultureAttribute(string culture)
    {
        _culture = culture;
    }
}
```

Now we'll modify our enumeration to include these attributes:

```
enum BookLanguage
{
    None = 0,
    [Culture("en-US")]
    [Culture("en-UK")]
    English = 1,
    [Culture("es-MX")]
    [Culture("es-ES")]
    Spanish = 2,
    [Culture("it-IT")]
    Italian = 3,
    [Culture("fr-FR")]
    [Culture("fr-BE")]
    French = 4,
};
```

Finally, we need to add the extension method to access these attributes:

```
static class CultureExtensions
{
    public static string[] GetCultures(this BookLanguage language)
    {
        //note: this will only work for single-value genres
        CultureAttribute[] attributes =
➥(CultureAttribute[])language.GetType().GetField(
➥language.ToString()).GetCustomAttributes(typeof(CultureAttribute),
```

```
                                               false);
        string[] cultures = new string[attributes.Length];
        for (int i = 0; i < attributes.Length; i++)
        {
            cultures[i] = attributes[i].Culture;
        }
        return cultures;
    }
}
```

Now to test it:

```
PrintCultures(BookLanguage.English);
PrintCultures(BookLanguage.Spanish);

static void PrintCultures(BookLanguage language)
{
    Console.WriteLine("Cultures for {0}:", language);
    foreach (string culture in language.GetCultures())
    {
        Console.WriteLine("\t" + culture);
    }
}
```

The following output is produced:

```
Cultures for English:
        en-UK
        en-US
Cultures for Spanish:
        es-MX
        es-ES
```

NOTE Before adding too much extra data on top of Enum values, make sure that you are not violating their lightweight nature. Consider if you actually need a `struct` to represent your data (perhaps with the Enum as an ID in the struct).

Enumeration Tips

The following list contains some best practices you should follow when using enumerations:

- If your enumerations must match external values (such as from a database), then explicitly assign a value to each enumeration member.

- Always use `[Flags]` when you need to combine multiple values into a single field.
- Flag enumerations must have values explicitly assigned that are unique powers of two (1, 2, 4, 8, 16, and so on) to work correctly.
- An enumeration should have a singular name if it is not used as flags, whereas flags should have plural names. See the `BookBinding` and `BookGenres` examples earlier in this chapter.
- Define a `None` value in each enumeration, with value of 0. This is especially important when using `[Flags]`.

CHAPTER 7

Strings

IN THIS CHAPTER

- Convert a String to Bytes (and Vice Versa)
- Create a Custom Encoding Scheme
- Compare Strings Correctly
- Change Case Correctly
- Detect Empty Strings
- Concatenate Strings: Should You Use `StringBuilder`?
- Concatenate Collection Items into a String
- Append a Newline Character
- Split a String
- Convert Binary Data to a String (Base-64 Encoding)
- Reverse Words
- Sort Number Strings Naturally

Strings are so fundamental a data type that their usage is often covered elsewhere, as it relates to other types. Nevertheless, some topics are specific to strings, and those are covered in this chapter.

Convert a String to Bytes (and Vice Versa)

Scenario/Problem: You need to convert text to and from a binary format.

Solution: The `System.Text` namespace defines a number of classes that help you work with textual data. To convert to and from bytes, use the `Encoding` class. Although it is possible to create your own text-encoding scheme, usually you will use one of the pre-created static members of the `Encoding` class, which represent the most common encoding standards, such as ASCII, Unicode, UTF-8, and so on.

The `GetBytes()` method will get the appropriate byte representation:

```
string myString = "C# Rocks!";
byte[] bytes = Encoding.ASCII.GetBytes(myString);
```

If you were to print out the string and the bytes, it would look like this:

```
Original string: C# Rocks!
ASCII bytes: 43-23-20-52-6F-63-6B-73-21
```

Using `Encoding.Unicode`, it would look like this:

```
Unicode bytes: 43-00-23-00-20-00-52-00-6F-00-63-00-6B-00-73-00-21-00
```

To convert back, use `Encoding.GetString()` and pass in the bytes:

```
string result = Encoding.ASCII.GetString(bytes);
```

This is all simple enough, but consider the string "C# Rocks!♪". The music note has no ASCII equivalent. This character will be converted to a question mark (?) if you convert to a byte format with no valid encoding, as in this example:

```
string myString = "C# Rocks! ♪";
byte[] bytes = Encoding.ASCII.GetBytes(myString);
string result = Encoding.ASCII.GetString(bytes);
Console.WriteLine("Round trip: {0}->{1}->{2}",
                  myString,
                  BitConverter.ToString(bytes),
                  result);
```

This has the following output:

```
Round trip: C# Rocks!♪->43-23-20-52-6F-63-6B-73-21-3F->C# Rocks!?
```

However, if we use Unicode encoding, it will all work out both ways:

```
string myString = "C# Rocks!?";
byte[] bytes = Encoding.Unicode.GetBytes(myString);
string result =
Encoding.Unicode.GetString(bytes);Console.WriteLine("Round trip: {0}-
>{1}->{2}",
                  myString,
                  BitConverter.ToString(bytes),
                  result);
```

Here's the output:

```
Round trip: C# Rocks!♪
➥->43-00-23-00-20-00-52-00-6F-00-63-00-6B-00-73-00-21-00-6B-26
➥->C# Rocks!♪
```

NOTE In memory, all strings are Unicode in .NET. It's only when you're writing strings to files, networks, databases, interop buffers, and other external locations that you need to worry about byte representation.

Create a Custom Encoding Scheme

Scenario/Problem: You need to translate strings to bytes in a custom manner.

Solution: Derive a class from `System.Text.Encoding` and implement the abstract methods. The Encoding class defines many overloads for both encoding and decoding strings, but they all eventually call a few fundamental methods and these are the only methods you need to define.

Much of the code in this example is argument validation, as stipulated by the MSDN documentation for this class.

The encoding algorithm is the famous substitution cipher, ROT13, where each letter is rotated 13 places to the right.

```
class Rot13Encoder : System.Text.Encoding
{
    //The encoder class defines many different overloads for conversion,
    //but they all end up calling these methods, so these are
    //all you need to implement
    public override int GetByteCount(char[] chars, int index, int count)
```

```
{
    if (chars == null)
    {
        throw new ArgumentNullException("chars");
    }
    if (index < 0)
    {
        throw new ArgumentOutOfRangeException("index");
    }
    if (count < 0)
    {
        throw new ArgumentOutOfRangeException("count");
    }
    if (index + count > chars.Length)
    {
        throw new ArgumentOutOfRangeException("index, count");
    }
    //we'll use one byte per character
    //(you could do whatever you want--
    //need 6 bits per character? you can do it)
    return count;
}

public override int GetBytes(char[] chars,
                             int charIndex,
                             int charCount,
                             byte[] bytes,
                             int byteIndex)
{
    if (chars == null)
        throw new ArgumentNullException("chars");
    if (bytes == null)
        throw new ArgumentNullException("bytes");
    if (charIndex < 0)
        throw new ArgumentOutOfRangeException("charIndex");
    if (charCount < 0)
        throw new ArgumentOutOfRangeException("charCount");
    if (charIndex + charCount > chars.Length) throw new
➥ArgumentOutOfRangeException("charIndex, charCount");
    if (bytes.Length - byteIndex < charCount)
➥throw new ArgumentException("Not enough bytes in destination");
    if (!AreValidChars(chars))
        throw new ArgumentException(
        "Only lower-case alphabetic characters allowed");
```

```
        for (int i = charIndex, dest = byteIndex;
             i < charIndex + charCount;
             ++i, ++dest)
        {
            //rebase to 'a' = 0
            int value = chars[i] - 'a';
            value = (value + 13) % 26;
            value += 'a';
            bytes[dest] = (byte)value;
        }

        //return the number of bytes written
        return charCount;
    }

    private bool AreValidChars(char[] chars)
    {
        foreach (char c in chars)
        {
            if (!(c >= 'a' && c <= 'z'))
                return false;
        }
        return true;
    }

    public override int GetCharCount(byte[] bytes, int index, int count)
    {
        if (bytes == null) throw new ArgumentNullException("bytes");
        if (index < 0) throw new ArgumentOutOfRangeException("index");
        if (count < 0) throw new ArgumentOutOfRangeException("count");
        if (index + count > bytes.Length)
➥throw new ArgumentOutOfRangeException("index, count");
        return count;
    }

    public override int GetChars(byte[] bytes,
                                 int byteIndex,
                                 int byteCount,
                                 char[] chars,
                                 int charIndex)
    {
        if (bytes == null)
           throw new ArgumentNullException("bytes");
        if (chars == null)
           throw new ArgumentNullException("chars");
```

```
        if (charIndex < 0)
           throw new ArgumentOutOfRangeException("charIndex");
        if (charIndex >= chars.Length)
➥throw new ArgumentOutOfRangeException("charIndex");
        if (byteIndex < 0)
            throw new ArgumentOutOfRangeException("byteIndex");
        if (byteCount < 0)
            throw new ArgumentOutOfRangeException("byteCount");
        if (byteIndex + byteCount > bytes.Length) throw new
➥ArgumentOutOfRangeException("byteIndex, byteCount");

        for (int i = byteIndex, dest = charIndex;
             i < byteIndex + byteCount;
             ++i, ++dest)
        {
            //rebase 'a' to 0
            int value = bytes[i] - 'a';
            value = (value + 13) % 26;
            value += 'a';
            chars[dest] = (char)value;
        }
        //return the number of characters written
        return byteCount;
    }

    public override int GetMaxByteCount(int charCount)
    {
        //since there is one byte per character, this is pretty easy
        return charCount;
    }

    public override int GetMaxCharCount(int byteCount)
    {
        return byteCount;
    }
}
```

A simple test demonstrates this (non)encryption encoder:

```
Rot13Encoder encoder = new Rot13Encoder();

string original = "hellocsharp";

byte[] bytes = encoder.GetBytes(original);

//if we assumed ASCII, what does it look like?
Console.WriteLine("Original: {0}", original);
```

```
Console.WriteLine("ASCII interpretation: {0}",
                  Encoding.ASCII.GetString(bytes));
Console.WriteLine("Rot13 interpretation: {0}",
                  encoder.GetString(bytes));
```

Here's the output:

```
Original: hellocsharp
ASCII interpretation: uryybpfunec
Rot13 interpretation: hellocsharp
```

NOTE The need for custom string encoding can show up in unusual places. I once worked on a system that needed to communicate with buoys via satellites. Because of space, the limited alphabet had to be encoded in 6 bits per character. It was easy to wrap this functionality into a custom `Encoder`-derived class for use in the application.

Compare Strings Correctly

Scenario/Problem: You need to compare two localized strings. A localized string is any string that the users see that may have been translated into their local language.

Solution: Always take culture into account and use the functionality provided in the .NET Framework. There are many ways to compare strings in C#. Some are better suited for localized text because strings can seem equivalent while having different byte values. This is especially true in non-Latin alphabets and when capitalization rules are not what you assume.

Here is a demonstration of the issue:

```
string a = "file";
string b = "FILE";
bool equalInvariant =
    string.Compare(a, b, true, CultureInfo.InvariantCulture) == 0;
bool equalTurkish =
    string.Compare(a, b, true,
                   CultureInfo.CreateSpecificCulture("tr-TR")) == 0;

Console.WriteLine("Are {0} and {1} equal?",a,b);
Console.WriteLine("Invariant culture: " +
                  (equalInvariant ? "yes" : "no"));
Console.WriteLine("Turkish culture: " +
                  (equalTurkish ? "yes" : "no"));
```

What is the output of this program?

```
Are file and FILE equal?
Invariant culture: yes
Turkish culture: no
```

As you can see, the culture can drastically change how strings are interpreted.

In general, you should use `String.Compare()` and supply the culture you want to use. For nonlocalized strings, such as internal program strings or settings names, using the invariant culture is acceptable.

Change Case Correctly

Scenario/Problem: You need to change the case of a localized string.

Solution: This is nearly the same issue as comparing two strings. You must specify the culture to do it correctly. Again, use the built-in functionality and remember the culture.

Using our Turkish example again, here is the sample code:

```
string original = "file";
Console.WriteLine("Original: "+original);
Console.WriteLine("Uppercase (invariant): " +
                  original.ToUpperInvariant());
Console.WriteLine("Uppercase (Turkish): " +
    original.ToUpper(CultureInfo.CreateSpecificCulture("tr-TR")));
```

What is the difference in output?

```
Original: file
Uppercase (invariant): FILE
Uppercase (Turkish): FILE
```

Seemingly nothing, but let's look at the bytes of the uppercase strings:

```
Bytes (invariant): 46-00-49-00-4C-00-45-00
Bytes   (Turkish): 46-00-30-01-4C-00-45-00
```

You can now see the difference, even though the visual representation is the same. The lesson here is that just because a character looks the same, it doesn't mean it is the same.

Detect Empty Strings

Scenario/Problem: You need to detect if a string contains content.

Solution: When handling string input, you generally need to be aware of four possible states:

1. String is null.
2. String is empty.
3. String contains nothing but whitespace.
4. String contains content.

The first two conditions are handled by the static method `String.IsNullOrEmpty()`, which has existed in .Net for a while.

.Net 4 adds `String.IsNullOrWhitespace()`, which also handles condition 3.

```
bool containsContent = !String.IsNullOrWhitespace(myString);
```

Concatenate Strings: Should You Use StringBuilder?

Scenario/Problem: You need to append a large number of strings together to form a single string. You have heard that `StringBuilder` should always be used.

Solution: Not necessarily. Use of `StringBuilder` has become somewhat of a dogmatic issue in the C# community, and some explanation is useful.

In C#, strings are immutable objects, meaning they cannot be changed once created. This has ramifications for string manipulation, but they are probably not as drastic as you might be led to believe. There are essentially two options for string concatenation: using plain `String` objects and using `StringBuilder`.

Here's an example using plain `string` objects:

```
string a = "Hello";
string b = ", ";
string c = "World";
string s = a + b + c;
```

Here's an example using `StringBuilder`:

```
StringBuilder sb = new StringBuilder();
sb.Append("Hello");
sb.Append(", ");
sb.Append("World");
```

Conventional wisdom tells you to use `StringBuilder` for concatenating strings, but that answer is too simplistic. In fact, the official guidelines gives as good guidance as we're likely to find. The following is from the MSDN documentation for `System.StringBuilder` (http://msdn.microsoft.com/en-us/library/system.text.stringbuilder.aspx):

> The performance of a concatenation operation for a `String` or `StringBuilder` object depends on how often a memory allocation occurs. A `String` concatenation operation always allocates memory, whereas a `StringBuilder` concatenation operation only allocates memory if the `StringBuilder` object buffer is too small to accommodate the new data. Consequently, the `String` class is preferable for a concatenation operation if a fixed number of `String` objects are concatenated. In that case, the individual concatenation operations might even be combined into a single operation by the compiler. A `StringBuilder` object is preferable for a concatenation operation if an arbitrary number of strings are concatenated; for example, if a loop concatenates a random number of strings of user input.

Running my own tests basically confirms this strategy. `StringBuilder` is only faster once we're dealing with a *lot* of strings, as Figure 7.1 shows. Despite string append being much slower, we're still talking about milliseconds either way.

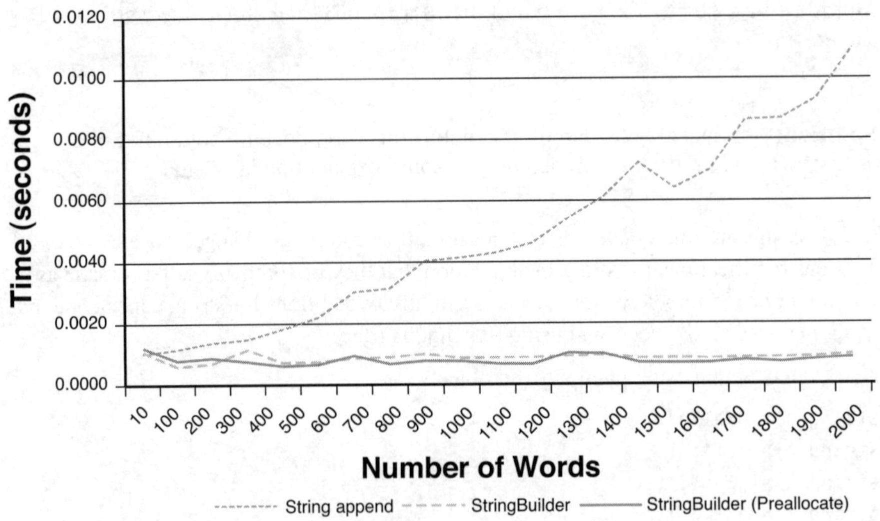

FIGURE 7.1
Using `StringBuilder` doesn't matter (for performance) when there are relatively few strings.

However, a caveat: All of this greatly depends on the size and number of your strings. Whenever performance is involved, there is only one rule: measure it.

You also need to keep in mind the number of objects created—when standard string concatenation is used, a new string is created at each concatenation. This can lead to an explosion of objects for the garbage collector to deal with.

You can perform your own timings with the StringBuilderTime project located in the code samples for this chapter.

In the end, you must measure and profile your own code to determine what's best in your scenario.

Concatenate Collection Items into a String

Scenario/Problem: You need to convert all the items in a collection into a single string.

Solution: There are a few options for this, depending on what you need. For simple concatenation, use the new String.Concat() method that takes a collection of any type and converts it to a string.

```
int[] vals = { 1, 2, 3, 4, 5, 6, 7, 8, 9, 0 };

Console.WriteLine(String.Concat(vals));
```

This gives the following output:

```
1234567890
```

If you want to separate the values with delimiters, use `String.Join`:

```
int[] vals = { 1, 2, 3, 4, 5, 6, 7, 8, 9, 0 };
Console.WriteLine(string.Join(", ", vals));
```

This produces the output:

```
1, 2, 3, 4, 5, 6, 7, 8, 9, 0
```

However, if you want to do this with objects, it gets trickier. Suppose the existence of a Person class:

```
class Person
{
    public string FirstName { get; set; }
    public string LastName { get; set; }
};
```

You can try to use the same code (with a required type parameter now):

```
Person[] people = new Person[]
{
    new Person() { FirstName = "Bill", LastName="Gates"},
    new Person() { FirstName = "Steve", LastName="Ballmer"},
    new Person() { FirstName = "Steve", LastName="Jobs"}
};
Console.WriteLine(string.Join<Person>(", ", people));
```

This produces this undesirable output:

```
ConsoleApplication2.Program+Person, ConsoleApplication2.Program+Person,
➥ConsoleApplication2.Program+Person
```

Instead, you can use an extension method on IEnumerable<T> that was introduced for LINQ (see Chapter 21, "LINQ") to accumulate just the properties you need. This example combines anonymous delegates with LINQ to pack a lot of functionality into very little code:

```
Console.WriteLine(people.Aggregate("",
        (output, next) =>
           output.Length > 0 ? output + ", " + next.LastName
                             : next.LastName));
```

This gives the following output:

```
Gates, Ballmer, Jobs
```

Append a Newline Character

Scenario/Problem: You need to insert a newline character in a string in a platform-agnostic way.

Solution: Consider that .NET works on many operating systems, all of which have different newline conventions. For example, Windows uses a carriage-return/line-feed pair, whereas Linux and Mac OS X use just line-feed. Here is the correct way to format a string with a newline:

```
string a = "My String Here" + Environment.NewLine;
```

`Environment.NewLine` will always return the correct string for the current environment.

Split a String

Scenario/Problem: You need to split a string into an array of strings, based on delimiters (characters or strings that specify where the divisions should be).

Solution: The String class contains a handy `Split` method. You can tell it what characters (or strings) to consider as delimiters and also give it some options (as demonstrated next).

```
string original =
   "But, in a larger sense, we can not dedicate--  we can not
➥consecrate--  we can not hallow--  this ground.";
char[] delims = new char[]{',','-',' ','.'};
string[] strings = original.Split(delims);
Console.WriteLine("Default split behavior:");
foreach (string s in strings)
{
    Console.WriteLine("\t{0}", s);
}
```

The following output is produced:

```
Default split behavior:
        But

        in
        a
        larger
        sense

        we
        can
        not
        dedicate-we
        can
        not
        consecrate-we
        can
        not
        hallow-this
        ground
```

Notice the gaps? Those are the points where two delimiters appear in a row. In this case, the `Split()` method emits an empty string. This can be useful if, say, you are parsing a data file consisting of comma-separated values and you need to know when a value was missing. Sometimes, though, you'll want to remove the empty strings. In that case, pass in the `StringSplitOptions.RemoveEmptyEntries` flag, as shown here:

```
strings = original.Split(delims, StringSplitOptions.RemoveEmptyEntries);
Console.WriteLine("StringSplitOptions.RemoveEmptyEntries:");
foreach (string s in strings)
{
    Console.WriteLine("\t{0}", s);
}
```

Here's the output:

```
StringSplitOptions.RemoveEmptyEntries:
        But
        in
        a
        larger
        sense
        we
        can
        not
        dedicate-we
        can
        not
        consecrate-we
        can
        not
        hallow-this
        ground
```

Convert Binary Data to a String (Base-64 Encoding)

Scenario/Problem: You need to convert binary data to base-64 encoded text, suitable for transmission in text-only protocols (such as SMTP for emails).

Solution: Use the `Convert.ToBase64String` method as Listing 7.1 shows.

LISTING 7.1 EncodeBase64Bad

```
using System;
using System.IO;

namespace EncodeBase64Bad
{
    class Program
    {
        static void PrintUsage()
        {
            Console.WriteLine("Usage: EncodeBase64Bad [sourceFile]");
        }

        static void Main(string[] args)
        {
            if (args.Length < 1)
            {
                PrintUsage();
                return;
            }

            string sourceFile = args[0];

            if (!File.Exists(sourceFile))
            {
                PrintUsage();
                return;
            }

            byte[] bytes = File.ReadAllBytes(sourceFile);
            Console.WriteLine(Convert.ToBase64String(bytes));
        }
    }
}
```

To use this program, run it with a filename on the command line. It will dump the base-64 equivalent to the console (or you can redirect it to a text file, if desired).

NOTE Notice I called this a "bad" implementation. That's because it reads the entire file into memory in one go and then writes it out as a single string. Try this on an enormous file, and you'll see why it's not such a good idea for a general file conversion utility. It would be better to perform the conversion in smaller chunks.

To convert back to binary from base-64, use the following:

```
byte[] bytes = Convert.FromBase64String(myBase64String);
```

Reverse Words

Scenario/Problem: You need to reverse the words or tokens in a string (for example, reverse the string "Hello World" to become "World Hello").

Solution: Perform a reversal of the entire string, character by character. Then find the parts containing words and reverse each part individually. Listing 7.2 shows an example.

LISTING 7.2 **Reverse Words in a String**

```
using System;

namespace ReverseWords
{
    class Program
    {
        static void Main(string[] args)
        {
            string original =
                "But, in a larger sense, we can not dedicate--  we can
➥not consecrate--  we can not hallow--  this ground.";

            Console.WriteLine("Original: " + original);
            Console.WriteLine("Reversed: " + ReverseWords(original));

            Console.ReadKey();
        }

        static string ReverseWords(string original)
        {
            //first convert the string to a character array since
            //we'll be needing to modify it extensively.
            char[] chars = original.ToCharArray();
            ReverseCharArray(chars, 0, chars.Length - 1);

            //now find consecutive characters and
            //reverse each group individually
            int wordStart = 0;
```

LISTING 7.2 **Reverse Words in a String** (continued)

```
            while (wordStart < chars.Length)
            {
                //skip past non-letters
                while (wordStart < chars.Length-1 &&
                       !char.IsLetter(chars[wordStart]))
                    wordStart++;
                //find end of letters
                int wordEnd = wordStart;
                while (wordEnd < chars.Length-1 &&
                       char.IsLetter(chars[wordEnd+1]))
                    wordEnd++;
                //reverse this range
                if (wordEnd > wordStart)
                {
                    ReverseCharArray(chars, wordStart, wordEnd);
                }
                wordStart = wordEnd + 1;
            }
            return new string(chars);
        }

        static void ReverseCharArray(char[] chars, int left, int right)
        {
            int l = left, r = right;
            while (l < r)
            {
                char temp = chars[l];
                chars[l] = chars[r];
                chars[r] = temp;
                l++;
                r--  ;
            }
        }
    }
}
```

Sort Number Strings Naturally

> **Scenario/Problem:** When you sort strings that contain numbers (such as the digits from 1 to 10), they are "computer sorted" (that is, 10 comes before 2), but you need them "naturally" sorted such that 10 comes in order after 9.

Solution: You must write your own string comparer to do the comparison correctly. You can either write a class that implements `IComparer<T>` or a method that conforms to the delegate `Comparison<T>` (see Chapter 15, "Delegates, Events, and Anonymous Methods," which discusses delegates). Listing 7.3 provides an example of the first option.

LISTING 7.3 **Natural Sorting**

```
using System;
using System.Collections.Generic;
using System.Diagnostics;

namespace NaturalSort
{
    class Program
    {
        static void Main(string[] args)
        {
            string[] originals = new string[]
            {
                "Part 1", "Part 2", "Part 3", "Part 4", "Part 5",
                "Part 6", "Part 7", "Part 8", "Part 9", "Part 10",
                "Part 11", "Part 12", "Part 13", "Part 14", "Part 15",
                "Part 16", "Part 17", "Part 18", "Part 19", "Part 20"
            };

            Console.WriteLine("Naive sort:");
            List<string> copy = new List<string>(originals);
            copy.Sort();
            foreach (string s in copy)
            {
                Console.WriteLine("\t{0}", s);
            }

            Console.WriteLine();
            Console.WriteLine("Natural Sort:");
            copy = new List<string>(originals);
            copy.Sort(new NaturalSorter());
            foreach (string s in copy)
            {
                Console.WriteLine("\t{0}", s);
            }
        }
    }
```

LISTING 7.3 **Natural Sorting** (continued)

```
class NaturalSorter : IComparer<string>
{
    //use a buffer for performance since we expect
    //the Compare method to be called a lot
    private char[] _splitBuffer = new char[256];

    public int Compare(string x, string y)
    {
        //first split each string into segments
        //of non-numbers and numbers
        IList<string> a = SplitByNumbers(x);
        IList<string> b = SplitByNumbers(y);

        int aInt, bInt;
        int numToCompare = (a.Count < b.Count) ? a.Count : b.Count;
        for (int i = 0; i < numToCompare; i++)
        {
            if (a[i].Equals(b[i]))
                continue;

            bool aIsNumber = Int32.TryParse(a[i], out aInt);
            bool bIsNumber = Int32.TryParse(b[i], out bInt);
            bool bothNumbers = aIsNumber && bIsNumber;
            bool bothNotNumbers = !aIsNumber && !bIsNumber;
            //do an integer compare
            if (bothNumbers) return aInt.CompareTo(bInt);
            //do a string compare
            if (bothNotNumbers) return a[i].CompareTo(b[i]);
            //only one is a number, which are
            //by definition less than non-numbers
            if (aIsNumber) return -1;
            return 1;
        }
        //only get here if one string is empty
        return a.Count.CompareTo(b.Count);
    }

    private IList<string> SplitByNumbers(string val)
    {
        System.Diagnostics.Debug.Assert(val.Length <= 256);
        List<string> list = new List<string>();
        int current = 0;
        int dest = 0;
        while (current < val.Length)
```

LISTING 7.3 **Natural Sorting** (continued)

```
            {
                //accumulate non-numbers
                while (current < val.Length &&
                        !char.IsDigit(val[current]))
                {
                    _splitBuffer[dest++] = val[current++];
                }
                if (dest > 0)
                {
                    list.Add(new string(_splitBuffer, 0, dest));
                    dest = 0;
                }
                //accumulate numbers
                while (current < val.Length &&
                        char.IsDigit(val[current]))
                {
                    _splitBuffer[dest++] = val[current++];
                }
                if (dest > 0)
                {
                    list.Add(new string(_splitBuffer, 0, dest));
                    dest = 0;
                }
            }
            return list;
        }
    }
}
```

Here is the output of the program:

```
Naive sort:
        Part 1
        Part 10
        Part 11
        Part 12
        Part 13
        Part 14
        Part 15
        Part 16
```

```
        Part 17
        Part 18
        Part 19
        Part 2
        Part 20
        Part 3
        Part 4
        Part 5
        Part 6
        Part 7
        Part 8
        Part 9

Natural Sort:
        Part 1
        Part 2
        Part 3
        Part 4
        Part 5
        Part 6
        Part 7
        Part 8
        Part 9
        Part 10
        Part 11
        Part 12
        Part 13
        Part 14
        Part 15
        Part 16
        Part 17
        Part 18
        Part 19
        Part 20
```

Note that although it's easier to split a string using regular expressions, this method is faster (at least in my case—you should always measure performance yourself when it's important), which has advantages when this method is called often during a sorting session. However, it is not thread-safe because the buffer is shared between all calls to `Compare()`.

NOTE The List<T> sort method also allows you to pass in a delegate to perform the sort. Because the example in this section requires a helper method and a buffer, using a delegate may not be the best solution in this particular case. However, in general, for one-off sorting algorithms, it's perfectly fine and can be implemented something like this (using a lambda expression for the delegate; see Chapter 15, "Delegates, Events, and Anonymous Methods"):

```
List<string> copy = new List<string>(originals);
copy.Sort((string x, string y) => {
    //reverse normal sort order
    return -x.CompareTo(y);
});
```

CHAPTER 8

Regular Expressions

IN THIS CHAPTER

- Search Text
- Extract Groups of Text
- Replace Text
- Match and Validate
- Help Regular Expressions Perform Better

Regular expressions provide an extremely powerful text-processing system that every programmer should at least be familiar with. This chapter is not a full tutorial on regular expression syntax, but if you are new to them, this will get you started with some useful tips.

Search Text

Scenario/Problem: You need an advanced text search where you can find patterns.

Solution: Using regular expressions gives you the power to find complex patterns in text. .NET's regular expression classes can be found in the System.Text.RegularExpressions namespace. A text search in its most fundamental form looks like this:

```
string source = "We few, we happy few, we band of brothers...";
Regex regex = new Regex("we");
MatchCollection coll = regex.Matches(source);
foreach (Match match in coll)
{
    Console.WriteLine("\t\"{0}\" at position {1}",
                      match.Value.Trim(), match.Index);
}
```

Here's the output:

```
        "we" at position 8
        "we" at position 22
```

A simple search like this isn't taking advantage of regular expressions, however. Here's a more interesting one:

```
//find all words 7 characters or longer
Regex regex = new Regex("[a-zA-Z]{7,}");
```

And here's the output:

```
        "brothers" at position 33
```

Extract Groups of Text

Scenario/Problem: You need to extract portions of text into named groups. Suppose you have a file that looks like this:

```
1234 Cherry Lane, Smalltown, USA
1235 Apple Tree Drive, Smalltown, USA
3456 Cherry Orchard Street, Smalltown, USA
```

Solution: Let's extract all the street names:

```
string file =
            "1234 Cherry Lane, Smalltown, USA" + Environment.NewLine +
            "1235 Apple Tree Drive, Smalltown, USA" +
             Environment.NewLine +
            "3456 Cherry Orchard Street, Smalltown, USA" +
             Environment.NewLine;

Regex regex = new Regex("^(?<HouseNumber>\\d+)\\s*(?<Street>
➥[\\w\\s]*), (?<City>[\\w]+),
➥ (?<Country>[\\w\\s]+)$", RegexOptions.Multiline);
MatchCollection coll = regex.Matches(file);
foreach (Match m in coll)
{
    string street = m.Groups["Street"].Value;
    Console.WriteLine("Street: {0}", street);
}
```

The following output is produced:

```
Street: Cherry Lane
Street: Apple Tree Drive
Street: Cherry Orchard Street
```

Replace Text

Scenario/Problem: You need to replace text according to a pattern.

Solution: You can do a straight replacement of text with regular expressions, like this:

```
//replace the word after "we" with "something"
Regex regex = new Regex("[wW]e\\s[a-zA-Z]+");
string result = regex.Replace(source, "we something");
```

There is a more powerful option, however. By using a `MatchEvaluator`, you can have complex text replacements that depend on the value of the match found. Here is a simple example where the word *we* is swapped with the word that appears after it:

```
static string SwapOrder(Match m)
{
    //put whatever the other word was first, then put " we"
```

```
    return m.Groups["OtherWord"].Value + " we";
}

...

string source = "We few, we happy few, we band of brothers...";
//put the word after we into its own group so we can extract it later
regex = new Regex("[wW]e\\s(?<OtherWord>[a-zA-Z]+)");

//pass in our own method for the evaluator to use
result = regex.Replace(source, new MatchEvaluator(SwapOrder));
Console.WriteLine("result: {0}", result);
```

This produces the following output:

```
result: few we, happy we few, band we of brothers
```

Match and Validate

Scenario/Problem: You need to validate user input according to well-known patterns.

Solution: This section contains some common validation expressions. The general usage, from which the sample output is taken, is as follows:

```
Regex regex = new Regex(pattern);
bool isMatch = regex.IsMatch(userString);
Console.WriteLine("{0} ? {1}", userString, isMatch?"ok":"bad");
```

To see the full example, look at the MatchAndValidate project in this chapter's accompanying source code.

Social Security Number

Validating these numbers is fairly simple. They are expressed as nine digits, optionally separated into groups with hyphens.

```
Regex = new Regex(@"^\d{3}\-?\d{2}\-?\d{4}$");
```

Sample output:

```
123456789 ? ok
123-45-6789 ? ok
111-11-1111 ? ok
123-45.678 ? bad
```

```
123.45.6789 ? bad
12.123.4444 ? bad
123.45.67890 ? bad
123.a5.6789 ? bad
just random text ? bad
```

Phone Number

Phone numbers are also commonly validated. The next example validates a standard 10-digit US telephone number.

```
Regex regex = new Regex(
    //xxx.xxx.xxxx and xxx-xxx-xxxx
    @"^((\d{3}[\-\.]?\d{3}[\-\.]?\d{4})|"+
    //xx.xx.xxx.xxx and xx-xx-xxx-xxx
    @"(\d{2}[\-\.]?\d{2}[\-\.]?\d{3}[\-\.]?\d{3}))"+
    "$"
);
```

Sample output:

```
123.456.7890 ? ok
123-456-7890 ? ok
1234567890 ? ok
123.4567890 ? ok
12.34.567.890 ? ok
123.456.78900 ? bad
123-456 ? bad
123-abc-7890 ? bad
```

Zip Codes

Zip codes can be either 5 digits or 9 digits, with an optional hyphen.

```
Regex regex = new Regex(@"^\d{5}(-?\d{4})?$");
```

Sample output:

```
12345 ? ok
12345-6789 ? ok
123456789 ? ok
12345- ? bad
1234 ? bad
1234-6789 ? bad
a234 ? bad
123456 ? bad
1234567890 ? bad
```

Dates

This regular expression validates US-format dates in the form MM/DD/YYYY.

```
Regex regex = new Regex (@"(0[1-9]|1[012])/
➥([1-9]|0[1-9]|[12][0-9]|3[01])/\d{4}");
```

Sample output:

```
12/25/2009 ? ok
01/25/2009 ? ok
1/2/2009 ? bad
25/12/2009 ? bad
2009/12/25 ? bad
13/25/2009 ? bad
12/25/09 ? bad
```

Match an Email (or Not)

So far, we've seen some simple examples of regular expression validation, but what about something a little more complex, such as an email address? As it happens, this isn't a little more complex—it's a lot more complex! You will see that as the syntax gets more complex, regular expressions can become quite large and unwieldy. In fact, it is not possible to do an absolutely correct email validation with regular expressions. That doesn't stop people from trying, though. If you do a web search, you will come across many regular expressions for email addresses that range from a few lines to a few pages.

Beware of turning to such things as a solution. Chances are, with such an enormous regular expression, you will not be able to understand it once written. There is also the possibility that the data format is just too complex and the regular expression can't capture all of it. Also, you do not want to be in the position of refusing to accept information from a user because she has an unusual email address. That's a user who may not come back! (You will notice that most websites don't validate email addresses anyway—they just ask the user to enter the address twice to make sure it's correct.)

If you do need to use large, unreadable regular expressions, ensure that you have *very* thorough unit tests to cover your input cases. With unit tests, you'll be able to modify the regular expression with confidence that you're not breaking existing functionality.

Help Regular Expressions Perform Better

Scenario/Problem: You want regular expressions to run faster.

Solution: If you tell .NET to compile them into their own assembly, they'll run a bit faster, especially for complex expressions. Here's an example:

```
Regex regex = new Regex(pattern, RegexOptions.Compiled);
```

CHAPTER 9

Generics

IN THIS CHAPTER

- Create a Generic List
- Create a Generic Method
- Create a Generic Interface
- Create a Generic Class
- Create a Generic Delegate
- Use Multiple Generic Types
- Constrain the Generic Type
- Convert `IEnumerable<Child>` to `IEnumerable<Parent>` (Covariance)
- Convert `IComparer<Child>` to `IComparer<Parent>` (Contravariance)
- Create Tuples (Pairs and More)

Generics are a way to declare types, interfaces, delegates, and methods in a type-agnostic way. For example, `IComparable<T>` defines an interface that specifies a comparison between objects of type `T`. The `T` is defined by you where needed.

One of the most common ways to use generics is in collection classes. Before generics, the ArrayList was commonly used to store a dynamic array of objects. ArrayList stored references to objects, so you had to always cast the items to the right type when pulling them out. Not so with generics. This topic deserves a chapter all its own (see Chapter 10, "Collections"), but is introduced here in the first section since it's by far the most common scenario.

The rest of this chapter shows the various ways to use generics, not specifically in collections.

Create a Generic List

Scenario/Problem: You need a dynamically sized array of objects of a specific type.

Solution: Use `List<T>` to create a list of objects of type T, as in this example:

```
class Person
{
    public string Name { get; set; }
    public string Address { get; set; }
};

static void Main(string[] args)
{
    List<Person> people = new List<Person>();
    people.Add(new Person()
         { Name = "Ben", Address = "1 Redmond Way, Redmond, WA 98052" });
    //no casting needed!
    Person p = people[0];
}
```

NOTE You should always default to using the generic collections rather than the older ArrayList-style collections from early versions of .NET.

See Chapter 10 for more information on generic collections of all types in .NET.

Create a Generic Method

Scenario/Problem: You need a method that can be called to perform the same work on different types of arguments.

Solution: Generics are specified with angle brackets that include the type name (usually T). T can then be used wherever a real type name is used, as in the following example:

```
using System;

namespace GenericMethods
{
    class Program
    {
        static void Main(string[] args)
        {
            int aInt = 13;
            int bInt = 26;
            string aString = "Hello";
            string bString = "World";

            Console.WriteLine("aInt: {0}, bInt: {1}", aInt, bInt);
            Console.WriteLine("aString: {0}, bString: {1}", aString,
                                bString);
            Console.WriteLine("Swap!");
            //call Swap with the specific types
            Swap<int>(ref aInt, ref bInt);
            Swap<string>(ref aString, ref bString);

            Console.WriteLine("aInt: {0}, bInt: {1}", aInt, bInt);
            Console.WriteLine("aString: {0}, bString: {1}", aString,
                                bString);

            Console.ReadKey();
        }

        private static void Swap<T>(ref T a, ref T b)
        {
            T temp = a;
```

```
            a = b;
            b = temp;
        }
    }
}
```

The following output is produced:

```
aInt: 13, bInt: 26
aString: Hello, bString: World
Swap!
aInt: 26, bInt: 13
aString: World, bString: Hello
```

Create a Generic Interface

Scenario/Problem: You need to create an interface that specifies behavior with respect to a user-supplied type.

Solution: Generics are commonly used on interfaces where the methods are defined with respect to a specific type, as in the following example:

```
//declare generic interface of T
interface IUnique<T>
{
    T Id { get; }
}
//implement interface with specific types
class MyObject : IUnique<int>
{
    private int _id;
    //implementation of interface's method
    public int Id
    {
        get { return _id; }
    }
}

class MyOtherObject : IUnique<string>
{
    private string _id;
```

```
    public string Id
    {
        get { return _id; }
    }
}
```

Create a Generic Class

Scenario/Problem: You need a class to operate on different types, but still want the benefits of strong typing.

Solution: This is similar to the declaration for interfaces. As an example, consider this indexing class with a (very) naive implementation for brevity:

```
//the object we want to add to our index
class Part
{
    private string _partId;
    private string _name;
    private string _description;
    private double _weight;

    public string PartId { get { return _partId; } }

    public Part(string partId,
                string name,
                string description,
                double weight)
    {
        _partId = partId;
        _name = name;
        _description = description;
        _weight = weight;
    }

    public override string ToString()
    {
        return string.Format("Part: {0}, Name: {1}, Weight: {2}", _
            partId, _name, _weight);
```

```
    }
}

//the actual indexer, which accepts the generic type
//note the type must be a class (not a value type)
class Indexer<T> where T:class
{
    struct ItemStruct
    {
        public string key;
        public T value;
        public ItemStruct(string key, T value)
        {
            this.key = key;
            this.value = value;
        }
    };

    List<ItemStruct> _items = new List<ItemStruct>();

    //T must be a class so that we can return null here if not found
    public T Find(string key)
    {
        foreach (ItemStruct itemStruct in _items)
        {
            if (itemStruct.key == key)
            {
                return itemStruct.value;
            }
        }
        return null;
    }

    public void Add(string key, T value)
    {
        _items.Add(new ItemStruct(key, value));
    }
}

//and a program to test it
class Program
{
    static void Main(string[] args)
    {
        Indexer<Part> indexer = new Indexer<Part>();
```

```
        Part p1 = new Part("1", "Part01", "The first part", 1.5);
        Part p2 = new Part("2", "Part02", "The second part", 2.0);

        indexer.Add(p1.PartId, p1);
        indexer.Add(p2.PartId, p2);

        Part p = indexer.Find("2");
        Console.WriteLine("Found: {0}", p.ToString());
    }
}
```

Create a Generic Delegate

Scenario/Problem: You need a delegate that operates on a specific type (delegates are discussed in more detail in Chapter 15, "Delegates, Events, and Anonymous Methods").

Solution: Delegates are like type-safe function pointers, and those types can also be generic.

```
class Program
{
    delegate T DoMath<T>(T a, T b);

    static void Main(string[] args)
    {
        DoMath<int> delegateInt = Add;
        int result1 = delegateInt(1, 2);
        Console.WriteLine("results of delegateInt(1, 2): {0}", result1);

        DoMath<double> delegateDouble = Multiply;
        double result2 = delegateDouble(1.5, 10.0);
        Console.WriteLine(
            "results of delegateDouble(1.5, 10.0): {0}",
            result2);

        Console.ReadKey();
    }

    static int Add(int a, int b)
    {
        return a + b;
    }
```

```
    static int Multiply(int a, int b)
    {
        return a * b;
    }

    static double Add(double a, double b)
    {
        return a + b;
    }

    static double Multiply(double a, double b)
    {
        return a * b;
    }
}
```

Use Multiple Generic Types

Scenario/Problem: You want to have more than one generic type on a method, interface, and so on.

Solution: Separate the types by commas within the brackets, as in this example:

```
interface SomeInterface<T, U>
{
    T GetSomething();
    DoSomething(U object);
}
```

NOTE Type parameters are sometimes labeled starting with T and using the alphabet from there on (there should not usually be more than a few type parameter arguments). However, you can also label them according to purpose. For example, `Dictionary<TKey, TValue>`.

Constrain the Generic Type

Scenario/Problem: You want to restrict the generic type to types with certain properties. These restrictions allow you and the compiler to then make certain assumptions about the type.

Solution: By adding certain constraints to the type, you are allowed to do more with it since the compiler can infer addition information. For example, by telling C# that T must be a reference type, you can assign null to an instance of type T.

To add a constraint, you add a where clause after the declaration, as in the examples in the following sections.

Constrain to a Reference Type

The class keyword is used to denote a reference type, as in this example:

```
class Indexer<T> where T : class
{
    public T DoSomething()
    {
        //now we can do this
        return null;
    }
}
Indexer<string> index1 = new Indexer<string>();//ok
Indexer<int> index2 = new Indexer<int>();//not allowed!
```

Constrain to a Value Type

Sometimes, you'll want to restrict interfaces or collections—for example, to value types only. You can do this with the struct keyword, as in this example:

```
class Indexer<T> where T : struct
{
    T val;
    public T DoSomething()
    {
        return val;
        //return null;//not allowed!
    }
}
Indexer<int> index1 = new Indexer<int>();//ok
Indexer<string> index2 = new Indexer<string>();//not allowed!
```

Note that even though the syntax says struct, any value type, including the built-in ones, is allowed.

Constrain to an Interface or Base Class

You can constrain to any type, whether it's an interface, base class, or a class itself. Anything that is that type or derived from that type will be valid. By doing this, the compiler allows you to call methods defined on the specified type. Here's an example:

```
class Indexer<T> where T: IComparable<T>
{
    public int Compare(T a, T b)
    {
        //since the compiler knows T is IComparable<T>,
        //we can do this:
        return a.CompareTo(b);
    }
}
//any object that implements IComparable<T> can
//be used in the Indexer<T> class
class MyObject : IComparable<MyObject>
{
    int _id;
    public override int CompareTo(MyObject other)
    {
        return _id.CompareTo(other._id);
    }
}
```

Constrain to a Type with a Default Constructor

If you need to create a new object of the unknown, generic type, you must tell the compiler that the type is restricted to those with a default (parameterless) constructor. You do this with a special usage of the new keyword, as shown here:

```
class Factory<T> where T : new()
{
    public T Create()
    {
        return new T();
    }
}
```

NOTE Creation of generic types can be problematic in some cases. You may find yourself needing to use factory methods to create the type instead of new:

```
class SomeClass<T, TFactory> where TFactory : new()
{
    public T CreateNew()
    {
        TFactory factory = new TFactory();
        return factory.Create<T>();
    }
}
```

Have Multiple Constraints

You can separate multiple constraints with commas. Note that, if present, `new()` must appear last in the list.

```
class MyClass<T>
    where T : IComparable<T>, new()
{
}
```

Constrain Multiple Type Arguments

You can apply constraints to as many type arguments as you desire.

```
class Temp<T, S>
    where T : IComparable<T>, new()
    where S : class, new()
{
}
```

Convert `IEnumerable<string>` to `IEnumerable<object>` (Covariance)

Scenario/Problem: You want to pass a generic collection to a method that only accepts `IEnumerable<object>` (or some other parent of your type). For example, suppose you want to do this:

```
interface IShape
{
    void Draw();
}

interface IRectangle : IShape
{
    void HitTest();
}

class Program
{
    static void Main(string[] args)
    {
        List<IRectangle> rects = new List<IRectangle>();

        DrawShapes(rects);
    }
```

```
    static void DrawShapes(IEnumerable<IShape> shapes)
    {
        foreach (IShape shape in shapes)
        {
            shape.Draw();
        }
    }
}
```

In previous versions of .NET, this was impossible.

Solution: In .NET 4, covariance and contravariance are supported on interfaces and delegates, so the preceding code will work as-is. This is known as covariance. It only works because `IEnumerable` is declared as `IEnumerable<out T>`, which means that you cannot give `T` as an input to any method on `IEnumerable`. This rule implies that any output of this collection can also be treated as a collection of the parent class of `T`, which makes sense since iterating over `IRectangle` is equivalent to iterating over `IShape`.

On the other hand, imagine if we had another type of shape, `ICircle, which is also derived from` IShape. The collection should *not* be treated as a collection of `IShape` for the purposes of insertion, because this would imply you could also add an `ICircle`, which is not the case, since it's really a collection of `IRectangle objects`. That's why `T` is declared as an out parameter: It only works when reading values out of the collection, not putting them in, and it explains why covariance can work in the preceding code example.

Convert `IComparer<Child>` to `IComparer<Parent>` (Contravariance)

Scenario/Problem: You need a more specific interface to refer to an object of less-specific type. For example, suppose the existence of these classes:

```
class Shape
{
    public int id;
}

class Rectangle : Shape
{

}

class ShapeComparer : IComparer<Shape>
{
```

```
    public int Compare(Shape x, Shape y)
    {
        return x.id.CompareTo(y.id);
    }
}
```

In your code, the following code snippet should intuitively work because any method that accepts a Shape should also accept a Rectangle:

```
ShapeComparer shapeComparer = new ShapeComparer();
IComparer<Rectangle> irc = shapeComparer;
```

However, prior to .NET 4, this did not work.

Solution: In .NET 4, IComparer<T> has been changed to IComparer<in T>, which means that objects of type T are used only as input parameters. Therefore, an object implementing this interface can be assigned to interfaces of a more derived type. This is called contravariance. The preceding code sample will now work.

For more on contravariance and to see how it applies to delegates, see Chapter 15.

Create Tuples (Pairs and More)

Scenario/Problem: A very common scenario in programming is that you want to group two or more variables to pass around as a unit. The Point class is a good example, as it groups X and Y coordinates into a single unit. The KeyValuePair<TKey,TValue> is another example.

Solution: Rather than creating your own class to handle tuples on a case-by-case basis, use the Tuple class:

```
var name = Tuple.Create("Ben", "Michael", "Watson");
string firstName = name.Item1;
```

Tuple values can be different types:

```
var partId = Tuple.Create(1, "Widget00001");
int partnum = partId.Item1;
string partName = partId.Item2;
```

There are `Create` methods from 1 to 8 arguments (singleton to octuple).

PART II

Handling Data

IN THIS PART

CHAPTER 10

Collections

IN THIS CHAPTER

- Pick the Correct Collection Class
- Initialize a Collection
- Iterate over a Collection Independent of Its Implementation
- Create a Custom Collection
- Create Custom Iterators for a Collection
- Reverse an Array
- Reverse a Linked List
- Get the Unique Elements from a Collection
- Count the Number of Times an Item Appears
- Implement a Priority Queue
- Create a Trie (Prefix Tree)

The intelligent use of collections is in many ways central to building large, well-factored applications. How you store and access your data can strongly influence or even determine everything else. Thus, it is crucial to get it right. This chapter contains tips for working with collections and creating your own.

Pick the Correct Collection Class

Scenario/Problem: You need to pick the correct type of collection for your data structure.

Solution: Use Tables 10.1 and 10.2 to help you decide which collection class to use.

Note that only the basic `Array` type cannot grow beyond its initial size. All the others will manage their internal storage such that objects can be added to it indefinitely (limited by memory, of course).

TABLE 10.1 **Generic Collections**

Type	Insert	Remove	Find	Grows	Allows Duplicates
`Array`	O(n)*	O(n)*	O(n)†	No	Yes
`List<T>`	O(n)*	O(n)	O(n)†	Yes	Yes
`LinkedList<T>`	O(1)	O(1)	O(n)	Yes	Yes
`SortedList<TKey, TValue>`‡	O(n)	O(n)	O(log n)	Yes	Keys:no, Values:yes
`Stack<T>`	O(1)	O(1)	O(n)	Yes	Yes
`Queue<T>`	O(1)	O(1)	O(n)	Yes	Yes
`HashSet<T>`	O(1)	O(1)	O(1)	Yes	No
`SortedSet<T>`	O(1)	O(1)	O(1)	Yes	No
`Dictionary<TKey, TValue>`	O(1)	O(1)	O(1)	Yes	Keys:no, Values:yes
SortedDictionary<TKey, TValue>‡	O(log n)	O(log n)	O(log n)	Yes	Keys:no, Values:yes

*O(1) if at the end.

†O(log n) if you keep the array sorted so you can use a binary search.

‡`SortedList` and `SortedDictionary` are similar in that both are implemented as a binary search tree. Both have similar retrieve times, but `SortedList` uses less memory, `SortedDictionary` has generally faster insertion and removal, and `SortedList` is faster at inserting already sorted data.

TABLE 10.2 **Nongeneric Collections with No Generic Equivalent**

Collection	Description
`ArrayList`	Similar to `List<object>`.
`BitArray`	Array of bit (Boolean) values. You can perform Boolean logic on this collection.
`BitVector32`	Like `BitArray`, but limited to (and optimized for) 32 bits.
`ListDictionary`	An implementation of `IDictionary` (association semantics) using a linked list. Designed for very small collections (10 or fewer elements). Operations are O(n).
`HybridDictionary`	Uses `ListDictionary` when there are few items, but switches to `Hashtable` when the collection grows.
`StringCollection`	Equivalent to `List<string>`.
`StringDictionary`	Equivalent to `Dictionary<string, string>`.

Use Concurrency-Aware Collections

Scenario/Problem: You need a collection that will be accessed by multiple threads simultaneously.

Solution: Either protect the access yourself using thread synchronization objects (see Chapter 23, "Threading and Asynchronous Programming") or use the collections in the `System.Collections.Concurrent` namespace. These include the following:

- `ConcurrentBag<T>` (similar to a set, but duplicates are allowed)
- `ConcurrentDictionary<TKey, TValue>`
- `ConcurrentLinkedList<T>`
- `ConcurrentQueue<T>`
- `ConcurrentStack<T>`

NOTE Beware of using these collections. Every access will be protected, which will greatly affect performance. Often, thread synchronization should be handled at a higher level than the collection.

Initialize a Collection

Scenario/Problem: You want to initialize a collection with some values at the time of declaration.

Solution: You can use object initialization syntax, used for class instances (see Chapter 1, “Type Fundamentals”) and arrays (See Chapter 3, “General Coding”), as in this example:

```
List<int> list = new List<int>() { 1, 2, 3, 4, 5 };
Dictionary<int, string> dict =
    new Dictionary<int, string>() { { 1, "One" }, { 2, "Two" } };
```

Iterate over a Collection Independently of Its Implementation

Scenario/Problem: You want to access all of a collection’s objects independently from how the collection is implemented.

Solution: Rather than writing loops with collection access by index or key, you can use the `foreach` construct to access any object that implements `IEnumerable` (or `IEnumerable<T>`).

```
int[] array = { 1, 2, 3, 4, 5 };
foreach (int n in array)
{
    Console.Write("{0} ", n);
}
Console.WriteLine();
List<DateTime> times = new List<DateTime>(
                       new DateTime[]{DateTime.Now, DateTime.UtcNow});
foreach (DateTime time in times)
{
    Console.WriteLine(time);
}

Dictionary<int, string> numbers = new Dictionary<int, string>();
numbers[1] = "One"; numbers[2] = "Two"; numbers[3] = "Three";
foreach (KeyValuePair<int, string> pair in numbers)
{
    Console.WriteLine("{0}", pair);
}
```

This program produces the following output:

```
1 2 3 4 5
12/27/2008 1:14:57 PM
12/27/2008 9:14:57 PM
```

```
[1, One]
[2, Two]
[3, Three]
```

Create a Custom Collection

Scenario/Problem: If the collections built into .NET are not sufficient, you need to create your own collection class.

Solution: So that they can play nicely with other components, all collections in .NET should implement a subset of the collection-related interfaces. Table 10.3 briefly describes the common interfaces as they relate to collections.

TABLE 10.3 **Collection Interfaces**

Interface	Description	Methods
`ICollection<T>`	Basic methods that pertain to most collection types. Inherits `IEnumerable<T>`.	`Add`, `Clear`, `Contains`, `CopyTo`, `Remove`
`IEnumerable<T>`	Specifies that the collection's objects can be enumerated using `foreach`.	`GetEnumerator`
IDictionary<TKey, TValue>	Allows access to collections by key/value pairs. Inherits from `ICollection<KeyValuePair <TKey, TValue>>`.	`ContainsKey`, `TryGetValue`
IList<T>	Specifies that the collection can be accessed by index. Inherits from `ICollection<T>`.	`IndexOf`, `Insert`, `RemoveAt`

Note that although not explicitly stated in the table for space purposes, any interface that inherits from another also includes the base interface's methods in its own definition.

The example I'll use over this and the next section implements a binary search tree, complete with three different traversals. We'll start with the basic definition:

```
class BinaryTree<T> : ICollection<T>, IEnumerable<T>
    where T:IComparable<T>
{
    //this inner class is private because
    //only the tree needs to know about it
    private class Node<T>
    {
        public T Value;
```

```
        //these are public fields so that we can use "ref" to simplify
        //the algorithms
        public Node<T> LeftChild;
        public Node<T> RightChild;

        public Node(T val)
        { this.Value = val; this.LeftChild = this.RightChild = null; }
        public Node(T val, Node<T> left, Node<T> right)
        { this.Value = val;
          this.LeftChild = left; this.RightChild = right; }
    }

    private Node<T> _root;
    private int _count = 0;
}
```

Because binary search trees depend on comparing items to get their ordering correct, we need to ensure that type T is comparable. We'll implement `ICollection<T>` and `IEnumerable<T>` on this collection (neither `IList<T>` nor `IDictionary<TKey, TValue>` seem to make sense with a binary search tree).

Here are the `ICollection<T>` methods:

```
public void Add(T item)
{
    AddImpl(new Node<T>(item), ref _root);
}

//a convenience method for adding multiple items at once
public void Add(params T[] items)
{
    foreach (T item in items)
    {
        Add(item);
    }
}
//recursively finds where new node should go in tree
private void AddImpl(Node<T> newNode, ref Node<T> parentNode)
{
    if (parentNode == null)
    {
        parentNode = newNode;
        _count++;
    }
    else
    {
        if (newNode.Value.CompareTo(parentNode.Value) < 0)
```

```
        {
            AddImpl(newNode, ref parentNode.LeftChild);
        }
        else
        {
            AddImpl(newNode, ref parentNode.RightChild);
        }
    }
}

public void Clear()
{
    _root = null;
    _count = 0;
}

public bool Contains(T item)
{
    foreach (T val in this)
    {
        if (val.CompareTo(item) == 0)
            return true;
    }
    return false;
}

public void CopyTo(T[] array, int arrayIndex)
{
    int index = arrayIndex;
    //InOrder will be defined below
    foreach(T val in InOrder)
    {
        array[index++] = val;
    }
}

public int Count { get { return _count; } }

public bool IsReadOnly { get { return false; } }

public bool Remove(T item)
{
    bool removed = RemoveImpl(item, ref _root) != null;
    if (removed)
    {
```

```
        _count--;
    }
    return removed;
}

private Node<T> RemoveImpl(T item, ref Node<T> node)
{
    if (node != null)
    {
        if (node.Value.CompareTo(item) > 0)
        {
            node.LeftChild = RemoveImpl(item, ref node.LeftChild);
        }
        else if (node.Value.CompareTo(item) < 0)
        {
            node.RightChild = RemoveImpl(item, ref node.RightChild);
        }
        else
        {
            if (node.LeftChild == null)
            {
                node = node.RightChild;
            }
            else if (node.RightChild == null)
            {
                node = node.LeftChild;
            }
            else
            {
                Node<T> successor = FindSuccessor(node);
                node.Value = successor.Value;
                node.RightChild =
                        RemoveImpl(successor.Value, ref node.RightChild);
            }
        }
        return node;
    }
    else
    {
        return null;
    }
}

// Find the next node after the passed-in node,
// while will be the left-most node on the right branch
```

```
private Node<T> FindSuccessor(Node<T> node)
{
    Node<T> currentNode = node.RightChild;
    while (currentNode.LeftChild != null)
    {
        currentNode = currentNode.LeftChild;
    }
    return currentNode;
}
```

So what about the `IEnumerable<T>` implementation? That deserves a topic of its own.

Create Custom Iterators for a Collection

Scenario/Problem: You need to create custom iterators for a collection, such as iterators to traverse the collection in different directions.

Solution: Recall that binary trees can be traversed in multiple ways: typically pre-order, in-order, and post-order. We can implement all three on our binary tree quite easily using public properties and the `yield return` keywords. The default will be in-order.

```
public IEnumerator<T> GetEnumerator()
{
    return InOrder.GetEnumerator();
}

System.Collections.IEnumerator
          System.Collections.IEnumerable.GetEnumerator()
{
    return this.GetEnumerator();
}

//Here are the iterators, each represented by a public property
//and a recursive function that does all the actual work
public IEnumerable<T> PreOrder
{
    get { return IteratePreOrder(_root); }
}

private IEnumerable<T> IteratePreOrder(Node<T> parent)
{
    if (parent != null)
```

```
    {
        yield return parent.Value;

        foreach(T item in IteratePreOrder(parent.LeftChild))
        {
            yield return item;
        }
        foreach(T item in IteratePreOrder(parent.RightChild))
        {
            yield return item;
        }
    }
}

public IEnumerable<T> PostOrder
{
    get { return IteratePostOrder(_root); }
}

private IEnumerable<T> IteratePostOrder(Node<T> parent)
{
    if (parent != null)
    {
        foreach (T item in IteratePostOrder(parent.LeftChild))
        {
            yield return item;
        }
        foreach (T item in IteratePostOrder(parent.RightChild))
        {
            yield return item;
        }
        yield return parent.Value;
    }
}

public IEnumerable<T> InOrder
{ get { return IterateInOrder(_root); } }

private IEnumerable<T> IterateInOrder(Node<T> parent)
{
    if (parent != null)
    {
        foreach (T item in IterateInOrder(parent.LeftChild))
        {
            yield return item;
```

```
        }

        yield return parent.Value;

        foreach (T item in IterateInOrder(parent.RightChild))
        {
            yield return item;
        }
    }
}
```

The `yield return` statement causes the magic. Under the hood, C# is generating code to track which item is the current one in the iteration. Thankfully, we can use this shorthand to avoid that mess.

Let's look at an example, given the binary tree definition shown in Figure 10.1.

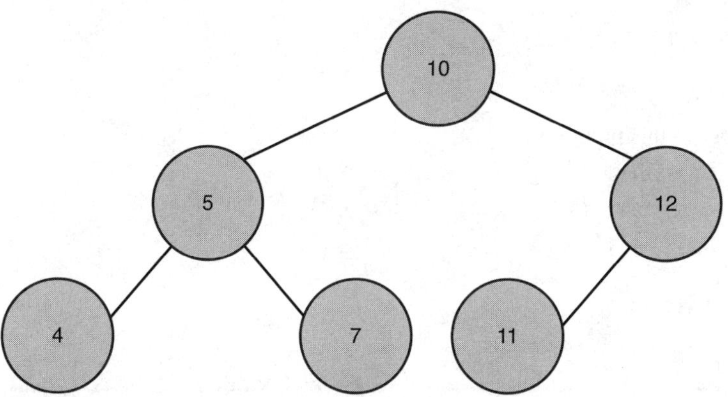

FIGURE 10.1
A binary search tree over which we'll iterate in each type of order.

The following sample code will iterate over the tree in each of the three orderings:

```
BinaryTree<int> tree = new BinaryTree<int>();
tree.Add(10, 5, 12, 4, 7, 11);

//Iterate over tree with each type of ordering
Console.Write("Pre-order: ");
foreach (int val in tree.PreOrder)
{
    Console.Write("{0} ", val);
}
Console.WriteLine();
Console.Write("Post-order: ");
foreach (int val in tree.PostOrder)
```

```
{
    Console.Write("{0} ", val);
}
Console.WriteLine();
Console.Write("In-order: ");
foreach (int val in tree.InOrder)
{
    Console.Write("{0} ", val);
}
Console.WriteLine();

//remove the root and see how the tree looks
Console.WriteLine("Removed Root");
tree.Remove(10);
Console.Write("In-order: ");
foreach (int val in tree.InOrder)
{
    Console.Write("{0} ", val);
}
```

Here is the output of this program:

```
Pre-order: 10 5 4 7 12 11
Post-order: 4 7 5 11 12 10
In-order: 4 5 7 10 11 12
Removed Root
In-order: 4 5 7 11 12
```

Reverse an Array

Scenario/Problem: You need to reverse the values in an array.

Solution: Reversing an array is a fairly common procedure. You can do this yourself, as in this example:

```
private static void Reverse<T>(T[] array)
{
    int left = 0, right = array.Length - 1;
    while (left < right)
    {
        T temp = array[left];
        array[left] = array[right];
        array[right] = temp;
        left++;
```

```
        right--;
    }
}
```

Or you can let the Reverse extension method do it for you:

```
int[] array = new int[5] {1,2,3,4,5};
IEnumerable<int> reversed = array.Reverse();
```

This will work on any `IEnumerable<T>` collection, but you won't get an array back. Instead, you will get an iterator object that will iterate through the original collection in reverse order.

What you do depends on what you need.

Reverse a Linked List

Scenario/Problem: You need to reverse a linked list.

Solution: Reversing a linked list is a bit more complicated because each node points to the next. Using our own node implementation, here is a way to quickly reverse the list by making each node point to its previous.

The following is the definition for a node:

```
class Node<T>
{
    public T Value { get; set; }
    public Node<T> Next { get; set; }
    public Node(T val) { this.Value = val; this.Next = null; }
}
```

Here is a method that will reverse a linked list of these nodes:

```
private static void ReverseList<T>(ref Node<T> head)
{
    Node<T> tail = head;
    //track the next node
    Node<T> p = head.Next;
    //make the old head the end of the line
    tail.Next = null;
    while (p != null)
    {
        //get the next one
        Node<T> n = p.Next;
        //set it to our current end
```

```
        p.Next = tail;
        //reset the end
        tail = p;
        p = n;
    }
    //the new head is where the tail is
    head = tail;
}
```

Get the Unique Elements from a Collection

Scenario/Problem: Given a collection of objects, you need to generate a new collection containing just one copy of each item.

Solution: To generate a collection without the duplicate items, you need to track which items are found in the collection, and only add them to the new collection if they haven't been seen before, as in this example:

```
private static ICollection<T> GetUniques<T>(ICollection<T> list)
{
    //use a dictionary to track whether you've seen an element yet
    Dictionary<T, bool> found = new Dictionary<T, bool>();
    List<T> uniques = new List<T>();
    //this algorithm will preserve the original order
    foreach (T val in list)
    {
        if (!found.ContainsKey(val))
        {
            found[val] = true;
            uniques.Add(val);
        }
    }
    return uniques;
}
```

Count the Number of Times an Item Appears

Scenario/Problem: You need to count the number of times each element appears in a collection.

Solution: This is quite similar to the previous section.

```
void CountUniques<T>(List<T> list)
{
    Dictionary<T, int> counts = new Dictionary<T, int>();
    List<T> uniques = new List<T>();
    foreach (T val in list)
    {
        if (counts.ContainsKey(val))
            counts[val]++;
        else
        {
            counts[val] = 1;
            uniques.Add(val);
        }
    }
    foreach (T val in uniques)
    {
        Console.WriteLine("{0} appears {1} time(s)", val, counts[val]);
    }
}
```

Implement a Priority Queue

Scenario/Problem: You need a priority queue that conforms to the standard collection interfaces.

Solution: The usual way to implement a priority queue is with a heap, and you can find a lot of examples of this on the Internet. One problem with such implementations is that it is problematic to implement `IEnumerable` on a heap because the heap does not maintain a strict ordering.

An alternate solution is to use existing collection classes to create a sorted set of queues. It's perhaps not as efficient, but works well for many applications.

Listing 10.1 contains the full code of a possible implementation of a priority queue.

LISTING 10.1 **PriorityQueue.cs**

```
using System;
using System.Collections;
using System.Collections.Generic;

namespace PriorityQueueDemo
{
    /*
```

LISTING 10.1 **PriorityQueue.cs** (continued)

```
    usually, priority queues are implemented as
    heaps, but this turns out to be problematic when
    we want to enumerate over the structure, as a heap
    does not maintain a strict order. Here's an alternate
    implementation using just existing data structures.
    */
    class PriorityQueue<TPriority, TObject>
      : ICollection, IEnumerable<TObject>
    {
        private SortedDictionary<TPriority, Queue<TObject>>
➥                   _elements;

        //same types of constructors as Queue<T> class

        public PriorityQueue()
        {
            _elements = new SortedDictionary<
                               TPriority,
                               Queue<TObject>>();
        }

        public PriorityQueue(IComparer<TPriority> comparer)
        {
            _elements = new SortedDictionary<
                               TPriority,
                               Queue<TObject>>(comparer);
        }

        public PriorityQueue(PriorityQueue<TPriority, TObject>
➥queue)
            :this()
        {
            foreach (var pair in queue._elements)
            {
                _elements.Add(
                    pair.Key,
                    new Queue<TObject>(pair.Value));
            }
        }

        public PriorityQueue(
           PriorityQueue<TPriority, TObject> queue,
           IComparer<TPriority> comparer)
            :this(comparer)
```

LISTING 10.1 **PriorityQueue.cs** (continued)

```
        {
            foreach (var pair in queue._elements)
            {
                _elements.Add(
                   pair.Key,
                   new Queue<TObject>(pair.Value));
            }
        }

        public void Enqueue(TPriority priority, TObject item)
        {
            Queue<TObject> queue = null;
            if (!_elements.TryGetValue(priority, out queue))
            {
                queue = new Queue<TObject>();
                _elements[priority] = queue;
            }
            queue.Enqueue(item);
        }

        public TObject Dequeue()
        {
            if (_elements.Count == 0)
            {
                throw new InvalidOperationException(
                 "The priority queue is empty");
            }
            SortedDictionary<TPriority, Queue<TObject>>.
➥Enumerator enumerator = _elements.GetEnumerator();
            //must succeed since we've already established
            //that there is at least one element
            enumerator.MoveNext();
            Queue<TObject> queue = enumerator.Current.Value;
            TObject obj = queue.Dequeue();
            //always make sure to remove empty queues
            if (queue.Count == 0)
            {
                _elements.Remove(enumerator.Current.Key);
            }
            return obj;
        }

        public IEnumerator<TObject> GetEnumerator()
        {
```

LISTING 10.1 **PriorityQueue.cs** (continued)

```
            foreach (var pair in _elements)
            {
                foreach (TObject obj in pair.Value)
                {
                    yield return obj;
                }
            }
        }

        IEnumerator IEnumerable.GetEnumerator()
        {
            return (this as IEnumerable<TObject>).
➥GetEnumerator();
        }

        public void CopyTo(Array array, int index)
        {
            if (array == null)
            {
                throw new ArgumentNullException("array");
            }
            if (index < 0)
            {
                throw new ArgumentOutOfRangeException("index");
            }
            if (array.Rank != 1)
            {
                throw new ArgumentException(
                  "Array needs to be of rank 1",
                  "array");
            }
            if (this.Count + index > array.Length)
            {
                throw new ArgumentException(
                 "There is not enough space in the array",
                 "array");
            }
            int currentIndex = index;
            foreach (var pair in _elements)
            {
                foreach (TObject obj in pair.Value)
                {
                    array.SetValue(obj, currentIndex++);
                }
```

LISTING 10.1 **PriorityQueue.cs** (continued)

```
            }
        }

        public int Count
        {
            get
            {
                int count = 0;
                foreach (var queue in _elements.Values)
                {
                    count += queue.Count;
                }
                return count;
            }
        }

        public bool IsSynchronized
        {
            get { return (_elements as ICollection).IsSynchronized;
                }
        }

        public object SyncRoot
        {
            get { return (_elements as ICollection).SyncRoot; }
        }
    }
}
```

Create a Trie (Prefix Tree)

Scenario/Problem: You need to quickly look up objects by a string key, and many of the keys are similar. For example, if you need an index of product titles, it is likely that many of them will start the same (Microsoft Windows, Microsoft Office, Microsoft SQL Server, and so on).

Solution: A trie structure is a good way to quickly look up data by using string prefixes. A trie is an n-ary tree where each child link represents the next part of the key and each leaf node represents the values indexed by the path to that node (see Figure 10.2).

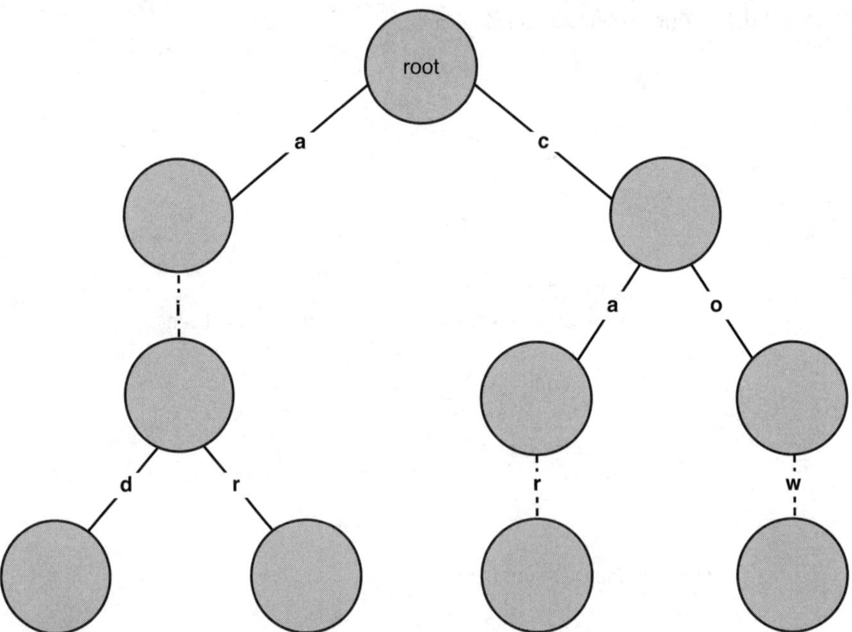

FIGURE 10.2
A trie's children represent the next part of the key, until you get to the leaf nodes where the values are stored. In this trie, the words air, aid, car, and cow are indexed.

A trie can be implemented using arrays if the key's alphabet is known beforehand, but in general a dictionary can be used to look up the next trie node.

The first class we need is a `TrieNode` that holds the values associated with the node, as well as links to children nodes.

```
//an inner class to actually contain values and the next nodes
class TrieNode<T>
{
    private Dictionary<char, TrieNode<T>> _next =
        new Dictionary<char, TrieNode<T>>();
    public ICollection<T> Values { get; private set; }

    public TrieNode()
    {
        this.Values = new List<T>();
        _next = new Dictionary<char, TrieNode<T>>();
    }

    public void AddValue(string key, int depth, T item)
    {
        if (depth < key.Length)
        {
```

```
            //keep creating/following nodes until
            //we reach the end of the key
            TrieNode<T> subNode;
            if (!_next.TryGetValue(key[depth], out subNode))
            {
                subNode = new TrieNode<T>();
                _next[key[depth]] = subNode;
            }
            subNode.AddValue(key, depth + 1, item);
        }
        else
        {
            Values.Add(item);
        }
    }

    //get the sub-node for the specific character
    public TrieNode<T> GetNext(char c)
    {
        TrieNode<T> node;
        if (_next.TryGetValue(c, out node))
            return node;
        return null;
    }

    //get all values in this node, and possibly all nodes under this one
    public ICollection<T> GetValues(bool recursive)
    {
        List<T> values = new List<T>();
        values.AddRange(this.Values);
        if (recursive)
        {
            foreach (TrieNode<T> node in _next.Values)
            {
                values.AddRange(node.GetValues(recursive));
            }
        }
        return values;
    }
}
```

Most of the functionality is in the `TrieNode`, but for convenience, there is a wrapper that hides some of the complexity:

```
class Trie<T>
{
    TrieNode<T> _root = new TrieNode<T>();
```

```
    public void AddValue(string key, T item)
    {
        _root.AddValue(key, 0, item);
    }

    public ICollection<T> FindValues(string key, bool recursive)
    {
        TrieNode<T> next = _root;
        int index = 0;
        //follow the key to the last node
        while (index < key.Length &&
            next.GetNext(key[index]) != null)
        {
            next = next.GetNext(key[index++]);
        }
        //only get values if we found the entire key
        if (index == key.Length)
        {
            return next.GetValues(recursive);
        }
        else
        {
            return new T[0];
        }
    }
}
```

For a test program, the sample code fills the trie from a list of words and searches for some patterns. You can see this program in the TrieDemo project in this chapter's source code. Here is the output:

```
Non-recursive lookup:
agonize

Recursive lookup:
agonize
agonized
agonizedlies
agonizedly
agonizer
agonizers
agonizes

Non-existent lookup:
Found 0 values
```

CHAPTER 11

Files and Serialization

IN THIS CHAPTER

- Create, Read, and Write Files
- Delete a File
- Combine Streams (Compress a File)
- Get a File Size
- Get File Security Description
- Check for File and Directory Existence
- Enumerate Drives
- Enumerate Directories and Files
- Browse for Directories
- Search for a File or Directory
- Manipulate File Paths
- Create Unique or Temporary Filenames
- Watch for File System Changes
- Get the Paths to My Documents, My Pictures, Etc.
- Serialize Objects
- Serialize to an In-Memory Stream
- Store Data when Your App Has Restricted Permissions

Almost every program at some point must interact with files or persisted data in some way. The foundation of nearly all such functionality is located in the `System.IO` namespace.

Create, Read, and Write Files

There are generally two modes to access files: text and binary. In text mode, the raw contents of a file are converted to `System.String` for easy manipulation in .NET. Binary files are just that—you get access to the raw, unfiltered bytes, and you can do what you want with them. We'll look at two simple programs that examine each type of file.

Most I/O in .NET is handled with the concept of streams, which are conceptual buffers of data that you can read from and write to in a linear fashion. Some streams (such as files) allow you to jump to an arbitrary location in the stream. Others (such as network streams) do not.

Create, Read, and Write a Text File

Scenario/Problem: You need to read and write a text file.

Solution: If you tell .NET that you are opening a text file, the underlying stream is wrapped in a text decoder called `StreamReader` or `StreamWriter` that can translate between UTF-8 text and the raw bytes.

Here is a sample program that writes its command-line arguments to a text file that you specify and then reads it back:

```
class Program
{
    static void Main(string[] args)
    {
        if (args.Length < 2)
        {
            Console.WriteLine(
        "Usage: ConsoleToFile filename output1 output2 output3 ...");
            return;
        }
        //write each command line argument to the file
        string destFilename = args[0];
        using (StreamWriter writer = File.CreateText(destFilename))
        {
            for (int i = 1; i < args.Length; i++)
            {
```

```
                writer.WriteLine(args[i]);
            }
        }
        Console.WriteLine("Wrote args to file {0}", destFilename);

        //just read back the file and dump it to the console
        using (StreamReader reader = File.OpenText(destFilename))
        {
            string line = null;
            do
            {
                line = reader.ReadLine();
                Console.WriteLine(line);
            } while (line != null);
        }
    }
}
```

NOTE For this and all succeeding code examples in this chapter, make sure you have `using System.IO;` at the top of your file, as it will not always be explicit in every code sample.

NOTE Files are shared resources, and you should take care to close them when done to return the resource back to the operating system. This is done using the Dispose Pattern, which is described in Chapter 22, "Memory Management." The `using` statements in the preceding code sample ensure that the files are closed at the end of each code block, regardless of any exceptions that occur within the block. You should consider this a best practice that you should always follow whenever possible.

Create, Read, and Write a Binary File

Scenario/Problem: You need to manipulate a file's bytes directly.

Solution: When you open files in binary mode, you get back a stream that you can control more precisely than with text. Here is very naive file copy program, but it demonstrates the point:

```
class Program
{
    static void Main(string[] args)
    {
        if (args.Length < 2)
```

```
        {
            Console.WriteLine(
             "Usage: FileCopy [SourceFile] [DestinationFile]");
            return;
        }

        string sourceFile = args[0];
        string destFile = args[1];
        const int BufferSize = 16384;
        byte[] buffer = new byte[BufferSize];

        int bytesCopied = 0;
        UInt64 totalBytes = 0;
        //open both files--the source file can be read shared, but not
        //the destination
        using (FileStream inStream = File.Open(
               sourceFile, FileMode.Open,
               FileAccess.Read, FileShare.Read))
        using (FileStream outStream = File.Open(
               destFile, FileMode.Create,
               FileAccess.Write, FileShare.None))
        {
            do
            {
                //must track how many bytes we actually read in
                bytesCopied = inStream.Read(buffer, 0, BufferSize);
                if (bytesCopied > 0)
                {
                    outStream.Write(buffer, 0, bytesCopied);
                    totalBytes += (UInt64)bytesCopied;
                }
            } while (bytesCopied > 0);
        }
        Console.WriteLine("{0:N0} bytes copied", totalBytes);
    }
}
```

Delete a File

Scenario/Problem: You need to delete a file.

Solution: The `File` class has a number of static methods you can use, one of them being `Delete()`.

```
File.Delete("Filename.txt");
```

NOTE If the file does not exist, no exception will be thrown. However, `DirectoryNotFoundException` is thrown if the directory does not exist.

Combine Streams (Compress a File)

Scenario/Problem: You want to pump one stream's output into another stream's input to achieve complex behavior, such as compressing a file as you write it out.

Solution: You can combine streams to accomplish rich behavior that can perform powerful transformations. Listing 11.1 shows a quick-and-dirty file compression utility.

LISTING 11.1 **CompressFile.cs**

```
using System;
using System.IO;
using System.IO.Compression;

namespace CompressFile
{
    class Program
    {
        static bool compress = false;
        static string sourceFile = null;
        static string destFile = null;
        const int BufferSize = 16384;

        static void Main(string[] args)
        {
            if (!ParseArgs(args))
            {
                Console.WriteLine(
             "CompressFile [compress|decompress] sourceFile destFile");
                return;
            }
```

LISTING 11.1 **CompressFile.cs** (continued)

```
            byte[] buffer = new byte[BufferSize];
            /* First create regular streams to both source and
             * destination files.
             * Then create a gzip stream that encapsulates
             * one or the other,depending on if we need to
             * compress or uncompress.
             * i.e. If we hook up the gzip stream to the
             * output file streamand then write bytes to it,
             * those bytes will be compressed.
             */
            using (Stream inFileStream =
➥File.Open(sourceFile, FileMode.Open,
➥FileAccess.Read, FileShare.Read))
            using (Stream outFileStream =
➥File.Open(destFile, FileMode.Create,
➥FileAccess.Write, FileShare.None))
            using (GZipStream gzipStream = new GZipStream(
                compress ? outFileStream : inFileStream,
                compress ? CompressionMode.Compress
                        : CompressionMode.Decompress))
            {
                Stream inStream = compress?inFileStream:gzipStream;
                Stream outStream = compress?gzipStream:outFileStream;

                int bytesRead = 0;
                do
                {
                    bytesRead = inStream.Read(buffer, 0, BufferSize);
                    outStream.Write(buffer, 0, bytesRead);
                } while (bytesRead > 0);
            }
        }

        private static bool ParseArgs(string[] args)
        {
            if (args.Length < 3)
                return false;

            if (string.Compare(args[0], "compress") == 0)
                compress = true;
            else if (string.Compare(args[0], "decompress") == 0)
                compress = false;
            else return false;
            sourceFile = args[1];
```

LISTING 11.1 **CompressFile.cs** (continued)

```
                destFile = args[2];
                return true;
            }
        }
    }
```

Get a File Size

Scenario/Problem: You want to retrieve a file's size.

Solution: The `FileInfo` class encapsulates data from the file system.

```
FileInfo info = new FileInfo(@"C:\Autoexec.bat");
long size = info.Length;
```

The `FileInfo` class contains many useful properties, such as creation and modification times, the directory, and file attributes such as hidden and archive in the `Attributes` property (an enumeration of `FileAttributes`).

Get File Security Description

Scenario/Problem: You want to retrieve security information for a file. Security descriptors can be attached to many types of objects, but some of the most common to deal with are files.

Solution: The System.Security namespace contains .NET classes related to security. The following code sample display security information about a file whose name is passed on the command line.

```
using System;
using System.IO;
using System.Security.AccessControl;
using System.Security.Principal;

namespace ShowFileSecurity
{
    class Program
    {
```

```
        static void Main(string[] args)
        {
            if (args.Length < 1)
            {
                Console.WriteLine("Usage: ShowFileSecurity filename");
                return;
            }
            string filename = args[0];
            FileInfo info = new FileInfo(filename);
            FileSecurity security = info.GetAccessControl();
            ShowSecurity(security);
        }

        private static void ShowSecurity(FileSecurity security)
        {
            AuthorizationRuleCollection coll =
                security.GetAccessRules(true, true, typeof(NTAccount));
            foreach (FileSystemAccessRule rule in coll)
            {
                Console.WriteLine("IdentityReference: {0}",
                  rule.IdentityReference);
                Console.WriteLine("Access control type: {0}",
                  rule.AccessControlType);
                Console.WriteLine("Rights: {0}", rule.FileSystemRights);
                Console.WriteLine("Inherited? {0}", rule.IsInherited);

                Console.WriteLine();
            }
        }
    }
}
```

You can run the program from the command line like this:

```
D:\code\ch11\ShowFileSecurity\bin\Debug>ShowFileSecurity.exe
➥ShowFileSecurity.pdb
```

It produces output similar to the following:

```
IdentityReference: Ben-Desktop\Ben
Access control type: Allow
Rights: FullControl
Inherited? True

IdentityReference: NT AUTHORITY\SYSTEM
Access control type: Allow
Rights: FullControl
Inherited? True
```

```
IdentityReference: BUILTIN\Administrators
Access control type: Allow
Rights: FullControl
Inherited? True
```

Check for File and Directory Existence

Scenario/Problem: You need to check if a file or directory exists before attempting to use it.

Solution: This snippet uses the static `Exists()` methods on `File` and `Directory` to check for existence:

```
string target = @"D:\Files";
if (File.Exists(target))
{
    Console.WriteLine("File {0} exists", target);
}
else if (Directory.Exists(target))
{
    Console.WriteLine("Directory {0} exists", target);
}
```

Enumerate Drives

Scenario/Problem: You want to get a list of all drives installed on the system.

Solution: The `DriveInfo` class provides static methods to retrieve this information.

```
DriveInfo[] drives = DriveInfo.GetDrives();
foreach (DriveInfo info in drives)
{
    Console.WriteLine("Name: {0} (RootDirectory: {1}",
                      info.Name, info.RootDirectory);
    Console.WriteLine("DriveType: {0}", info.DriveType);
    Console.WriteLine("IsReady: {0}", info.IsReady);
    //you'll get an exception if you try to read some
    //info when the drive isn't ready
    if (info.IsReady)
```

```
    {
        Console.WriteLine("VolumeLabel: {0}", info.VolumeLabel);

        Console.WriteLine("DriveFormat: {0}", info.DriveFormat);
        Console.WriteLine("TotalSize: {0:N0}", info.TotalSize);
        Console.WriteLine("TotalFreeSpace: {0:N0}", info.TotalFreeSpace);
        Console.WriteLine("AvailableFreeSpace: {0:N0}",
                          info.AvailableFreeSpace);
    }

    Console.WriteLine();
}
```

This code produces the following output on my system (edited to show only unique drives):

```
Name: A:\ (RootDirectory: A:\)
DriveType: Removable
IsReady: False

Name: C:\ (RootDirectory: C:\)
DriveType: Fixed
IsReady: True
VolumeLabel:
DriveFormat: NTFS
TotalSize: 160,045,199,360
TotalFreeSpace: 81,141,878,784
AvailableFreeSpace: 81,141,878,784

Name: F:\ (RootDirectory: F:\)
DriveType: CDRom
IsReady: False

Name: H:\ (RootDirectory: H:\)
DriveType: Removable
IsReady: False
```

Enumerate Directories and Files

Scenario/Problem: You need to get a (possibly recursive) list of all directories or files.

Solution: `DirectoryInfo` can retrieve a list of subdirectories and files inside of it.

```
string root = @"C:\";
//old way--get all strings up front
DirectoryInfo di = new DirectoryInfo(root);
DirectoryInfo[] directories = di.GetDirectories("*",
                                      SearchOption.AllDirectories);

//new in .Net 4--use an enumerator
di = new DirectoryInfo(root);
//to get files, use di.EnumerateFiles with the same type of arguments
IEnumerable<DirectoryInfo> dirInfo =  di.EnumerateDirectories("*",
                                           SearchOption.AllDirectories);
foreach (DirectoryInfo info in dirInfo)
{
    Console.WriteLine(info.Name);
}
```

NOTE Be aware that you can easily get a `SecurityException` while enumerating files and folders, especially if you're not running as an administrator.

Browse for Directories

Scenario/Problem: You need to allow the user to select a folder.

Solution: Use the `FolderBrowserDialog` class in `System.Windows.Forms`. This example is from the BrowseForDirectories project in the sample code for this chapter.

```
FolderBrowserDialog fbd = new FolderBrowserDialog();
if (fbd.ShowDialog() == DialogResult.OK)
{
    textBoxFilename1.Text = fbd.SelectedPath;
}
```

NOTE There is no WPF-equivalent of this dialog, but you can use it from WPF as well.

Search for a File or Directory

Scenario/Problem: You need to find a file or directory by name, possibly with wildcards.

Solution: The `DirectoryInfo` object contains many useful functions, among them the ability to search the file system for files and folders containing a search pattern. The search pattern can contain wildcards, just as if you were using the command prompt.

Listing 11.2 provides a simple example that searches a directory tree for any file or directory that matches the input pattern.

LISTING 11.2 **Searching for a File or Directory**

```
using System;
using System.Collections.Generic;
using System.IO;

namespace Find
{
    class Program
    {
        static bool _folderOnly = false;
        static string _startFolder;
        static string _searchTerm;

        static void Main(string[] args)
        {
            if (!ParseArgs(args))
            {
                PrintUsage();
                return;
            }
            Console.WriteLine("Searching {0} for \"{1}\" {2}",
                _startFolder, _searchTerm,
                _folderOnly ? "(folders only)" : "");
            DoSearch();
        }

        private static void DoSearch()
        {
            DirectoryInfo di = new DirectoryInfo(_startFolder);
```

LISTING 11.2 **Searching for a File or Directory** (continued)

```
        DirectoryInfo[] directories = di.GetDirectories(_searchTerm,
                SearchOption.AllDirectories);
        int numResults = directories.Length;
        PrintSearchResults(directories);
        if (!_folderOnly)
        {
            FileInfo[] files = di.GetFiles(
                         _searchTerm,
                         SearchOption.AllDirectories);
            PrintSearchResults(files);
            numResults += files.Length;
        }

        Console.WriteLine("{0:N0} results found", numResults);
    }

    private static void PrintSearchResults(
                            DirectoryInfo[] directories)
    {
          foreach(DirectoryInfo di in directories)
        {
            Console.WriteLine("{0}\t{1}\t{2}",
             di.Name, di.Parent.FullName, "D");
        }
    }

    private static void PrintSearchResults(FileInfo[] files)
    {
         foreach(FileInfo fi in files)
        {
            Console.WriteLine("{0}\t{1}\t{2}",
             fi.Name, fi.DirectoryName, "F");
        }
    }

    static void PrintUsage()
    {
        Console.WriteLine(
         "Usage: Find [-directory] SearchTerm StartFolder");
        Console.WriteLine("Ex: Find -directory code D:\\Projects");
        Console.WriteLine("* wildcards are accepted");

    }
```

LISTING 11.2 **Searching for a File or Directory** (continued)

```
        static bool ParseArgs(string[] args)
        {
            if (args.Length < 2)
            {
                return false;
            }
            if (string.Compare(args[0], "-directory") == 0)
            {
                _folderOnly = true;
                if (args.Length < 3)
                    return false;
            }
            _startFolder = args[args.Length - 1];
            _searchTerm = args[args.Length - 2];
            return true;
        }
    }
}
```

Here's the program output (your results will likely vary):

```
D:\code\ch11\Find\bin\Debug>Find *media* "c:\Program Files" > temp.txt
Searching c:\Program Files for "*media*"
Windows Media Player          c:\Program Files                          D
VideoMediaHandler.dll         c:\Program Files\Movie Maker              F
VideoMediaHandler.dll.mui     c:\Program Files\Movie Maker\en-US        F
3 results found
```

NOTE You may get an "access denied" error while running this program when the search runs across a folder you don't have permission to access. One way to handle this is to change the search options to `SearchOption.TopDirectoryOnly`, track the subdirectories in a stack, and perform the recursive search yourself, handling the possible exceptions along the way.

Manipulate File Paths

Scenario/Problem: You need to combine a filename with a directory name, or extract certain parts of a path.

Solution: You should almost never need to manually parse a path in C#. Instead, use the `System.IO.Path` class to perform your manipulation. This class has only static methods.

Table 11.1 details most of the methods and properties available to you.

TABLE 11.1 **Path Methods and Properties**

Method	Input	Output
`GetDirectoryName()`	C:\Windows\System32\xcopy.exe	C:\Windows\System32
`GetExtension()`	C:\Windows\System32\xcopy.exe	.exe
`GetFileName()`	C:\Windows\System32\xcopy.exe	xcopy.exe
`GetFileNameWithoutExtension()`	C:\Windows\System32\xcopy.exe	xcopy
`GetFullPath()`	xcopy.exe	C:\Windows\System32\xcopy.exe
`Root()`	C:\Windows\System32\xcopy.exe	C:\
`HasExtension()`	C:\Windows\System32\xcopy.exe	True
`IsPathRooted()`	C:\Windows\System32\xcopy.exe	True
`IsPathRooted()`	xcopy.exe	False
`RandomFileName()`	N/A	rq33lkoe.vwi
`GetInvalidFileNameChars()`	N/A	*A long list of characters that are not allowed in filenames*
`GetInvalidPathChars()`	N/A	*A long list of characters that are not allowed in paths*
`AltDirectorySeparatorChar`	N/A	'/'
`DirectorySeparatorChar`	N/A	'\'
`PathSeparator`	N/A	';'
`VolumeSeparatorChar`	N/A	':'

There are two additional useful methods. `Path.Combine()` will take two or more strings and combine them into a single path, inserting the correct directory separator characters where necessary. Here's an example:

```
string path = Path.Combine(@"C:\Windows\", "System32", "xcopy.exe ");
```

This results in the path having the value `"C:\Windows\System32\xcopy.exe "`.

The second method, `Path.ChangeExtension()`, does just what you think it would. Here's an example:

```
string path = Path.ChangeExtension(@"C:\Windows\System32\xcopy.exe ",
➥"bin");
```

The new value of path is `"C:\Windows\System32\xcopy.bin"`. Note that this does not change the file on the disk—it's just in the string.

Create Unique or Temporary Filenames

Scenario/Problem: You need an arbitrarily named file for temporary purposes.

Solution: Rather than trying to figure out where the user's temporary directory is, generating a random filename, and then creating a file, you can just use the following:

```
//tempFileName is the full path of a 0-byte file in the temp directory.
string tempFileName = Path.GetTempFileName();
using (StreamWriter writer = File.OpenText(tempFileName))
{
    writer.WriteLine("data");
}
```

On one run on my system, `GetTempFileName()` produced the following value:

```
C:\Users\Ben\AppData\Local\Temp\tmp96B7.tmp
```

If you don't need the file to actually be created, you can get just a random filename (no path) by using the following:

```
string fileName = Path.GetRandomFileName();
//fileName: fup5cwk4.355
```

Watch for File System Changes

Scenario/Problem: You want your application to be notified when changes occur in the file system, such as when files are created or modified.

Solution: Many file systems provide ways for the operating system to notify programs when files and directories change. .NET provides the `System.IO.FileSystemWatcher` class to listen to these events.

```
class Program
{
    static void Main(string[] args)
    {
        if (args.Length < 1)
        {
            Console.WriteLine("Usage: WatchForChanges [FolderToWatch]");
```

```
            return;
        }

        System.IO.FileSystemWatcher watcher =
          new System.IO.FileSystemWatcher();
        watcher.Path = args[0];
        watcher.NotifyFilter = System.IO.NotifyFilters.Size |
            System.IO.NotifyFilters.FileName |
            System.IO.NotifyFilters.DirectoryName |
            System.IO.NotifyFilters.CreationTime;
        watcher.Filter = "*.*";
        watcher.Changed += watcher_Change;
        watcher.Created += watcher_Change;
        watcher.Deleted += watcher_Change;
        watcher.Renamed +=
          new System.IO.RenamedEventHandler(watcher_Renamed);

        Console.WriteLine(
         "Manipulate files in {0} to see activity...", args[0]);

        watcher.EnableRaisingEvents = true;

        while (true) { Thread.Sleep(1000); }
    }

    static void watcher_Change(object sender,
                                System.IO.FileSystemEventArgs e)
    {
        Console.WriteLine("{0} changed ({1})", e.Name, e.ChangeType);
    }

    static void watcher_Renamed(object sender,
                                 System.IO.RenamedEventArgs e)
    {
        Console.WriteLine("{0} renamed to {1}", e.OldName, e.Name);
    }
}
```

Here's some sample output (during a create, rename, and delete of the file temp.txt):

```
D:\code\ch11\WatchForChanges\bin\Debug>WatchForChanges.exe d:\
Manipulate files in d:\ to see activity...
temp.txt changed (Created)
temp.txt changed (Changed)
temp.txt renamed to temp.rename
temp.rename changed (Deleted)
```

You can also call `watcher.WaitForChange()`, which will wait until something happens before returning, but usually the event-based mechanism will work for you.

Get the Paths to My Documents, My Pictures, Etc.

Scenario/Problem: You need to get the path of a user's special folders, such as his documents folder.

Solution: You should never hard-code the paths. Not only can different versions of the OS have different folder names, but the user can change these folders to be in whatever location he wants. Use `Environment.GetFolder()` with the `Environment.SpecialFolder` enumeration to retrieve the actual folder on the disk. The following code will print the entire list:

```
foreach (Environment.SpecialFolder folder in
➥Enum.GetValues(typeof(Environment.SpecialFolder)))
{
    string path = Environment.GetFolderPath(folder);
    Console.WriteLine("{0}\t==>\t{1}", folder, path);
}
```

NOTE In general, you should put your application's data in the LocalApplicationData (nonroaming) or ApplicationData (roaming) folder. That is what these folders are meant for. Examine them on your own computer to see how other software uses them. You should never write program data to ProgramFiles or anywhere file security is an issue. The ApplicationData directory will be replicated on all computers to which the user logs on in a domain, so avoid putting unnecessary data there. Starting with Windows Vista, the operating system enforces file security much more strongly, and an application that doesn't pay attention to security issues can break.

Serialize Objects

Scenario/Problem: You want to store .NET objects in a binary form suitable for storage or transmission via a network.

Solution: The easy way to allow a type to be serialized is to just put the attribute `[Serializable]` in front of the type definition. .NET provides three built-in serialization formatters: SOAP, binary, and XML. XML serialization is handled a little differently and will be discussed in its own chapter (see Chapter 14, "XML"). For the examples in this chapter, I chose SOAP because it can be represented in text. But you can easily substitute the `BinaryFormatter` class.

Serialize Objects Using `SerializableAttribute`

Let's do this to our `Vertex3d` class from Chapter 2, "Creating Versatile Types." For simplicity, I've created a simplified version of the `struct` for use here:

```
[Serializable]
public struct Vertex3d
{
    private double _x;
    private double _y;
    private double _z;

    public double X
    {
        get { return _x; }
        set { _x = value; }
    }

    public double Y
    {
        get { return _y; }
        set { _y = value; }
    }

    public double Z
    {
        get { return _z; }
        set { _z = value; }
    }

    public Vertex3d(double x, double y, double z)
    {
        _x = x;
        _y = y;
        _z = z;
    }
}
```

The following code can serialize and output it for us:

```
Vertex3d v = new Vertex3d(1.0, 2.0, 3.0);

byte[] bytes = new byte[1024];
string result = "";
//you can serialize to any arbitrary stream--I'm using MemoryStream
//just to make it easier to display
using (MemoryStream ms = new MemoryStream(bytes))
```

```
{
    SoapFormatter formatter = new SoapFormatter();
    formatter.Serialize(ms, v);
    //translate the bytes into a string we can understand
    result = Encoding.UTF8.GetString(bytes, 0, (int)ms.Position);
}

Console.WriteLine("Vertex: {0}", v);
Console.WriteLine("Serialized to SOAP: " +
                  Environment.NewLine + result);
```

Here's the output:

```
Serialized to SOAP:
<SOAP-ENV:Envelope xmlns:xsi="http://www.w3.org/2001/XMLSchema-instance"
➥xmlns:xsd="http://www.w3.org/2001/XMLSchema" xmlns:SOAP-
➥ENC="http://schemas.xmlsoap.org/soap/encoding/" xmlns:SOAP-
➥ENV="http://schemas.xmlsoap.org/soap/envelope/"xmlns:clr="http://schemas
➥.microsoft.com/soap/encoding/clr/1.0" SOAP-
➥ENV:encodingStyle="http://schemas.xmlsoap.org/soap/encoding/">
<SOAP-ENV:Body>
<a1:Vertex3d id="ref-1"
➥xmlns:a1="http://schemas.microsoft.com/clr/nsassem/SerializeVertex/
➥SerializeVerte
➥x%2C%20Version%3D1.0.0.0%2C%20Culture%3Dneutral
➥%2C%20PublicKeyToken%3Dnull">
<_x>1</_x>
<_y>2</_y>
<_z>3</_z>
</a1:Vertex3d>
</SOAP-ENV:Body>
</SOAP-ENV:Envelope>
```

All of that, with no effort other than adding `[Serializable]`. Actually, not quite true. This version of Vertex3d doesn't contain the `int? _id` field that was present in the original code. Serialization formatters don't know what to do with that. If you want to be able to serialize classes that contain data that can't be automatically formatted, you have to do a little more work, as you'll see in the next section.

Serialize Objects by Implementing `ISerializable`

In order to serialize more complex data (often such as collections), you need to take control of the serialization process. We'll do this by implementing the `ISerializable` interface and also defining a serializing constructor.

Modify the code from the previous section with the following additions:

```
[Serializable]
public struct Vertex3d : ISerializable
{
    private int? _id;

    public int? Id
    {
        get
        {
            return _id;
        }
        set
        {
            _id = value;
        }
    }
...
    //notice that the constructor is private. If this were a class,
    //it should be protected so derived classes could access it
    private Vertex3d(SerializationInfo info, StreamingContext context)
    {
        if (info == null)
            throw new ArgumentNullException("info");
        //custom handling of our nullable id field
        int tempId = info.GetInt32("id");
        if (tempId != 0)
            _id = tempId;
        else
            _id = null;
        _x = info.GetInt32("x");
        _y = info.GetInt32("y");
        _z = info.GetInt32("z");
    }

    public void GetObjectData(SerializationInfo info,
                              StreamingContext context)
    {
        info.AddValue("id", _id.HasValue ? _id.Value : 0);
        info.AddValue("x", _x);
        info.AddValue("y", _y);
        info.AddValue("z", _z);
    }
}
```

Serialize to an In-Memory Stream

Scenario/Problem: You need to serialize data to a buffer in memory, rather than a network stream or file.

Solution: The preceding serialization example did this, but I'll cover it in this section as well.

```
byte[] bytes = new byte[1024];
using (MemoryStream ms = new MemoryStream(bytes))
{
    //write to stream using any method you like that accepts a stream
}
//manipulate the bytes however you want, including converting them to
//text using the Encoding class if the data is textual
```

Store Data when Your App Has Restricted Permissions

Scenario/Problem: You need to save application and user data even when the app has no permission to access the local computer, such as when it's running from the Internet security zone.

Solution: Use Isolated Storage. This is kind of like a virtual file system that .NET associates with an assembly, user, application domain, application (when using ClickOnce only), or a combination of these items. By using Isolated Storage, you can give programs the ability to store information without giving them access to the real file system.

Here's a simple example that creates a subdirectory and a text file:

```
using System;
using System.IO;
using System.IO.IsolatedStorage;

namespace IsolatedStorageDemo
{
    class Program
    {
        static void Main(string[] args)
        {
```

```
            Console.WriteLine("Run with command line arg -r
➥to remove isolated storage for this app/user");

            //get the isolated storage for this appdomain + user
            using (IsolatedStorageFile file =
                    IsolatedStorageFile.GetUserStoreForDomain())
            {
                //setup directory
                if (!file.DirectoryExists("Dummy"))
                {
                    file.CreateDirectory("Dummy");
                }
                Console.WriteLine("Accesses:");
                //read and write to a file in the directory
                using (IsolatedStorageFileStream stream =
                       file.OpenFile(@"Dummy\accesses.txt",
                       System.IO.FileMode.OpenOrCreate))
                using (TextReader reader = new StreamReader(stream))
                using (TextWriter writer = new StreamWriter(stream))
                {
                    string line = null;
                    do
                    {
                        line = reader.ReadLine();
                        if (line != null)
                        {
                            Console.WriteLine(line);
                        }
                    } while (line != null);

                    writer.WriteLine(DateTime.Now.ToString());
                }
                if (args.Length > 0 && args[0] == "-r")
                {
                    Console.WriteLine(
➥"Removing isolated storage for this user/app-domain");
                    file.Remove();
                }
            }

            Console.ReadKey();
        }
    }
}
```

After a few runs, the output looks like this:

```
Run with command line arg -r to remove isolated storage
for this app/user
Accesses:
7/4/2009 4:02:08 PM
7/4/2009 4:02:16 PM
7/4/2009 4:02:22 PM
7/4/2009 4:02:28 PM
```

CHAPTER 12

Networking and the Web

IN THIS CHAPTER

- Resolve a Hostname to an IP Address
- Get This Machine's Hostname and IP Address
- Ping a Machine
- Get Network Card Information
- Create a TCP/IP Client and Server
- Send an Email via SMTP
- Download Web Content via HTTP
- Upload a File with FTP
- Strip HTML of Tags
- Embed a Web Browser in Your Application
- Consume an RSS Feed
- Produce an RSS Feed Dynamically in IIS
- Communicate Between Processes on the Same Machine (WCF)
- Communicate Between Two Machines on the Same Network (WCF)
- Communicate over the Internet (WCF)
- Discover Services During Runtime (WCF)

It is a rare application these days that does not have some functionality tied to the Internet. The software world is increasingly connected, and much software is expected to have some networking functionality, even if it is as simple as checking for updates to itself.

Good networking is hard, but this chapter will get you well on your way with some basics and some not-so-basics.

Resolve a Hostname to an IP Address

Scenario/Problem: You need to translate a hostname, such as microsoft.com, to its IP addresses.

Solution: The `System.Net` namespace contains much of the functionality you'll see in this chapter, including such basics as the `IPAddress` and `Dns` classes.

```
string host = "www.microsoft.com";
//note that a host can have multiple IP addresses
IPAddress[] addresses = Dns.GetHostAddresses(host);
foreach (IPAddress addr in addresses)
{
    Console.Write("\t{0}", addr);
}
```

Here is the output from a sample run of a few common hostnames:

```
www.microsoft.com
        207.46.19.254   207.46.19.190
www.live.com
        204.2.160.40    204.2.160.49
www.google.com
        208.67.219.230  208.67.219.231
www.yahoo.com
        209.131.36.158
```

Get This Machine's Hostname and IP Address

Scenario/Problem: You want to retrieve the current machine's hostname and IP addresses.

Solution: In addition to the solution in the previous section, all you need to do is make one additional call to get the current hostname:

```
string hostname = Dns.GetHostName();
Console.WriteLine("Hostname: {0}", hostname);
IPAddress[] addresses = Dns.GetHostAddresses(hostname);
foreach (IPAddress addr in addresses)
{
    Console.WriteLine("IP Address: {0} ({1})",
                        addr.ToString(), addr.AddressFamily);
}
```

Here is the output on my machine. Notice the IPv6 addresses in the list:

```
Hostname: Ben-Desktop
IP Address: fe80::2c4c:372:e7ee:35b7%14 (InterNetworkV6)
IP Address: fe80::c1aa:9268:a7f0:a203%8 (InterNetworkV6)
IP Address: 192.168.1.2 (InterNetwork)
IP Address: 2001:0:4137:9e50:2c4c:372:e7ee:35b7 (InterNetworkV6)
```

Ping a Machine

Scenario/Problem: You need to detect network or host availability.

Solution: .NET has a ping interface that supports synchronous and asynchronous operations:

```
System.Net.NetworkInformation.Ping ping =
   new System.Net.NetworkInformation.Ping();
System.Net.NetworkInformation.PingReply reply = ping.Send("yahoo.com");
Console.WriteLine("address: {0}", reply.Address);
Console.WriteLine("options: don't fragment: {0}, TTL: {1}",
                  reply.Options.DontFragment, reply.Options.Ttl);
Console.WriteLine("rountrip: {0}ms", reply.RoundtripTime);
Console.WriteLine("status: {0}", reply.Status);
```

NOTE Many networks are configured to not allow pings outside their local networks. You should handle catch `PingException` when using this functionality and look at the inner exception to see the specific reason a failure occurs. Look at the MSDN documentation for the `Send()` method for more possible exceptions.

The output is as follows:

```
address: 69.147.114.224
options: don't fragment: False, TTL: 49
rountrip: 111ms
status: Success
```

Get Network Card Information

Scenario/Problem: You need to retrieve the low-level information about all the network adaptors in the computer.

Solution: The `System.Net.NetworkInformation.NetworkInterface` class provides this functionality.

```
NetworkInterface[] nics = NetworkInterface.GetAllNetworkInterfaces();
foreach (NetworkInterface nic in nics)
{
    //basically, there are just a bunch of properties to query
    Console.WriteLine("ID: {0}", nic.Id);
    Console.WriteLine("Name: {0}", nic.Name);
    Console.WriteLine("Physical Address: {0}",
                      nic.GetPhysicalAddress());
    IPInterfaceProperties props = nic.GetIPProperties();
    PrintIPCollection("DHCP Servers: ", props.DhcpServerAddresses);
}
```

For the complete code, see the NicInfo project in the accompanying code.

Here is some sample output (for just one adaptor):

```
ID: {6B124BB0-CFBE-4DA8-831E-3FD323733CD4}
Name: Local Area Connection
Description: Marvell Yukon 88E8053 PCI-E Gigabit Ethernet Controller
Type: Ethernet
Status: Up
Speed: 100000000
Supports Multicast: True
Receive-only: False
Physical Address: 000129A4C39B
DHCP Servers:
DNS Servers: 208.67.222.222 208.67.220.220
```

Create a TCP/IP Client and Server

Scenario/Problem: You have a situation in which an existing transfer protocol doesn't meet your needs. For example, if HTTP is too simplistic, SOAP is too heavy, RPC is too complex, and you can't use the Windows Communication Foundation (WCF), you may need to design your own application-level protocol on top of TCP/IP.

Solution: .NET makes creating a TCP/IP client and server very easy. Let's do the server first (see Listing 12.1). The logic is pretty easy to follow:

- Run in a loop. Inside the loop, wait for a connection.
- Once a connection is achieved, spawn a thread to handle it.
- Receive a message.
- Send a response.
- Close the connection and return from the thread.

LISTING 12.1 **TCP Server**

```
using System;
using System.Net.Sockets;
using System.Net;
using System.Text;
using System.Threading;

namespace TcpServer
{
    class Program
    {
        static void Main(string[] args)
        {
            IPAddress localhost = IPAddress.Parse("127.0.0.1");
            TcpListener listener =
               new System.Net.Sockets.TcpListener(localhost, 1330);
            listener.Start();

            while (true)
            {
                Console.WriteLine("Waiting for connection");
                //AcceptTcpClient waits for a connection from the client
                TcpClient client = listener.AcceptTcpClient();
                //start a new thread to handle this connection so we can
                //go back to waiting for another client
                Thread thread = new Thread(
                      new ParameterizedThreadStart(HandleClientThread));
                thread.Start(client);
            }
        }

        static void HandleClientThread(object obj)
        {
            TcpClient client = obj as TcpClient;
```

LISTING 12.1 TCP Server (continued)

```
            bool done = false;
            while (!done)
            {
                string received = ReadMessage(client);
                Console.WriteLine("Received: {0}", received);
                done = received.Equals("bye");
                if (done) SendResponse(client, "BYE");
                else SendResponse(client, "OK");
            }
            client.Close();
            Console.WriteLine("Connection closed");
        }

        private static string ReadMessage(TcpClient client)
        {
            byte[] buffer = new byte[256];
            int totalRead = 0;
            //read bytes until stream indicates there are no more
            do
            {
                int read = client.GetStream().Read(buffer, totalRead,
                               buffer.Length - totalRead);
                totalRead += read;
            } while (client.GetStream().DataAvailable);

            return Encoding.Unicode.GetString(buffer, 0, totalRead);
        }

        private static void SendResponse(TcpClient client,
                                         string message)
        {
            //make sure the other end decodes with the same format!
            byte[] bytes = Encoding.Unicode.GetBytes(message);
            client.GetStream().Write(bytes, 0, bytes.Length);
        }
    }
}
```

The only way to stop this server is with Ctrl+C (which is fairly standard for console servers).

Next, the client (see Listing 12.2). Its logic is similarly easy:

- Connect to the server.
- Loop until an exit is signaled.

- Send a message.
- Read a response.
- If the response is "BYE," signal an exit.

LISTING 12.2 **TCP Client**

```
using System;
using System.Text;
using System.Net;
using System.Net.Sockets;

namespace TcpClientTest
{
    class Program
    {
        static void Main(string[] args)
        {
            TcpClient client = new TcpClient("127.0.0.1", 1330);
            bool done = false;
            Console.WriteLine("Type 'bye' to end connection");
            while (!done)
            {
                Console.Write("Enter a message to send to server: ");
                string message = Console.ReadLine();

                SendMessage(client, message);

                string response = ReadResponse(client);
                Console.WriteLine("Response: " + response);
                done = response.Equals("BYE");
            }
        }

        private static void SendMessage(TcpClient client,
                                        string message)
        {
            //make sure the other end encodes with the same format!
            byte[] bytes = Encoding.Unicode.GetBytes(message);
            client.GetStream().Write(bytes, 0, bytes.Length);
        }

        private static string ReadResponse(TcpClient client)
        {
            byte[] buffer = new byte[256];
            int totalRead = 0;
```

LISTING 12.2 **TCP Client** (continued)

```
            //read bytes until there are none left
            do
            {
                int read = client.GetStream().Read(buffer, totalRead,
                    buffer.Length - totalRead);
                totalRead += read;
            } while (client.GetStream().DataAvailable);
            return Encoding.Unicode.GetString(buffer, 0, totalRead);
        }
    }
}
```

NOTE Raw TCP/IP is still useful, but if you can use WCF, it is far superior and easier to develop. It's described later in this chapter, beginning with the section "Communicate Between Processes on the Same Machine (WCF)."

Send an Email via SMTP

Scenario/Problem: You need to send emails via SMTP.

Solution: SMTP stands for Simple Mail Transport Protocol and is a simple, well-defined protocol for exchanging emails with an SMTP server. Thankfully, the specifics of the protocol are handled for you in the `System.Net.Mail.SmtpClient` class. Figure 12.1 shows an SMTP client.

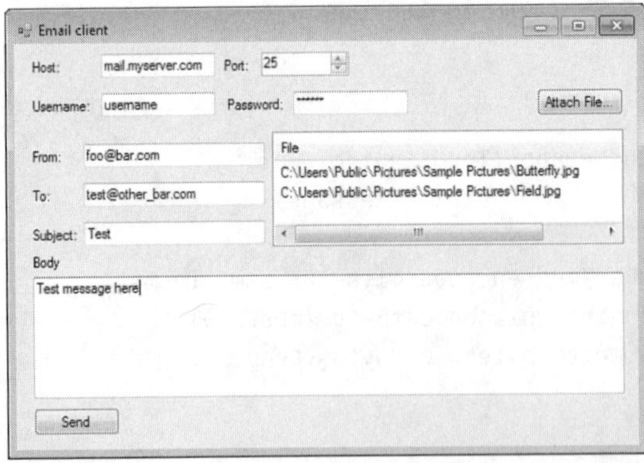

FIGURE 12.1
It's very easy to create a simple SMTP client with full attachment support.

To see a full example of a simple email program, look at the `EmailClient` code example for this chapter. Here is just the method for sending email:

```
private void SendEmail(string host, int port,
    string username, string password,
    string from, string to,
    string subject, string body,
    ICollection<string> attachedFiles)
{
    //A MailMessage object must be disposed!
    using (MailMessage message = new MailMessage())
    {
        message.From = new MailAddress(from);
        message.To.Add(to);
        message.Subject = subject;
        message.Body = body;
        foreach (string file in attachedFiles)
        {
            message.Attachments.Add(new Attachment(file));
        }

        SmtpClient client = new SmtpClient(host, port);
        //if your SMTP server requires a password,
        //the following line is important
        client.Credentials = new NetworkCredential(username, password);
        //this send is synchronous. You can also choose
        //to send asynchronously
        client.Send(message);
    }
}
```

NOTE The `MailMessage` class must be disposed after you send it. I once noticed strange problems with mail not going out immediately when I neglected to do this.

Download Web Content via HTTP

Scenario/Problem: You need to download a web page or file from the Web.

Solution: The System.Net.WebClient class provides most of the functionality you will ever need, as demonstrated in the following example:

```
string url = "http://www.microsoft.com";
string outputfile = "temp.html";

using (WebClient client = new WebClient())
{
    //could also do: byte[] bytes = client.DownloadData(url);
    try
    {
        client.DownloadFile(url, outputfile);
    }
    catch (WebException ex)
    {
        Console.WriteLine(ex.Message);
    }
}
```

This is very easy to do, but `DownloadFile` is a synchronous method, which means it will wait until the file is done before returning. This isn't great if you want to allow the user to do other things in the meanwhile (or to be able to cancel the transfer). For a better solution, continue to the next section.

Download Web Content Asynchronously

Scenario/Problem: You need to download web content with the ability to cancel it, and without blocking your own thread while the content finishes. See Figure 12.2 for an example of a program that allows you to cancel an asynchronous download.

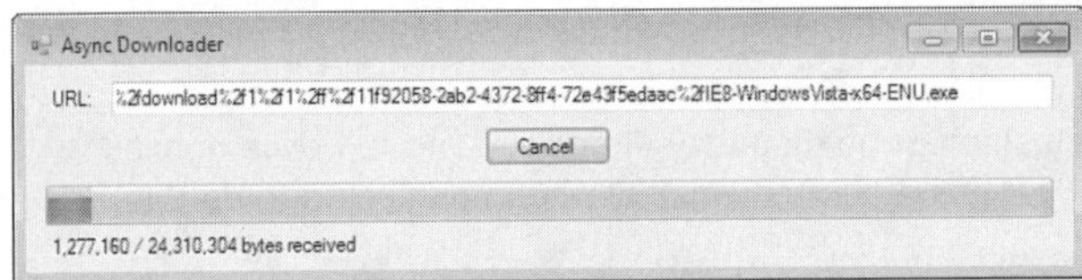

FIGURE 12.2
Asynchronous operations allow you to view progress and give the user a chance to cancel the operation.

Solution: Here's a rundown of how the asynchronous model works in this instance:

- Listen to events that will notify you of the download status.
- Start the download event with an `-Async` method.
- Do other stuff (even if it's just listen for a button click to cancel).
- In the event handlers for the download events, respond to the download progress (or completion).

Listing 12.3 shows a portion of the code for our sample application. To run this sample, please see the WebDownloaderAsync project in this chapter's sample code.

LISTING 12.3 **Asynchronous Web Downloader**

```
using System;
using System.ComponentModel;
using System.Text;
using System.Windows.Forms;
using System.Net;

namespace WebDownloaderAsync
{
    public partial class Form1 : Form
    {
        WebClient _client = null;
        bool _downloading = false;//for tracking what button does

        public Form1()
        {
            InitializeComponent();
        }

        private void buttonDownload_Click(object sender, EventArgs e)
        {
            if (!_downloading)
            {
                _client = new WebClient();
                //listen for events so we know when things happen
                _client.DownloadProgressChanged +=
                   _client_DownloadProgressChanged;
                _client.DownloadDataCompleted +=
                   _client_DownloadDataCompleted;

                try
                {
                    //start downloading and immediately return
                    _client.DownloadDataAsync(new Uri(textBoxUrl.Text));
                    //now our program can do other stuff while we wait!
                    _downloading = true;
                    buttonDownload.Text = "Cancel";
                }
                catch (UriFormatException ex)
                {
                    MessageBox.Show(ex.Message);
                    _client.Dispose();
```

LISTING 12.3 **Asynchronous Web Downloader** (continued)

```
            }
            catch (WebException ex)
            {
                MessageBox.Show(ex.Message);
                _client.Dispose();
            }
        }
        else
        {
            _client.CancelAsync();
        }
    }

    void _client_DownloadProgressChanged(object sender,
            DownloadProgressChangedEventArgs e)
    {
        progressBar.Value = e.ProgressPercentage;
        labelStatus.Text =
              string.Format("{0:N0} / {1:N0} bytes received",
                            e.BytesReceived,
                            e.TotalBytesToReceive);
    }

    void _client_DownloadDataCompleted(object sender,
➥DownloadDataCompletedEventArgs e)
    {
        //now the file is done downloading
        if (e.Cancelled)
        {
            progressBar.Value = 0;
            labelStatus.Text = "Cancelled";
        }
        else if (e.Error != null)
        {
            progressBar.Value = 0;
            labelStatus.Text = e.Error.Message;
        }
        else
        {
            progressBar.Value = 100;
            labelStatus.Text = "Done!";
        }
        //don't forget to dispose our download client!
        _client.Dispose();
```

LISTING 12.3 **Asynchronous Web Downloader** (continued)

```
            _downloading = false;
             buttonDownload.Text = "Download";
            //access data in e.Result
        }
    }
}
```

Upload a File with FTP

Scenario/Problem: You need to download a file from an FTP site.

Solution: FTP is an old, but ever-popular file transfer mechanism, and .NET supports it out of the box with the WebClient, which will see the "ftp://" part of the URL and internally use a FtpWebRequest to perform the communication.

```
string host = "ftp.myFtpSite.com";
string username = "anonymous";
string password = "your@email.com";
string file = "myLocalFile.txt";
if (!host.StartsWith("ftp://"))
{
    host = "ftp://" + host;
}
Uri uri = new Uri(host);
System.IO.FileInfo info = new System.IO.FileInfo(file);
string destFileName = host + "/" + info.Name;
try
{
    //yes, even though this is FTP, we can use the WebClient
    //it will see the ftp:// and use the appropriate protocol
    //internally
    WebClient client = new WebClient();
    client.Credentials = new NetworkCredential(username, password);
    byte[] response = client.UploadFile(destFileName, file);
    if (response.Length > 0)
    {
        Console.WriteLine("Response: {0}",
                          Encoding.ASCII.GetString(response));
    }
}
```

```
catch (WebException ex)
{
    Console.WriteLine(ex.Message);
}
```

There is also an asynchronous version of `UploadFile`.

Strip HTML of Tags

Scenario/Problem: You have a string containing the complete contents of a web page and want to strip away everything but the content.

Solution: A common practice of analyzing web data sources when they do not provide an API for structured access is to scrape the web pages themselves. This is an imprecise process and prone to easy breakage, but sometimes still useful. One part of this process that could be useful is to remove the HTML content, leaving just the text on the page. This could also be useful in a simple web-indexing application. You can use regular expressions to accomplish this (see Chapter 8, "Regular Expressions," for more information):

```
private string StripHtml(string source)
{
    string[] patterns = {
        @"<(.|\n)*?>",            //general HTML tags
        @"<script.*?</script>"   //script tags
                        };
    string stripped = source;
    foreach (string pattern in patterns)
    {
        stripped = System.Text.RegularExpressions.Regex.Replace(
                       stripped, pattern, string.Empty);
    }

    return stripped;
}
```

Embed a Web Browser in Your Application

Scenario/Problem: You want to enable users to browse the Internet (or an intranet site) directly in your application. Alternatively, you just want to be able to render HTML with a standard browser rendering engine.

Solution: You can use the Internet Explorer component included with .NET. In Visual Studio, it shows up under Common Controls in the Form Designer.

You can use the WebBrowser control just like you would any other control and arrange it how you want. Figure 12.3 shows an example of a simple browser.

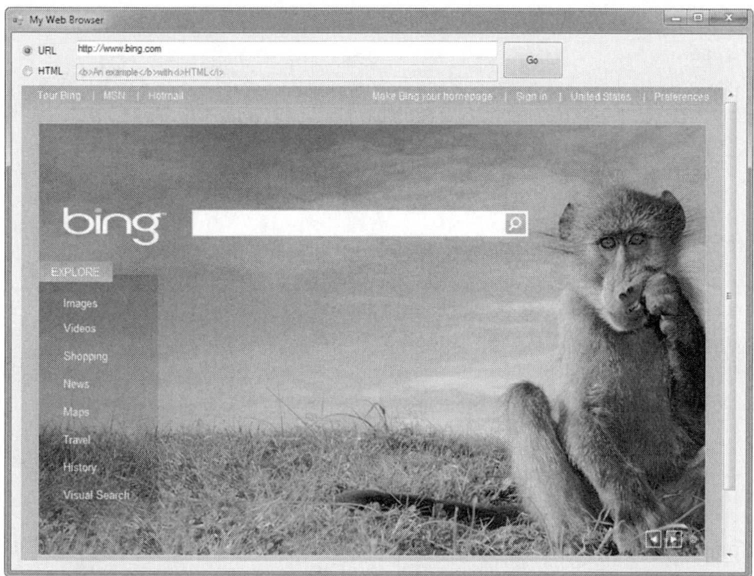

FIGURE 12.3
It is quite simple to create your own web browser by using the existing functionality from Internet Explorer.

Listing 12.4 provides a snippet of the code that manipulates the browser control.

LISTING 12.4 **Custom Web Browser**

```
using System;
using System.ComponentModel;
using System.Windows.Forms;

namespace WebBrowser
{
    public partial class Form1 : Form
    {
        public Form1()
        {
            InitializeComponent();
        }
```

LISTING 12.4 **Custom Web Browser** (continued)

```
        private void buttonGo_Click(object sender, EventArgs e)
        {
            if (radioButtonUrl.Checked)
            {
                this.webBrowser1.Navigate(textBoxUrl.Text);
            }
            else
            {
                this.webBrowser1.DocumentText = textBoxHTML.Text;
            }
        }

        private void OnRadioCheckedChanged(object sender, EventArgs e)
        {
            textBoxUrl.Enabled = radioButtonUrl.Checked;
            textBoxHTML.Enabled = radioButtonHTML.Checked;
        }
    }
}
```

As you can see, it's equally easy to show your own content or anything on the Web. However, the renderer is always Internet Explorer, regardless of what you put around it (just right-click on a page to see the standard IE context menu). Keep this in mind when dealing with JavaScript, for example.

Consume an RSS Feed

Scenario/Problem: You need to parse RSS content in your application.

Solution: An RSS feed is merely an XML file generated at regular intervals, consumed by an application that knows what to do with it. Therefore, it's really just putting together pieces you already know: web download and XML parsing.

The accompanying source code for this chapter contains two projects: RssLib and RssReader. The following sample is from RssLib and contains some simple feed parsing code.

```
using System;
using System.Collections.Generic;
using System.Linq;
using System.Text;
using System.IO;
```

```
using System.Xml;
using System.Net;
using System.Globalization;

namespace RssLib
{
    public class Channel
    {
        public string Title { get; set; }
        public string Link { get; set; }
        public string Description { get; set; }
        public CultureInfo Culture { get; set; }
        public List<Item> Items { get; set; }
    }

    public class Item
    {
        public string Title { get; set; }
        public string Link { get; set; }
        public string Comments { get; set; }
        public string PubDate { get; set; }
        public string Description { get; set; }
    }

    public class Feed
    {
        public Channel Read(string url)
        {
            WebRequest request = WebRequest.Create(url);

            WebResponse response = request.GetResponse();
            XmlDocument doc = new XmlDocument();
            try
            {
                doc.Load(response.GetResponseStream());
                Channel channel = new Channel();
                XmlElement rssElem = doc["rss"];
                if (rssElem == null) return null;
                XmlElement chanElem = rssElem["channel"];

                if (chanElem != null)
                {
                    //only read a few of the many possible fields
                    channel.Title = chanElem["title"].InnerText;
                    channel.Link = chanElem["link"].InnerText;
```

```
                channel.Description =
                    chanElem["description"].InnerText;
                channel.Culture =
➥CultureInfo.CreateSpecificCulture(chanElem["language"].InnerText);
                channel.Items = new List<Item>();
                XmlNodeList itemElems =
                  chanElem.GetElementsByTagName("item");
                foreach (XmlElement itemElem in itemElems)
                {
                    Item item = new Item();
                    item.Title = itemElem["title"].InnerText;
                    item.Link = itemElem["link"].InnerText;
                    item.Description =
                       itemElem["description"].InnerText;
                    item.PubDate = itemElem["pubDate"].InnerText;
                    item.Comments = itemElem["comments"].InnerText;
                    channel.Items.Add(item);
                }
            }
            return channel;
        }
        catch (XmlException)
        {
            return null;
        }
    }

    public void Write(Stream stream, Channel channel)
    {
        XmlWriter writer = XmlTextWriter.Create(stream);
        writer.WriteStartElement("rss");
        writer.WriteAttributeString("version", "2.0");
        writer.WriteStartElement("channel");
        writer.WriteElementString("title", channel.Title);
        writer.WriteElementString("link", channel.Link);
        writer.WriteElementString("description",
                                  channel.Description);
        writer.WriteElementString("language",
                                  channel.Culture.ToString());
        foreach (Item item in channel.Items)
        {
            writer.WriteStartElement("item");
            writer.WriteElementString("title", item.Title);
            writer.WriteElementString("link", item.Link);
            writer.WriteElementString("description",
```

```
                                               item.Description);
                    writer.WriteElementString("pubDate", item.PubDate);
                    writer.WriteEndElement();
                }

                writer.WriteEndElement();
                writer.WriteEndElement();

                writer.Flush();
            }
        }
    }
```

Here’s a short sample of how this library is used:

```
private void buttonLoad_Click(object sender, EventArgs e)
{
    LoadFeed(textBoxFeed.Text);
}

private void LoadFeed(string url)
{
    listViewEntries.Items.Clear();

    RssLib.Channel channel = _feed.Read(url);
    this.Text = "RSS Reader - " + channel.Title;

    foreach (RssLib.Item item in channel.Items)
    {
        ListViewItem listViewItem = new
            ListViewItem(item.PubDate.ToString());
        listViewItem.SubItems.Add(item.Title);
        listViewItem.SubItems.Add(item.Link);
        listViewItem.Tag = item;
        listViewEntries.Items.Add(listViewItem);
    }
}
```

To see the full example, look at the RssReader application in the sample code for this chapter.

In a complete implementation, RSS can have many more fields than are presented here. See http://www.rssboard.org/rss-specification for the full specification of required and optional elements.

Produce an RSS Feed Dynamically in IIS

Scenario/Problem: You want to generate an RSS feed dynamically from a content database.

Solution: You already have all the pieces you need to actually create the feed: It's merely an XML file, after all. The more important question is this: When do you generate it?

There are a few options:

- Each time content is created or updated.
- On a regular schedule (once an hour, for example).
- On each request (possibly with caching).

An example of the last option is to create a custom handler for IIS.

In a class library project, define this class:

```
class RssGenerator : System.Web.IHttpHandler
{
    RssLib.Feed feed = new RssLib.Feed();

    #region IHttpHandler Members

    public bool IsReusable
    {
        get { return true; }
    }

    public void ProcessRequest(System.Web.HttpContext context)
    {
        context.Response.ContentType = "application/xml";
        CreateFeedContent(context.Response.OutputStream);
    }

    #endregion

    private void CreateFeedContent(Stream outStream)
    {
        RssLib.Channel channel = GetFeedFromDB();

        feed.Write(outStream, channel);
```

```
    }

    private RssLib.Channel GetFeedFromDB()
    {
        using (IDataReader reader = CreateDataSet().CreateDataReader())
        {
            RssLib.Channel channel = new RssLib.Channel();
            channel.Title = "Test Feed";
            channel.Link = "http://localhost";
            channel.Description = "A sample RSS generator";
            channel.Culture = CultureInfo.CurrentCulture;
            channel.Items = new List<RssLib.Item>();
            while (reader.Read())
            {
                RssLib.Item item = new RssLib.Item();
                item.Title = reader["title"] as string;
                item.Link = reader["link"] as string;
                item.PubDate = reader["pubDate"] as string;
                item.Description = reader["description"] as string;
                channel.Items.Add(item);
            }
            return channel;
        }
    }

    private static DataSet CreateDataSet()
    {
        DataSet dataSet = new DataSet();
        //get results from database and populate DataSet
        return dataSet;
    }
}
```

To use this in a web project, you must modify the web project's `web.config` to reference it:

```
<httpHandlers>
    ...
    <!-- type="Namespace.ClassName,AssemblyName" -->
    <add verb="GET" path="feed.xml"
         type="IISRssHandler.RssGenerator,IISRssHandler"/>
</httpHandlers>
```

Now, whenever you access the project's feed.xml file via a web browser, the handler will intercept the request and run your code to generate the RSS.

NOTE Rather than generate the results on each request, you may want to implement a simple caching system—only generate if the results haven't been generated in the last 10 minutes or so; otherwise, use the previous results.

To see the web example in action, run the WebAppForRSS project in the sample source code.

Communicate Between Processes on the Same Machine (WCF)

Scenario/Problem: You need to communicate with a process running on the same machine.

Solution: Use Windows Communication Foundation (WCF) with named pipe bindings.

Before WCF, you had many, many communications choices, including COM, DCOM, .NET Remoting, SOAP, TCP/IP, HTTP, named pipes, and more. WCF wraps all of those into a single framework. It separates *what* you communicate from *how* you communicate. As you'll see, you can change from using named pipes to HTTP with only configuration changes.

WCF was designed from the ground up to unify communication technologies under a single framework. This allows your apps to be resilient to change when you need to modify how they communicate. In addition, you get an enormous amount of supporting abilities like security, auditing, extensibility, and more. If you need to use more than one protocol, you can interact with both of them through the common interface of WCF rather than worrying about protocol specifics. WCF can be in command-line apps, GUIs, Windows services, or IIS components.

WCF is a large enough topic for its own book (or series of books), but we'll present enough to get you started.

A WCF app generally has three components:

- A service interface and implementation. This can be implemented in the same assembly as the server, but it can be useful to keep it in a separate assembly so that it can be used in multiple hosts if needed.
- A server that hosts the service implementation.
- A client that calls the server via a proxy class that implements the library's interfaces.

This section will handle each component in turn.

Define the Service Interface

The service in this example will be a simple file server that implements three methods to retrieve directory and file data for the client. The methods are defined in an interface inside a class library that the server references and implements.

```
using System;
using System.ServiceModel;

namespace FileServiceLib
{
    [ServiceContract]
    public interface IFileService
    {
        [OperationContract]
        string[] GetSubDirectories(string directory);

        [OperationContract]
        string[] GetFiles(string directory);

        [OperationContract]
        int RetrieveFile(string filename, int amountToRead,
                         out byte[] bytes);
    }
}
```

The attributes on the interface and methods tell WCF that these should be part of the service.

The implementation is simple:

```
using System;
using System.ServiceModel;
using System.IO;

namespace FileServiceLib
{
    public class FileService : FileServiceLib.IFileService
    {
        //just because it's a file service doesn't mean that you have to
        //actually use the real underlying file system--you could make
        //your own virtual file system

        public string[] GetSubDirectories(string directory)
        {
            return System.IO.Directory.GetDirectories(directory);
        }
```

```
        public string[] GetFiles(string directory)
        {
            return System.IO.Directory.GetFiles(directory);
        }

        public int RetrieveFile(string filename, int amountToRead,
                                out byte[] bytes)
        {
            bytes = new byte[amountToRead];
            using (FileStream stream = File.OpenRead(filename))
            {
                return stream.Read(bytes, 0, amountToRead);
            }
        }
    }
}
```

See the FileServiceLib project in the accompanying source code.

Create the Server

In this case, the server is going to be a console application for simplicity. You could just as easily make it part of a Windows service or run it under IIS.

```
using System;
using System.ServiceModel;
using FileServiceLib;

namespace WCFHost
{
    class Program
    {
        static void Main(string[] args)
        {
            Console.WriteLine("FileService Host");
            //tell WCF to start our service using the
            //info in app.config file
            using (ServiceHost serviceHost =
                    new ServiceHost(typeof(FileServiceLib.FileService)))
            {
                serviceHost.Open();

                Console.ReadLine();
            }
        }
    }
}
```

The configuration file is where the action is. In this case, it tells WCF to use named pipes to communicate with clients, which is ideal for processes located on the same machine.

```
<?xml version="1.0" encoding="utf-8" ?>
<configuration>
  <system.serviceModel>
    <services>
      <service name="FileServiceLib.FileService"
               behaviorConfiguration="FileServiceMEXBehavior">
        <endpoint address=""
                  binding="netNamedPipeBinding"
                  contract="FileServiceLib.IFileService"/>
        <!-- a MEX endpoint allows WCF to exchange
             metadata about your connection -->
        <endpoint address="mex"
                  binding="mexNamedPipeBinding"
                  contract="IMetadataExchange"/>-->
        <host>
          <baseAddresses>
            <add baseAddress="net.pipe://localhost/FileService"/>
          </baseAddresses>
        </host>
      </service>
    </services>
    <behaviors>
      <serviceBehaviors>
        <behavior name="FileServiceMEXBehavior">
          <serviceMetadata  />
        </behavior>
      </serviceBehaviors>
    </behaviors>
  </system.serviceModel>
</configuration>
```

See the WCFHost project in the accompanying source code.

Create the Client

To allow the client to communicate with the server seamlessly, without any knowledge of the underlying protocols, you need a *proxy* class, which converts normal method calls into WCF commands that eventually translate into bytes that go over the connection to the server. You could create this class by hand, but it's easier to start up the server and run a utility to generate it for you.

The file svcutil.exe ships with the Windows SDK. It generates two files: a C# code file with the proxy class implementation, and a configuration file to use in the client.

My copy of svcutil.exe is located in C:\Program Files (x86)\Microsoft SDKs\Windows\v7.0A\bin\. Your location may vary. After starting the server, I ran the following command at the console:

```
D:\>"C:\Program Files (x86)\Microsoft SDKs\Windows\v7.0A\bin\
➥SvcUtil.exe "
➥net.pipe://localhost/FileService /out:FileServiceLib_Proxy.cs
➥/config:app.config
```

NOTE Visual Studio can also generate a proxy class for you in the Add Service Reference dialog box. However, if you have multiple developers working on a project, you should stick to using svcutil.exe because Visual Studio generates additional metadata files that also need to be checked in, but these can be different on different machines, which can cause headaches. It's better to just avoid it completely.

NOTE The proxy is generated for the interface and is the same regardless of which protocol is used. This allows you to make protocol changes in the configuration without having to rebuild the application.

In this example, the client will be a WinForms app that allows you to call each service method and then shows the results.

First, add both of the svcutil.exe-generated files to the project. The app.config file looks similar to this:

```
<?xml version="1.0" encoding="utf-8"?>
<configuration>
    <system.serviceModel>
        <bindings>
            <netNamedPipeBinding>
                <binding name="NetNamedPipeBinding_IFileService"
                        closeTimeout="00:01:00"
                    openTimeout="00:01:00" receiveTimeout="00:10:00"
                    sendTimeout="00:01:00"
                    transactionFlow="false" transferMode="Buffered"
                    transactionProtocol="OleTransactions"
                    hostNameComparisonMode="StrongWildcard"
                    maxBufferPoolSize="524288"
                    maxBufferSize="65536" maxConnections="10"
                    maxReceivedMessageSize="65536">
                    <readerQuotas maxDepth="32"
                        maxStringContentLength="8192"
                        maxArrayLength="16384"
                        maxBytesPerRead="4096"
                        maxNameTableCharCount="16384" />
                    <security mode="Transport">
                        <transport protectionLevel="EncryptAndSign" />
```

```
                </security>
            </binding>
        </netNamedPipeBinding>
    </bindings>
    <client>
        <endpoint address="net.pipe://localhost/FileService"
                  binding="netNamedPipeBinding"
                  bindingConfiguration
                    = "NetNamedPipeBinding_IFileService"
                  contract="IFileService"
            name="NetNamedPipeBinding_IFileService">
            <identity>
                <userPrincipalName value="Ben-Desktop\Ben" />
            </identity>
        </endpoint>
    </client>
  </system.serviceModel>
</configuration>
```

The proxy class has the name `FileServiceClient`, so to instantiate and use it looks something like this:

```
using System;
using System.ComponentModel;
using System.Linq;
using System.Text;
using System.Windows.Forms;

namespace WCFClient
{
    public partial class Form1 : Form
    {
        FileServiceClient fsClient = null;

        public Form1()
        {
            InitializeComponent();

            fsClient = new FileServiceClient();
        }

        private void buttonGetSubDirs_Click(object sender, EventArgs e)
        {
            SetResults(fsClient.GetSubDirectories(
                                        textBoxGetSubDirs.Text));
        }
```

```
        private void buttonGetFiles_Click(object sender, EventArgs e)
        {
            SetResults(fsClient.GetFiles(textBoxGetFiles.Text));
        }

        private void buttonGetFileContents_Click(object sender,
                                                 EventArgs e)
        {
            int bytesToRead = (int)numericUpDownBytesToRead.Value;
            byte[] buffer = new byte[bytesToRead];
            int bytesRead =
               fsClient.RetrieveFile(out buffer,
                                     textBoxRetrieveFile.Text,
                                     bytesToRead);

            if (bytesRead > 0)
            {
                //just assume ASCII for this example
                string text = Encoding.ASCII.GetString(buffer,
                                                       0,
                                                       bytesRead);
                SetResults(text);
            }
        }

        private void SetResults(string[] results)
        {
            //use LINQ to concat the results easily
            textBoxOutput.Text =
               results.Aggregate((a, b) => a + Environment.NewLine + b);
        }

        private void SetResults(string results)
        {
            textBoxOutput.Text = results;
        }
    }
}
```

Figure 12.4 shows the client running on the same machine as the server.

There is a lot more to WCF, but the power of the framework should be apparent.

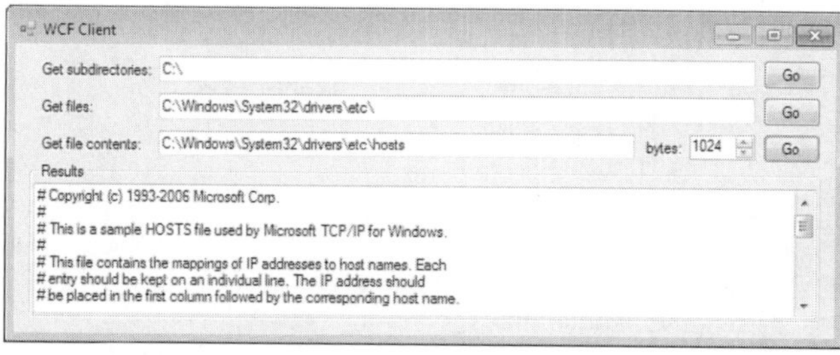

FIGURE 12.4
The client communicates via the server over named pipes.

Communicate Between Two Machines on the Same Network (WCF)

Scenario/Problem: You want to communicate with a process on a machine located on the same network.

Solution: Use WCF with a TCP/IP binding.

Starting with the result from the previous section, all you need to do is change the configuration information in both the server and the client. In fact, you could just have multiple endpoints on the server and allow clients to connect however they desire.

Here's the server's app.config:

```
<?xml version="1.0" encoding="utf-8" ?>
<configuration>
  <system.serviceModel>
    <services>
      <service name="WCFHost.FileService"
               behaviorConfiguration="FileServiceMEXBehavior">
        <endpoint address=""
                  binding="netTcpBinding"
                  contract="FileServiceLib.IFileService"/>
        <endpoint address="mex"
                  binding="mexTcpBinding"
                  contract="IMetadataExchange"/>
        <host>
          <baseAddresses>
            <add baseAddress="net.tcp://localhost:8080/FileService"/>
```

```
          </baseAddresses>
        </host>
      </service>

    </services>
    <behaviors>
      <serviceBehaviors>
        <behavior name="FileServiceMEXBehavior">
          <serviceMetadata  />
        </behavior>
      </serviceBehaviors>
    </behaviors>
  </system.serviceModel>
</configuration>
```

The client's app.config is similarly modified:

```
<?xml version="1.0" encoding="utf-8"?>
<configuration>
    <system.serviceModel>
        <bindings>
          <netTcpBinding>
            <binding name="netTcpBinding_IFileService" />
          </netTcpBinding>
        </bindings>
        <client>
          <endpoint address="net.tcp://remote-pc:8080/FileService"
                    binding="netTcpBinding"
                    bindingConfiguration="netTcpBinding_IFileService"
                    contract="IFileService"
                    name="netTcpBinding_IFileService"/>
        </client>
    </system.serviceModel>
</configuration>
```

NOTE To adequately test this on a modern operating system, you may have to create a firewall exception to allow connections to the server.

That's it. With just a configuration change, the underlying protocol completely changes and you can communicate over the network.

Communicate over the Internet (WCF)

Scenario/Problem: You want to communicate with a service on the Internet.

Solution: Use an HTTP binding with WCF.

Again, this is just a configuration change in our working WCF service.

Here's the server's app.config:

```
<?xml version="1.0" encoding="utf-8" ?>
<configuration>
  <system.serviceModel>
    <services>
      <service name="WCFHost.FileService"
               behaviorConfiguration="FileServiceMEXBehavior">
        <endpoint address=""
                  binding="basicHttpBinding"
                  contract="FileServiceLib.IFileService"/>

        <endpoint address="mex"
                  binding="mexHttpBinding"
                  contract="IMetadataExchange"/>
        <host>
          <baseAddresses>
            <add baseAddress="http://localhost:8080/FileService"/>
          </baseAddresses>
        </host>
      </service>

    </services>
    <behaviors>
      <serviceBehaviors>
        <behavior name="FileServiceMEXBehavior">
        <!-- Allows metadata to be viewed via a web
             browser or other HTTP request -->
          <serviceMetadata httpGetEnabled="true" />
        </behavior>
      </serviceBehaviors>
    </behaviors>
  </system.serviceModel>
</configuration>
```

NOTE To be able to enable an HTTP endpoint under Vista or Windows 7, you need to run this command as an administrator:

```
netsh http add urlacl url=http://+:PORT/
➥user=MYMACHINE\UserName
```

Here's an example:

```
netsh http add urlacl url=http://+:8080/ user=BEN-PC\Ben
```

The client's app.config is shown next:

```
<?xml version="1.0" encoding="utf-8"?>
<configuration>
    <system.serviceModel>
        <bindings>
          <basicHttpBinding>
            <binding name="BasicHttpBinding_IFileService"
                closeTimeout="00:01:00"
                openTimeout="00:01:00"
                receiveTimeout="00:10:00"
                sendTimeout="00:01:00"
                allowCookies="false" bypassProxyOnLocal="false"
                hostNameComparisonMode="StrongWildcard"
                maxBufferSize="65536" maxBufferPoolSize="524288"
                maxReceivedMessageSize="65536"
                messageEncoding="Text"
                textEncoding="utf-8"
                transferMode="Buffered"
                useDefaultWebProxy="true">
              <readerQuotas maxDepth="32" maxStringContentLength="8192"
                  maxArrayLength="16384"
                  maxBytesPerRead="4096" maxNameTableCharCount="16384" />
              <security mode="None">
                <transport clientCredentialType="None"
                           proxyCredentialType="None"
                           realm="" />
                <message clientCredentialType="UserName"
                         algorithmSuite="Default" />
              </security>
            </binding>
          </basicHttpBinding>
        </bindings>
        <client>
            <endpoint address="http://localhost:8080/FileService"
                binding="basicHttpBinding"
                bindingConfiguration="BasicHttpBinding_IFileService"
```

```
                contract="IFileService"
                name="BasicHttpBinding_IFileService" />
        </client>
    </system.serviceModel>
</configuration>
```

Discover Services During Runtime (WCF)

Scenario/Problem: You want clients to dynamically discover available hosts on a network.

Solution: In .NET 4, you can use the `System.ServiceModel.Discovery.DiscoveryClient` class to find all the endpoints on the network that implement the interface you're looking for. Once you bind to an address, use of the service's proxy class is the same as before.

Implement Discoverable Host

The code for the host is exactly the same:

```
using System;
using System.ServiceModel;

namespace WCFDiscoverableHost
{
    class Host
    {
        static void Main(string[] args)
        {
            Console.WriteLine("FileService Host (Discoverable)");

            using (ServiceHost serviceHost = new
                    ServiceHost(typeof(FileServiceLib.FileService)))
            {
                serviceHost.Open();

                Console.ReadLine();
            }
        }
    }
}
```

The configuration has a few new items in it, however:

```
<?xml version="1.0" encoding="utf-8" ?>
<configuration>
  <system.serviceModel>
    <services>
      <service name="FileServiceLib.FileService"
               behaviorConfiguration="fileservice">

        <endpoint address=""
                  binding="netTcpBinding"
                  contract="FileServiceLib.IFileService"
                  behaviorConfiguration="dynEPBehavior"/>

        <endpoint name="udpDiscovery" kind="udpDiscoveryEndpoint"/>

        <endpoint address="mex"
                  binding="mexTcpBinding" contract="IMetadataExchange"/>
        <host>
          <baseAddresses>
            <add baseAddress="net.tcp://localhost:8080/FileService"/>
          </baseAddresses>
        </host>
      </service>
    </services>
    <behaviors>
      <serviceBehaviors>
        <behavior name="fileservice">
          <serviceMetadata />
          <serviceDiscovery />
        </behavior>
      </serviceBehaviors>
      <endpointBehaviors>
        <behavior name="dynEPBehavior">
          <endpointDiscovery />
        </behavior>
      </endpointBehaviors>
    </behaviors>

  </system.serviceModel>
</configuration>
```

Implement Dynamic Client

To keep the code concise, this client will also be implemented as console application.

```
using System;
using System.Collections.Generic;
using System.ServiceModel;
using System.ServiceModel.Discovery;

namespace WCFDiscoverableClient
{
    class Client
    {
        static void Main(string[] args)
        {
            DiscoveryClient client =
               new DiscoveryClient(new UdpDiscoveryEndpoint());

            //find all the endpoints available
            //-- you can also call this method asynchronously
            FindCriteria criteria =
               new FindCriteria(typeof(FileServiceLib.IFileService));
            FindResponse response = client.Find(criteria);

            //bind to one of them
            FileServiceClient svcClient = null;
            foreach (var endpoint in response.Endpoints)
            {
                svcClient = new FileServiceClient();
                svcClient.Endpoint.Address = endpoint.Address;
                break;
            }
            //call the service
            if (svcClient != null)
            {
                string[] dirs = svcClient.GetSubDirectories(@"C:\");
                foreach (string dir in dirs)
                {
                    Console.WriteLine(dir);
                }
            }
            Console.ReadLine();
        }
    }
}
```

The configuration is simpler:

```
<?xml version="1.0" encoding="utf-8" ?>
<configuration>
  <system.serviceModel>
    <client>
      <endpoint name="fileServiceEndpoint"
                address=""
                binding="netTcpBinding"
                contract="IFileService"/>
      <endpoint name="udpDiscoveryEndpoint"
                kind="udpDiscoveryEndpoint"/>
    </client>
  </system.serviceModel>
</configuration>
```

CHAPTER 13

Databases

IN THIS CHAPTER

- Create a New Database in Visual Studio
- Connect and Retrieve Data
- Insert Data into a Database Table
- Delete Data from a Table
- Run a Stored Procedure
- Use Transactions
- Bind Data to a Control Using a DataSet
- Detect if Database Connection Is Available
- Automatically Map Data to Objects with the Entity Framework

Most applications deal with data in some manner. Often, such data resides in a relational database such as SQL Server, Oracle, or MySQL (among many others).

This chapter covers some of the basics of database access from .NET. If you do not have a database to play around with, I recommend either SQL Server Express Edition or MySql Community Edition, either of which can be found via your favorite search engine. Both databases have components that allow you create and edit databases directly from Visual Studio.

All the examples use a database called TestDB, with a single table called Books. The first section will walk through creating this in SQL Server.

Create a New Database from Visual Studio

Scenario/Problem: You want to create a new database from Visual Studio.

Solution: First, make sure you have SQL Server (the Express Edition is fine) or another database server installed. Although SQL Server will automatically integrate with Visual Studio, you may have to download additional components to allow third-party databases to work inside Visual Studio. This section will assume you are using SQL Server.

1. Open Server Explorer (Ctrl+W, L or from the View menu).
2. Right-click Data Connections and choose Create New SQL Server Database.
3. Pick your server instance from the drop-down box and select the appropriate authentication method (usually chosen when you set up the server).
4. Type in a name—for example, "TestDB"—and hit OK.
5. Expand the new database that was created for you.
6. Right-click Tables and select Add New Table.
7. Configure the table similar to what is shown in Figure 13.1.
8. Close the window and give the table the name Books.
9. To add data, right-click the created table and select Show Table Data. You can see the values I added in Figure 13.2.

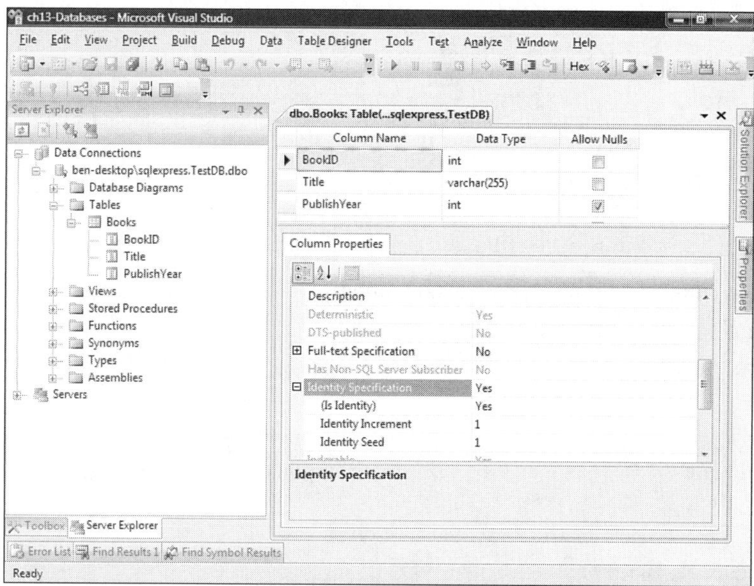

FIGURE 13.1

In order to run the examples in this chapter, you will need to create a test database and table similar to the one shown here.

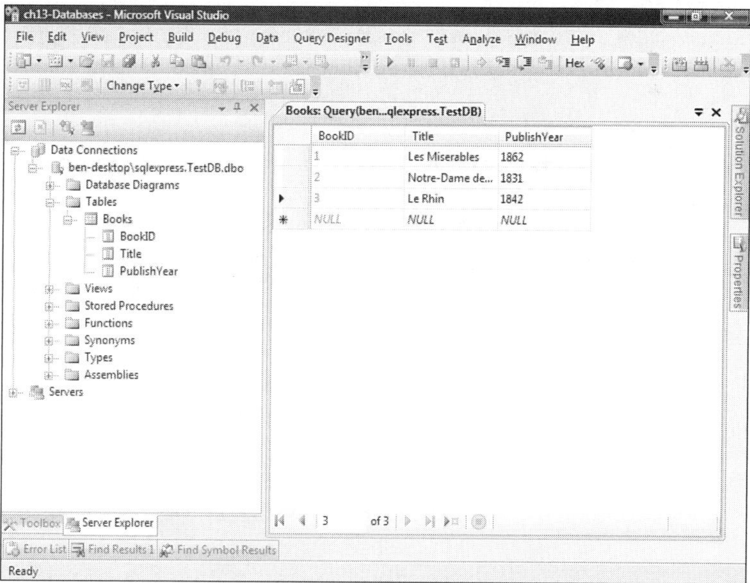

FIGURE 13.2

You can insert whatever data you want into the table.

Connect and Retrieve Data

Scenario/Problem: You need to connect to a database and run a simple query against it.

Solution: Most database access is based around the following set of steps:

1. Create a connection using a connection string.
2. Create a command using SQL syntax.
3. Execute the command upon connection and possibly get data back.

We'll see specific examples of this in the following sections. Most code samples in this chapter require the `System.Data.SqlClient` namespace, even though it's not always explicitly referenced in the code samples.

Connect to SQL Server

.NET ships with a connector for SQL Server, so we'll start with an example of that:

```
static void Main(string[] args)
{
    try
    {
        string connectionString = GetConnectionString();
        using (SqlConnection conn = new SqlConnection(connectionString))
        {
            conn.Open();
            //don't forget to pass the connection object to the command
            using (SqlCommand cmd = new SqlCommand(
                          "SELECT * FROM Books", conn))
            using (SqlDataReader reader = cmd.ExecuteReader())
            {
                //SqlDataReader reads the rows one at a
                //time from the database
                //as you request them
                while (reader.Read())
                {
                    Console.WriteLine("{0}\t{1}\t{2}",
                                      reader.GetInt32(0),
                                      reader.GetString(1),
                                      reader.GetInt32(2));
                }
            }
        }
```

```
    }
    catch (SqlException ex)
    {
        Console.Write(ex);
    }
}

//you shouldn't store connection strings in source code, but this is
//to illustrate SQL access, so I'm keeping it simple
static string GetConnectionString()
{
    //change data source to point to your local copy of SQL Server
    return @"Data source=BEN-DESKTOP\SQLEXPRESS;Initial Catalog=TestDB;
➥Integrated Security=SSPI";
}
```

Here is the output:

```
1       Les Miserables  1862
2       Notre-Dame de Paris     1831
3       Le Rhin 1842
```

Connect to MySQL

Sun (who owns MySQL at the time of this writing) provides .NET connectors for accessing MySQL databases. You have two options for installation:

- Use the installer, which will put the MySql.Data.dll into the Global Assembly Cache (GAC), from which all MySQL-enabled applications can access it.
- Put the MySql.Data.dll into your project and reference it directly from the file system.

In the accompanying source code, I chose the second option. Although this is a somewhat personal choice, I feel it's best to have as few external dependencies for the project as possible.

Once you add a reference to the component, the code is nearly identical to the SQL Server version:

```
static void Main(string[] args)
{
    try
    {
        string connectionString = GetConnectionString();
        //basically, it's all the same, but with "My"
        //in front of everything
        using (MySqlConnection conn =
```

```
                new MySqlConnection(connectionString))
        {
            conn.Open();
            using (MySqlCommand cmd = new MySqlCommand(
                          "SELECT * FROM Books", conn))
            using (MySqlDataReader reader = cmd.ExecuteReader())
            {
                while (reader.Read())
                {
                    Console.WriteLine("{0}\t{1}\t{2}",
                                      reader.GetInt32(0),
                                      reader.GetString(1),
                                      reader.GetInt32(2));
                }
            }
        }
    }
    catch (MySqlException ex)
    {
        Console.Write(ex);
    }
}
//you shouldn't store connection strings in source code, but this is
//to illustrate SQL access, so I'm keeping it simple
static string GetConnectionString()
{
    return @"Data source=localhost;Initial Catalog=TestDB;
➥user=ben;password=password;";
}
```

Structure Your Program to Be Database-Agnostic

Scenario/Problem: You need your program to work with multiple database servers.

Solution: Notice how similar the MySQL and SQL Server code is? That's because all data connectors in .NET derive from a common set of interfaces and classes. If there is a possibility of switching database servers, it's a good idea to abstract out as much as possible, as in the following simplistic example.

```
enum DatabaseServerType { SqlServer, MySQL };

static void PrintUsage()
```

```
{
    Console.WriteLine("ConnectToEither.exe [SqlServer | MySql]");
}

static void Main(string[] args)
{
    DatabaseServerType dbType;

    if (args.Length < 1)
    {
        PrintUsage();
        return;
    }
    if (string.Compare("SqlServer", args[0]) == 0)
    {
        dbType = DatabaseServerType.SqlServer;
    }
    else if (string.Compare("MySQL", args[0]) == 0)
    {
        dbType = DatabaseServerType.MySQL;
    }
    else
    {
        PrintUsage();
        return;
    }
    try
    {
        string connectionString = GetConnectionString(dbType);
        using (DbConnection conn = CreateConnection(dbType,
                                                     connectionString))
        {
            conn.Open();
            using (DbCommand cmd = CreateCommand(dbType,
                                                 "SELECT * FROM Books",
                                                 conn))
            using (IDataReader reader = cmd.ExecuteReader())
            {
                while (reader.Read())
                {
                    Console.WriteLine("{0}\t{1}\t{2}",
                                      reader.GetInt32(0),
➥ reader.GetString(1), reader.GetInt32(2));
                }
            }
```

```
        }
    }
    catch (DbException ex)
    {
        Console.Write(ex);
    }
    Console.WriteLine("Press any key to exit...");
    Console.ReadKey();
}

static string GetConnectionString(DatabaseServerType dbType)
{
    switch (dbType)
    {
        case DatabaseServerType.SqlServer:
            return @"Data source=BEN-DESKTOP\SQLEXPRESS;
➥Initial Catalog=TestDB; Integrated Security=SSPI";
        case DatabaseServerType.MySQL:
            return @"Data source=localhost;
➥Initial Catalog=TestDB;user=ben;password=password;";
    }
    throw new InvalidOperationException();
}

private static DbConnection CreateConnection(DatabaseServerType dbType,
➥string connectionString)
{
    switch (dbType)
    {
        case DatabaseServerType.SqlServer:
            return new System.Data.SqlClient.SqlConnection(
                                              connectionString);
        case DatabaseServerType.MySQL:
            return new MySql.Data.MySqlClient.MySqlConnection(
                                              connectionString);
    }
    throw new InvalidOperationException();
}

private static string CreateSelectString(DatabaseServerType dbType)
{
    //be aware that different servers have slightly
    //different SQL syntax for many things
    //for a simple select like we're doing, the syntax is the same
    return "SELECT * FROM Books";
```

```
}

private static DbCommand CreateCommand(DatabaseServerType dbType,
➥string query, DbConnection conn)
{
    switch (dbType)
    {
        case DatabaseServerType.SqlServer:
            //we have to cast the connections because the commands
            //only work on the correct connection
            return new System.Data.SqlClient.SqlCommand(query,
➥conn as System.Data.SqlClient.SqlConnection);
        case DatabaseServerType.MySQL:
            return new MySql.Data.MySqlClient.MySqlCommand(query,
➥conn as MySql.Data.MySqlClient.MySqlConnection);
    }
    throw new InvalidOperationException();
}
```

NOTE When you use the base classes for database access, you are limited to the common functionality provided by all database systems. Even then, you may run into trouble where one database doesn't support the entire interface. Even if you make your codebase largely database-agnostic, you may still have to provide some database-specific functionality.

NOTE In a real system, you will likely need to do much more work to get truly useful database-agnostic code. Databases consist of many things, such as triggers, views, stored procedures, and much more, so obtaining complete agnosticism can be quite a bit of work.

Insert Data into a Database Table

Scenario/Problem: You need to insert data into a table.

Solution: Most applications need to write some kind of data to a database as well as read it.

```
try
{
    string connectionString = GetConnectionString();
    using (SqlConnection conn = new SqlConnection(connectionString))
```

```
    {
        conn.Open();
        using (SqlCommand cmd = new SqlCommand(
➥"INSERT INTO Books (Title, PublishYear) VALUES (@Title, @PublishYear)"
➥, conn))
        {
            cmd.Parameters.Add(new SqlParameter("@Title", "Test Book"));
            cmd.Parameters.Add(new SqlParameter("@PublishYear",
                                                "2010"));
            //we use the ExecuteNonQuery because we don't get rows
            //back during an insert
            int rowsAffected = cmd.ExecuteNonQuery();
            Console.WriteLine("{0} rows affected by insert",
                              rowsAffected);
        }
    }
}
catch (SqlException ex)
{
    Console.Write(ex);
}
```

NOTE Most SQL objects wrap external resources, thus the extensive use of `using` statements in database code.

NOTE You should always use the `SqlCommand` object, with parameters, to execute your code. Using these objects will prevent dreaded SQL injection attacks. If you execute raw SQL statements, especially with user input in them, it's an invitation for your database to be stolen or destroyed.

Delete Data from a Table

Scenario/Problem: You need to delete data from a table.

Solution: Delete is a dangerous operation, but it is sometimes necessary. Executing it is just as simple in .NET.

```
try
{
    string connectionString = GetConnectionString();
    using (SqlConnection conn = new SqlConnection(connectionString))
```

```
    {
        conn.Open();
        //delete the rows we inserted above
        using (SqlCommand cmd = new SqlCommand(
➥"DELETE FROM Books WHERE Title LIKE '%Test%'", conn))
        {
            int rowsAffected = cmd.ExecuteNonQuery();
            Console.WriteLine("{0} rows affect by delete",
                                rowsAffected);
        }
    }
}
catch (SqlException ex)
{
    Console.Write(ex);
}
```

NOTE Do you really need to delete data? Removing data from a database can be difficult, especially when you have lots of tables referring to others. You might be surprised at how often it is easier to just leave data in the database and have a field called "IsDeleted" to mark whether the record represents active data.

However, do your due diligence: Sometimes there are laws that require certain types of data to be deleted after a certain amount of time.

Run a Stored Procedure

Scenario/Problem: You need to execute a stored procedure in the database.

Solution: Stores procedures are something like methods stored on the server, and .NET supports them by settings the `CommandType` on the `SqlCommand` object. For this example, I created a simple stored procedure in my SQL Server database to return a list of books sorted by publishing year.

```
ALTER PROCEDURE dbo.GetSortedBooks
AS
    SELECT * FROM Books ORDER BY PublishYear
    RETURN
```

Executing a stored procedure is very similar to executing a query, as shown here:

```
string connectionString = GetConnectionString();
using (SqlConnection conn = new SqlConnection(connectionString))
```

```
{
    conn.Open();
    //don't forget to pass the connection object to the command
    using (SqlCommand cmd = new SqlCommand("GetSortedBooks", conn))
    {
        //we set the command type so the command object can interpret
        //the query text as a stored proc
        cmd.CommandType = System.Data.CommandType.StoredProcedure;
        using (SqlDataReader reader = cmd.ExecuteReader())
        {
            //SqlDataReader reads the rows one at a time from the
            //database as you request them
            while (reader.Read())
            {
                Console.WriteLine("{0}\t{1}\t{2}", reader.GetInt32(0),
➥ reader.GetString(1), reader.GetInt32(2));
            }
        }
    }
}
```

Use Transactions

Scenario/Problem: You need to use database transactions to guarantee multiple operations are treated as an atomic unit—that is, they either all succeed or all fail.

Solution: You can create a new transaction from a connection object. You then need to include that transaction with each command you execute.

```
try
{
    //GetConnectionString is from a previous example
    string connectionString = GetConnectionString();
    using (SqlConnection conn = new SqlConnection(connectionString))
    {
        conn.Open();

        Console.WriteLine("Before attempted inserts: ");
        using (SqlCommand cmd = new SqlCommand("SELECT * FROM Books",
                                               conn))
        using (SqlDataReader reader = cmd.ExecuteReader())
        {
```

```
            while (reader.Read())
            {
                Console.WriteLine("{0}\t{1}\t{2}", reader.GetInt32(0),
➥ reader.GetString(1), reader.GetInt32(2));
            }
        }

        using (SqlTransaction transaction = conn.BeginTransaction())
        {
            try
            {
                using (SqlCommand cmd = new SqlCommand(
➥"INSERT INTO Books (Title, PublishYear) VALUES ('Test', 2010)",
➥conn, transaction))
                {
                    cmd.ExecuteNonQuery();//this should work
                }

                using (SqlCommand cmd = new SqlCommand(
➥"INSERT INTO Books (Title, PublishYear) VALUES ('Test', 'Oops')",
➥conn, transaction))
                {
                    cmd.ExecuteNonQuery();//this should NOT work
                }
                //if we got here, everything worked,
                //so go ahead and commit
                transaction.Commit();
            }
            catch (SqlException )
            {
                Console.WriteLine("Exception occurred, rolling back");
                transaction.Rollback();
            }
        }
        Console.WriteLine("After attempted inserts");
        using (SqlCommand cmd = new SqlCommand("SELECT * FROM Books",
                                               conn))
        using (SqlDataReader reader = cmd.ExecuteReader())
        {
            while (reader.Read())
            {
                Console.WriteLine("{0}\t{1}\t{2}", reader.GetInt32(0),
➥ reader.GetString(1), reader.GetInt32(2));
            }
        }
```

```
    }
}
catch (SqlException ex)
{
    Console.Write(ex);
}
```

The following output demonstrates that even though the first `INSERT` was perfectly fine, it never gets added because the second `INSERT` in the same transaction failed:

```
Before attempted inserts:
1       Les Miserables  1862
2       Notre-Dame de Paris     1831
3       Le Rhin 1842
Exception occurred, rolling back
After attempted inserts
1       Les Miserables  1862
2       Notre-Dame de Paris     1831
3       Le Rhin 1842
```

Bind Data to a Control Using a DataSet

Scenario/Problem: You want to easily display data from a database table on a form.

Solution: This section introduces the powerful technique of binding data to onscreen controls and allowing .NET to manage the interaction between them.

All database binding functionality relies on data sets. Technically, a data set can be any `IEnumerable` collection, but often you can use the `DataSet` class, which allows you to store relational data in memory. `DataSet` objects can be populated from a database, after which the connection to the database can be safely closed.

Bind Data to a Control in Windows Forms

This code assumes the form contains a single `DataGridView` control: See the DataBindingWinForms project for this chapter for the complete source code, including all the UI stuff I neglected to copy here.

```
public partial class Form1 : Form
{
    DataSet _dataSet;
```

```
    public Form1()
    {
        InitializeComponent();

        _dataSet = CreateDataSet();
        dataGridView.DataSource = _dataSet.Tables["Books"];
    }

    protected override void OnFormClosing(FormClosingEventArgs e)
    {
        _dataSet.Dispose();
    }

    private DataSet CreateDataSet()
    {
        string connectionString = @"Data source=BEN-DESKTOP\SQLEXPRESS;
➥Initial Catalog=TestDB;Integrated Security=SSPI";
        using (SqlConnection conn = new SqlConnection(connectionString))
        {
            conn.Open();
            using (SqlCommand cmd =
                    new SqlCommand("SELECT * FROM Books", conn))
            using (SqlDataAdapter adapter = new SqlDataAdapter())
            {
                //adapters know how to talk to specific database servers
                adapter.TableMappings.Add("Table", "Books");
                adapter.SelectCommand = cmd;
                DataSet dataSet = new DataSet("Books");
                //put all the rows into the dataset
                adapter.Fill(dataSet);
                return dataSet;
            }
        }
    }
}
```

Figure 13.3 demonstrates the `DataGridView` control when it's hooked up to our sample database.

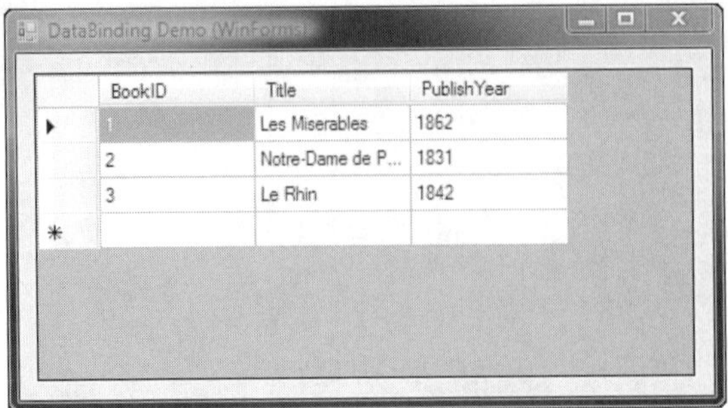

FIGURE 13.3
The `DataGridView` control is an easy way to display table data directly from the database.

Update Database from DataSet

Scenario/Problem: Because the `DataGridView` allows you to edit the cell values, you want to push the changes made back to the database.

Solution: To do this, you need to make sure the `DataSet` knows the syntax of an `UPDATE` command. Then you need to call `Update()` on the adapter object. This code extends the previous example by adding the `UpdateCommand` to the `DataSet` and adding a button to trigger the update.

```
public partial class Form1 : Form
{
    IDataAdapter _adapter;
    DataSet _dataSet;
    IDbConnection _conn;

    public Form1()
    {
        InitializeComponent();

        buttonUpdate.Enabled = false;

        CreateDataSet();

        dataGridView1.DataSource = _dataSet.Tables["Books"];
        dataGridView1.CellEndEdit +=
            new DataGridViewCellEventHandler(OnCellEdit);
```

```
        buttonUpdate.Click += new EventHandler(buttonUpdate_Click);
    }

    protected override void OnClosing(CancelEventArgs e)
    {
        _dataSet.Dispose();
        _conn.Dispose();
    }

    private void CreateDataSet()
    {
        string connectionString =
          @"Data source=BEN-DESKTOP\SQLEXPRESS;InitialCatalog=TestDB;
➥Integrated Security=SSPI";
        SqlConnection conn = new SqlConnection(connectionString);

        SqlCommand selectCmd = new SqlCommand("SELECT * FROM Books",
                                              conn);
        SqlCommand updatecmd = new SqlCommand(
          "UPDATE BOOKS SET Title=@Title, PublishYear=@PublishYear WHERE
➥BookID=@BookID",
          conn);
        //must add parameters so the DataSet can supply the
        //right values for the columns
        updatecmd.Parameters.Add("@BookID", SqlDbType.Int, 4, "BookID");
        updatecmd.Parameters.Add("@Title", SqlDbType.VarChar,
                                 255, "Title");
        updatecmd.Parameters.Add("@PublishYear", SqlDbType.Int,
                                 4, "PublishYear");

        SqlDataAdapter adapter = new SqlDataAdapter();

        adapter.TableMappings.Add("Table", "Books");
        adapter.SelectCommand = selectCmd;
        adapter.UpdateCommand = updatecmd;
        _conn = conn;
        _adapter = adapter;
        _dataSet = new DataSet("Books");

        //put all the rows into the dataset
        _adapter.Fill(_dataSet);
    }
```

```
    private void OnCellEdit(object sender, DataGridViewCellEventArgs e)
    {
        buttonUpdate.Enabled = true;
    }

    private void buttonUpdate_Click(object sender, EventArgs e)
    {
        _adapter.Update(_dataSet);
        buttonUpdate.Enabled = false;
    }
}
```

Bind Data to a Control in WPF

WPF offers much more flexible formatting capabilities than Windows Forms, but for this example, we'll stick to the same type of display as before. See the DatabindingWPF sample project for the complete code.

Here's the Extensible Application Markup Language (XAML) code for the window:

```
<Window x:Class="DataBindingWPF.Window1"
    xmlns="http://schemas.microsoft.com/winfx/2006/xaml/presentation"
    xmlns:x="http://schemas.microsoft.com/winfx/2006/xaml"
    Title="Data Binding Demo (WPF)" Height="301" Width="477">
    <Grid>
        <ListView Name="listView1">
            <ListView.View>
                <GridView>
                    <GridViewColumn Header="ID" Width="35"
➥DisplayMemberBinding="{Binding Path=BookID}"/>
                    <GridViewColumn Header="Title" Width="200"
➥DisplayMemberBinding="{Binding Path=Title}"/>
                    <GridViewColumn Header="Published" Width="70"
➥DisplayMemberBinding="{Binding Path=PublishYear}"/>
                </GridView>
            </ListView.View>
        </ListView>
    </Grid>
</Window>
```

Here's the code-behind for the window:

```
public partial class Window1 : Window
{
    DataSet _dataSet;
    public Window1()
```

```
    {
        InitializeComponent();

        _dataSet = CreateDataSet();
        listView1.DataContext = _dataSet.Tables["Books"];
        Binding binding = new Binding();
        listView1.SetBinding(ListView.ItemsSourceProperty, binding);
    }

    protected override void
       OnClosing(System.ComponentModel.CancelEventArgs e)
    {
        _dataSet.Dispose();
    }

    private DataSet CreateDataSet()
    {
        string connectionString = @"Data source=BEN-DESKTOP\SQLEXPRESS;
➥Initial Catalog=TestDB;Integrated Security=SSPI";
        using (SqlConnection conn = new SqlConnection(connectionString))
        {
            conn.Open();
            using (SqlCommand cmd =
               new SqlCommand("SELECT * FROM Books", conn))
            using (SqlDataAdapter adapter = new SqlDataAdapter())
            {
                adapter.TableMappings.Add("Table", "Books");
                adapter.SelectCommand = cmd;
                DataSet dataSet = new DataSet("Books");
                //put all the rows into the dataset
                adapter.Fill(dataSet);
                return dataSet;
            }
        }
    }
}
```

Figure 13.4 shows the WPF version of the `DataGrid` with our database's data.

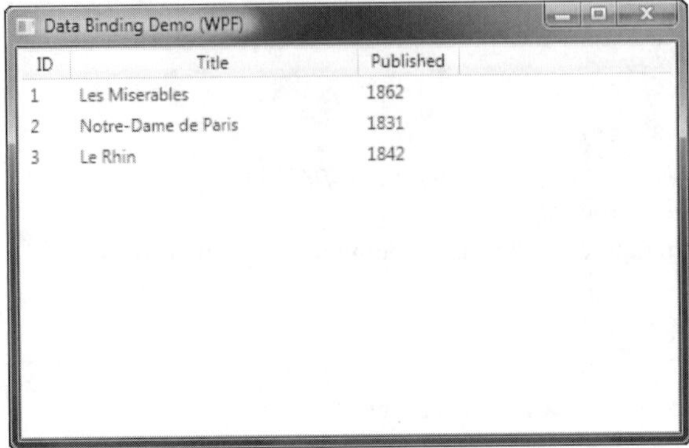

FIGURE 13.4
In WPF, any control can have its values bound to a data source.

Bind Data to a Control in ASP.NET

Data binding is similarly easy in ASP.NET. You can rely on the GridView control.

Here's the HTML:

```
<%@ Page Language="C#" AutoEventWireup="true"
    CodeBehind="Default.aspx.cs" Inherits="DataBindingWeb._Default" %>
<!DOCTYPE html PUBLIC "-//W3C//DTD XHTML 1.0 Transitional//EN"
➥"http://www.w3.org/TR/xhtml1/DTD/xhtml1-transitional.dtd">
<html xmlns="http://www.w3.org/1999/xhtml" >
<head runat="server">
    <title></title>
</head>
<body>
    <form id="form1" runat="server">
    <div>
    Database Results:
        <asp:GridView ID="GridView1" runat="server">
        </asp:GridView>
    </div>
    </form>
</body>
</html>
```

And here's the code-behind:

```
public partial class _Default : System.Web.UI.Page
{
    private DataSet _dataSet;

    protected void Page_Load(object sender, EventArgs e)
    {
```

```
            _dataSet = CreateDataSet();
            GridView1.DataSource = _dataSet.Tables["Books"];
            GridView1.DataBind();
        }

        private DataSet CreateDataSet()
        {
            string connectionString = @"Data source=BEN-DESKTOP\SQLEXPRESS;
➥Initial Catalog=TestDB;Integrated Security=SSPI";
            using (SqlConnection conn = new SqlConnection(connectionString))
            {
                conn.Open();
                using (SqlCommand cmd =
                  new SqlCommand("SELECT * FROM Books", conn))
                using (SqlDataAdapter adapter = new SqlDataAdapter())
                {
                    adapter.TableMappings.Add("Table", "Books");
                    adapter.SelectCommand = cmd;
                    DataSet dataSet = new DataSet("Books");
                    //put all the rows into the dataset
                    adapter.Fill(dataSet);
                    return dataSet;
                }
            }
        }
    }
```

Figure 13.5 shows our by-now familiar grid of data, this time in a web page.

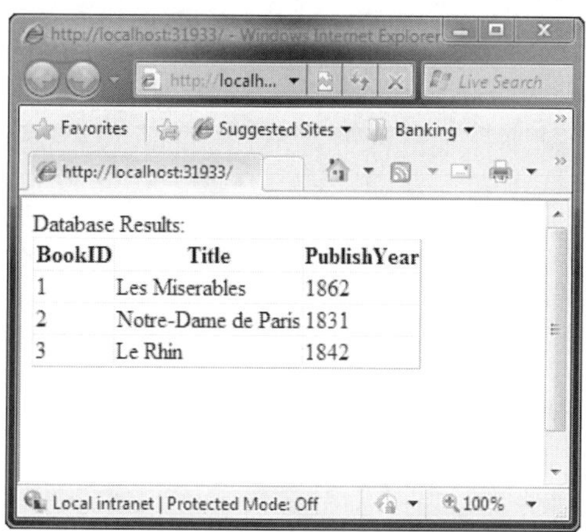

FIGURE 13.5
Binding to ASP.NET's GridView control is just as easy as in Windows Forms.

Detect if Database Connection Is Available

Scenario/Problem: Your application operates in an environment where the database connection can be unreliable and you want your program to pause operations if it detects a problem.

Solution: Ideally, you would want to ensure that databases can't disappear from the network, but sometimes you need to be extra cautious.

Here's a simple function that tries to open a connection and returns a Boolean value depending on whether it was successful or not:

```
private static bool TestConnection()
{
    try
    {
        using (SqlConnection conn =
           new SqlConnection(GetConnectionString()))
        {
            conn.Open();
            return (conn.State == ConnectionState.Open);
        }
    }
    catch (SqlException)
    {
        return false;
    }
    catch (InvalidOperationException)
    {
        return false;
    }
}
```

NOTE Using this won't guarantee the database is available for you—after all, the server could fail right after this method returns true. Ultimately, your code must be very robust in the face of failure. Nevertheless, I have found this code useful on a network where there was a reliably inconsistent connection to the database.

Automatically Map Data to Objects with the Entity Framework

Scenario/Problem: You want to access database data through .NET objects with having to create your own data object library.

Solution: Use the Entity Framework to automatically map database tables and their relationships to objects you can use in C# code.

The Entity Framework is Microsoft's Object-Relational Mapping library and is fully integrated with Visual Studio.

To create an object for the Books table introduced earlier in this chapter, follow these steps:

1. Right-click your project, select Add, New Item.
2. Select ADO.NET Entity Data Model and give it the name Books.edmx. Click Add.
3. In the Entity Data Model Wizard that comes up, select "Generate From Database" and click Next.
4. Select the database. from the drop-down list.
5. For the value under "Save entity connection settings in App.Config as:" type BookEntities.
6. Click Next.
7. Check the Books table.
8. Set the Model Namespace to "BookModel" and click Finish.

This will create the Book and BookEntities object for you. The following sections will demonstrate how to use them.

Get a List of All Entities

The BookEntities represents the interface to the collection. The following code prints out all values in the table via the entity collection:

```
//get a list of all entities
BookEntities entities = new BookEntities();
foreach (var book in entities.Books)
{
    Console.WriteLine("{0}, {1}   {2}",
                      book.ID, book.Title, book.PublishYear);
}
```

This is the output:

```
1, Les Miserables   1862
2, Notre-Dame de Paris   1831
3, Le Rhin   1842
```

Create a New Entity

To create a new Book, just declare the object and set its properties before adding it to the entity collection. In this case, since ID is an auto-incrementing property, you don't need to set it.

```
BookEntities entities = new BookEntities();
Book newBook = new Book();
newBook.Title = "C# 4 How-to";
newBook.PublishYear = 2010;
entities.AddToBooks(newBook);
entities.SaveChanges();
```

Look Up an Entity

You can use the `ObjectQuery<T>` class to create queries for you, as in this sample:

```
ObjectQuery<Book> bookQuery =
   new ObjectQuery<Book>(
     "SELECT VALUE Book FROM BookEntities.Books AS Book",
         entities).Where("it.ID = 1");
```

However, this syntax becomes awkward very quickly. Instead, you should use LINQ, which is discussed in Chapter 21. The equivalent query would looks like this:

```
var books = from book in entities.Books
            where book.ID == 1
            select book;
```

Delete an Entity

To delete an entity, pass it to the entity list's `DeleteObject` method:

```
BookEntities entities = new BookEntities();

//create a new entity
Book newBook = new Book();
newBook.Title = "C# 4 How-to";
newBook.PublishYear = 2010;
entities.AddToBooks(newBook);
entities.SaveChanges();

entities.DeleteObject(newBook);
entities.SaveChanges();
```

CHAPTER 14

XML

IN THIS CHAPTER

- Serialize an Object to and from XML
- Write XML from Scratch
- Read an XML File
- Validate an XML Document
- Query XML Using XPath
- Transform Database Data to XML
- Transform XML to HTML

XML has become the *lingua franca* of information exchange. There is hardly a technology anymore that doesn't use XML data in some way, whether it's an import/export format, a native database format, or just configuration data.

This is due in part to its very nature. XML stands for *eXtensible Markup Language*, and it's eminently flexible and suited to a wide variety of tasks.

.NET supports XML in many ways, from a multitude of ways to read, parse, and search, to creation and validation.

Most samples in this chapter use the `System.XML` namespace.

Serialize an Object to and from XML

Scenario/Problem: You want to output your .NET objects in an XML-equivalent representation and load them back.

Solution: Automatic object serialization is the easiest way to translate between XML and your binary objects. The biggest caveat is that it only works on public types and public data members in those types. Given that, let's look at an example with some test classes:

```
public class Person
{
    public string FirstName { get; set; }
    public char MiddleInitial { get; set; }
    public string LastName { get; set; }

    public DateTime BirthDate { get; set; }
    public double HighschoolGPA { get; set; }

    public Address Address {get;set;}

    //to be XML serialized, the type must have
    //a parameterless constructor
    public Person() { }

    public Person(string firstName, char middleInitial, string lastName,
        DateTime birthDate, double highSchoolGpa, Address address)
    {
        this.FirstName = firstName;
        this.MiddleInitial = middleInitial;
        this.LastName = lastName;
        this.BirthDate = birthDate;
        this.HighschoolGPA = highSchoolGpa;
        this.Address = address;
    }
```

```
    public override string ToString()
    {
        return FirstName + " " + MiddleInitial + ". " + LastName +
                               ", DOB:" +BirthDate.ToShortDateString() +
            ", GPA: " + this.HighschoolGPA
            + Environment.NewLine + Address.ToString();
    }
}

//sorry, don't feel like listing out 50 states :)
public enum StateAbbreviation {RI, VA, SC, CA, TX, UT, WA};

public class Address
{
    public string AddressLine1 { get; set; }
    public string AddressLine2 { get; set; }
    public string City { get; set; }
    public StateAbbreviation State { get; set; }
    public string ZipCode { get; set; }

    public Address() { }

    public Address(string addressLine1, string addressLine2,
        string city, StateAbbreviation state, string zipCode)
    {
        this.AddressLine1 = addressLine1;
        this.AddressLine2 = addressLine2;
        this.City = city;
        this.State = state;
        this.ZipCode = zipCode;
    }

    public override string ToString()
    {
        return AddressLine1 + Environment.NewLine + AddressLine2 +
            Environment.NewLine + City+", "+State+" "+ ZipCode;
    }
}
```

Notice that nothing in here has anything to do with XML. These are just application data objects.

To serialize (and then deserialize), use code similar to the following:

```
Person person = new Person("John", 'Q', "Public",
    new DateTime(1776, 7, 4), 3.5,
```

```
    new Address("1234 Cherry Lane", null, "Smalltown",
        StateAbbreviation.VA,"10000"));

Console.WriteLine("Before serialize:" + Environment.NewLine +
    person.ToString());

XmlSerializer serializer = new XmlSerializer(typeof(Person));
//for demo purposes, just serialize to a string
StringBuilder sb = new StringBuilder();
using (StringWriter sw = new StringWriter(sb))
{
    //the actual serialization
    serializer.Serialize(sw, person);
    Console.WriteLine(Environment.NewLine + "XML:"+Environment.NewLine +
        sb.ToString()+Environment.NewLine);
}

using (StringReader sr = new StringReader(sb.ToString()))
{
    //deserialize from text back into binary
    Person newPerson = serializer.Deserialize(sr) as Person;
    Console.WriteLine("After deserialize:" + Environment.NewLine +
        newPerson.ToString());
}
```

Here’s the output:

```
Before serialize:
John Q. Public, DOB:7/4/1776, GPA: 3.5
1234 Cherry Lane

Smalltown, VA 10000

XML:
<?xml version="1.0" encoding="utf-16"?>
<Person xmlns:xsi="http://www.w3.org/2001/XMLSchema-instance"
➥xmlns:xsd="http:/
www.w3.org/2001/XMLSchema">
  <FirstName>John</FirstName>
  <MiddleInitial>81</MiddleInitial>
  <LastName>Public</LastName>
  <BirthDate>1776-07-04T00:00:00</BirthDate>
  <HighschoolGPA>3.5</HighschoolGPA>
  <Address>
    <AddressLine1>1234 Cherry Lane</AddressLine1>
    <City>Smalltown</City>
    <State>VA</State>
```

```
    <ZipCode>10000</ZipCode>
  </Address>
</Person>

After deserialize:
John Q. Public, DOB:7/4/1776, GPA: 3.5
1234 Cherry Lane

Smalltown, VA 10000
```

Notice that the `XmlSerializer` correctly handled the `null` value of `AddressLine2`.

Control Object Serialization

> **Scenario/Problem:** You need to control the serialization process, perhaps by ignoring a certain property in your class, changing the element names, or determining whether something is an element or an attribute.

Solution: Use of `XmlSerializer` is a largely automated process, but there are some easy ways to modify the XML to fit your needs. For example, suppose you modify the `Person` class with these attributes:

```
[XmlIgnore]
public char MiddleInitial { get; set; }

[XmlElement("DOB")]
public DateTime BirthDate { get; set; }

[XmlAttribute("GPA")]
public double HighschoolGPA { get; set; }
```

You get this output:

```
Before serialize:
John Q. Public, DOB:7/4/1776, GPA: 3.5
1234 Cherry Lane

Smalltown, VA 10000

XML:
<?xml version="1.0" encoding="utf-16"?>
<Person xmlns:xsi="http://www.w3.org/2001/XMLSchema-instance"
➥        xmlns:xsd="http://
www.w3.org/2001/XMLSchema" GPA="3.5">
  <FirstName>John</FirstName>
  <LastName>Public</LastName>
```

```
  <DOB>1776-07-04T00:00:00</DOB>
  <Address>
    <AddressLine1>1234 Cherry Lane</AddressLine1>
    <City>Smalltown</City>
    <State>VA</State>
    <ZipCode>10000</ZipCode>
  </Address>
</Person>

After deserialize:
John  . Public, DOB:7/4/1776, GPA: 3.5
1234 Cherry Lane

Smalltown, VA 10000
```

Although other attributes can give you more control, these three are the most common.

Write XML from Scratch

When creating XML from scratch, there are, in general, two methods you can use:

- Write out each element and attribute in order, from start to finish.
- Build up a document object model (DOM).

There are tradeoffs between these two methods. Basically, it's between speed and efficiency in working with the data. Building up a DOM in memory allows you to easily work with any nodes, but it takes up a lot of resources and is slow. Just writing out the elements is very fast, but this can be harder for more complex data models. Examples of both are shown in this section.

Write XML Using `XmlDocument`

Scenario/Problem: You want to build up an XML document from scratch using a rich set of tools that represent the document object model.

Solution: The `XmlDocument` class is the in-memory version of XML's node structure.

```
XmlDocument doc = new XmlDocument();
XmlElement bookElem = doc.CreateElement("Book");
bookElem.SetAttribute("PublishYear", "2009");
XmlElement titleElem = doc.CreateElement("Title");
titleElem.InnerText = "Programming, art or engineering?";
XmlElement authorElem = doc.CreateElement("Author");
```

```
authorElem.InnerText = "Billy Bob";
bookElem.AppendChild(titleElem);
bookElem.AppendChild(authorElem);
doc.AppendChild(bookElem);

StringBuilder sb = new StringBuilder();
//you could write to a file or any stream just as well
using (StringWriter sw = new StringWriter(sb))
using (XmlTextWriter xtw = new XmlTextWriter(sw))
{
    //if you don't specify this, the XML will be a single
    //long line of unbroken XML—better for transmission,
    //but not console
    xtw.Formatting = Formatting.Indented;
    doc.WriteContentTo(xtw);
    Console.WriteLine(sb.ToString());
}
```

Write XML Using `XmlWriter`

Scenario/Problem: You want to create XML from scratch in a very fast, forward-only manner.

Solution: Use an `XmlWriter`. By doing so, you're taking on the responsibility of figuring out the correct relationships among subnodes, the start and end of tags, and where attributes should go.

```
StringBuilder sb = new StringBuilder();
using (StringWriter sw = new StringWriter(sb))
using (XmlTextWriter xtw = new XmlTextWriter(sw))
{
    xtw.Formatting = Formatting.Indented;

    xtw.WriteStartElement("Book");

    xtw.WriteAttributeString("PublishYear", "2009");
    xtw.WriteStartElement("Title");
    xtw.WriteString("Programming, art or engineering?");
    xtw.WriteEndElement();

    xtw.WriteStartElement("Author");
    xtw.WriteString("Billy Bob");
    xtw.WriteEndElement();
```

```
    xtw.WriteEndElement();
}

Console.WriteLine(sb.ToString());
```

Read an XML File

The tradeoffs inherent in generating an XML file with the two different methods exist even more obviously when reading one in. If the XML file is large and complex, using `XmlDocument` could be painfully slow. On the other hand, using `XmlTextReader` is very fast, but puts all the onus of tracking state on you. Only you can decide how to resolve these tradeoffs.

Read an XML File Using `XmlDocument`

Scenario/Problem: You need to read in an XML document, and either the document is not too large or you're not concerned about performance.

Solution: The `XmlDocument` class contains methods for loading XML from files, streams, or strings.

```
class Program
{
    const string sourceXml =
        "<Book PublishYear=\"2009\">"+
        "<Title>Programming, art or engineering?</Title>"+
        "<Author>Billy Bob</Author>"+
        "</Book>";

    static void Main(string[] args)
    {
        XmlDocument doc = new XmlDocument();
        doc.LoadXml(sourceXml);

        Console.WriteLine("Publish Year: {0}",
➥doc.GetElementsByTagName("Book")[0].Attributes["PublishYear"].Value);
        Console.WriteLine("Author: {0}",
➥doc.GetElementsByTagName("Author")[0].InnerText);
    }
}
```

Read an XML File Using `XmlTextReader`

Scenario/Problem: You need to read in an XML document. You are concerned about performance, don't need the document object model, and can easily create the object structure yourself.

Solution: Use the `XmlTextReader` class, which can read from a variety of sources. In this case, because the source XML is in a string, you need to use a `StringReader` to convert it into a stream for the `XmlTextReader`.

```
class Program
{
    const string sourceXml =
        "<Book PublishYear=\"2009\">" +
        "<Title>Programming, art or engineering?</Title>" +
        "<Author>Billy Bob</Author>" +
        "</Book>";

    static void Main(string[] args)
    {
        string publishYear = null, author = null;
        using (StringReader reader = new StringReader(sourceXml))
        using (XmlTextReader xmlReader = new XmlTextReader(reader))
        {
            while (xmlReader.Read())
            {
                if (xmlReader.NodeType == XmlNodeType.Element)
                {
                    if (xmlReader.Name == "Book")
                    {
                        if (xmlReader.MoveToAttribute("PublishYear"))
                        {
                            publishYear = xmlReader.Value;
                        }
                    }
                    else if (xmlReader.Name == "Author")
                    {
                        xmlReader.Read();
                        author = xmlReader.Value;
                    }
                }
            }
        }
```

```
        Console.WriteLine("Publish Year: {0}", publishYear);
        Console.WriteLine("Author: {0}", author);
    }
}
```

You can easily see how this method involves a bit more code. Again, it's all about tradeoffs.

> **NOTE** Once, while working on an application that read a few large XML files (3MB or so in my case) on startup, I gave the app an instant performance boost merely by switching from using `XmlDocument` to `XmlTextReader`.

Validate an XML Document

Scenario/Problem: You want to validate an XML document against its schema.

Solution: XML documents can be validated in a number of ways, one common way being the use of XML schemas.

Suppose you have a schema file defined like this:

```
<?xml version="1.0" encoding="utf-8"?>
<xs:schema elementFormDefault="qualified"
    xmlns:xs="http://www.w3.org/2001/XMLSchema">
  <xs:element name="Book" >
    <xs:complexType >
      <xs:sequence>
        <xs:element name="Title" type="xs:string"/>
        <xs:element name="Author" type="xs:string"/>
      </xs:sequence>
      <xs:attribute name="PublishYear" type="xs:gYear" />
    </xs:complexType>
  </xs:element>
</xs:schema>
```

The following code will validate the XML snippet against the previous schema, assuming it was in the file XmlBookSchema.xsd:

```
//this XML fails validation because Author and Title elements
//are out of order
const string sourceXml =
    "<?xml version='1.0'?>" +
    "<Book PublishYear=\"2009\">" +
```

```
    "<Author>Billy Bob</Author>" +
    "<Title>Programming, art or engineering?</Title>" +
    "</Book>";

static void Main(string[] args)
{
    XmlSchemaSet schemaSet = new XmlSchemaSet();
    schemaSet.Add(null, "XmlBookSchema.xsd");
    XmlReaderSettings settings = new XmlReaderSettings();
    settings.ValidationType = ValidationType.Schema;
    settings.Schemas = schemaSet;
    settings.ValidationEventHandler +=
➥new ValidationEventHandler(Settings_ValidationEventHandler);

    using (StringReader reader = new StringReader(sourceXml))
    using (XmlReader xmlReader = XmlTextReader.Create(reader, settings))
    {
        while (xmlReader.Read()) ;
    }

    Console.WriteLine("Validation complete");

    Console.ReadKey();
}

static void Settings_ValidationEventHandler(object sender,
                                            ValidationEventArgs e)
{
    Console.WriteLine("Validation failed: "+e.Message);
}
```

Query XML Using XPath

Scenario/Problem: You need to query a document for specific information by using the XML query language XPath.

Solution: In addition to reading XML the traditional way, via `XmlDocument` or `XmlTextReader`, you can use `XPathDocument` and related classes to query XML using XPath, a query language defined for XML.

Here is our source XML file (`LesMis.xml`):

```
<?xml version="1.0" encoding="utf-8" ?>
<Book>
  <Title>Les Misérables</Title>
  <Author>Victor Hugo</Author>
  <Source Retrieved="2009-02-14T00:00:00">
    <URL>http://www.gutenberg.org/files/135/135.txt</URL>
  </Source>
  <Chapters>
    <Chapter>M. Myriel</Chapter>
    <Chapter>M. Myriel becomes M. Welcome</Chapter>
    <Chapter>A Hard Bishopric for a Good Bishop</Chapter>
    <Chapter>Monseigneur Bienvenu made his Cassocks last too long
➥</Chapter>
    <Chapter>Who guarded his House for him</Chapter>
    <Chapter>Cravatte</Chapter>
    <Chapter>Philosophy after Drinking</Chapter>
    <Chapter>The Brother as depicted by the Sister</Chapter>
    <Chapter>The Bishop in the Presence of an Unknown Light</Chapter>
    <Chapter>A Restriction</Chapter>
    <Chapter>The Solitude of Monseigneur Welcome</Chapter>
    <Chapter>What he believed</Chapter>
    <Chapter>What he thought</Chapter>
    <Chapter>...far too many more...</Chapter>
  </Chapters>
</Book>
```

This code will perform a query for all the chapter names:

```
XPathDocument doc = new XPathDocument("LesMis.xml");
XPathNavigator navigator = doc.CreateNavigator();
XPathNodeIterator iter = navigator.Select("/Book/Chapters/Chapter");
while (iter.MoveNext())
{
    Console.WriteLine("Chapter: {0}", iter.Current.Value);
}
Console.WriteLine("Found {0} chapters",
                  navigator.Evaluate("count(/Book/Chapters/Chapter)"));
```

Here is the output:

```
Chapter: M. Myriel
Chapter: M. Myriel becomes M. Welcome
Chapter: A Hard Bishopric for a Good Bishop
```

```
Chapter: Monseigneur Bienvenu made his Cassocks last too long
Chapter: Who guarded his House for him
Chapter: Cravatte
Chapter: Philosophy after Drinking
Chapter: The Brother as depicted by the Sister
Chapter: The Bishop in the Presence of an Unknown Light
Chapter: A Restriction
Chapter: The Solitude of Monseigneur Welcome
Chapter: What he believed
Chapter: What he thought
Chapter: ...far too many more...
Found 14 chapters
```

Transform Database Data to XML

Scenario/Problem: You want to translate information in relational tables (in a database) into XML, perhaps for transmission to another application.

Solution: Using some of the knowledge you gained from the chapter on databases, you can grab a DataSet, which has a nice WriteXml() method.

```
XmlDocument doc = new XmlDocument();
DataSet dataSet = new DataSet("Books");
using (SqlConnection conn = new SqlConnection(GetConnectionString()))
using (SqlCommand cmd = new SqlCommand("SELECT * FROM Books", conn))
using (SqlDataAdapter adapter = new SqlDataAdapter(cmd))
{
    adapter.Fill(dataSet);
}

StringBuilder sb = new StringBuilder();
using (StringWriter sw = new StringWriter(sb))
{
    dataSet.WriteXml(sw);
}

Console.WriteLine(sb.ToString());
```

If we run this on our sample table from the database chapter, we get the following:

```
<Books>
  <Table>
    <BookID>1</BookID>
    <Title>Les Miserables</Title>
    <PublishYear>1862</PublishYear>
  </Table>
  <Table>
    <BookID>2</BookID>
    <Title>Notre-Dame de Paris</Title>
    <PublishYear>1831</PublishYear>
  </Table>
  <Table>
    <BookID>3</BookID>
    <Title>Le Rhin</Title>
    <PublishYear>1842</PublishYear>
  </Table>
</Books>
```

Transform XML to HTML

Scenario/Problem: You want to transform XML data into an easily understood report formatted with HTML.

Solution: This is done using XML Transforms, which .NET supports out of the box.

Using the earlier XML file with chapter headings from *Les Misérables*, let's add another file, an XML transformation file that includes the HTML and XML template tags to insert the data (see Listing 14.1).

LISTING 14.1 **BookTransform.xslt**

```
<?xml version="1.0" encoding="utf-8"?>
<xsl:stylesheet version="1.0"
     xmlns:xsl="http://www.w3.org/1999/XSL/Transform"
     xmlns:msxsl="urn:schemas-microsoft-com:xslt"
     exclude-result-prefixes="msxsl">
```

LISTING 14.1 **BookTransform.xslt** (continued)

```
        <xsl:output method="xml" indent="yes"/>
          <xsl:template match="/">
            <html>
              <head>
                <title>
                  <xsl:value-of select="/Book/Title"/>
                </title>
              </head>
              <body>
                <b>Author:</b><xsl:value-of
➥select="/Book/Author"/><br></br>
                Chapters:
                <table border="1">
                  <xsl:for-each select="/Book/Chapters/Chapter">
                    <tr>
                      <td>
                        <xsl:value-of select="."/>
                      </td>
                    </tr>
                  </xsl:for-each>
                </table>
              </body>
            </html>
          </xsl:template>
</xsl:stylesheet>
```

Here is some simple code to perform the transformation and display the resulting HTML file:

```
XslCompiledTransform transform = new XslCompiledTransform();
transform.Load("BookTransform.xslt");
transform.Transform("LesMis.xml", "LesMis.html");

//view web page in a browser
Process.Start("LesMis.html");
```

The results are displayed in Figure 14.1.

FIGURE 14.1

Using `XslCompiledTransform`, you can produce quick HTML reports directly from XML data.

PART III

User Interaction

IN THIS PART

CHAPTER 15

Delegates, Events, and Anonymous Methods

IN THIS CHAPTER

- Decide Which Method to Call at Runtime
- Subscribe to an Event
- Publish an Event
- Ensure UI Updates Occur on UI Thread
- Assign an Anonymous Method to a Delegate
- Use Anonymous Methods as Quick-and-Easy Event Handlers
- Take Advantage of Contravariance

Although not directly related to user interaction per se, delegates and events form the fundamental building blocks upon which the GUI layer operates.

Delegates and events, in particular, are a way of decoupling various parts of your program. For example, by creating events for your components, they can signal changes in themselves, without needing to care about the interfaces of external components that are interested in finding out about those changes.

Anonymous methods and lambda expressions are in some ways merely simplifications of syntax when dealing with delegates.

Decide Which Method to Call at Runtime

Scenario/Problem: You need to be able to decide which method gets called at runtime.

Solution: Declare a delegate that matches the signature of the target methods. In C#, delegates are kind of like object-oriented, type-safe function pointers. They can also be generic. This example shows how delegates can be aggregated and stored like any other piece of data, and then executed.

```
class Program
{
    delegate T MathOp<T>(T a, T b);

    static void Main(string[] args)
    {
        //yes, this is an array of methods--
        //that all conform to MathOp<T> delegate
        List<MathOp<double>> opsList = new List<MathOp<double>>();

        opsList.Add(Add);
        opsList.Add(Divide);
        opsList.Add(Add);
        opsList.Add(Multiply);

        double result = 0.0;
        foreach (MathOp<double> op in opsList)
        {
            result = op(result, 3);
        }
        Console.WriteLine("result = {0}", result);
    }

    static double Divide(double a, double b)
    {
```

```
        return a / b;
    }

    static double Multiply(double a, double b)
    {
        return a * b;
    }

    static double Add(double a, double b)
    {
        return a + b;
    }
}
```

Call Multiple Methods with a Single Delegate

Scenario/Problem: You want multiple methods to be called with a single delegate invocation.

Solution: All delegates are automatically what are called *multicast delegates*, which means that you can assign multiple target methods to them. This is done using the += operator.

```
class Program
{
    delegate void FormatNumber(double number);

    static void Main(string[] args)
    {
        //assign three target methods to this delegate
        FormatNumber format = FormatNumberAsCurrency;
        format += FormatNumberWithCommas;
        format += FormatNumberWithTwoPlaces;

        //invoke all three in succession
        format(12345.6789);
    }

    static void FormatNumberAsCurrency(double number)
    {
        Console.WriteLine("A Currency: {0:C}", number);
    }
```

```
    static void FormatNumberWithCommas(double number)
    {
        Console.WriteLine("With Commas: {0:N}", number);
    }

    static void FormatNumberWithTwoPlaces(double number)
    {
        Console.WriteLine("With 3 places: {0:.###}", number);
    }
}
```

NOTE In the first delegate example, the delegate methods returned values. This is perfectly legal for multicast delegates, but the return value for non-`void` delegate invocations will be the return value of the final method called. This is rather nondeterministic, so most delegates are of return type `void`.

Subscribe to an Event

Scenario/Problem: You want to subscribe to an event and run your own handler method whenever the event is raised.

Solution: Use .NET's event-handling syntax to add your handler to the event's delegate list.

This example subscribes to the Button's `Click` event:

```
public partial class Form1 : Form
{
    public Form1()
    {
        InitializeComponent();

        //add our own method to the button's Click delegate list
        button1.Click += new EventHandler(button1_Click);
    }

    void button1_Click(object sender, EventArgs e)
    {
        MessageBox.Show("This is too easy");
    }
}
```

Stop Subscription to an Event

Scenario/Problem: You no longer want to listen to an event that you've previously subscribed.

Solution: Use the `-=` syntax to remove your event handler. Here's an example:

```
button1.Click -= new EventHandler(button1_Click);
```

Publish an Event

Scenario/Problem: You want to notify external components of changes in your class.

Solution: Create an event in your class that anyone else can subscribe to. You should follow the established event-raising pattern established in the .NET Framework, as demonstrated in the following example.

This example simulates the loading of program data on a second thread, which notifies the main thread when it's complete:

```
class ProgramData
{
    private DateTime _startTime;

    /* Follow this pattern when defining your own events:
     * -public event
     * -protected virtual On... function that triggers the event
     */
    public event EventHandler<EventArgs> LoadStarted;
    protected virtual void OnLoadStarted()
    {
        if (LoadStarted != null)
        {
            //no custom data, so just use empty EventArgs
            LoadStarted(this, EventArgs.Empty);
        }
    }

    public event EventHandler<ProgramDataEventArgs> LoadEnded;
    protected virtual void OnLoadEnded(TimeSpan loadTime)
```

```
    {
        if (LoadEnded != null)
        {
            LoadEnded(this, new ProgramDataEventArgs(loadTime));
        }
    }

    public void BeginLoad()
    {
        _startTime = DateTime.Now;
        Thread thread = new Thread(new ThreadStart(LoadThreadFunc));
        thread.Start();
        //raise LoadStarted event
        OnLoadStarted();
    }

    private void LoadThreadFunc()
    {
        //simulate work
        Thread.Sleep(5000);
        //raise LoadEnded event
        OnLoadEnded(DateTime.Now - _startTime);
    }
}

//your own EventArgs classes must be derived from EventArgs proper
class ProgramDataEventArgs : EventArgs
{
    public TimeSpan LoadTime { get; private set; }
    public ProgramDataEventArgs(TimeSpan loadTime)
    {
        this.LoadTime = loadTime;
    }
}
public partial class Form1 : Form
{
    ProgramData _data;

    public Form1()
    {
        InitializeComponent();

        _data = new ProgramData();
        _data.LoadStarted +=
           new EventHandler<EventArgs>(_data_LoadStarted);
```

```
        _data.LoadEnded +=
           new EventHandler<ProgramDataEventArgs>(_data_LoadEnded);

        _data.BeginLoad();
    }

    void _data_LoadStarted(object sender, EventArgs e)
    {
        if (this.InvokeRequired)
        {
            //if we're not on the UI thread, call recursively,
            //but on the UI thread
            Invoke(new EventHandler<EventArgs>(_
                         data_LoadStarted), sender, e);
        }
        else
        {
            textBoxLog.AppendText("Load started" + Environment.NewLine);
        }
    }

    void _data_LoadEnded(object sender, ProgramDataEventArgs e)
    {
        if (this.InvokeRequired)
        {
            Invoke(new EventHandler<ProgramDataEventArgs>(_
                         data_LoadEnded), sender, e);
        }
        else
        {
            textBoxLog.AppendText(string.Format("Load ended (elapsed:
➥{0})" + Environment.NewLine, e.LoadTime));
        }
    }
}
```

Ensure UI Updates Occur on UI Thread

Scenario/Problem: Whenever you try to update a UI element in response to an event that occurred on a separate thread, you get an exception.

Solution: You must invoke the required method on the UI thread.

Because of the way they're implemented internally, Windows UI elements must be accessed on the same thread that created them. Previous frameworks (such as MFC) didn't enforce this so much, but .NET does. Windows Forms and WPF handle this slightly differently.

In WinForms

In WinForms, you can check if you're running on the UI thread by polling `InvokeRequired` on any UI element. If it's true, you need to switch to the main thread by calling `Invoke()` and passing it a delegate.

In practice, there are a few ways to do this, but an easy way (from the previous example) is demonstrated in the `data_LoadStarted` event handler:

```
public Form1()
{
    InitializeComponent();

    _data = new ProgramData();
    _data.LoadStarted += new EventHandler<EventArgs>(_data_LoadStarted);
    _data.LoadEnded +=
            new EventHandler<ProgramDataEventArgs>(_data_LoadEnded);

    _data.BeginLoad();
}

void _data_LoadStarted(object sender, EventArgs e)
{
    if (this.InvokeRequired)
    {
        //if we're not on the UI thread, call recursively,
        //but on the UI thread
        Invoke(new EventHandler<EventArgs>(_
                    data_LoadStarted), sender, e);
    }
    else
    {
        textBoxLog.AppendText("Load started" + Environment.NewLine);
    }
}
```

In WPF

In WPF, the concept is similar. Each WPF element has a property called `Dispatcher`. By comparing the `Dispatcher`'s thread to the current thread, you can tell when you need to call `Invoke`. The following example demonstrates this in a simple WPF app (see the WpfInvoke sample project):

```
using System;
using System.Windows;
using System.Windows.Controls;
using System.Threading;

namespace WpfInvoke
{
    public partial class MainWindow : Window
    {
        public MainWindow()
        {
            InitializeComponent();

            //startup second thread to do the updating
            Thread thread = new Thread(new ThreadStart(ThreadProc));
            thread.IsBackground = true;
            thread.Start();
        }

        private void ThreadProc()
        {
            int val = 0;
            while (true)
            {
                ++val;
                UpdateValue(val);
                Thread.Sleep(200);
            }
        }

        private delegate void UpdateValueDelegate(int val);

        private void UpdateValue(int val)
        {
            if (Dispatcher.Thread != Thread.CurrentThread)
            {
                Dispatcher.Invoke(new UpdateValueDelegate(UpdateValue),
                  val);
            }
            else
            {
                textBlock.Text = val.ToString("N0");
            }
        }
    }
}
```

Assign an Anonymous Method to a Delegate

Scenario/Problem: You have a short snippet of code you want to run but don't need the overhead of a full method.

Solution: Use the anonymous method syntax to assign a block of code to a delegate.

```
delegate int MathOp(int a, int b);

...

MathOp op = delegate(int a, int b) { return a + b; };

int result = MathOp(13,14);
```

Use Anonymous Methods as Quick-and-Easy Event Handlers

Scenario/Problem: You need a quick-and-easy event handler, with no need for a name.

Solution: Assign an anonymous method to the delegate using syntax like that in the following example:

```
public partial class Form1 : Form
{
    Point prevPt = Point.Empty;
    public Form1()
    {
        InitializeComponent();

        this.MouseMove += delegate(object sender, MouseEventArgs e)
            {
                if (prevPt != e.Location)
                {
                    this.textBox1.AppendText(
                      string.Format("MouseMove: ({0},{1})"
                          + Environment.NewLine, e.X, e.Y));
                    prevPt = e.Location;
```

```
                }
            };

        this.MouseClick += delegate(object sender, MouseEventArgs e)
        { this.textBox1.AppendText(
                string.Format("MouseClick: ({0},{1}) {2}"
            + Environment.NewLine, e.X, e.Y, e.Button)); };

        //don't need the method args? don't include them
        this.MouseDown += delegate
➥{this.textBox1.AppendText("MouseDown"+Environment.NewLine);};
        this.MouseUp += delegate { this.textBox1.AppendText("MouseUp"
➥+ Environment.NewLine); };
    }
}
```

Figure 15.1 demonstrates the AnonymousMethods sample project, from the sample code for this chapter.

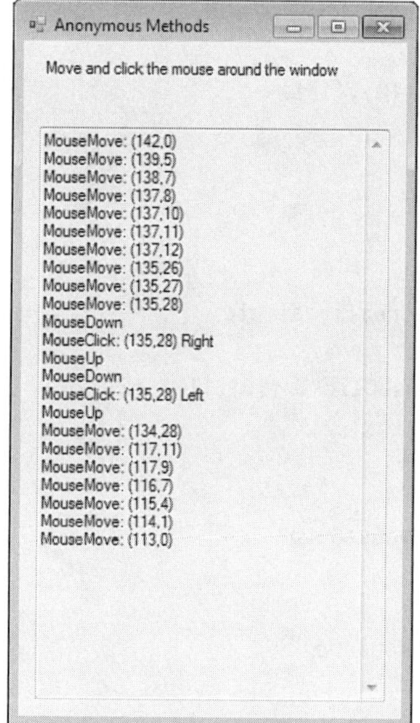

FIGURE 15.1
Anonymous methods often make sense for quick event handlers.

Use Lambda Expression Syntax for Anonymous Methods

Scenario/Problem: You want an anonymous method with simplified syntax.

Solution: Use the lambda expression syntax for anonymous methods. Lambda expressions can be used for anonymous methods, as well as to create expression trees in LINQ. This code does the same thing as the previous example:

```
public partial class Form1 : Form
{
    Point prevPt = Point.Empty;
    public Form1()
    {
        InitializeComponent();
        //the type of the arguments can be inferred by the compiler
        this.MouseMove += (sender, e) =>
        {
            if (prevPt != e.Location)
            {
                this.textBox1.AppendText(
                  string.Format("MouseMove: ({0},{1})"
➥+ Environment.NewLine, e.X, e.Y));
                prevPt = e.Location;
            }
        };

        //a single-line lambda expression is really simple
        this.MouseClick += (sender, e) =>
➥this.textBox1.AppendText(string.Format("MouseClick: ({0},{1}) {2}" +
➥Environment.NewLine, e.X, e.Y, e.Button));

        this.MouseDown += (sender,e) =>
                  this.textBox1.AppendText("MouseDown"
              + Environment.NewLine);
        this.MouseUp += (sender, e) =>
                  this.textBox1.AppendText("MouseUp"
              + Environment.NewLine);
    }
}
```

Take Advantage of Contravariance

Scenario/Problem: In previous versions of .NET, there were situations where delegates did not behave as expected. For example, a delegate with a type parameter of a base class should be assignable to delegates of a more derived type parameter because any delegate that is callable with the base class should also be callable with the derived class. The following code sample demonstrates the issue:

Given these class definitions:

```
class Shape
{
    public void Draw() { Console.WriteLine("Drawing shape"); }
};

class Rectangle : Shape
{
    public void Expand() { /*...*/ }
};
```

And given this delegate and method:

```
delegate void ShapeAction< T>(T shape);

static void DrawShape(Shape shape)
{
    if (shape != null)
    {
        shape.Draw();
    }
}
```

You would expect this scenario to work:

```
ShapeAction<Shape> action = DrawShape;
ShapeAction<Rectangle> rectAction2 = action;
```

After all, `DrawShape` can take any type of `Shape`, including `Rectangle`. Unfortunately, this scenario did not work as expected.

Solution: In .NET 4, contravariance on delegates fixed this to enable you to assign less-specific delegates to more-specific delegates, as long as the type parameter T is declared as “in,” which means the delegate does not return T. In the following code, the delegate’s type parameter has been modified with `in`.

```
class Shape
{
    public void Draw() { Console.WriteLine("Drawing shape"); }
};

class Rectangle : Shape
{
    public void Expand() { /*...*/ }
};

class Program
{
    delegate void ShapeAction<in T>(T shape);

    static void DrawShape(Shape shape)
    {
        if (shape != null)
        {
            shape.Draw();
        }
    }

    static void Main(string[] args)
    {
        //this should obviously be ok
        ShapeAction<Shape> action = DrawShape;
        action(new Rectangle());

        /* Intuitively, you know any method that
         * conforms to a ShapeAction<Shape> delegate
         * should also work on a Rectangle because
         * Rectangle is a type of Shape.
         *
         * It's always possible to assign a less derived _method_
         * to a more-derived delegate, but until .NET 4
         * you could not assign a less-derived _delegate_ to
         * a more-derived delegate: an important distinction.
         *
         * Now, as long as the type parameter is marked as "in"
         * you can.
         */

        //this was possible before .NET 4
        ShapeAction<Rectangle> rectAction1 = DrawShape;
        rectAction1(new Rectangle());
```

```
        //this was NOT possible before .NET 4
        ShapeAction<Rectangle> rectAction2 = action;
        rectAction2(new Rectangle());

        Console.ReadKey();
    }
}
```

CHAPTER 16

Windows Forms

IN THIS CHAPTER

- Create Modal and Modeless Forms
- Add a Menu Bar
- Disable Menu Items Dynamically
- Add a Status Bar
- Add a Toolbar
- Create a Split Window Interface
- Inherit a Form
- Create a User Control
- Use a Timer
- Use Application and User Configuration Values
- Use ListView Efficiently in Virtual Mode
- Take Advantage of Horizontal Wheel Tilt
- Cut and Paste
- Automatically Ensure You Reset the Wait Cursor

Windows Forms is the direct evolutionary step of Win32 programming and Microsoft Foundation Classes (MFC). It is relatively easy to learn and use for long-time programmers.

Because Windows Forms applications have a lot of code that is generated and maintained for you by Visual Studio, many of the examples in this chapter require things that are not presented in the book. For the complete, runnable examples, please see the sample projects for this chapter on the book's Web site.

Create Modal and Modeless Forms

Scenario/Problem: You need to create a window that must be dealt with before the user can continue using the application, or you want to create a window that the user can keep up while using the rest of the application.

Solution: Two types of forms are available: modal and modeless. Modal forms must be dealt with and dismissed before the rest of the application can be used, whereas modeless forms can stick around while the user goes back and forth to other forms (see Figure 16.1).

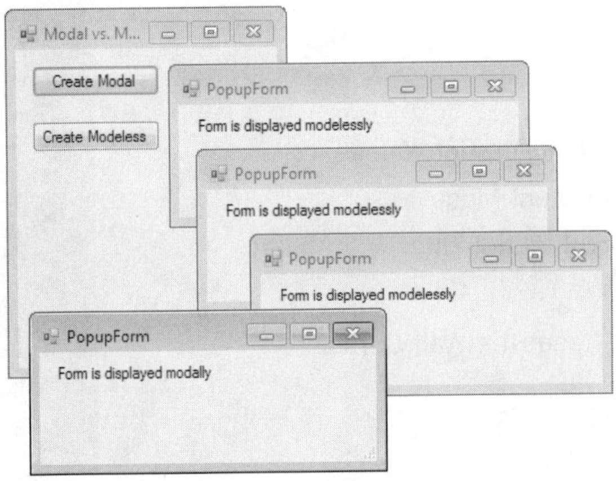

FIGURE 16.1
Modeless windows can remain active, but only a single modal window can appear at a time.

In .NET, there is a difference in how the forms are launched:

```
//show form modally
PopupForm form = new PopupForm();
form.ShowDialog(this);
```

and

```
//show form modelessly
PopupForm form = new PopupForm();
//setting the parent will allow better behavior of child and parent
```

```
//windows, especially when dealing with active windows and minimization
form.Show(this);
```

See the Modal vs. Modeless example in the sample source code.

Add a Menu Bar

Scenario/Problem: You want to provide a menu system in your application.

Solution: This section starts an example that will be used over the next few sections. In the example, you'll build up a very, very simple file browser application, complete with menus, status bar, toolbar, and a split pane window (see Figure 16.2).

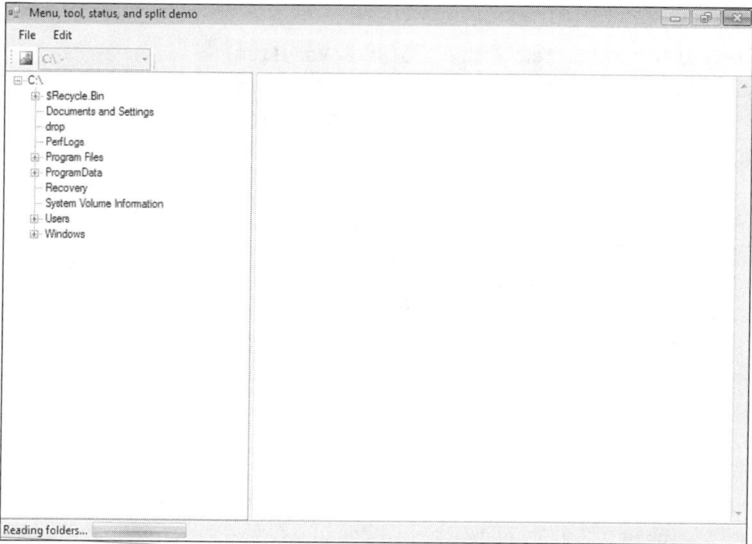

FIGURE 16.2
Windows Forms has a number of controls that make it easy to create standard interfaces.

All of these are instances of controls that can be placed inside a ToolStripContainer, which is a convenient layout control that allows easy placement of controls on all sides of a form.

NOTE Controls derived from ToolStrip are far more powerful than their predecessors. For example, not only can they host standard text items and buttons, but they can host combo boxes, progress bars, and more—anything that is derived from ToolStripItem.

Here is some sample code to demonstrate the initialization of the menu bar and its placement in the ToolStripContainer:

```
//in class Form1
private ToolStripContainer toolStripContainer;
private MenuStrip menuStrip;
private ToolStripMenuItem fileToolStripMenuItem;
private ToolStripMenuItem exitToolStripMenuItem;
private ToolStripMenuItem editToolStripMenuItem;
private ToolStripMenuItem copyToolStripMenuItem;
private TextBox textView;

private void InitializeComponent()
{
    ...
    this.toolStripContainer = new ToolStripContainer();
    this.menuStrip = new MenuStrip();
    this.fileToolStripMenuItem = new ToolStripMenuItem();
    this.exitToolStripMenuItem = new ToolStripMenuItem();
    this.editToolStripMenuItem = new ToolStripMenuItem();
    this.copyToolStripMenuItem = new ToolStripMenuItem();

 // Menu strip
    this.menuStrip.Dock = DockStyle.None;
    this.menuStrip.Items.AddRange(
    new ToolStripItem[] { this.fileToolStripMenuItem,
                          this.editToolStripMenuItem});
    this.menuStrip.Name = "menuStrip";
    //so it comes before toolbar in tab order
    this.menuStrip.TabIndex = 0;

 // File menu
 this.fileToolStripMenuItem.DropDownItems.AddRange(
         new ToolStripItem[] {this.exitToolStripMenuItem});
    this.fileToolStripMenuItem.Name = "fileToolStripMenuItem";
    this.fileToolStripMenuItem.Text = "&File";

 // exit menu item
    this.exitToolStripMenuItem.Name = "exitToolStripMenuItem";
    this.exitToolStripMenuItem.ShortcutKeys =
      ((Keys)((Keys.Alt | Keys.F4)));
    this.exitToolStripMenuItem.Text = "E&xit";
    this.exitToolStripMenuItem.Click += new
      EventHandler(exitToolStripMenuItem_Click);
```

```
// edit menu item
    this.editToolStripMenuItem.DropDownItems.AddRange(
        new ToolStripItem[] {this.copyToolStripMenuItem});
    this.editToolStripMenuItem.Name = "editToolStripMenuItem";
    this.editToolStripMenuItem.Text = "&Edit";
    this.editToolStripMenuItem.DropDownOpening += new
      EventHandler(editToolStripMenuItem_DropDownOpening);

    // copyToolStripMenuItem
    this.copyToolStripMenuItem.Name = "copyToolStripMenuItem";
    this.copyToolStripMenuItem.Text = "&Copy";
    this.copyToolStripMenuItem.Click += new
EventHandler(copyToolStripMenuItem_Click);

    //put the menu into the top portion of the ToolStripContainer
    this.toolStripContainer.TopToolStripPanel.Controls.Add(
                                                this.menuStrip);
    this.toolStripContainer.Dock = DockStyle.Fill;
    this.toolStripContainer.Name = "toolStripContainer";
    ...
}
```

Here are two of the menu item handlers:

```
void exitToolStripMenuItem_Click(object sender, EventArgs e)
{
    Application.Exit();
}

void copyToolStripMenuItem_Click(object sender, EventArgs e)
{
    if (textView.SelectionLength > 0)
    {
        textView.Copy();
    }
}
```

We'll look at the other menu event handlers in the next section.

NOTE In larger applications, you may want to derive your own class from ToolStripMenuItem so that you can associate your own state data, such as for command handling or document workspace context.

Disable Menu Items Dynamically

Scenario/Problem: You want to disable menu items when the command they represent is not valid in the current context. For example, Cut and Paste should only be enabled if text is selected.

Solution: If a menu item is not valid, it should be disabled as a clue to the user.

```
//respond to the DropDownOpening on the *parent*
//of the item you'll want to disable
void editToolStripMenuItem_DropDownOpening(object sender, EventArgs e)
{
    // check program state for whether this menu should be enabled
    this.copyToolStripMenuItem.Enabled = (textView.SelectionLength > 0);
}
```

Add a Status Bar

Scenario/Problem: You want to provide the user some information about program state.

Solution: Adding a status bar is just as easy as adding a menu. Add this to your code:

```
private StatusStrip statusStrip;
private ToolStripStatusLabel toolStripStatusLabel;
private ToolStripProgressBar toolStripProgressBar;

private void InitializeComponent()
{
    ...
    this.statusStrip = new StatusStrip();
    this.toolStripProgressBar = new ToolStripProgressBar();
    this.toolStripStatusLabel = new ToolStripStatusLabel();

this.statusStrip.Items.AddRange(
        new ToolStripItem[] {
            this.toolStripStatusLabel, this.toolStripProgressBar});
    this.statusStrip.Name = "statusStrip";
    this.statusStrip.Text = "statusStrip";
```

```
    this.toolStripStatusLabel.Name = "toolStripStatusLabel";
    this.toolStripStatusLabel.Text = "Ready";

    this.toolStripProgressBar.Name = "toolStripProgressBar";
    this.toolStripProgressBar.Size = new System.Drawing.Size(100, 16);
    this.toolStripProgressBar.Style = ProgressBarStyle.Continuous;

this.toolStripContainer.BottomToolStripPanel.Controls.Add(
                                            this.statusStrip);
    ...
}
```

Add a Toolbar

Scenario/Problem: You want to provide graphical buttons to invoke common commands in your application.

Solution: Add this code to your form to add a toolbar underneath the menu:

```
private ToolStrip toolStrip;
private ToolStripButton toolStripButtonExit;
private ToolStripSeparator toolStripSeparator1;
private ToolStripComboBox toolStripComboBoxDrives;

private void InitializeComponents()
{
    ...
    this.toolStrip.Dock = System.Windows.Forms.DockStyle.None;
    this.toolStrip.Location = new System.Drawing.Point(3, 24);
    this.toolStrip.Name = "toolStrip";
    this.toolStrip.Size = new System.Drawing.Size(164, 25);
    this.toolStrip.TabIndex = 1;

this.toolStripButtonExit.DisplayStyle =
       System.Windows.Forms.ToolStripItemDisplayStyle.Image;
    this.toolStripButtonExit.Image =
        ((System.Drawing.Image)(resources.GetObject(
                              "toolStripButtonExit.Image")));
    this.toolStripButtonExit.ImageTransparentColor =
                              System.Drawing.Color.Magenta;
    this.toolStripButtonExit.Name = "toolStripButtonExit";
    this.toolStripButtonExit.Size = new System.Drawing.Size(23, 22);
    this.toolStripButtonExit.Text = "Exit";
```

```
    this.toolStripButtonExit.Click +=
      new System.EventHandler(this.toolStripButtonExit_Click);

this.toolStripSeparator1.Name = "toolStripSeparator1";
    this.toolStripSeparator1.Size = new System.Drawing.Size(6, 25);

this.toolStripComboBoxDrives.DropDownStyle =
      System.Windows.Forms.ComboBoxStyle.DropDownList;
    this.toolStripComboBoxDrives.Name = "toolStripComboBoxDrives";
    this.toolStripComboBoxDrives.Size =
            new System.Drawing.Size(121, 25);
    this.toolStripComboBoxDrives.SelectedIndexChanged +=
      new System.EventHandler(
            this.toolStripComboBoxDrives_SelectedIndexChanged);
    ...
}
```

Here are the event handlers:

```
void toolStripButtonExit_Click(object sender, EventArgs e)
{
    Application.Exit();
}

void toolStripComboBoxDrives_SelectedIndexChanged(object sender,
                                                   EventArgs e)
{
    /* handle the combo box*/
}
```

Create a Split Window Interface

Scenario/Problem: You want to be able to dynamically resize a portion of your interface. A very popular UI interface element is the split window, with an adjustable bar between the two panes.

Solution: .NET provides the SplitContainer for just this. You can even nest SplitContainers inside of other SplitContainers to achieve more complex layouts.

In our sample program, let's add a SplitContainer with a TreeView on the left and a TextView on the right:

```
private SplitContainer splitContainer;
private TextBox textView;
private TreeView treeView;

private void InitializeComponent()
{
    ...
    this.splitContainer = new System.Windows.Forms.SplitContainer();
    this.treeView = new System.Windows.Forms.TreeView();
    this.textView = new System.Windows.Forms.TextBox();

this.toolStripContainer.ContentPanel.Controls.Add(this.splitContainer);

this.splitContainer.Dock = System.Windows.Forms.DockStyle.Fill;
    this.splitContainer.Location = new System.Drawing.Point(0, 0);
    this.splitContainer.Name = "splitContainer";

    //add to left side
    this.splitContainer.Panel1.Controls.Add(this.treeView);

    //add to right side
    this.splitContainer.Panel2.Controls.Add(this.textView);
    this.splitContainer.Size = new System.Drawing.Size(840, 369);
    this.splitContainer.SplitterDistance = 280;
    this.splitContainer.TabIndex = 2;

this.treeView.Dock = System.Windows.Forms.DockStyle.Fill;
    this.treeView.Location = new System.Drawing.Point(0, 0);
    this.treeView.Name = "treeView";
    this.treeView.Size = new System.Drawing.Size(280, 369);
    this.treeView.TabIndex = 0;
    this.treeView.AfterSelect +=
      new System.Windows.Forms.TreeViewEventHandler(
                              this.treeView_AfterSelect);

this.textView.Dock = System.Windows.Forms.DockStyle.Fill;
    this.textView.Multiline = true;
    this.textView.Name = "textView";
    this.textView.ScrollBars = System.Windows.Forms.ScrollBars.Both;
}
```

To review the full source for this example, see the ToolAndStatusAndSplit example in the accompanying source code.

Inherit a Form

Scenario/Problem: You want a master form to lay out common controls and use child forms to customize the layout or add more controls.

Solution: Form inheritance works similarly to regular class inheritance. You can put common behavior in the base form and then specialize and augment it in inherited forms. Figure 16.3 demonstrates this by adding more columns to the ListView in the InheritedForm window.

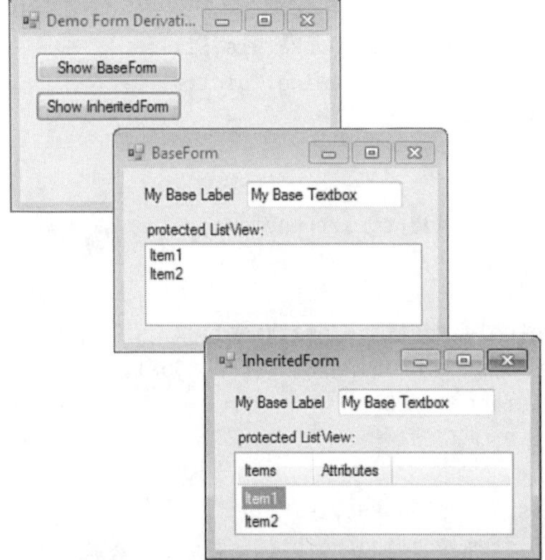

FIGURE 16.3
An inherited form contains everything in the base form plus new elements.

To modify UI elements from the base form, you must make them public or protected.

Listings 16.1 and 16.2 come from the DerivedForms example in this chapter's source code.

LISTING 16.1 **BaseForm.cs**

```
using System;
using System.ComponentModel;
using System.Windows.Forms;

namespace DerivedForms
{
    public partial class BaseForm : Form
    {
        private System.Windows.Forms.Label label1;
        private System.Windows.Forms.TextBox textBox1;
```

LISTING 16.1 **BaseForm.cs** (continued)

```
        protected System.Windows.Forms.ListView listView1;
        private System.Windows.Forms.Label label2;

        private System.ComponentModel.IContainer components = null;

        public BaseForm()
        {
            InitializeComponent();
        }

        protected override void Dispose(bool disposing)
        {
            if (disposing && (components != null))
            {
                components.Dispose();
            }
            base.Dispose(disposing);
        }

        private void InitializeComponent()
        {
            System.Windows.Forms.ListViewItem listViewItem3 =
             new System.Windows.Forms.ListViewItem("Item1");
            System.Windows.Forms.ListViewItem listViewItem4 =
             new System.Windows.Forms.ListViewItem("Item2");
            this.label1 = new System.Windows.Forms.Label();
            this.textBox1 = new System.Windows.Forms.TextBox();
            this.listView1 = new System.Windows.Forms.ListView();
            this.label2 = new System.Windows.Forms.Label();
            this.SuspendLayout();
            // label1
            this.label1.AutoSize = true;
            this.label1.Location = new System.Drawing.Point(13, 13);
            this.label1.Name = "label1";
            this.label1.Size = new System.Drawing.Size(77, 13);
            this.label1.TabIndex = 0;
            this.label1.Text = "My Base Label";
            // textBox1
            this.textBox1.Location = new System.Drawing.Point(96, 10);
            this.textBox1.Name = "textBox1";
            this.textBox1.Size = new System.Drawing.Size(120, 20);
            this.textBox1.TabIndex = 1;
            this.textBox1.Text = "My Base Textbox";
            // listView1
```

LISTING 16.1 BaseForm.cs (continued)

```
            this.listView1.Items.AddRange(
                    new System.Windows.Forms.ListViewItem[] {
                                                listViewItem3,
                                                listViewItem4});
            this.listView1.Location = new System.Drawing.Point(16, 56);
            this.listView1.Name = "listView1";
            this.listView1.Size = new System.Drawing.Size(215, 62);
            this.listView1.TabIndex = 2;
            this.listView1.UseCompatibleStateImageBehavior = false;
            this.listView1.View = System.Windows.Forms.View.List;
            // label2
            this.label2.AutoSize = true;
            this.label2.Location = new System.Drawing.Point(16, 39);
            this.label2.Name = "label2";
            this.label2.Size = new System.Drawing.Size(97, 13);
            this.label2.TabIndex = 3;
            this.label2.Text = "protected ListView:";
            // BaseForm
            this.AutoScaleDimensions =
                  new System.Drawing.SizeF(6F, 13F);
            this.AutoScaleMode =
                  System.Windows.Forms.AutoScaleMode.Font;
            this.ClientSize = new System.Drawing.Size(243, 130);
            this.Controls.Add(this.label2);
            this.Controls.Add(this.listView1);
            this.Controls.Add(this.textBox1);
            this.Controls.Add(this.label1);
            this.Name = "BaseForm";
            this.StartPosition =
             System.Windows.Forms.FormStartPosition.CenterParent;
            this.Text = "BaseForm";
            this.ResumeLayout(false);
            this.PerformLayout();
        }
    }
}
```

LISTING 16.2 InheritedForm.cs

```
using System;
using System.ComponentModel;
using System.Windows.Forms;
```

LISTING 16.2 **InheritedForm.cs** (continued)

```
namespace DerivedForms
{
    public partial class InheritedForm : DerivedForms.BaseForm
    {
        private System.Windows.Forms.ColumnHeader columnHeader1;
        private System.Windows.Forms.ColumnHeader columnHeader2;
        private CheckBox checkBox1;

        private System.ComponentModel.IContainer components = null;

        public InheritedForm()
        {
            InitializeComponent();
        }

        protected override void Dispose(bool disposing)
        {
            if (disposing && (components != null))
            {
                components.Dispose();
            }
            base.Dispose(disposing);
        }

        private void InitializeComponent()
        {
            this.columnHeader1 =
                  new System.Windows.Forms.ColumnHeader();
            this.columnHeader2 =
                  new System.Windows.Forms.ColumnHeader();
            this.checkBox1 = new System.Windows.Forms.CheckBox();
            this.SuspendLayout();
            // listView1 - we can add columns
            //because listView1 is protected
            this.listView1.Columns.AddRange(
                     new System.Windows.Forms.ColumnHeader[] {
                                  this.columnHeader1,
                                  this.columnHeader2});
            this.listView1.Location = new System.Drawing.Point(15, 57);
            this.listView1.View = System.Windows.Forms.View.Details;
            // columnHeader1
            this.columnHeader1.Text = "Items";
            // columnHeader2
```

LISTING 16.2 **InheritedForm.cs** (continued)

```
            this.columnHeader2.Text = "Attributes";
            // checkBox1 - we can add whatever new fields we want
            this.checkBox1.AutoSize = true;
            this.checkBox1.Location = new System.Drawing.Point(19, 126);
            this.checkBox1.Name = "checkBox1";
            this.checkBox1.Size = new System.Drawing.Size(107, 17);
            this.checkBox1.TabIndex = 4;
            this.checkBox1.Text = "Added checkbox";
            this.checkBox1.UseVisualStyleBackColor = true;
            // InheritedForm
            this.AutoScaleDimensions =
                    new System.Drawing.SizeF(6F, 13F);
            this.ClientSize = new System.Drawing.Size(243, 149);
            this.Controls.Add(this.checkBox1);
            this.Name = "InheritedForm";
            this.Text = "InheritedForm";
            this.Controls.SetChildIndex(this.checkBox1, 0);
            this.Controls.SetChildIndex(this.listView1, 0);
            this.ResumeLayout(false);
            this.PerformLayout();
        }
    }
}
```

Create a User Control

Scenario/Problem: You need to create a custom, reusable UI control.

Solution: Sometimes the built-in Windows Forms controls don't provide the functionality you need. You can create your own control that can be anything from a mere combination of existing controls behind your own interface, to custom drawings or themes.

This rather long example provides a custom control that combines a track bar, a numeric control, a label, and a drawing to enable the user to select a single color component value:

```
using System;
using System.Collections.Generic;
using System.ComponentModel;
using System.Drawing;
using System.Windows.Forms;
```

```
namespace CustomControl
{
    public enum RGBSelection
    {
        R,G,B
    };

    public partial class MyCustomControl : UserControl
    {
        //the controls
        private System.ComponentModel.IContainer components = null;
        private System.Windows.Forms.Label labelLabel;
        private System.Windows.Forms.NumericUpDown numericUpDownValue;
        private System.Windows.Forms.TrackBar trackBarValue;

        protected override void Dispose(bool disposing)
        {
            if (disposing && (components != null))
            {
                components.Dispose();
            }
            base.Dispose(disposing);
        }

        private void InitializeComponent()
        {
            this.labelLabel = new System.Windows.Forms.Label();
            this.numericUpDownValue =
                    new System.Windows.Forms.NumericUpDown();
            this.trackBarValue = new System.Windows.Forms.TrackBar();
            ((System.ComponentModel.ISupportInitialize)
➥(this.numericUpDownValue)).BeginInit();
            ((System.ComponentModel.ISupportInitialize)
➥(this.trackBarValue)).BeginInit();
            this.SuspendLayout();
            // labelLabel
            this.labelLabel.AutoSize = true;
            this.labelLabel.Location = new System.Drawing.Point(4, 4);
            this.labelLabel.Name = "labelLabel";
            this.labelLabel.Size = new System.Drawing.Size(71, 13);
            this.labelLabel.TabIndex = 0;
            this.labelLabel.Text = "Dummy Label";
            // numericUpDownValue
            this.numericUpDownValue.Location =
                    new System.Drawing.Point(175, 20);
```

```
            this.numericUpDownValue.Name = "numericUpDownValue";
            this.numericUpDownValue.Size =
                    new System.Drawing.Size(41, 20);
            this.numericUpDownValue.TabIndex = 1;
            // trackBarValue
            this.trackBarValue.Location =
                    new System.Drawing.Point(7, 20);
            this.trackBarValue.Name = "trackBarValue";
            this.trackBarValue.Size = new System.Drawing.Size(162, 45);
            this.trackBarValue.TabIndex = 2;
            // MyCustomControl
            this.AutoScaleDimensions =
                    new System.Drawing.SizeF(6F, 13F);
            this.AutoScaleMode =
                    System.Windows.Forms.AutoScaleMode.Font;
            this.Controls.Add(this.trackBarValue);
            this.Controls.Add(this.numericUpDownValue);
            this.Controls.Add(this.labelLabel);
            this.Name = "MyCustomControl";
            this.Size = new System.Drawing.Size(216, 65);
            ((System.ComponentModel.ISupportInitialize)
➥(this.numericUpDownValue)).EndInit();
            ((System.ComponentModel.ISupportInitialize)
➥(this.trackBarValue)).EndInit();
            this.ResumeLayout(false);
            this.PerformLayout();
        }

        public RGBSelection ColorPart {get;set;}

        public string Label
        {
            get
            {
                return labelLabel.Text;
            }
            set
            {
                labelLabel.Text = value;
            }
        }
        //overall value of the control
        public int Value
```

```
{
    get
    {
        return (int)numericUpDownValue.Value;
    }
    set
    {
        numericUpDownValue.Value = (int)value;
    }
}

public event EventHandler<EventArgs> ValueChanged;

public MyCustomControl()
{
    InitializeComponent();

    numericUpDownValue.Minimum = 0;
    numericUpDownValue.Maximum = 255;
    trackBarValue.Minimum = 0;
    trackBarValue.Maximum = 255;

    trackBarValue.TickFrequency = 10;

    numericUpDownValue.ValueChanged
          += numericUpDownValue_ValueChanged;
    trackBarValue.ValueChanged += trackBarValue_ValueChanged;
}
//if either the trackbar or the numeric control changes value
//we need to update the other to keep the control
//internally consistent
void trackBarValue_ValueChanged(object sender, EventArgs e)
{
    if (sender != this)
    {
        numericUpDownValue.Value = trackBarValue.Value;
        OnValueChanged();
    }
}

void numericUpDownValue_ValueChanged(object sender, EventArgs e)
{
    if (sender != this)
```

```
            {
                trackBarValue.Value = (int)numericUpDownValue.Value;
                OnValueChanged();
            }
        }

        protected void OnValueChanged()
        {
            Refresh();
            if (ValueChanged != null)
            {
                ValueChanged(this, EventArgs.Empty);
            }
        }

        protected override void OnPaint(PaintEventArgs e)
        {
            base.OnPaint(e);
            //the only part we need to draw is the ellipse in our color
            Rectangle rect = new Rectangle(numericUpDownValue.Left, 5,
➥numericUpDownValue.Width, numericUpDownValue.Bounds.Top - 10);

            int r = 0, g = 0, b = 0;
            switch (ColorPart)
            {
                case RGBSelection.R:
                    r = Value;
                    break;
                case RGBSelection.G:
                    g = Value;
                    break;
                case RGBSelection.B:
                    b = Value;
                    break;
            }
            Color c = Color.FromArgb(r,g,b);
            using (Brush brush = new SolidBrush(c))
            {
                e.Graphics.FillEllipse(brush, rect);
            }
        }
    }
}
```

You can now reuse this control easily in forms, as shown in Figure 16.4, which demonstrates a color picking application that combines three of our controls.

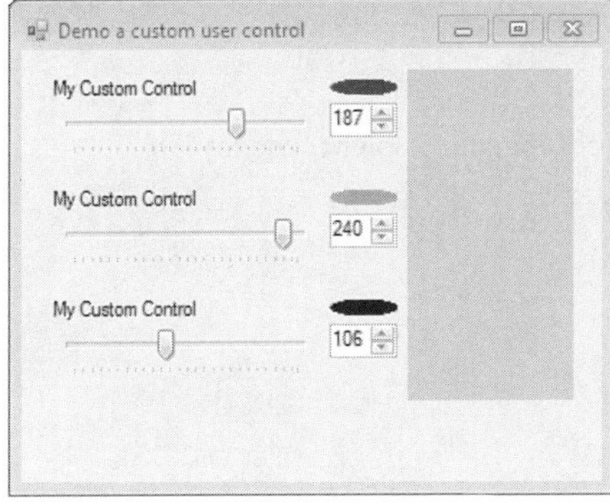

FIGURE 16.4
Create user controls to enable more complex, reusable interfaces.

Use a Timer

Scenario/Problem: You want to call a function at regular intervals, or just once after a specified interval.

Solution: Use a timer. .NET provides many types of timers, but perhaps one of the most common and easiest to use is the `System.Windows.Forms.Timer` class, which uses the normal event-handling mechanism to notify users when it ticks.

Here's a simple example that alternates the text in a Label every second. The Button and Label are defined in Form's code-behind file, which you can find in the TimerDemo sample project for this chapter.

```
public partial class Form1 : Form
{
    private Timer _timer;
    bool _tick = true;
    bool _stopped = true;

    public Form1()
    {
        InitializeComponent();

        _timer = new Timer();
        _timer.Interval = 1000;//1 second
        _timer.Tick += new EventHandler(_timer_Tick);
    }

    void _timer_Tick(object sender, EventArgs e)
    {
        labelOutput.Text = _tick ? "Tick" : "Tock";
```

```
        _tick = !_tick;
    }

    private void buttonStart_Click(object sender, EventArgs e)
    {
        if (_stopped)
        {
            _timer.Enabled = true;
            buttonStart.Text = "&Stop";
        }
        else
        {
            _timer.Enabled = false;
            buttonStart.Text = "&Start";
        }
        _stopped = !_stopped;
    }
}
```

NOTE Be wary of the accuracy of timers. This timer is implemented using the normal event model and is not designed to be super-accurate. For a more accurate timer, you can use the one discussed in Chapter 23, "Threads, Asynchronous, and Parallel Programming." Even then, however, don't put all your trust in its accuracy. Windows is not a real-time operating system and is therefore not guaranteed to honor strict timing requests.

Use Application and User Configuration Values

Scenario/Problem: You want to store application-level and user-specific configuration settings.

Solution: Configuration settings are often the bane of a programmer's existence, and they are implemented as an afterthought. Thankfully, .NET takes some of the sting out with some built-in classes. These classes enjoy direct IDE support in Visual Studio.

Most new GUI projects automatically create a settings file for you, but if you need to create one, follow these steps:

1. Right-click your project in the Solution Explorer.
2. Select Add, New Item.
3. Find the entry for Settings File and highlight it (see Figure 16.5).

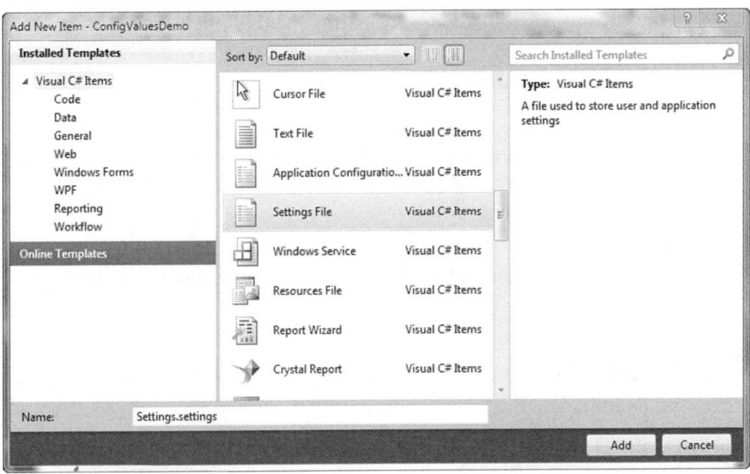

FIGURE 16.5
Add a settings file in Visual Studio.

4. Give it a meaningful name. (Settings.settings usually works for me.)

5. Once you have a new settings file, double-click it in the Solution Explorer to open the settings editor (see Figure 16.6).

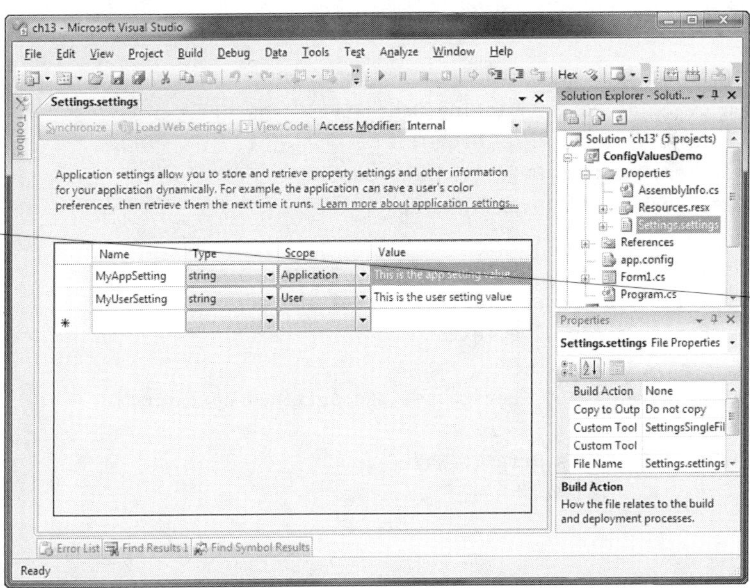

FIGURE 16.6
You can add user- and application-level settings in Visual Studio's settings editor.

Table 16.1 describes the differences between user settings and application settings.

TABLE 16.1 **The Scope of the Configuration Settings**

Setting	Description
Application	All instances and users are affected by these settings. They cannot be changed during runtime. The configurations live in the file located with the executable.
User	The settings can be changed on a user basis. They can be changed during runtime. The settings file is stored in the user's application data directory.

Behind the scenes, Visual Studio will generate properties of the correct type for your code to use. Here's an example:

```
public partial class Form1 : Form
{
    public Form1()
    {
        InitializeComponent();
        //load the settings into our UI
        this.textBoxAppConfigValue.Text =
             Properties.Settings.Default.MyAppSetting;
        this.textBoxUserConfigValue.Text =
             Properties.Settings.Default.MyUserSetting;
    }

    //save settings when we close
    protected override void OnClosing(CancelEventArgs e)
    {
        Properties.Settings.Default.MyUserSetting =
            textBoxUserConfigValue.Text;

        //can't do this--app settings are read-only!
        //Properties.Settings.Default.MyAppSetting =
        //textBoxAppConfigValue.Text;

        //better save if you want to see the settings next time
        //the app runs
        Properties.Settings.Default.Save();
    }
}
```

For a demo and the full source code, see the ConfigValuesDemo project in this chapter's sample code.

Use ListView Efficiently in Virtual Mode

Scenario/Problem: Have you ever tried to enter over a few thousand items into a ListView control? If so, you know that it does not perform well. However, it is possible to efficiently list over, say 100,000,000 items in a ListView without it choking.

Solution: The key is to use ListView's virtual mode, which uses callbacks to retrieve the data it needs to display.

You should use virtual mode intelligently to avoid continually re-creating objects that the garbage collector will need to clean up. For this reason, the following sample code sets up a simple caching system where ListViewItem objects are reused when the ListView needs to update which items it is currently displaying:

```
public partial class Form1 : Form
{
    //our simple cache of items
    private List<ListViewItem> _listViewItemCache =
                new List<ListViewItem>();
    //needed so we can map the index in the
    //list view to the index in our cache
    private int _topIndex = -1;

    public Form1()
    {
        InitializeComponent();

        listView.VirtualMode = true;
        listView.VirtualListSize = (int)numericUpDown1.Value;
        listView.CacheVirtualItems += new
➥CacheVirtualItemsEventHandler(listView_CacheVirtualItems);
        listView.RetrieveVirtualItem += new
➥RetrieveVirtualItemEventHandler(listView_RetrieveVirtualItem);
    }
    //called when the ListView is about to display a new range of items
    void listView_CacheVirtualItems(object sender,
                                    CacheVirtualItemsEventArgs e)
    {
        _topIndex = e.StartIndex;
        //find out if we need more items
        //(note we never make the list smaller--not a very good cache)
        int needed = (e.EndIndex - e.StartIndex) + 1;
        if (_listViewItemCache.Capacity < needed)
```

```
        {
            int toGrow = needed - _listViewItemCache.Capacity;
            //adjust the capacity to the target
            _listViewItemCache.Capacity = needed;
            //add the new cached items
            for (int i = 0; i < toGrow; i++)
            {
                _listViewItemCache.Add(new ListViewItem());
            }
        }
    }

    void listView_RetrieveVirtualItem(object sender,
                                     RetrieveVirtualItemEventArgs e)
    {
        int cacheIndex = e.ItemIndex - _topIndex;
        if (cacheIndex >= 0 && cacheIndex < _listViewItemCache.Count)
        {
            e.Item = _listViewItemCache[cacheIndex];
            //we could set the text to any data we want,
            //based on e.ItemIndex let's just show
            //the item index and the cache index for simplicity
            e.Item.Text = e.ItemIndex.ToString() + " --> " +
                          cacheIndex.ToString();
            //e.Item.Tag = some arbitrary object
        }
        else
        {
            //this can happen occasionally, but you won't see it
            e.Item = _listViewItemCache[0];
            e.Item.Text = "Oops";
        }
    }
    //update the size of our list on demand
    private void numericUpDown1_ValueChanged(object sender, EventArgs e)
    {
        listView.VirtualListSize = (int)numericUpDown1.Value;
    }
}
```

To see the full source code, including the code-behind for the controls, look at the VirtualListView project in the accompanying source.

Take Advantage of Horizontal Wheel Tilt

Scenario/Problem: Most mice these days come with a scroll wheel, which is fairly well supported by most controls. Some mice, however, also come with a horizontal "tilt" wheel capability. The support for this is a little more spotty. If you have a form with automatic scrollbars, both the mouse scrolling and tilt scrolling will work fine. However, if you instead want scrolling in a custom control, you'll find the horizontal scrolling isn't there.

Solution: This support could be added in future versions of .NET, but until then, here is an example of how to achieve this functionality in a control derived from Panel by taking over some of the underlying Win32 processing:

```
abstract class Win32Messages
{
    //taken from winuser.h
    public const int WM_MOUSEWHEEL = 0x020a;

    //taken from winuser.h (Vista or Server 2008 and up required!)
    public const int WM_MOUSEHWHEEL = 0x020e;
}

class Win32Constants
{
    //taken from winuser.h in the Platform SDK
    public const int MK_LBUTTON = 0x0001;
    public const int MK_RBUTTON = 0x0002;
    public const int MK_SHIFT = 0x0004;
    public const int MK_CONTROL = 0x0008;
    public const int MK_MBUTTON = 0x0010;
    public const int MK_XBUTTON1 = 0x0020;
    public const int MK_XBUTTON2 = 0x0040;

    public const int WHEEL_DELTA = 120;

    //(Vista or Server 2008 and up required!)
    public const int SPI_GETWHEELSCROLLCHARS = 0x006C;
}

class TiltAwarePanel : Panel
{
    //FYI: There is a .Net SystemParameters class in WPF,
    //but not in Winforms
    [DllImport("user32.dll", SetLastError = true)]
```

```
    [return: MarshalAs(UnmanagedType.Bool)]
    static extern bool SystemParametersInfo(uint uiAction, uint uiParam,
➥ref uint pvParam, uint fWinIni);

    private int _wheelHPos = 0;
    private readonly uint HScrollChars = 1;
    //scrolling is in terms of lines and characters, which is app-defined
    private const int CharacterWidth = 8;

    public event EventHandler<MouseEventArgs> MouseHWheel;

    public TiltAwarePanel()
    {
        //get the system's values for horizontal scrolling
        if (!SystemParametersInfo(
             Win32Constants.SPI_GETWHEELSCROLLCHARS, 0,
             ref HScrollChars, 0))
        {
            throw new InvalidOperationException(
                           "Unsupported on this platform");
        }
    }

    protected void OnMouseHWheel(MouseEventArgs e)
    {
        //we have to accumulate the value
        _wheelHPos += e.Delta;
        //this method
        while (_wheelHPos >= Win32Constants.WHEEL_DELTA)
        {
            ScrollHorizontal((int)HScrollChars * CharacterWidth);
            _wheelHPos -= Win32Constants.WHEEL_DELTA;
        }

        while (_wheelHPos <= -Win32Constants.WHEEL_DELTA)
        {
            ScrollHorizontal(-(int)HScrollChars * CharacterWidth);
            _wheelHPos += Win32Constants.WHEEL_DELTA;
        }

        if (MouseHWheel != null)
        {
            MouseHWheel(this, e);
        }
```

```
        Refresh();
    }

    private void ScrollHorizontal(int delta)
    {
        AutoScrollPosition =
          new Point(
                -AutoScrollPosition.X + delta,
              -AutoScrollPosition.Y);
    }

    protected override void WndProc(ref Message m)
    {
        if (m.HWnd == this.Handle)
        {
            switch (m.Msg)
            {
                case Win32Messages.WM_MOUSEHWHEEL:
                    OnMouseHWheel(CreateMouseEventArgs(m.WParam,
                                                m.LParam));
                    //0 to indicate we handled it
                    m.Result = (IntPtr)0;
                    return;
                default:
                    break;
            }
        }
        base.WndProc(ref m);
    }

    private MouseEventArgs CreateMouseEventArgs(IntPtr wParam,
                                            IntPtr lParam)
    {
        int buttonFlags = LOWORD(wParam);
        MouseButtons buttons = MouseButtons.None;
        buttons |= ((buttonFlags & Win32Constants.MK_LBUTTON) != 0)?
➥MouseButtons.Left:0;
        buttons |= ((buttonFlags & Win32Constants.MK_RBUTTON) != 0) ?
➥MouseButtons.Right : 0;
        buttons |= ((buttonFlags & Win32Constants.MK_MBUTTON) != 0) ?
➥MouseButtons.Middle : 0;
        buttons |= ((buttonFlags & Win32Constants.MK_XBUTTON1) != 0) ?
➥MouseButtons.XButton1 : 0;
        buttons |= ((buttonFlags & Win32Constants.MK_XBUTTON2) != 0) ?
➥MouseButtons.XButton2 : 0;
```

```
        int delta = (Int16)HIWORD(wParam);
        int x = LOWORD(lParam);
        int y = HIWORD(lParam);

        return new MouseEventArgs(buttons, 0, x, y, delta);
    }

    private static Int32 HIWORD(IntPtr ptr)
    {
        Int32 val32 = ptr.ToInt32();
        return ((val32 >> 16) & 0xFFFF);
    }

    private static Int32 LOWORD(IntPtr ptr)
    {
        Int32 val32 = ptr.ToInt32();
        return (val32 & 0xFFFF);
    }
}

//main form, which includes the above panel
//see the HorizTiltWheelDemo project for the full source code
public partial class Form1 : Form
{
    [DllImport("user32.dll", CharSet = CharSet.Auto)]
    private static extern IntPtr SendMessage(IntPtr hWnd,
                                             int msg,
                                             IntPtr wp,
                                             IntPtr lp);

    public Form1()
    {
        InitializeComponent();

        panel1.MouseHWheel
            += new EventHandler<MouseEventArgs>(panel1_MouseHWheel);
    }

    void panel1_MouseHWheel(object sender, MouseEventArgs e)
    {
        label1.Text = string.Format("H Delta: {0}", e.Delta);
    }

    protected override void WndProc(ref Message m)
    {
```

```
        //send all mouse wheel messages to panel
        switch (m.Msg)
        {
            case Win32Messages.WM_MOUSEWHEEL:
            case Win32Messages.WM_MOUSEHWHEEL:
                SendMessage(panel1.Handle, m.Msg, m.WParam, m.LParam);
                m.Result = IntPtr.Zero;
                break;
        }
        base.WndProc(ref m);
    }
}
```

Look at the full HorizTiltWheelDemo project in the accompanying sample source code for the all the code.

Cut and Paste

Scenario/Problem: You need to place items on the clipboard.

Solution: There is a simple way and a simpler way to do this, depending on your requirements—if you need to put multiple formats to the clipboard simultaneously or if only one will do. I'll cover each method in the following sections, as well as how to put your own custom objects on the clipboard.

Cut and Paste a Single Data Type

The naive way to cut and paste is to simply use the methods `Clipboard.SetText()`, `Clipboard.SetImage()`, and so on.

```
//puts the text "Hello, there!" on the clipboard
Clipboard.SetText("Hello, there!");
Bitmap bitmap = Bitmap.FromFile(@"C:\MyImage.bmp");
//puts the contents of C:\MyImage.bmp onto the clipboard
Clipboard.SetImage(bitmap);

//to retrieve it
Image image = Clipboard.GetImage();
string text = Clipboard.GetText();
```

Cut and Paste Text and Images Together

Many programs support more advanced clipboard functionality. For example, when you copy text to the clipboard from Microsoft Word, it copies that text in many formats simultaneously, including plain text, Word format, HTML, and even an image of the text you can paste into a graphics program! This is a built-in feature of the Windows clipboard that you can take advantage of. When pasting, it is up to each program to decide what format to ask for by default, or even to give the user a choice.

Here is how to put both text and an image on the clipboard:

```
Bitmap bitmap = Bitmap.FromFile(@"C:\MyImage.bmp");
DataObject obj = new DataObject();
obj.SetText("Hello, there!");
obj.SetImage(bitmap);
Clipboard.SetDataObject(obj);
```

Determine What Formats Are on the Clipboard

To determine what formats are available for you to paste, the `Clipboard` class defines some static methods:

```
Clipboard.ContainsAudio();
Clipboard.ContainsFileDropList();
Clipboard.ContainsImage();
Clipboard.ContainsText();
```

These all return a `bool`. There is also a `ContainsData` method, which is used to determine if a custom format is present. This is used in the next section.

To determine what formats are present, you can use this code:

```
IDataObject obj = Clipboard.GetDataObject();
if (obj != null)
{
    foreach (string format in obj.GetFormats())
    {
        Console.WriteLine(format);
    }
}
```

Running this code after I copied this sentence from Microsoft Word yielded the following output:

```
Object Descriptor
Rich Text Format
HTML Format
System.String
UnicodeText
Text
EnhancedMetafile
MetaFilePict
Embed Source
```

```
Link Source
Link Source Descriptor
ObjectLink
Hyperlink
```

Cut and Paste User-Defined Objects

If your program is, for example, a CAD program for widgets, chances are you will want to support cut and paste functionality on widgets. You have two options:

- Transform your widgets into a standard clipboard format (such as text) and put that on the clipboard. Then translate it back when pasting.
- Put arbitrary binary data on the clipboard and then serialize and deserialize your class (with minimal effort).

The good news is that the second option is easy to use.

Suppose you have a ListView containing the name, sex, and age of various people. To put these rows on the clipboard, define an intermediary class that is serializable:

```
[Serializable]
class MyClipboardItem
{
    //We must have a unique name to identify
    //our data type on the clipboard
    //we're naming it this, but we'll actually store a list of these
    public const string FormatName =
        "HowToCSharp.ch16.ClipboardDemo.MyClipboardItem";
    public static readonly DataFormats.Format Format;
    static MyClipboardItem()
    {
        Format = DataFormats.GetFormat(FormatName);
    }

    public string Name { get; set; }
    public string Sex { get; set; }
    public string Age { get; set; }

    public MyClipboardItem(string name, string sex, string age)
    {
        this.Name = name;
        this.Sex = sex;
        this.Age = age;
    }
}
```

When you want to put it on the clipboard, you can do something like this, assuming the existence of a ListView that contains this information:

```
private void CopyAllFormats()
{
    DataObject obj = new DataObject();
    obj.SetText(GetText()); //get text version of rows
    obj.SetImage(GetBitmap()); //get bitmap version of rows
    //get our own data form of the rows
   //--note that is a list of our items, not just a single item
    obj.SetData(MyClipboardItem.Format.Name, RowsToClipboardItems());
    Clipboard.SetDataObject(obj);
}

private string GetText()
{
    StringBuilder sb = new StringBuilder(256);
    foreach (ListViewItem item in listView1.SelectedItems)
    {
        sb.AppendFormat("{0},{1},{2}", item.Text,
                                       item.SubItems[1].Text,
                                       item.SubItems[2].Text);
        sb.AppendLine();
    }
    return sb.ToString();
}

private Bitmap GetBitmap()
{
    Bitmap bitmap = new Bitmap(listView1.Width, listView1.Height);
    listView1.DrawToBitmap(bitmap, listView1.ClientRectangle);
    return bitmap;
}

private List<MyClipboardItem> RowsToClipboardItems()
{
    List<MyClipboardItem> clipItems = new List<MyClipboardItem>();
    foreach (ListViewItem item in listView1.SelectedItems)
    {
        clipItems.Add(
            new MyClipboardItem(item.Text, item.SubItems[1].Text,
                                item.SubItems[2].Text)
            );
    }
    return clipItems;
}
```

To retrieve the custom data type from the clipboard, use this:

```
private void buttonPasteToList_Click(object sender, EventArgs e)
{
    if (Clipboard.ContainsData(MyClipboardItem.Format.Name))
    {
        IList<MyClipboardItem> items = GetItemsFromClipboard();
        foreach (MyClipboardItem item in items)
        {
            AddPerson(item.Name, item.Sex, item.Age);
        }
    }
    else
    {
        MessageBox.Show(
           "Nothing on the clipboard in the right format!");
    }
}
private void AddPerson(string name, string sex, string age)
{
    ListViewItem item = new ListViewItem(name);
    item.SubItems.Add(sex);
    item.SubItems.Add(age);

    listView1.Items.Add(item);
}

IList<MyClipboardItem> GetItemsFromClipboard()
{
    object obj = Clipboard.GetData(MyClipboardItem.Format.Name);
    return obj as IList<MyClipboardItem>;
}
```

See the ClipboardDemo sample project, which demonstrates the use of the clipboard with text, image, and custom data.

Automatically Ensure You Reset the Wait Cursor

Scenario/Problem: During long-running operations, you should use the wait cursor to indicate to the user that he should not expect to be able to use the program during the operation.

However, what about this situation?

```
Cursor oldCursor = this.Cursor;
this.Cursor = Cursors.WaitCursor;
//do work
throw new Exception("Ooops, something happened!");
//uh-oh, the old cursor never gets set back!
this.Cursor = oldCursor;
```

In this case, an error prohibits the cursor from being set back to normal.

Solution: Although you could wrap this in a `try...finally` block, here is a simple hack that shortcuts this by using the `IDisposable` interface:

```
class AutoWaitCursor : IDisposable
{
    private Control _target;
    private Cursor _prevCursor = Cursors.Default;

    public AutoWaitCursor(Control control)
    {
        if (control == null)
        {
            throw new ArgumentNullException("control");
        }
        _target = control;
        _prevCursor = _target.Cursor;
        _target.Cursor = Cursors.WaitCursor;
    }

    public void Dispose()
    {
        _target.Cursor = _prevCursor;
    }
}
```

Now you can just do the following, and the cursor is automatically reset:

```
using (new AutoWaitCursor(this))
{
    //do  work...
    throw new Exception();
}
```

CHAPTER 17

Graphics with Windows Forms and GDI+

IN THIS CHAPTER

- Understand Colors
- Use the System Color Picker
- Convert Colors Between RGB to HSV
- Draw Shapes
- Create Pens
- Create Custom Brushes
- Use Transformations
- Draw Text
- Draw Text Diagonally
- Draw Images
- Draw Transparent Images
- Draw to an Off-Screen Buffer
- Access a Bitmap's Pixels Directly for Performance
- Draw with Anti-Aliasing
- Draw Flicker-Free
- Resize an Image
- Create a Thumbnail of an Image
- Take a Multiscreen Capture
- Get the Distance from the Mouse Cursor to a Point
- Determine if a Point Is Inside a Rectangle
- Determine if a Point Is Inside a Circle
- Determine if a Point Is Inside an Ellipse
- Determine if Two Rectangles Intersect
- Print and Print Preview

If you're familiar with Win32 and the Graphics Device Interface (GDI), GDI+ will be very recognizable to you. It is just what the name implies: GDI with a little extra. GDI+ is a very basic method of drawing custom graphics in your application that is quite easy to learn.

Understand Colors

Color definitions are implemented using the `System.Drawing.Color` struct. This is basically just a wrapper around four 1-byte values: red, green, blue, and alpha (for transparency).

```
Color color = Color.FromArgb(255, 255, 255, 255); // opaque pure white
```

For well-known colors, you can use one of the many static properties on the `Color` struct:

```
Color color = Color.White;
```

> **NOTE** Be aware that named colors are different from colors you define yourself! What do you think the value of this expression is?
>
> ```
> bool e = Color.White.Equals(Color.FromArgb(255, 255, 255));
> ```
>
> `e` is false, even though they are visually equivalent colors.

There are properties to access each color component:

```
int red = color.R;
```

Use the System Color Picker

Scenario/Problem: You need to provide the user with a basic ability to pick colors.

Solution: A built-in color picker is available (see Figure 17.1):

```
Color c = Color.FromArgb(25, 50, 75);
System.Windows.Forms.ColorDialog cdg =
            new System.Windows.Forms.ColorDialog();
cdg.Color = c;
if (cdg.ShowDialog() == DialogResult.OK)
{
    c = cdg.Color;
}
```

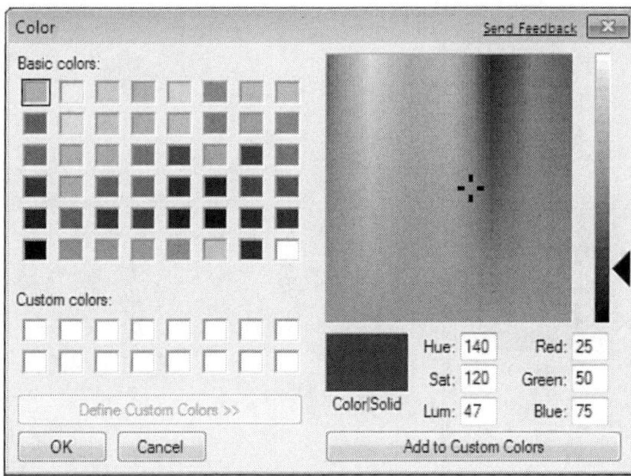

FIGURE 17.1
The system color picker gives you quick-and-easy access to a basic color-selection interface.

Convert Colors Between RGB to HSV

Scenario/Problem: You want to give the user the option to specify colors in the more natural HSV format.

The RGB format that colors use in computers is extremely convenient—for computers. Not so much for humans, where HSV (hue, saturation, value) is more intuitive and easier to control.

Most decent paint programs allow you to control color in either format, and you should give your users the same freedom.

Solution: The science and math behind color and how to convert it is beyond the scope of this book. There are plenty of explanations on the Internet.

The ColorConverter sample app, shown in Figure 17.2, puts this conversion code to use in a nifty form that demonstrates some useful UI techniques. It uses `LinearGradientBrushes` generously to indicate the effect of changing each slider. The full code for this app is not presented in the book but is in the ColorConverter sample application in the accompanying source code for this chapter.

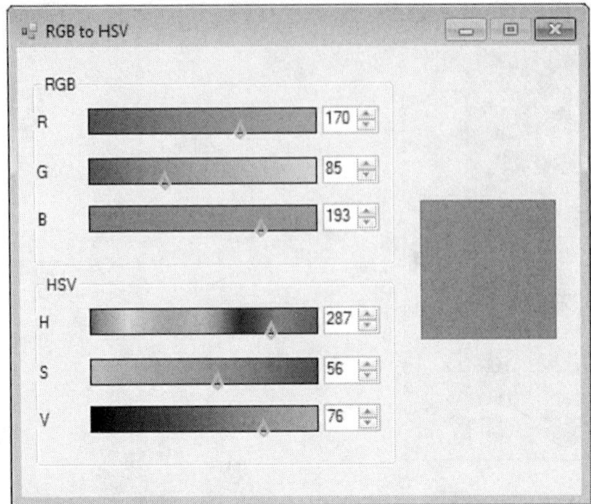

FIGURE 17.2
A color-selection form that demonstrates the relationship between RGB and HSV.

Convert RGB to HSV

```
/// <summary>
/// Convert RGB to HSV
/// </summary>
/// <param name="color">The RGB color.</param>
/// <param name="hue">The hue.</param>
/// <param name="saturation">The saturation.</param>
/// <param name="value">The value.</param>
/// <remarks>
/// Based on code from "Building a Color Picker with GDI+
/// in Visual Basic.Net or C#" byKen Getz
/// http://msdn.microsoft.com/en-us/magazine/cc164113.aspx
/// </remarks>
public static void RgbToHsv(Color rgbColor,
    out int hue, out int saturation, out int value)
{
    double r = rgbColor.R / 255.0;
    double g = rgbColor.G / 255.0;
    double b = rgbColor.B / 255.0;

    //get the min and max of all three components
    double min = Math.Min(Math.Min(r, g), b);
    double max = Math.Max(Math.Max(r,g), b);

    double v = max;
    double delta = max - min;
    double h=0, s=0;
```

```
    if (max == 0 || delta == 0)
    {
        //we've either got black or gray
        s = h = 0;
    }
    else
    {
        s = delta / max;
        if (r == max)
        {
            h = (g-b)/delta;
        }
        else if (g == max)
        {
            h = 2 + (b-r) / delta;
        }
        else
        {
            h = 4 + (r-g) / delta;
        }
    }
    //scale h to 0 -360
    h *= 60;
    if (h < 0)
    {
        h += 360.0;
    }
    hue = (int)h;
    //scale saturation and value to 0-100
    saturation = (int)(s * 100.0);
    value = (int)(v * 100.0);
}
```

Convert HSV to RGB

```
/// <summary>
/// HSVs to RGB.
/// </summary>
/// <param name="hue">The hue (0-360).</param>
/// <param name="saturation">The saturation (0-100).</param>
/// <param name="value">The value (0-100).</param>
/// <returns>The RGB color equivalent</returns>
/// <remarks>
/// Based on code from "Building a Color Picker with GDI+ in
/// Visual Basic.Net or C#" by Ken Getz
/// http://msdn.microsoft.com/en-us/magazine/cc164113.aspx
/// </remarks>
```

```
public static Color HsvToRgb(int hue, int saturation, int value)
{
    double h = hue;
    double s = saturation / 100.0;
    double v = value / 100.0;

    double r=0, g=0, b=0;
    if (s == 0)
    {
        //no saturation = gray
        r = g = b = v;
    }
    else
    {
        double sector = h / 60;
        int sectorNumber = (int)Math.Floor(sector);
        double sectorPart = sector - sectorNumber;

        //three axes of color
        double p = v * (1 - s);
        double q = v * (1 - (s * sectorPart));
        double t = v * (1 - (s * (1 - sectorPart)));

        switch (sectorNumber)
        {
            case 0://dominated by red
                r = v;
                g = t;
                b = p;
                break;
            case 1://dominated by green
                r = q;
                g = v;
                b = p;
                break;
            case 2:
                r = p;
                g = v;
                b = t;
                break;
            case 3://dominated by blue
                r = p;
                g = q;
                b = v;
                break;
```

```
            case 4:
                r = t;
                g = p;
                b = v;
                break;
            case 5://dominated by red
                r = v;
                g = p;
                b = q;
                break;
        }
    }
    return Color.FromArgb((int)(r * 255), (int)(g * 255),
                                          (int)(b * 255));
}
```

Draw Shapes

Scenario/Problem: You need to draw primitive shapes on the screen.

Solution: For most shapes, you have the option of drawing them filled or as an outline. This code demonstrates how to draw 10 different shapes as both outline and filled, where applicable (see Figure 17.3).

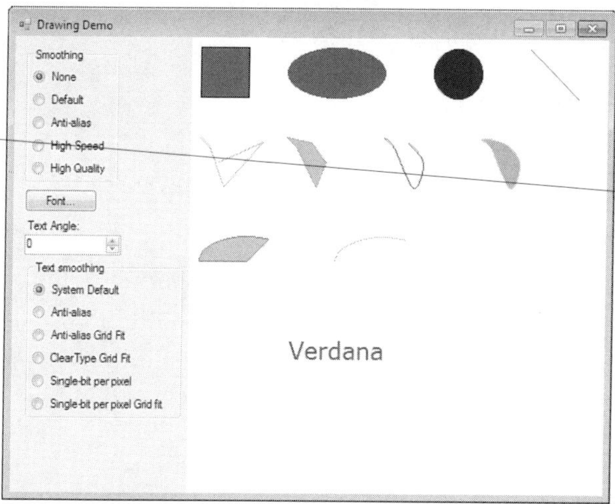

FIGURE 17.3
Basic shapes are easy in GDI+. The following sections discuss text and smoothing.

Drawing usually takes place in the OnPaint routine of a Control or Form.

```
protected override void OnPaint(PaintEventArgs e)
{
    base.OnPaint(e);

    //a filled shape with a border is actually two shapes
    e.Graphics.FillRectangle(Brushes.Red, 10, 10, 50, 50);
    e.Graphics.DrawRectangle(Pens.Black, 10, 10, 50, 50);

    e.Graphics.FillEllipse(Brushes.Green, 100, 10, 100, 50);
    e.Graphics.DrawEllipse(Pens.DarkGreen, 100, 10, 100, 50);

    //a circle is just an ellipse with equal width and height
    e.Graphics.FillEllipse(Brushes.Blue, 250, 10, 50, 50);
    e.Graphics.DrawEllipse(Pens.DarkBlue, 250, 10, 50, 50);

    //a single line
    e.Graphics.DrawLine(Pens.SteelBlue, 350, 10, 400, 60);

    //a series of connected lines
    Point[] linesPoints = new Point[] {
        new Point(10,100),
        new Point(20, 110),
        new Point(35, 150),
        new Point(75, 105),
        new Point(30, 125)};

    e.Graphics.DrawLines(Pens.SpringGreen, linesPoints);

    //a polygon (closed series of lines)
    Point[] polygonPoints = new Point[] {
        new Point(100,100),
        new Point(110,110),
        new Point(130,150),
        new Point(140,125),
        new Point(125,105)};

    e.Graphics.FillPolygon(Brushes.Tan, polygonPoints);
    e.Graphics.DrawPolygon(Pens.DarkGoldenrod, polygonPoints);

    //a curve that goes through each point
    //aka cardinal spline
    Point[] curvePoints = new Point[] {
        new Point(200,100),
        new Point(210,110),
```

```
        new Point(230,150),
        new Point(240,125),
        new Point(225,105)};

    e.Graphics.DrawCurve(Pens.Purple, curvePoints);

    Point[] closedCurvePoints = new Point[] {
        new Point(300,100),
        new Point(310,110),
        new Point(330,150),
        new Point(340,125),
        new Point(325,105)};

    e.Graphics.FillClosedCurve(Brushes.LightCoral, closedCurvePoints);
    e.Graphics.DrawClosedCurve(Pens.PowderBlue, closedCurvePoints);

    e.Graphics.FillPie(Brushes.LawnGreen, 10, 200, 100, 50, 180, 135);
    e.Graphics.DrawPie(Pens.DarkOliveGreen, 10, 200, 100, 50, 180, 135);

    e.Graphics.DrawArc(Pens.Plum, 150, 200, 100, 50, 180, 135);
}
```

NOTE In general, you use pens in the `Draw*` methods and brushes in the `Fill*` methods. As you'll see in the next section, however, pens can be made to mimic brushes in some respects.

Although the examples in this chapter, for simplicity's sake, generally put much of the painting code directly in `OnPaint()` or methods called from `OnPaint()`, for performance reasons you should endeavor to perform as much work outside of `OnPaint()` as possible. For example, put size calculations in `OnSize()` instead.

Create Pens

Scenario/Problem: You need to customize the pens used to draw shapes on the screen, such as making them thicker or a different color.

Solution: There are quite a few options you have for pen creation, as this code demonstrates:

```
Point[] points = new Point[]
    {
        new Point(5,10),
        new Point(50, 10),
        new Point (10, 50)
```

```
    };
LinearGradientBrush gradientBrush =
       new LinearGradientBrush(new Point(0, 0),
                               new Point(50, 50),
                               Color.Red, Color.Yellow);
HatchBrush hatchBrush = new HatchBrush(HatchStyle.DashedVertical,
➥Color.Green, Color.Transparent);
Pen[] pens;

public Form1()
{
    InitializeComponent();

    pens = new Pen[]
    {
        new Pen(Color.Red),
        new Pen(Color.Green, 4),     //width 4 pen
        new Pen(Color.Purple, 2),    //dash-dot pen
        new Pen(gradientBrush, 6),   //gradient pen
        new Pen(gradientBrush,6),    //rounded join and end cap
        new Pen(hatchBrush, 6)       //hatch pen
    };

    pens[2].DashStyle = DashStyle.DashDot;

    pens[4].EndCap = LineCap.Round;
    pens[4].LineJoin = LineJoin.Round;
}

protected override void OnPaint(PaintEventArgs e)
{
    base.OnPaint(e);

    //draw each set of lines in its own "box"
    const int boxWidth = 100;
    const int boxHeight = 100;

    for (int i = 0; i < pens.Length; i++)
    {
        e.Graphics.TranslateTransform(
            (i % 4) * boxWidth,
            (i / 4) * boxHeight);
        e.Graphics.DrawLines(pens[i], points);
        e.Graphics.ResetTransform();
    }
}
```

This code produces the output shown in Figure 17.4.

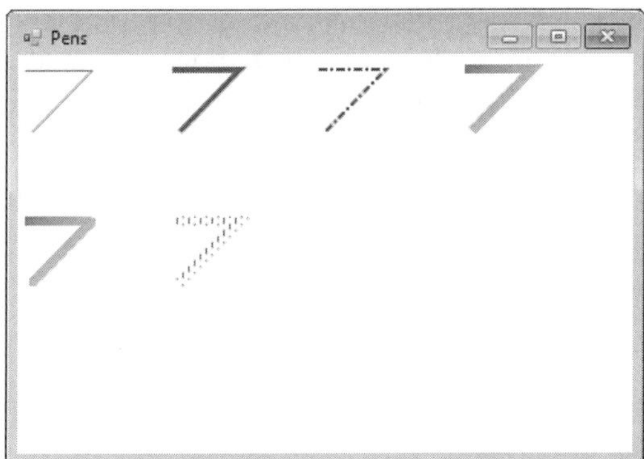

FIGURE 17.4
You can customize many aspects of pens, such as color, thickness, style, join type, and end caps. You can even make a pen take on the aspects of a brush!

NOTE Pens and brushes are GDI objects, which use operating system resources. Therefore, they must be disposed when you're done with them:

```
protected override void Dispose(bool disposing)
{
    if (disposing && (components != null))
    {
        components.Dispose();
        foreach(Pen pen in pens)
        {
            pen.Dispose();
        }
        hatchBrush.Dispose();
        gradientBrush.Dispose();
    }
    base.Dispose(disposing);
}
```

Create Custom Brushes

Scenario/Problem: You need to customize the brush used to fill shapes on the screen, such as specifying a different color or giving it a gradient.

Solution: Like pens, brushes can be extremely customized in color and style. Brushes can be made from hatch patterns, bitmaps, and gradients (see Figure 17.5).

```
Brush[] brushes;

const int boxSize = 175;
Rectangle ellipseRect = new Rectangle(0, 0, boxSize, boxSize);
GraphicsPath path = new GraphicsPath();

public Form1()
{
    InitializeComponent();

    path.AddRectangle(ellipseRect);

    brushes = new Brush[]
    {
        new SolidBrush(Color.Red),
        new HatchBrush(HatchStyle.Cross,
                       Color.Green,
                       Color.Transparent),
        //Elements is an image resource I added to the project
        new TextureBrush(Properties.Resources.Elements),
        //just tell .Net the start color and the
        //end color and it will figure out the rest!
        new LinearGradientBrush(ellipseRect, Color.LightGoldenrodYellow,
                                Color.ForestGreen, 45),
                                new PathGradientBrush(path)
    };

    //path gradient brushes are not as straight forward as others--
    //read more about them in the MSDN docs
    (brushes[4] as PathGradientBrush).SurroundColors =
➥new Color[] { Color.ForestGreen, Color.AliceBlue, Color.Aqua };
    (brushes[4] as PathGradientBrush).CenterColor = Color.Fuchsia;

}

protected override void OnPaint(PaintEventArgs e)
{
    base.OnPaint(e);

    ellipseRect.Inflate(-10, -10);

    for (int i=0;i<brushes.Length;i++)
    {
        e.Graphics.TranslateTransform(
            (i % 3) * boxSize,
```

```
            (i / 3) * boxSize);
        e.Graphics.FillEllipse(brushes[i], ellipseRect);
        e.Graphics.ResetTransform();
    }
}

protected override void Dispose(bool disposing)
{
    if (disposing && (components != null))
    {
        components.Dispose();
        foreach(Brush brush in brushes)
        {
            brush.Dispose();
        }
        path.Dispose();
    }
    base.Dispose(disposing);
}
```

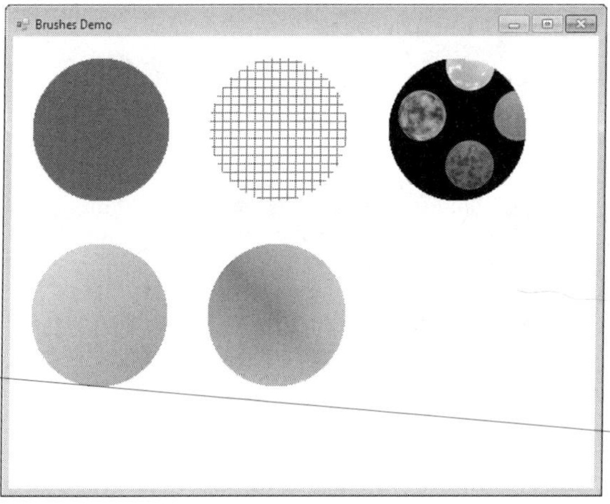

FIGURE 17.5
You can have many types of brushes, including solid colors, hatches, images, and various types of gradients.

Use Transformations

Scenario/Problem: You need to manipulate the location, size, or shape of a large portion of your drawing.

Suppose, for example, you have a line drawing consisting of a thousand points. What if you want to rotate that drawing 30 degrees? How could you do that? Would you change every single point? You could, but I don't recommend it.

Alternatively, suppose you have a shape you want to draw in multiple places on the screen at once. It doesn't make sense to have multiple copies of the object in memory just to draw in different places.

Solution: Both scenarios are easily handled with transformations, which are mathematical ways of manipulating coordinates with matrices. Thankfully, .NET has a lot of built-in functionality that hides much of the complexity of transformations, as shown in the following sections.

Translate

Translation is linearly moving an object. Its size and orientation remain unchanged.

```
Rectangle ellipseRect = new Rectangle(25, 25, 100, 50);

// Translation
// move it 100 pixels down
e.Graphics.TranslateTransform(0, 100);
e.Graphics.FillEllipse(Brushes.Blue, ellipseRect);
e.Graphics.ResetTransform();
```

Rotate

The rotation amount is specified in degrees and is similar in usage to translation.

```
// Rotation, angles are in degrees
e.Graphics.RotateTransform(-15);
e.Graphics.FillEllipse(Brushes.Red, ellipseRect);
e.Graphics.ResetTransform();
```

Translate and Rotate

When you combine transformations, the order is vitally important. Try some experimentation to see the difference.

```
// Translation + Rotation
// notice the order! it's important
e.Graphics.TranslateTransform(100, 100);
e.Graphics.RotateTransform(-15);
e.Graphics.FillEllipse(Brushes.Purple, ellipseRect);
e.Graphics.ResetTransform();
```

Scale

Scaling is just resizing an object along the X and Y dimensions.

```
// Scale
//make it twice as long and 3/4 as wide
e.Graphics.ScaleTransform(2.0f, 0.75f);
e.Graphics.FillEllipse(Brushes.Green, ellipseRect);
e.Graphics.ResetTransform();
```

Shear

All of these transformations are really just matrixes. For a shear transformation, we need to use a matrix directly.

```
// we can also use any arbitrary matrix
// to transform the graphics
Font font = new Font("Verdana", 16.0f);
Matrix matrix = new Matrix();
matrix.Shear(0.5f, 0.25f);
e.Graphics.Transform = matrix;
e.Graphics.DrawString("Hello, Shear", font, Brushes.Black, 0, 0);
e.Graphics.ResetTransform();
```

Figure 17.6 shows the results of all of these transformations.

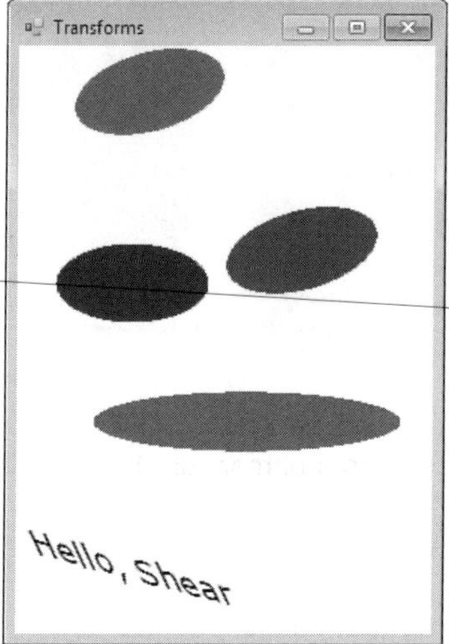

FIGURE 17.6
Transformations can save you a lot of drudgery when manipulating graphics.

Draw Text

Scenario/Problem: You need to draw text on the screen.

Solution: To draw text, you must specify the font and a brush with which to render it.

```
Font _textFont = new Font("Verdana", 18.0f);
//pass in the string you wish to render (in this case,
//the name of the font, followed by the font, a brush, and location
e.Graphics.DrawString(_textFont.Name, _textFont,
                      Brushes.DarkMagenta, 0, 0);
```

Draw Text Diagonally

Scenario/Problem: You need to draw text in any orientation other than horizontal.

Solution: Use transformations to accomplish this:

```
private Font font = new Font("Verdana", 18.0f);
e.Graphics.TranslateTransform(100, 300);
e.Graphics.RotateTransform(15);
e.Graphics.DrawString("My text here", font,
                      Brushes.DarkMagenta, 0, 0);
e.Graphics.ResetTransform();
```

Draw Images

Scenario/Problem: You need to draw an image, such as a bitmap, on the screen.

Solution: .NET provides an almost bewildering array of overloaded methods for drawing an image. Here is a sampling of some common ones:

```
//grab images from embedded resources
Image smallImage = Properties.Resources.Elements_Small;
Image largeImage = Properties.Resources.Elements_Large;
```

```
//draw normally
e.Graphics.DrawImage(smallImage, 10, 10);

//draw resized--interpolating pixels according to the current mode
// there are many algorithms for image resizing
e.Graphics.InterpolationMode =_InterpolationMode.Bicubic;
e.Graphics.DrawImage(smallImage, 250, 100, 400, 400);

//draw a subsection
Rectangle sourceRect = new Rectangle(400,400,200,200);
Rectangle destRect = new Rectangle(10, 200,
                                   sourceRect.Width, sourceRect.Height);
e.Graphics.DrawImage(Properties.Resources.Elements_Large,
                     destRect, sourceRect, GraphicsUnit.Pixel);
```

The sample program, shown in Figure 17.7, lets you choose the resizing interpolation mode so that you can easily see the difference interactively.

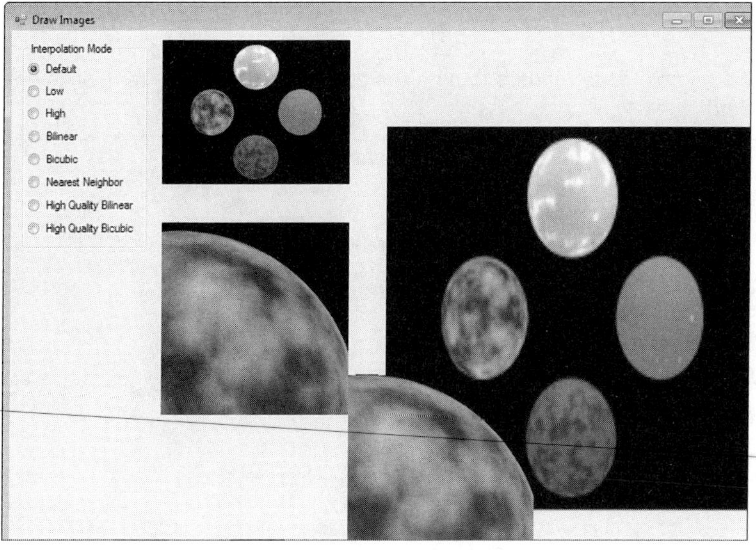

FIGURE 17.7
There are many powerful image-rendering methods available to you.

Draw Transparent Images

Scenario/Problem: You want to draw an image with "holes" that allow the background to show through.

Solution: Notice in Figure 17.7 that one image is painted without the black background, allowing you to see the other images behind it. This is achieved with a transparency key.

```
//draw same subsection and interpret black as transparent
ImageAttributes imageAttributes = new ImageAttributes();
imageAttributes.SetColorKey(Color.Black, Color.Black,
                            ColorAdjustType.Bitmap);
destRect.Offset(200, 150);
e.Graphics.DrawImage(largeImage, destRect, sourceRect.X, sourceRect.Y,
    sourceRect.Width, sourceRect.Height,
    GraphicsUnit.Pixel, imageAttributes);
```

Draw to an Off-Screen Buffer

Scenario/Problem: You want to draw GDI+ primitives to a bitmap for later display, printing, saving, or copying.

Solution: This sample code renders to both the screen and a bitmap for placement on the clipboard:

```
protected override void OnPaint(PaintEventArgs e)
{
    base.OnPaint(e);

    Render(e.Graphics);
}

//can be called with a Graphics object
private void Render(Graphics graphics)
{
    graphics.FillEllipse(Brushes.Red, 10, 10, 100, 50);
}

private void button1_Click(object sender, EventArgs e)
{
    using (Bitmap bitmap =
             new Bitmap(ClientSize.Width, ClientSize.Height))
    using (Graphics graphics = Graphics.FromImage(bitmap))
    {
        Render(graphics);
        Clipboard.SetImage(bitmap);
    }
}
```

See the DrawToBitmap sample in the projects for this chapter for the complete example.

NOTE In some applications, you will find that you need to render output to multiple types of devices. In such cases, you should factor out the code that does the actual drawing into something that can be called independently of the actual output device.

Access a Bitmap's Pixels Directly for Performance

Scenario/Problem: You need to manipulate individual pixels in a bitmap image.

Solution: The `Bitmap` class provides handy `GetPixel()` and `SetPixel()` methods, which are okay for small changes, but if you need to do a large-scale transformation of a bitmap's pixels, you'll need to access the image data directly.

This example shows how to manipulate an image's pixels by copying to a new image and halving the brightness:

```
//pictureBoxSource is a PictureControl that
//contains the image resource
Bitmap sourceImg = new Bitmap(pictureBoxSource.Image);

Bitmap destImg = new Bitmap(sourceImg.Width, sourceImg.Height);

Rectangle dataRect =
    new Rectangle(0,0, sourceImg.Width, sourceImg.Height);
BitmapData sourceData =
    sourceImg.LockBits(dataRect, ImageLockMode.ReadOnly,
➥PixelFormat.Format32bppArgb);
BitmapData destData =
    destImg.LockBits(dataRect, ImageLockMode.WriteOnly,
    PixelFormat.Format32bppArgb);

IntPtr sourcePtr = sourceData.Scan0;
IntPtr destPtr = destData.Scan0;
byte[] buffer = new byte[sourceData.Stride];

for (int row = 0; row < sourceImg.Height; row++)
{
    // yes, we could copy the whole bitmap in one go,
    // but want to demonstrate the point
```

```
    System.Runtime.InteropServices.Marshal.Copy(
        sourcePtr, buffer, 0, sourceData.Stride);

    //fiddle with the bits
    for (int i = 0; i < buffer.Length; i+=4)
    {
        //each pixel is represented by 4 bytes
        //last byte is transparency, which we'll ignore
        buffer[i + 0] /= 2;
        buffer[i + 1] /= 2;
        buffer[i + 2] /= 2;
    }

    System.Runtime.InteropServices.Marshal.Copy(
        buffer, 0, destPtr, destData.Stride);
    sourcePtr = new IntPtr(sourcePtr.ToInt64() + sourceData.Stride);
    destPtr = new IntPtr(destPtr.ToInt64() + destData.Stride);
}
sourceImg.UnlockBits(sourceData);
destImg.UnlockBits(destData);
```

See the BitmapDirect sample project for the full source code. It shows the difference in time to copy and change a bitmap with this method versus using `GetPixel` and `SetPixel`.

What's the difference in performance, you ask? In my informal tests with a 1600×1200 image, using `GetPixel()` and `SetPixel()` took 3 to 5 seconds. Locking the bits and performing the manipulation directly took less than half a second.

> **NOTE** Be careful. Locking bits in memory is not something you want to do haphazardly. When you lock memory, you prevent the .NET memory system from moving it, which can interfere with garbage collection and optimum memory usage. Use it when you need it, but don't keep locked memory around indefinitely.

Draw with Anti-Aliasing

> **Scenario/Problem:** You want to eliminate jagged edges (called the "jaggies") from diagonal and curved lines.

These edges appear because typical output devices are limited-resolution devices that are oriented horizontally and vertically.

Solution: You can easily eliminate most jagged edges by instructing the graphics context to smooth edges. Figure 17.8 shows an enlarged version of this so you can see what is happening:

```
e.Graphics.SmoothingMode = SmoothingMode.HighQuality;
//do your drawing with e.Graphics object
```

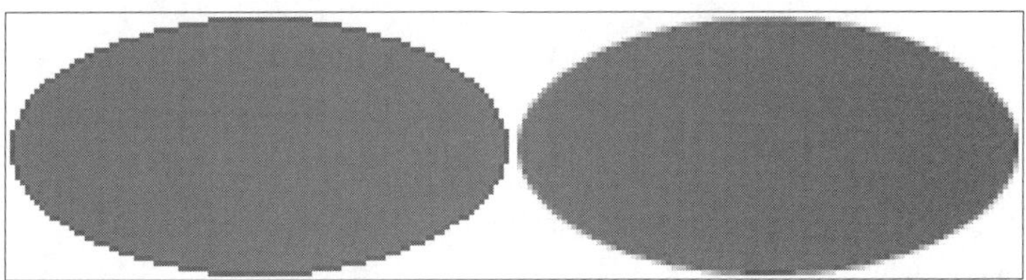

FIGURE 17.8
Anti-aliasing works by blurring the edges by combining colors of pixels with those of their neighbors to achieve a smooth blending effect, as this enlarged comparison shows.

Because text has its own set of issues (such as actually changing the amount of space it takes up, for example), it has a separate setting:

```
//ClearType should look best on an LCD
//You could also choose AntiAlias, or other options
e.Graphics.TextRenderingHint = TextRenderingHint. ClearTypeGridFit;
```

The DrawingDemo (refer to Figure 17.3) sample project allows you to see the differences between the various anti-aliasing options for both graphics and text.

Draw Flicker-Free

Scenario/Problem: Drawing the screen takes too long and is causing flicker.

Solution: The `Control` class defines a protected property called `DoubleBuffered`. It is set to `false` by default. To use it, you must derive your own control from `Control` (or another control that is in turn derived from `Control`) and set it to `true`.

```
class DrawPanel : Panel
{
    ...
    //make this public to expose it to configuration in the UI
    public new bool DoubleBuffered
    {
        get
```

```
        {
            return base.DoubleBuffered;
        }
        set
        {
            base.DoubleBuffered = value;
        }
    }
    ...
}
```

The difference in drawing behavior is quite dramatic, as you'll see if you run the FlickerFree sample code.

NOTE I have had very good results with the built-in `DoubleBuffered` capability, but if for some reason you want to control the process, you can always implement it yourself by using the technique described in "Draw to an Off-Screen Buffer" earlier in the chapter.

Resize an Image

Scenario/Problem: You need to resize an image.

Solution: By combining information from the preceding sections about drawing images and drawing to a bitmap, you can easily resize an image.

```
Bitmap resizedBmp = null;
try
{
    Image image = Image.FromFile(args[0]);

    resizedBmp = new Bitmap(image, new Size(100, 100));

    resizedBmp.Save(@"C:\NewImage.bmp", image.RawFormat);
}
finally
{
    if (resizedBmp!=null)
    {
        resizedBmp.Dispose();
    }
}
```

NOTE There are many algorithms for image resizing, and if you want something other than whatever `Bitmap` does, you have to implement the algorithm yourself with direct manipulation of the bitmap.

Create a Thumbnail of an Image

Scenario/Problem: You want to quickly generate a thumbnail of an image, possibly asynchronously (for use in a web page, for example). Thumbnails don't have to be as high quality as a resized image.

Solution: Use `Image`'s `GetThumbnailImage` method.

This sample code figures out what the correct proportional size should be, given a maximum size:

```
static void Main(string[] args)
{
    /* Parse arguments ... */
    int maxSize = 100;
    string outputFile = @"C:\output_thumb.bmp";
    try
    {
        Image image = Image.FromFile(args[0]);

        Size size = CalculateThumbSize(image.Size, maxSize);

        Image thumbnail = image.GetThumbnailImage(
                    size.Width, size.Height,
           ThumbnailAbortCallback, IntPtr.Zero);
        thumbnail.Save(outputFile);

    }
    catch (OutOfMemoryException ex)
    {
        Console.WriteLine(ex);
    }
    catch (FileNotFoundException ex)
    {
        Console.WriteLine(ex);
    }
}
```

```
//called by image processor to know if it should stop the resizing
//could be useful with large images
private static bool ThumbnailAbortCallback()
{
    return false;
}

//get the proportional size of the resulting image,
//based on the maxSize the user passed in
private static Size CalculateThumbSize(Size size, int maxSize)
{
    if (size.Width > size.Height)
    {
        return new Size(maxSize,
➥(int)(((double)size.Height / (double)size.Width) * maxSize));
    }
    else
    {
        return new Size(
➥(int)(((double)size.Width / (double)size.Height) * maxSize), maxSize);
    }
}
```

Take a Multiscreen Capture

Scenario/Problem: You need to capture the contents of all screens in a multimonitor environment. (Taking screenshots is an important part of many logging systems—both legal and illegal!—as well as fodder for screen savers.)

Solution: .NET makes the task of taking a multiscreen capture quite easy. You just need to figure out the bounds of each screen and then tell the Graphics object to copy pixels from those bounds.

```
Image _image = null;
private void buttonCapture_Click(object sender, EventArgs e)
{
    this.Visible = false;
    //wait for window to be hidden so that we don't see our
    //own window in the screen capture
    Thread.Sleep(500);
    _image = CaptureScreen();
    this.Visible = true;
}
```

```
private Image CaptureScreen()
{
    //combine bounds of all screens
    Rectangle bounds = GetScreenBounds();

    Bitmap bitmap = new Bitmap(bounds.Width, bounds.Height);
    using (Graphics graphics = Graphics.FromImage(bitmap))
    {
        graphics.CopyFromScreen(bounds.Location, new Point(0, 0),
                                bounds.Size);
    }
    return bitmap;
}

private Rectangle GetScreenBounds()
{
    Rectangle rect = new Rectangle();
    foreach (Screen screen in Screen.AllScreens)
    {
        rect = Rectangle.Union(rect, screen.Bounds);
    }
    return rect;
}
```

Figure 17.9 shows the ScreenCapture utility before capture.

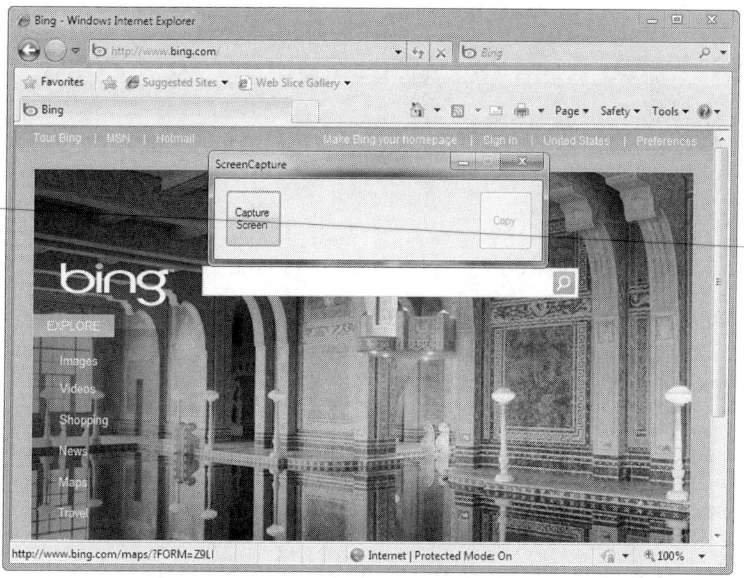

FIGURE 17.9
A view of our simple screen capture application before taking clicking capture.

Figure 17.10 shows the resulting image. Notice that the utility is not visible because we hid it before taking the capture.

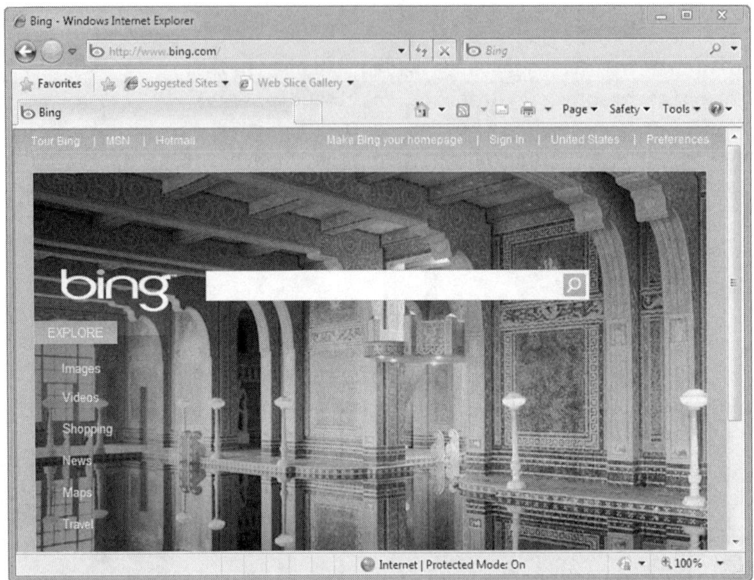

FIGURE 17.10
The image that results from our capture.

Get the Distance from the Mouse Cursor to a Point

Scenario/Problem: You need the distance in pixels from the mouse cursor to an arbitrary point on the screen.

Solution: This is just your old algebra class's Pythagorean theorem in action:

```
double DistanceFromCenter(Point location)
{
    Point center = new Point(ClientSize.Width / 2,
                             ClientSize.Height / 2);

    /*
     * Distance calculation is basically the Pythagorean theorem:
     *
     * d = sqrt(dx^2 + dy^2) where dx and dy are the
     * differences between the points
     */
```

```
    int dx = location.X - center.X;
    int dy = location.Y - center.Y;
    return Math.Sqrt(dx * dx + dy * dy);
}
```

See the HitTesting sample project for this chapter to see this and the following solutions in action.

Determine if a Point Is Inside a Rectangle

Scenario/Problem: You need to determine if the user clicked inside a rectangle.

Solution: The Rectangle struct provides the Contains method, which can do this. However, if you need to do this on your own, the code is simple:

```
class MyRectangle{
    private int _left, _top, _width, _height;

    //...

    public override bool HitTest(System.Drawing.Point location)
    {
        return location.X >= _left && location.X <= _left + _width
            && location.Y >= _top && location.Y <= _top + _height;
    }
}
```

Determine if a Point Is Inside a Circle

Scenario/Problem: You need to determine if the user clicked inside a circle on the screen.

Solution: This is a specific application of the distance-to-a-point calculation discussed previously.

```
class MyCircle{
    private Point _center;
    private int _radius;
```

```
    //...

    public override bool HitTest(System.Drawing.Point location)
    {
        /* X^2 + Y^2 = R^2 is the formula for a circle.
         * where R is the radius
         * A point is in the circle if X^2 + Y^2 <= R^2
         *
         * This formula assumes the circle's location is 0,0
         * so be sure to normalize to that
         */
        Point normalized = new Point(location.X - _center.X,
                                     location.Y - _center.Y);

        return (normalized.X * normalized.X +
               normalized.Y * normalized.Y)
               <= (_radius * _radius);
    }
}
```

NOTE Just looking at the formula for a circle, you might be tempted to call `Math.Sqrt` on the left side (and thus turn it into the Pythagorean theorem) rather than square the radius. However, which do you think is faster—a square root function or a multiplication? The answer is that multiplication is usually a *few orders of magnitude* faster than most square root functions.

Graphics code is often full of optimizations like this to avoid unnecessary processing cycles.

Determine if a Point Is Inside an Ellipse

Scenario/Problem: You need to determine if the user clicked inside an ellipse.

Solution: This is similar to the circle hit test, but it uses a more general formula:

```
class MyEllipse
{
    private Point _center;
    private int _xRadius;
    private int _yRadius;
```

```
    //...

    public override bool HitTest(System.Drawing.Point location)
    {
        if (_xRadius <= 0.0 || _yRadius <= 0.0)
            return false;
        /* This is a more general form of the circle equation
         *
         * X^2/a^2 + Y^2/b^2 <= 1
         */

        Point normalized = new Point(location.X - _center.X,
                                     location.Y - _center.Y);

        return ((double)(normalized.X * normalized.X)
                / (_xRadius * _xRadius)) +
➥((double)(normalized.Y * normalized.Y) / (_yRadius * _yRadius))
            <= 1.0;
    }
}
```

Determine if Two Rectangles Intersect

Scenario/Problem: You need to determine if two rectangles intersect each other.

Solution: The `Rectangle` class provides `IntersectsWith()`, which you can use as follows:

```
Rectangle rect1 = new Rectangle(0, 0, 100, 50);
Rectangle rect2 = new Rectangle(25, 25, 100, 50);

bool intersects = rect1.IntersectsWith(rect2);
```

If you want to actually get the rectangle that describes the intersection of two others, you can use the following:

```
Rectangle rect3 = rect1.Intersect(rect2);
```

Print and Print Preview

Scenario/Problem: You need to print content from your application.

Solution: Printing in .NET is similar to just displaying on the screen. Here's an example that uses an array of `Process` objects as a data source to print from.

We first derive from `PrintDocument`:

```
class ProcessPrintDocument : PrintDocument
{
    private Font _pageHeaderFont, _rowHeaderFont, _rowTextFont;
    float _pageHeaderHeight, _rowHeaderHeight, _rowHeight;

    bool _disposed = false;

    int _currentPage = 0;
    int _currentRow = 0;

    const int ColumnWidth = 150;

    private IList<Process> _processes;

    public ProcessPrintDocument(IList<Process> processes)
    {
        _processes = processes;

        _pageHeaderFont = new Font("Arial", 14.0f);
        _rowHeaderFont = new Font("Arial", 10.0f,
                             FontStyle.Bold | FontStyle.Underline);
        _rowTextFont = new Font("Verdana", 10.0f);
    }

    protected override void Dispose(bool disposing)
    {
        if (!_disposed)
        {
            if (disposing)
            {
                _pageHeaderFont.Dispose();
                _rowHeaderFont.Dispose();
                _rowTextFont.Dispose();
            }
```

```
            base.Dispose(disposing);
        }
        _disposed = true;
    }

    protected override void OnBeginPrint(PrintEventArgs e)
    {
        base.OnBeginPrint(e);
        //do any initial setup here
    }

    protected override void OnEndPrint(PrintEventArgs e)
    {
      base.OnEndPrint(e);
        //do any initial finish work here
    }

    protected override void OnPrintPage(PrintPageEventArgs e)
    {
        base.OnPrintPage(e);

        _pageHeaderHeight = e.Graphics.MeasureString("A",
                                _pageHeaderFont).Height;
        _rowHeaderHeight = e.Graphics.MeasureString("A",
                                _rowHeaderFont).Height;
        _rowHeight = e.Graphics.MeasureString("A",
                                _rowTextFont).Height;

        _currentPage++;

        PrintPageHeader(e);

        PrintContent(e);

        PrintPageFooter(e);

        //this is important! You won't get more
        //pages if you don't set this.
        //Also important to set it to false at
        //some point, so you don't print forever!
        e.HasMorePages = (_currentRow < _processes.Count - 1);
    }

    private void PrintPageHeader(PrintPageEventArgs e)
    {
```

```
    //find where we should print our header
    Rectangle headerRect = new Rectangle(e.PageBounds.Left,
                                         e.PageBounds.Top,
        e.PageBounds.Right - e.PageBounds.Left,
        e.MarginBounds.Top - e.PageBounds.Top);
    if (headerRect.Height < 50)
    {
        headerRect.Height = 50;
    }
    StringFormat headerFormat = new StringFormat();
    headerFormat.LineAlignment = StringAlignment.Center;
    headerFormat.Alignment = StringAlignment.Center;

    string headerText = string.Format("Processes - page {0}",
                                      _currentPage);
    e.Graphics.DrawString(headerText,
                          _pageHeaderFont,
                          Brushes.Black,
     headerRect, headerFormat);
}

private void PrintPageFooter(PrintPageEventArgs e)
{
    //let's draw an image just because we can
    PointF location = new PointF(e.MarginBounds.Left,
                                 e.MarginBounds.Bottom);
    int height = e.PageBounds.Bottom - e.MarginBounds.Bottom;
    RectangleF rect = new RectangleF(location,
             new Size (e.MarginBounds.Width, height));
    //add an image to your project's resources called SampleImage
    e.Graphics.DrawImage(Properties.Resources.SampleImage, rect);
}

private void PrintContent(PrintPageEventArgs e)
{
    PointF currentLoc = new Point(e.MarginBounds.Left,
                                  e.MarginBounds.Top);

    PrintRowHeader(e, ref currentLoc);
    bool lastRow = false, lastRowOnPage = false;
    while (!lastRow && !lastRowOnPage)
    {
        currentLoc.Y += _rowHeight;
        currentLoc.X = e.MarginBounds.Left;
        lastRow = (_currentRow == _processes.Count - 1);
```

```
            lastRowOnPage =
             (currentLoc.Y + _rowHeight > e.MarginBounds.Bottom);
            if (currentLoc.Y + _rowHeight < e.MarginBounds.Bottom)
            {
                PrintRow(e, _currentRow, ref currentLoc);
                _currentRow++;
            }
        }
    }

    private void PrintRowHeader(PrintPageEventArgs e,
                                ref PointF currentLoc)
    {
        string[] columnHeaders = { "Process", "PID",
                                   "Working Set", "Base Priority" };

        foreach (string header in columnHeaders)
        {
            RectangleF rect = new RectangleF(currentLoc.X, currentLoc.Y,
                      ColumnWidth, _rowHeight);
            e.Graphics.DrawString(header, _rowHeaderFont,
                                  Brushes.Black, rect);
            currentLoc.X += ColumnWidth;
        }
    }

    private void PrintRow(PrintPageEventArgs e,
                          int _currentRow,
                          ref PointF currentLoc)
    {
        Process proc = _processes[_currentRow];
        RectangleF destRect = new RectangleF(currentLoc,
                 new SizeF(ColumnWidth, _rowHeight));

e.Graphics.DrawString(_currentRow.ToString()+" " + proc.ProcessName,
                 _rowTextFont, Brushes.Black, destRect);
        destRect.Offset(ColumnWidth, 0);

        e.Graphics.DrawString(proc.Id.ToString(),
                              _rowTextFont,
                              Brushes.Black,
                              destRect);
        destRect.Offset(ColumnWidth, 0);
```

```
        e.Graphics.DrawString(proc.WorkingSet64.ToString("N0"),
                               _rowTextFont,
                   Brushes.Black, destRect);
        destRect.Offset(ColumnWidth, 0);

        e.Graphics.DrawString(proc.BasePriority.ToString(),
                               _rowTextFont,
                  Brushes.Black, destRect);
        destRect.Offset(ColumnWidth, 0);
    }
}
```

Printing and Print Preview are now merely a matter of passing this document class to the appropriate .NET Framework classes:

```
private void buttonPrint_Click(object sender, EventArgs e)
{
    ProcessPrintDocument printDoc =
        new ProcessPrintDocument(Process.GetProcesses());
    PrintDialog pd = new PrintDialog();
    pd.Document = printDoc;
    pd.UseEXDialog = true;

    if (pd.ShowDialog() == DialogResult.OK)
    {
        printDoc.Print();
    }
}

private void buttonPrintPreview_Click(object sender, EventArgs e)
{
    ProcessPrintDocument printDoc =
        new ProcessPrintDocument(Process.GetProcesses());
    PrintPreviewDialog dlg = new PrintPreviewDialog();
    dlg.Document = printDoc;
    dlg.ShowDialog(this);
}
```

Figure 17.11 shows the Print Preview window from this sample application.

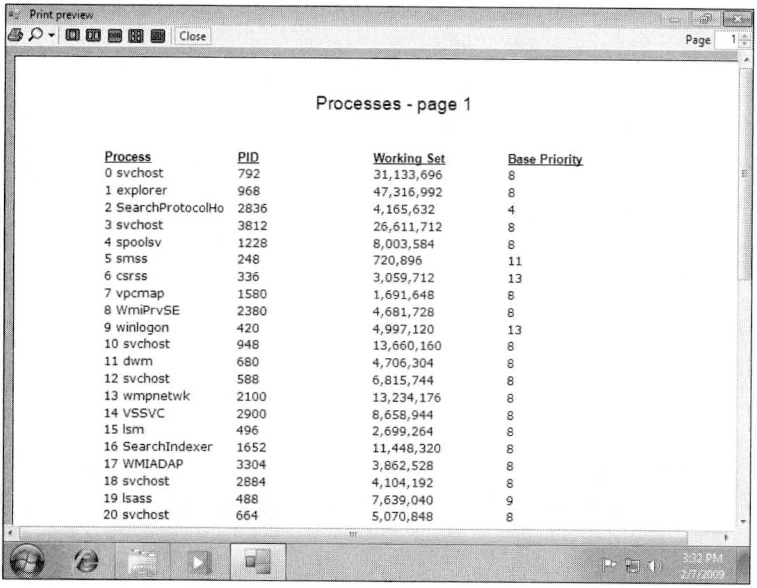

Print preview

Close Page 1

Processes - page 1

Process	PID	Working Set	Base Priority
0 svchost	792	31,133,696	8
1 explorer	968	47,316,992	8
2 SearchProtocolHo	2836	4,165,632	4
3 svchost	3812	26,611,712	8
4 spoolsv	1228	8,003,584	8
5 smss	248	720,896	11
6 csrss	336	3,059,712	13
7 vpcmap	1580	1,691,648	8
8 WmiPrvSE	2380	4,681,728	8
9 winlogon	420	4,997,120	13
10 svchost	948	13,660,160	8
11 dwm	680	4,706,304	8
12 svchost	588	6,815,744	8
13 wmpnetwk	2100	13,234,176	8
14 VSSVC	2900	8,658,944	8
15 lsm	496	2,699,264	8
16 SearchIndexer	1652	11,448,320	8
17 WMIADAP	3304	3,862,528	8
18 svchost	2884	4,104,192	8
19 lsass	488	7,639,040	9
20 svchost	664	5,070,848	8

3:32 PM 2/7/2009

FIGURE 17.11
Print Preview is easy to accomplish in C#.

CHAPTER 18

WPF

IN THIS CHAPTER

- Show a Window
- Choose a Layout Method
- Add a Menu Bar
- Add a Status Bar
- Add a Toolbar
- Use Standard Commands
- Use Custom Commands
- Enable and Disable Commands
- Expand and Collapse a Group of Controls
- Respond to Events
- Separate Look from Functionality
- Use Triggers to Change Styles at Runtime
- Format Values During Data Binding
- Convert Values to a Different Type During Data Binding
- Bind to a Collection
- Specify How Bound Data Is Displayed
- Define the Look of Controls with Templates
- Animate Element Properties
- Render 3D Geometry
- Put Video on a 3D Surface
- Put Interactive Controls onto a 3D Surface
- Use WPF in a WinForms App
- Use WinForms in a WPF Application

First, there was plain-old Win32: C interfaces and a lot of work to get anything done. MFC wrapped up some of the complexity into an object-oriented framework, but it was a fairly thin layer on top of Win32. .NET's Windows Forms was a more elegant attempt at abstracting away the old C interfaces, but they were still there somewhere.

Windows Presentation Foundation (WPF) throws all of that away and gives you a completely new framework from which to build user interfaces. It is designed to be hardware-accelerated to take advantage of today's modern graphics cards.

As with any new framework, there is a lot to learn. However, especially in the case of WPF, the payoff is huge. You can do things in WPF with little effort that would previously require you to learn a specialized graphics API, such as DirectX.

WPF is nearly boundless in the amount you could learn, but the examples and tips in this chapter will get you well on your way to creating astounding interfaces in far less time than with the older framework.

Show a Window

Scenario/Problem: You need to display a simple window in WPF. As with most applications, you usually need to start with a window.

Solution: Although most things in WPF can be expressed as either XAML or code, most examples will use XAML as much as possible.

Here's the code in Window1.xaml:

```
<Window x:Class="WpfTextEditor.Window1"
    xmlns="http://schemas.microsoft.com/winfx/2006/xaml/presentation"
    xmlns:x="http://schemas.microsoft.com/winfx/2006/xaml"
    Title="WPF Text Editor" Height="300" Width="300"
    >
</Window>
```

The corresponding code in Window1.xaml.cs is even simpler:

```
public partial class Window1 : Window
{
    public Window1()
    {
        InitializeComponent();
    }
}
```

The base Windows class's `InitializeComponent` method will do the XAML parsing and present the window.

This and the next few sections build up a simple WPF-based text editor, complete with menu, toolbar, status bar, and commands.

Choose a Layout Method

Scenario/Problem: You need to position controls in your window.

Solution: WPF is all about automatic layout. You should rarely need to manually position UI elements. This makes it much easier to deal with dynamic content and internationalization, for example. WPF provides a number of layout controls for you, which are detailed in Table 18.1. You should rarely need to build your own.

TABLE 18.1 **WPF Layout Controls**

Name	Description
DockPanel	Elements can be attached to any of the four sides, and the last element takes up the rest of the space. Popular for top-level window layout.
Grid	Each child specifies a cell it should appear in, including spanning multiple cells. A very good option for laying out elements in an ordered, table-like manner.
Uniform Grid	Similar to Grid, but each cell is the same size.
StackPanel	Orders elements one after the other, either horizontally or vertically.
WrapPanel	A little like StackPanel, but wraps around to the beginning when the end of the layout space is reached.
Canvas	Allows explicit positioning of elements. This is most like the old way of doing things. It allows absolute control but does not give you the benefits many of the other layout controls do.

Nearly any interface can be composed of combinations of these layouts. The examples in this chapter use Grid, StackPanel, and DockPanel.

Add a Menu Bar

Scenario/Problem: You need to add a menu bar to a WPF window.

Solution: Many WPF examples show off the 3D capabilities, or its advanced data-binding features, but WPF excels at standard interfaces (menu bar, toolbar, status bar) just as easily, so we'll start there before moving on to the more "wow" capabilities.

Let's add a simple menu definition to the bare window:

```
<Window x:Class="WpfTextEditor.Window1"
    xmlns="http://schemas.microsoft.com/winfx/2006/xaml/presentation"
    xmlns:x="http://schemas.microsoft.com/winfx/2006/xaml"
    Title="WPF Text Editor" Height="300" Width="300"
    xmlns:local="clr-namespace:WpfTextEditor">

    <!-- The DockPanel takes up the whole window
         and all elements go inside it. -->
    <DockPanel Name="dockPanel1" VerticalAlignment="Stretch"
➥HorizontalAlignment="Stretch">
        <Menu DockPanel.Dock="Top" Height="Auto">
            <MenuItem Header="_File">
                <MenuItem Header="_Exit"/>
            </MenuItem>
            <MenuItem Header="_Edit">
                <MenuItem Header="_Copy" />
                <MenuItem Header="C_ut" />
                <MenuItem Header="_Paste" />
            </MenuItem>
            <MenuItem Header="_View">
                <MenuItem  Header="_Wordwrap" IsCheckable="True"
                           Name="menuItemWordWrap" />
            </MenuItem>
        </Menu>
        <TextBox AcceptsReturn="True" SpellCheck.IsEnabled="True"
                 Name="textBox"
                 HorizontalScrollBarVisibility="Auto"
                 VerticalScrollBarVisibility="Auto">
        </TextBox>
    </DockPanel>
</Window>
```

NOTE Note the underscores (_) in front of some of the letters in the menu. These indicate that the following character should be a shortcut character. In Win32-style programming, you would use an ampersand (&), but that has a special meaning in XML (of which XAML is derivative), so the underscore is used instead.

This menu doesn't really do anything except be visible, so let's add a few more UI elements and then hook everything up with commands.

Add a Status Bar

Scenario/Problem: You need to add a status bar to the bottom of a WPF window.

Solution: The StatusBar can easily be docked to the bottom of the DockPanel, as shown in this example:

```
<Window x:Class="WpfTextEditor.Window1"
    ...
    <DockPanel Name="dockPanel1" VerticalAlignment="Stretch"
➥HorizontalAlignment="Stretch">
        <Menu DockPanel.Dock="Top" Height="Auto">
       ...
        </Menu>
        <StatusBar DockPanel.Dock="Bottom">
            <TextBlock><TextBlock
➥Text="{Binding ElementName=textBox, Path=Text.Length}"/>
➥characters</TextBlock>
        </StatusBar>
       ...
    </DockPanel>
</Window>
```

The StatusBar contains a TextBlock that binds to the Text's `Length` property of the TextBox. Data binding is discussed later in this chapter.

NOTE One of the great powers of WPF is that because it's not tied to Win32 in any way, you have a lot more freedom over layout. You can make your StatusBar contain a button, a menu, or a custom control if you want. The layout system is completely flexible. You can embed text boxes in buttons, and movies into check boxes (if you wanted to do such an odd thing), among many, many other things.

Add a Toolbar

Scenario/Problem: You want to add toolbar to a WPF window.

Solution: Toolbars are the same concept as in Windows Forms but come with the flexibility inherent in all WPF controls:

```
<Window x:Class="WpfTextEditor.Window1"
    ...
    <DockPanel Name="dockPanel1" VerticalAlignment="Stretch"
➥HorizontalAlignment="Stretch">
        <Menu DockPanel.Dock="Top" Height="Auto">
        ...
        </Menu>
        <ToolBarTray DockPanel.Dock="Top">
            <ToolBar >
                <Button >
                        <Image Source="Resources\Copy.png"
                               Opacity="1" />
                </Button>
                <!-- On a toolbar, CheckBox will appear
                     as a toggle button -->
                <!-- Bind the checked state to the
                     menu item's check state -->
                <CheckBox IsChecked="{Binding Mode=TwoWay,
                                  ElementName=menuItemWordWrap,
                               Path=IsChecked}" >
                        <Image Source="Resources\WordWrap.png"
                               OpacityMask="White" />
                </CheckBox>
            </ToolBar>
        </ToolBarTray>
        <StatusBar DockPanel.Dock="Bottom">
        ...
    </DockPanel>
</Window>
```

The toolbar is docked to the top, and because it comes after the menu, it will appear right below it.

Use Standard Commands

Scenario/Problem: You want to respond to a command from a menu, toolbar, or keystroke.

Solution: WPF ships with a number of standard command handlers that work with the standard controls. For example, associating a Copy menu item with the built-in Copy command automatically enables the command when the focus is in a TextBox.

```
<Window x:Class="WpfTextEditor.Window1"
    ... >
    <DockPanel Name="dockPanel1" VerticalAlignment="Stretch"
➥HorizontalAlignment="Stretch">
        <Menu DockPanel.Dock="Top" Height="Auto">
            ...
            <MenuItem Header="_Edit">
                <MenuItem Header="_Copy" Command="Copy"/>
                <MenuItem Header="_Cut" Command="Cut"/>
                <MenuItem Header="_Paste" Command="Paste"/>
            </MenuItem>
            ...
        </Menu>
        <ToolBarTray DockPanel.Dock="Top">
            <ToolBar >
                <Button Command="ApplicationCommands.Copy">
                        <Image Source="Resources\Copy.png"
                              Opacity="1" />
                </Button>
                ...
            </ToolBar>
        </ToolBarTray>
        ...
    </DockPanel>
</Window>
```

Use Custom Commands

Scenario/Problem: You need to create your own, application-specific commands.

Solution: Commands are commonly grouped into static classes for easy reference. Here, we define two commands:

```
public class WpfTextEditorCommands
{
    public static RoutedUICommand ExitCommand;
    public static RoutedUICommand WordWrapCommand;

    static WpfTextEditorCommands()
    {
        InputGestureCollection exitInputs =
               new InputGestureCollection();
        exitInputs.Add(new KeyGesture(Key.F4, ModifierKeys.Alt));
```

```
        ExitCommand = new RoutedUICommand("Exit application",
            "ExitApplication",
            typeof(WpfTextEditorCommands), exitInputs);

        WordWrapCommand = new RoutedUICommand("Word wrap", "WordWrap",
            typeof(WpfTextEditorCommands));
    }
}
```

These commands can now be used in command bindings and attached to event handlers:

```
public partial class Window1 : Window
{
    public Window1()
    {
        InitializeComponent();

        //setup handlers for our custom commands
        CommandBinding cmdBindingExit = new
➥CommandBinding(WpfTextEditorCommands.ExitCommand);
        cmdBindingExit.Executed += new
➥ExecutedRoutedEventHandler(cmdBindingExit_Executed);

        CommandBinding cmdBindingWordWrap = new
➥CommandBinding(WpfTextEditorCommands.WordWrapCommand);
        cmdBindingWordWrap.Executed += new
➥ExecutedRoutedEventHandler(cmdBindingWordWrap_Executed);

        this.CommandBindings.Add(cmdBindingExit);
        this.CommandBindings.Add(cmdBindingWordWrap);
    }

    void cmdBindingWordWrap_Executed(object sender,
                                     ExecutedRoutedEventArgs e)
    {
        textBox.TextWrapping =
           ((textBox.TextWrapping == TextWrapping.NoWrap) ?
               TextWrapping.Wrap : TextWrapping.NoWrap);
    }

    void cmdBindingExit_Executed(object sender, ExecutedRoutedEventArgs e)
    {
        Application.Current.Shutdown();
    }
}
```

And the XAML to hook them up is as follows:

```
<Window x:Class="WpfTextEditor.Window1"
    ... >
    <DockPanel Name="dockPanel1" VerticalAlignment="Stretch"
                                 HorizontalAlignment="Stretch">
        <Menu DockPanel.Dock="Top" Height="Auto">
            <MenuItem Header="_File">
                <MenuItem Header="_Exit"
                   Command="local:WpfTextEditorCommands.ExitCommand"/>
            </MenuItem>
            ...
            <MenuItem Header="_View">
                <MenuItem  Header="_Wordwrap" IsCheckable="True"
                           Name="menuItemWordWrap"
                  Command="local:WpfTextEditorCommands.WordWrapCommand"/>
            </MenuItem>
        </Menu>
        <ToolBarTray DockPanel.Dock="Top">
            <ToolBar >
                ...
                <CheckBox IsChecked="{Binding Mode=TwoWay,
                                      ElementName=menuItemWordWrap,
                              Path=IsChecked}"
                  Command="local:WpfTextEditorCommands.WordWrapCommand">
                        <Image Source="Resources\WordWrap.png"
                               OpacityMask="White" />
                </CheckBox>
            </ToolBar>
        </ToolBarTray>
        ...
    </DockPanel>
</Window>
```

Our nearly complete application, shown in Figure 18.1, requires little effort to implement but demonstrates some of WPF's powerful techniques, such as data binding and commands.

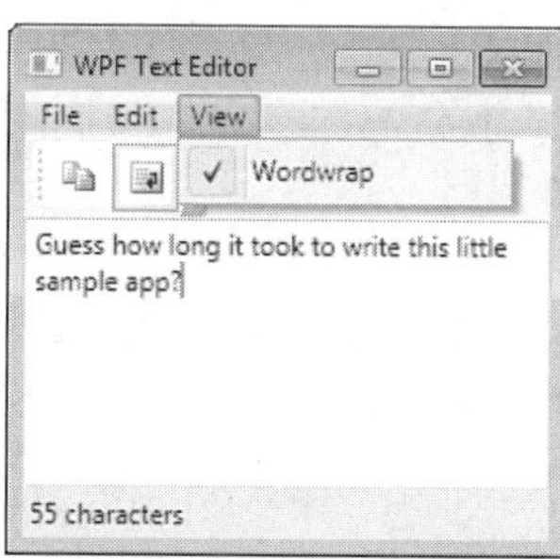

FIGURE 18.1
Our nearly complete application.

Enable and Disable Commands

Scenario/Problem: You need to selectively enable and disable commands, depending on the state of your application.

Solution: To complete this basic editor, let's give it the dubious feature of disabling the Exit command if text has been entered (see Figure 18.2).

```
public partial class Window1 : Window
{
    public Window1()
    {
        InitializeComponent();

        //setup handlers for our custom commands
        CommandBinding cmdBindingExit =
            new CommandBinding(WpfTextEditorCommands.ExitCommand);
        cmdBindingExit.Executed +=
            new ExecutedRoutedEventHandler(cmdBindingExit_Executed);
        cmdBindingExit.CanExecute +=
            new CanExecuteRoutedEventHandler(cmdBindingExit_CanExecute);

        //...
    }

    void cmdBindingExit_CanExecute(object sender,
                                   CanExecuteRoutedEventArgs e)
    {
        e.CanExecute = textBox.Text.Length == 0;
    }
}
```

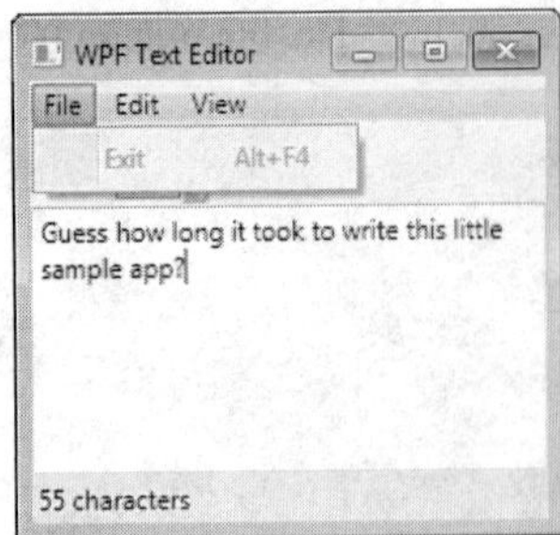

FIGURE 18.2
Disabling a command automatically grays out menu items and disables toolbar buttons.

Expand and Collapse a Group of Controls

Scenario/Problem: You have a group of controls that you want to be able to collapse when not in use.

Solution: An Expander is similar to a GroupBox in that it lets you group related elements under a common header. An Expander, however, also allows you to collapse the group to save UI space.

Here is one of the Expander elements from the ImageViewer sample app (see Figure 18.3):

```
<Expander Header="Image Info" IsExpanded="True" x:Name="imageInfoGroup">
    <Grid DockPanel.Dock="Left">
        <Grid.ColumnDefinitions>
            <ColumnDefinition/>
            <ColumnDefinition/>
        </Grid.ColumnDefinitions>
        <Grid.RowDefinitions>
            <RowDefinition/>
            <RowDefinition/>
            <RowDefinition/>
        </Grid.RowDefinitions>
        <Label Grid.Row="0" Grid.Column="0">Filename</Label>
        <TextBox IsReadOnly="True" Grid.Row="0" Grid.Column="1"
                 Text="{Binding Path=FileName, Mode=OneWay}"/>
        <Label Grid.Row="1" Grid.Column="0">Width</Label>
        <TextBox IsReadOnly="True" Grid.Row="1" Grid.Column="1"
                 Text="{Binding Path=Width,
                               Mode=OneWay,
                               Converter={StaticResource
➥formattingConverter}, ConverterParameter=\{0:N0\}}"/>
        <Label Grid.Row="2" Grid.Column="0">Height</Label>
        <TextBox IsReadOnly="True" Grid.Row="2" Grid.Column="1"
                 Text="{Binding Path=Height, Mode=OneWay,
                       Converter={StaticResource formattingConverter},
➥ConverterParameter=\{0:N0\}}"/>
    </Grid>
</Expander>
```

FIGURE 18.3
An Expander element allows you to easily group and hide related child elements.

Respond to Events

Scenario/Problem: You need to respond to WPF events

Solution: The ImageViewer example defines two RadioButton elements. The `RadioButton` class has a `Checked` event. To assign an event handler in XAML, you can merely assign the name of the function to the event's name:

```
<RadioButton Content="No caption" IsChecked="True"
             Checked="OnTemplateOptionChecked"
➥Name="radioButtonNoCaption" FontStyle="Normal" />
<RadioButton Content="With Caption" IsChecked="False"
             Checked="OnTemplateOptionChecked"
➥Name="radioButtonWithCaption" />
```

The event handler looks quite similar to ones in standard .NET event handling:

```
private void OnTemplateOptionChecked(object sender, RoutedEventArgs e)
{
    /* We'll add a method body below in the section on control templates
*/
}
```

NOTE WPF elements use RoutedEvents, which are like regular .NET events with a bunch of features added onto them. They are required because WPF elements can have many layers of embedding. For example, if you embed a StackPanel, a TextBlock, and an Image inside a button and you click on the image, you still want it to seem to your application like a button was clicked, not the image.

RoutedEvents come in a few flavors: direct, bubbling, and tunneling.

Direct events are similar to .NET events: Only the source element itself can call event handlers.

Bubbling events are the most common in the WPF UI. The event starts with the source element and "bubbles" up to its parent, and its parent in turn, and so on.

Tunneling events start at the element root and travel downward to the source element.

Separate Look from Functionality

Scenario/Problem: You want to separate the look of a control from what it does and be able to change the look independently.

Solution: The Web introduced the concept of separating visual style from functionality to many developers. WPF uses the same idea with its powerful style system.

Styles are resources that can be defined in dedicated resource files or in an element's own resource section.

```
<Window x:Class="ImageViewer.Window1"
...
    >
    <Window.Resources>
        <Style TargetType="{x:Type Label}">
            <Setter Property="FontSize" Value="12.0" />
        </Style>
    </Window.Resources>
    ...
</Window>
```

This simple style merely sets the FontSize property of a Label to 12.

NOTE Because the Style in this example specifies a TargetType but does not specify a name, it applies to all Label elements in its scope. You could alternatively name the style with <Style x:Key="MyStyle" ... /> and apply it to a specific Label with <Label Style="{StaticResource MyStyle}" ... />.

Use Triggers to Change Styles at Runtime

Scenario/Problem: You want events in the UI to cause an element's style to change at runtime.

Solution: Triggers are a powerful functionality that can cause certain things to happen when events occur or data changes. They can be used in particular with styles to cause visual changes in response to the user's input.

This example modifies the same Label style as before to change the look when the user hovers the mouse over it (see Figure 18.4).

```
<Window x:Class="ImageViewer.Window1"
...
    >
    <Window.Resources>
    ...
        <Style TargetType="{x:Type Label}">
            <Setter Property="FontSize" Value="12.0" />
            <Style.Triggers>
                <Trigger Property="IsMouseOver" Value="True">
                    <Setter Property="Label.FontWeight" Value="Bold" />
                    <Setter Property="Label.FontSize" Value="14.0" />
                    <Setter Property="Label.Background"
                            Value="LightBlue" />
                </Trigger>
            </Style.Triggers>
        </Style>
    ...
    </Window.Resources>
    ...
</Window>
```

FIGURE 18.4
You can use triggers to cause visual changes to appear in response to user actions.

Bind Control Properties to Another Object

Scenario/Problem: You want to associate a bit of UI with some data and have the UI update automatically when the data changes.

Solution: We already have some simple data binding in the preceding examples. It is, in fact, *hard* to do WPF without using data binding, because that is what it naturally wants to do.

For binding to work, the binding must be associated with a `DataContext`. Elements search up their parent tree for the closest `DataContext`. Data binding is relative to that, unless explicitly stated otherwise (using `ElementName` or `RelativeSource`).

For the ImageViewer sample application, a data object was created specifically for data binding and set to the window's `DataContext`.

Listings 18.1 and 18.2 demonstrate data binding with a drag-and-drop image viewer. Every time an image is dropped on the application, a new `ImageInfoViewModel` is created and assigned to the window's `DataContext` property. The view model abstracts away the actual model (the image) and presents a simple class that can be used in data binding for the UI. For more on the view model and the overall design pattern here, see Chapter 25, "Application Patterns and Tips."

LISTING 18.1 **ImageInfoViewModel.cs**

```
using System;
using System.Collections.Generic;
using System.Windows.Media.Imaging;
using System.IO;
using System.ComponentModel;

namespace ImageViewer
{
    public class ImageInfoViewModel
    {
        private BitmapImage _image;

        public BitmapImage Image
        {
            get
            {
                return _image;
            }
        }
        public string FileName
        {
            get
```

LISTING 18.1 **ImageInfoViewModel.cs** (continued)

```
            {
                return Path.GetFileName(_image.UriSource.LocalPath);
            }
        }
        public int Width
        {
            get
            {
                return (int)_image.PixelWidth;
            }
        }

        public int Height
        {
            get
            {
                return (int)_image.PixelHeight;
            }
        }

        public ICollection<KeyValuePair<string, object>> AllProperties
        {
            get
            {
                return CreateProperties();
            }
        }

        public ImageInfoViewModel(BitmapImage image)
        {
            _image = image;
        }

        private IDictionary<string, object> CreateProperties()
        {
            Dictionary<string, object> properties =
                        new Dictionary<string, object>();
            properties["Width"] = _image.PixelWidth;
            properties["Height"] = _image.PixelHeight;
            properties["DpiX"] = _image.DpiX;
            properties["DpiY"] = _image.DpiY;
            properties["BitsPerPixel"] = _image.Format.BitsPerPixel;
            properties["Format"] = _image.Format.ToString();
            return properties;
        }
    }
}
```

LISTING 18.2 **Window1.xaml.cs**

```
using System;
using System.Collections.Generic;
using System.Linq;
using System.Text;
using System.Windows;
using System.Windows.Controls;
using System.Windows.Data;
using System.Windows.Documents;
using System.Windows.Input;
using System.Windows.Media;
using System.Windows.Media.Imaging;
using System.Windows.Navigation;
using System.Windows.Shapes;
using System.Windows.Media.Animation;

namespace ImageViewer
{
    /// <summary>
    /// Interaction logic for Window1.xaml
    /// </summary>
    public partial class Window1 : Window
    {
        private static DependencyProperty ImageInfoProperty;
        static Window1()
        {
            ImageInfoProperty = DependencyProperty.Register("ImageInfo",
                typeof(ImageInfoViewModel), typeof(Window1));
        }

        public ImageInfoViewModel ImageInfo
        {
            get
            {
                return (ImageInfoViewModel)GetValue(ImageInfoProperty);
            }
            set
            {
                SetValue(ImageInfoProperty, value);
                //set data context so data binding works
                DataContext = value;
            }
        }

        public Window1()
        {
```

LISTING 18.2 **Window1.xaml.cs** (continued)

```
            InitializeComponent();
        }

        protected override void OnDragEnter(DragEventArgs e)
        {
            base.OnDragEnter(e);

            //is it a list of files?
            if (e.Data.GetDataPresent(DataFormats.FileDrop))
            {
                e.Effects = DragDropEffects.Copy;
            }
            else
            {
                e.Effects = DragDropEffects.None;
            }
        }

        protected override void OnDrop(DragEventArgs e)
        {
            base.OnDrop(e);
            if (e.Data.GetDataPresent(DataFormats.FileDrop))
            {
                foreach(string path in (string[])e.Data.GetData(
➥                      DataFormats.FileDrop))
                {
                    //grab first image
                    try
                    {
                        BitmapImage image =
                          new BitmapImage(new Uri(path));
                        ImageInfoViewModel model =
                          new ImageInfoViewModel(image);
                        this.ImageInfo = model;
                    }
                    catch (Exception )
                    {
                    }
                }
            }
        }
    }
}
```

Here's a part of the XAML that binds elements to the `ImageInfoViewModel` object:

```
<Expander Header="Image Info" IsExpanded="True" x:Name="imageInfoGroup">
    <Grid DockPanel.Dock="Left">
        <Grid.ColumnDefinitions>
            <ColumnDefinition/>
            <ColumnDefinition/>
        </Grid.ColumnDefinitions>
        <Grid.RowDefinitions>
            <RowDefinition/>
            <RowDefinition/>
            <RowDefinition/>
        </Grid.RowDefinitions>
        <Label Grid.Row="0" Grid.Column="0">Filename</Label>
        <TextBox IsReadOnly="True" Grid.Row="0" Grid.Column="1"
                 Text="{Binding Path=FileName, Mode=OneWay}"/>
        <Label Grid.Row="1" Grid.Column="0">Width</Label>
        <TextBox IsReadOnly="True" Grid.Row="1" Grid.Column="1"
                 Text="{Binding Path=Width, Mode=OneWay}"/>
        <Label Grid.Row="2" Grid.Column="0">Height</Label>
        <TextBox IsReadOnly="True" Grid.Row="2" Grid.Column="1"
                 Text="{Binding Path=Height, Mode=OneWay}"/>
    </Grid>
</Expander>
```

Every time you drag an image onto the ImageViewer application, the UI will update with information about that image automatically when the `ImageInfo` property is set.

Format Values During Data Binding

Scenario/Problem: You need to apply formatting to the bound value.

Solution: Starting in .NET 3.5 SP1, you can use the `StringFormat` property.

```
<TextBox IsReadOnly="True" Grid.Row="1" Grid.Column="1"
         Text="{Binding Path=Width, Mode=OneWay, StringFormat=N0}"/>
```

Convert Values to a Different Type During Data Binding

Scenario/Problem: You want to convert one type to another in data binding. For example, you could bind a control's color to some text.

Solution: Define a converter class derived from IValueConverter and implement one or both methods:

```
class FilenameToColorConverter : IValueConverter
{
    public object Convert(object value,
                          Type targetType,
                          object parameter,
                  System.Globalization.CultureInfo culture)
    {
        if (string.IsNullOrEmpty(value as string))
        {
            return Brushes.Red;
        }
        else
        {
            return Brushes.Green;
        }
    }

    public object ConvertBack(object value,
                              Type targetType,
                              object parameter,
                      System.Globalization.CultureInfo culture)
    {
        //you only need to implement this for two-way conversions
        throw new NotImplementedException();
    }
}
```

In your window XAML, define a resource and specify the converter where needed. In the following example, the background color is bound to the filename with this converter so that it becomes red if the filename is null:

```
<Window x:Class="ImageViewer.Window1"
    xmlns="http://schemas.microsoft.com/winfx/2006/xaml/presentation"
    xmlns:x="http://schemas.microsoft.com/winfx/2006/xaml"
    xmlns:local="clr-namespace:ImageViewer"
        Title="Image Viewer" Height="426" Width="537" AllowDrop="True"
    Name="MainWindow"
    >
    <Window.Resources>
        <local:FilenameToColorConverter x:Key="fileColorConverter"/>
        ...
    </Window.Resources>
    ...
```

```
    <TextBox IsReadOnly="True" Grid.Row="0" Grid.Column="1"
             Text="{Binding Path=FileName, Mode=OneWay}"
             Background="{Binding Path=FileName, Mode=OneWay,
                         Converter={StaticResource
                                    fileColorConverter}}"/>
</Window>
```

Bind to a Collection

Scenario/Problem: Some elements display a collection of items. You want to bind this to a data source.

Solution: Binding to a collection of items is fairly straightforward. You can declare XAML like this:

```
<Expander Header="All Properties" IsExpanded="False"
          x:Name="allPropertiesGroup">
    <ListBox
        <!-- AllProperties is defined as
             ICollection<KeyValuePair<string, object>> in
             ImageInfoViewModel -->
        ItemsSource="{Binding Path=AllProperties}"
        />
</Expander>
```

However, because WPF doesn't know how to display each item in the collection, it's just going to call `ToString()` on each item. To customize the display, you need to define a data template, which is covered in the next section.

Specify How Bound Data Is Displayed

Scenario/Problem: You need to control the way bound items are displayed.

Solution: You can use a data template. Data templates are defined as resources:

```
<Window.Resources>
<DataTemplate x:Key="dataItemTemplate">
    <Grid>
        <Grid.ColumnDefinitions>
            <ColumnDefinition Width="80"/>
            <ColumnDefinition Width="*"/>
```

```
        </Grid.ColumnDefinitions>
        <Label Content="{Binding Path=Key, Mode=OneWay}"
               Grid.Column="0"/>
        <TextBox Text="{Binding Path=Value, Mode=OneWay}"
                 IsReadOnly="True"
                 Grid.Column="1"
                 HorizontalContentAlignment="Left"
                 HorizontalAlignment="Left" />
    </Grid>
</DataTemplate>
</Window.Resources>
```

Then modify the ListBox's ItemTemplate property to refer to it:

```
<Expander Header="All Properties" IsExpanded="False"
          x:Name="allPropertiesGroup">
    <ListBox
        ItemsSource="{Binding Path=AllProperties}"
        ItemTemplate="{StaticResource dataItemTemplate}"
        />
</Expander>
```

The result is an attractive display of an arbitrary number of collection items, as previously seen in Figure 18.4.

Define the Look of Controls with Templates

Scenario/Problem: You want to set a control's look according to one or more templates and be able to change them at runtime.

Solution: If you look closely at Figures 18.3 and 18.4, you'll see that the latter shows a caption under the image, whereas the former does not. This is accomplished with control templates.

The two ControlTemplates are defined, as usual, in the resources:

```
<Window.Resources>
    <ControlTemplate x:Key="imageTemplate"
                     TargetType="{x:Type ContentControl}"
                     x:Name="imageControlTemplate">
        <Image Source="{Binding Path=Image}" />
    </ControlTemplate>

    <ControlTemplate x:Key="imageWithCaptionTemplate"
                     TargetType="{x:Type ContentControl}">
```

```
        <Grid>
            <Grid.RowDefinitions>
                <RowDefinition Height="*"/>
                <RowDefinition Height="Auto"/>
            </Grid.RowDefinitions>
            <Image Source="{Binding Path=Image}" Grid.Row="0"/>
            <TextBlock Text="{Binding Path=FileName}"
                       HorizontalAlignment="Center"
                       FontSize="16"
                       Grid.Row="1"/>
        </Grid>
    </ControlTemplate>
</Window.Resources>
```

And the default template is set in the element's definition:

```
<Window
    ...
    >
    ...
    <DockPanel>
   ...
      <ContentControl Template="{DynamicResource imageTemplate}"
                      Name="controlDisplay"/>
    </DockPanel>
</Window>
```

An event handler (discussed previously) on the radio buttons causes the template to be switched:

```
private void OnTemplateOptionChecked(object sender, RoutedEventArgs e)
{
    if (radioButtonNoCaption != null && controlDisplay!= null)
    {
        if (radioButtonNoCaption.IsChecked == true)
        {
            controlDisplay.Template =
              (ControlTemplate)FindResource("imageTemplate");
        }
        else
        {
            controlDisplay.Template =
      (ControlTemplate)FindResource("imageWithCaptionTemplate");
        }
    }
}
```

Animate Element Properties

Scenario/Problem: You want to change UI properties over time.

Solution: As far as WPF is concerned, animation is the change of an element's properties over time. For example, you could change the x position of a button from 1 to 100 over, say, 5 seconds. This would have the effect of moving the button on the screen during that time. You can animate any dependency property in WPF.

The ImageViewer application uses a single animation to fade in the left-side panel over 5 seconds when the application starts. Figure 18.5 shows the application with it faded in about halfway.

First, define the storyboard with animation in the Window's resources:

```
<Window.Resources>
    <Storyboard x:Key="FadeInLeftPanel"
        Storyboard.TargetName="LeftPanel">
        <!-- Double refers to the Type of the property -->
        <DoubleAnimation
            Storyboard.TargetProperty="Opacity"
            From="0.0" To="1.0" Duration="0:0:5" />
    </Storyboard>
</Window.Resources>
```

Once the animation is defined, you need to start with a trigger:

```
<Window>
    <Window.Resources>
        ...
    </Window.Resources>

    <Window.Triggers>
        <EventTrigger
                RoutedEvent="Window.Loaded">
            <BeginStoryboard
                    Storyboard="{StaticResource FadeInLeftPanel}" />
        </EventTrigger>
    </Window.Triggers>
    ...
</window>
```

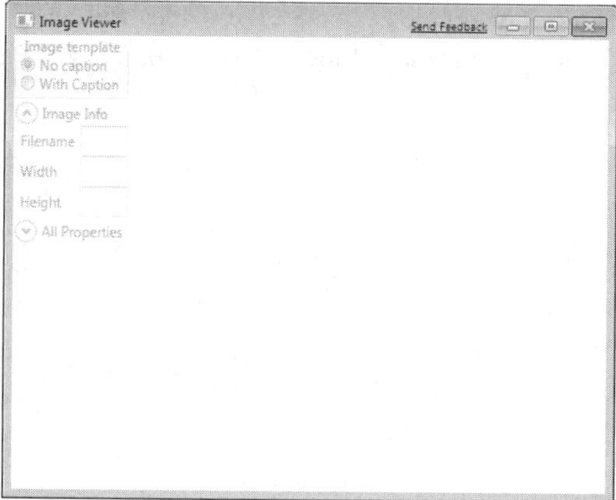

FIGURE 18.5
This image shows the sidebar fading in during program startup.

Render 3D Geometry

Scenario/Problem: You want to render 3D geometry.

Solution: Starting in this section, you'll see that WPF provides the unprecedented ability to merge 3D graphics with standard user interface elements and multimedia.

Effectively using 3D graphics requires learning a little about cameras, lighting, materials, and coordinate systems. Thankfully, WPF makes a lot of this very easy.

This simple demonstration creates a cube, complete with color and lighting, as seen in Figure 18.6

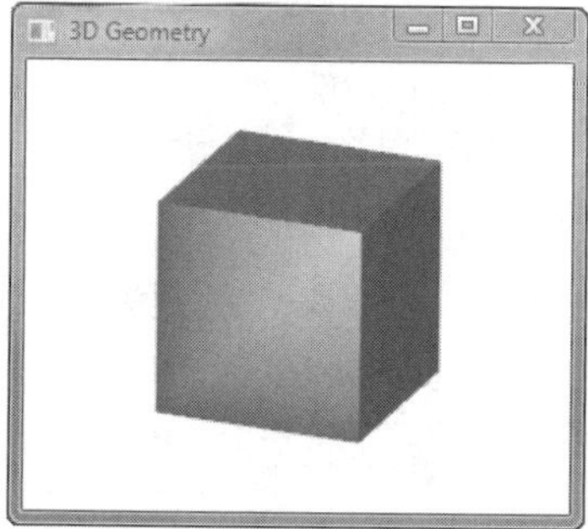

FIGURE 18.6
This cube demonstrates simple lighting and texture usage.

First, the geometry needs to be defined. For our simple examples, the shapes will be defined in the `Window.Resources` sections. Here is the definition for the six faces of the cube:

```
<Window.Resources>
    <MeshGeometry3D
        x:Key="faceNear"
        Positions="-1,-1,1 1,-1,1 1,1,1 -1,1,1"
        TriangleIndices="0 1 2 0 2 3"
        TextureCoordinates="0,1 1,1 1,0 0,0"
        Normals="0,0,1 0,0,1 0,0,1 0,0,1"/>
    <MeshGeometry3D
        x:Key="faceFar"
        Positions="-1,-1,-1 1,-1,-1 1,1,-1 -1,1,-1"
        TriangleIndices="0 1 2 0 2 3" />
    <MeshGeometry3D
        x:Key="faceLeft"
        Positions="-1,-1,-1 -1,-1,1 -1,1,1 -1,1,-1"
        TriangleIndices="0 1 2 0 2 3"/>
    <MeshGeometry3D
        x:Key="faceRight"
        Positions="1,-1,1 1,-1,-1 1,1,-1 1,1,1"
        TriangleIndices="0 1 2 0 2 3"/>
    <MeshGeometry3D
        x:Key="faceTop"
        Positions="-1,1,1 1,1,1 1,1,-1 -1,1,-1"
        TriangleIndices="0 1 2 0 2 3"/>
    <MeshGeometry3D
        x:Key="faceBottom"
        Positions="-1,-1,-1 1,-1,-1 1,-1,1 -1,-1,1"
        TriangleIndices="0 1 2 0 2 3"/>

    <MaterialGroup x:Key="defaultMaterial">
        <DiffuseMaterial Brush="Red" />
        <SpecularMaterial SpecularPower="30" Brush="Yellow" />
    </MaterialGroup>
</Window.Resources>
```

The actual placement of these mesh geometries is done inside a `Viewport3D` element:

```
<Grid>
    <!-- 3-D elements need to go inside a Viewport3D -->
    <Viewport3D x:Name="Viewport">
        <!-- Camera -->
        <Viewport3D.Camera>
            <OrthographicCamera
```

```
        Width="5"
        Position="4,4,10"
        LookDirection="-0.4,-0.4,-1"
        UpDirection="0,1,0" />
    </Viewport3D.Camera>

    <ModelVisual3D>
        <ModelVisual3D.Content>
            <GeometryModel3D
        Geometry="{StaticResource faceNear}"
        Material="{StaticResource defaultMaterial}" />
        </ModelVisual3D.Content>
    </ModelVisual3D>
    <ModelVisual3D>
        <ModelVisual3D.Content>
            <GeometryModel3D
            Geometry="{StaticResource faceFar}"
            Material="{StaticResource defaultMaterial}"/>
        </ModelVisual3D.Content>
    </ModelVisual3D>
    <ModelVisual3D>
        <ModelVisual3D.Content>
            <GeometryModel3D
            Geometry="{StaticResource faceLeft}"
            Material="{StaticResource defaultMaterial}"/>
        </ModelVisual3D.Content>
    </ModelVisual3D>
    <ModelVisual3D>
        <ModelVisual3D.Content>
            <GeometryModel3D
            Geometry="{StaticResource faceRight}"
            Material="{StaticResource defaultMaterial}"/>
        </ModelVisual3D.Content>
    </ModelVisual3D>
    <ModelVisual3D>
        <ModelVisual3D.Content>
            <GeometryModel3D
            Geometry="{StaticResource faceTop}"
            Material="{StaticResource defaultMaterial}"/>
        </ModelVisual3D.Content>
    </ModelVisual3D>
    <ModelVisual3D>
        <ModelVisual3D.Content>
            <GeometryModel3D
            Geometry="{StaticResource faceBottom}"
```

```
            Material="{StaticResource defaultMaterial}"/>
        </ModelVisual3D.Content>
    </ModelVisual3D>

    <!-- Lights -->

    <ModelVisual3D>
        <ModelVisual3D.Content>
            <PointLight Position="5,10,5" Color="White"/>
        </ModelVisual3D.Content>
    </ModelVisual3D>

    <ModelVisual3D>
        <ModelVisual3D.Content>
            <AmbientLight Color="Gray"/>
        </ModelVisual3D.Content>
    </ModelVisual3D>

    <ModelVisual3D>
        <ModelVisual3D.Content>
            <SpotLight Color="White" Position="0,0,3"
                       Direction="0,0,-1"/>
        </ModelVisual3D.Content>
    </ModelVisual3D>
  </Viewport3D>
</Grid>
```

Put Video on a 3D Surface

Scenario/Problem: You want to put some media onto a 3D surface.

Solution: A plain-old cube is great, but what about one of those cube faces playing a movie (or showing an image, or any other WPF element)? Now, that is pretty cool. WPF makes this almost too easy.

```
<Window x:Class="MovieIn3D.Window1"
    xmlns="http://schemas.microsoft.com/winfx/2006/xaml/presentation"
    xmlns:x="http://schemas.microsoft.com/winfx/2006/xaml"
    xmlns:interactive3D="clr-namespace:_3DTools;assembly=3DTools"
    Title="Movie and Controls in 3D"
    Height="480" Width="640" Loaded="Window_Loaded">
    <Window.Resources>
```

```
        <MeshGeometry3D
            x:Key="movieSurface"
            Positions="-1,-1,1 1,-1,1 1,1,1 -1,1,1"
            TriangleIndices="0 1 2 0 2 3"
            TextureCoordinates="0,1 1,1 1,0 0,0"
            Normals="0,0,1 0,0,1 0,0,1 0,0,1" />
        <MeshGeometry3D
            x:Key="controlSurface"
            Positions="1,-1,1 1,-1,-1 1,1,-1 1,1,1"
            TriangleIndices="0 1 2 0 2 3"
            TextureCoordinates="0,1 1,1 1,0 0,0"
            Normals="1,0,0 1,0,0 1,0,0 1,0,0"/>
        <MeshGeometry3D
            x:Key="faceTop"
            Positions="-1,1,1 1,1,1 1,1,-1 -1,1,-1"
            TriangleIndices="0 1 2 0 2 3"
            TextureCoordinates="0,1 1,1 1,0 0,0"/>
    </Window.Resources>
    <Grid>
        <Viewport3D x:Name="Viewport">
            <Viewport3D.Camera>
                <OrthographicCamera
            Width="5"
            Position="4,4,10"
            LookDirection="-0.4,-0.4,-1"
            UpDirection="0,1,0" />
            </Viewport3D.Camera>

            <ModelVisual3D>
                <ModelVisual3D.Content>
                    <GeometryModel3D
                       Geometry="{StaticResource movieSurface}">
                        <GeometryModel3D.Material>
                            <MaterialGroup>
                                <DiffuseMaterial Brush="LightBlue"/>
                                <DiffuseMaterial >
                                    <DiffuseMaterial.Brush>
                                        <!-- A VisualBrush can
                                          include any WPF element-->
                                        <VisualBrush>
                                            <VisualBrush.Visual>
                                                <MediaElement
➥x:Name="mediaPlayer" LoadedBehavior="Manual"/>
                                            </VisualBrush.Visual>
                                        </VisualBrush>
```

```
                                        </DiffuseMaterial.Brush>
                                    </DiffuseMaterial>
                                </MaterialGroup>
                            </GeometryModel3D.Material>
                        </GeometryModel3D>
                    </ModelVisual3D.Content>
                </ModelVisual3D>

                <!-- Lights -->
                <ModelVisual3D>
                    <ModelVisual3D.Content>
                        <PointLight Position="5,10,5" Color="White"/>
                    </ModelVisual3D.Content>
                </ModelVisual3D>

                <ModelVisual3D>
                    <ModelVisual3D.Content>
                        <AmbientLight Color="Gray"/>
                    </ModelVisual3D.Content>
                </ModelVisual3D>

                <ModelVisual3D>
                    <ModelVisual3D.Content>
                        <SpotLight Color="White"
                         Position="0,0,3" Direction="0,0,-1"/>
                    </ModelVisual3D.Content>
                </ModelVisual3D>
            </Viewport3D>
        </Grid>
</Window>
```

The movie can be loaded into the `MediaElement` with code like this:

```
mediaPlayer.Source = new Uri(filename);
mediaPlayer.Play();
```

In the next section, we'll hook it up to some controls, also in 3D.

> **NOTE** Yes, the ability to do this kind of stuff is pretty neat, but don't go overboard. A movie pasted on to a 3D surface might make sense as part of a presentation, in a store kiosk, or perhaps as supporting material or as an animation to bring the movie to the foreground, but it's probably not the best scenario for watching a whole movie. Just because you *can* do something doesn't always mean you *should*.

Put Interactive Controls onto a 3D Surface

Scenario/Problem: You can easily put any WPF element onto a 3D surface using the VisualBrush demonstrated earlier, but you won't have interaction that way.

Solution: For that, Microsoft has released 3D Tools for Windows Presentation Foundation, available at http://3dtools.codeplex.com/. This package includes objects that wrap around WPF elements and translate the 3D environment into something the elements can understand.

In this example, let's add some file selection and playback controls to our crazy video player (see Figure 18.7). You will also need to add a reference to the 3DTools.dll assembly in your project.

FIGURE 18.7
A cube playing a slideshow video, with working controls. I dare you to try this in Windows Forms.

Here is the complete code:

```
<Window x:Class="MovieIn3D.Window1"
    xmlns="http://schemas.microsoft.com/winfx/2006/xaml/presentation"
    xmlns:x="http://schemas.microsoft.com/winfx/2006/xaml"
    xmlns:interactive3D="clr-namespace:_3DTools;assembly=3DTools"
    Title="Movie and Controls in 3D"
    Height="480" Width="640" Loaded="Window_Loaded">
    <Window.Resources>
        <MeshGeometry3D
```

```
        x:Key="movieSurface"
        Positions="-1,-1,1 1,-1,1 1,1,1 -1,1,1"
        TriangleIndices="0 1 2 0 2 3"
        TextureCoordinates="0,1 1,1 1,0 0,0"
        Normals="0,0,1 0,0,1 0,0,1 0,0,1" />
    <MeshGeometry3D
        x:Key="controlSurface"
        Positions="1,-1,1 1,-1,-1 1,1,-1 1,1,1"
        TriangleIndices="0 1 2 0 2 3"
        TextureCoordinates="0,1 1,1 1,0 0,0"
        Normals="1,0,0 1,0,0 1,0,0 1,0,0"/>
    <MeshGeometry3D
        x:Key="faceTop"
        Positions="-1,1,1 1,1,1 1,1,-1 -1,1,-1"
        TriangleIndices="0 1 2 0 2 3"
        TextureCoordinates="0,1 1,1 1,0 0,0"/>
</Window.Resources>
<Grid>
    <interactive3D:Interactive3DDecorator>
        <Viewport3D x:Name="Viewport">
            <Viewport3D.Camera>
                <OrthographicCamera
            Width="5"
            Position="4,4,10"
            LookDirection="-0.4,-0.4,-1"
            UpDirection="0,1,0" />
            </Viewport3D.Camera>

            <ModelVisual3D>
                <ModelVisual3D.Content>
                    <GeometryModel3D
                      Geometry="{StaticResource movieSurface}">
                        <GeometryModel3D.Material>
                            <MaterialGroup>
                                <DiffuseMaterial Brush="LightBlue"/>
                                <DiffuseMaterial >
                                    <DiffuseMaterial.Brush>
                                        <VisualBrush>
                                            <VisualBrush.Visual>
                                                <MediaElement
➥x:Name="mediaPlayer" LoadedBehavior="Manual"/>
                                            </VisualBrush.Visual>
                                        </VisualBrush>
                                    </DiffuseMaterial.Brush>
                                </DiffuseMaterial>
                            </MaterialGroup>
```

```
                </GeometryModel3D.Material>
            </GeometryModel3D>
        </ModelVisual3D.Content>
    </ModelVisual3D>
    <interactive3D:InteractiveVisual3D Geometry=
      "{StaticResource controlSurface}">
        <interactive3D:InteractiveVisual3D.Visual>
            <StackPanel>
                <Button Content="Play"
                  x:Name="buttonPlay" Click="OnPlay"/>
                <Button Content="Pause"
                  x:Name="buttonPause" Click="OnPause"/>
                <Button Content="Stop"
                  x:Name="buttonStop" Click="OnStop"/>
            </StackPanel>
        </interactive3D:InteractiveVisual3D.Visual>
    </interactive3D:InteractiveVisual3D>
    <interactive3D:InteractiveVisual3D
         Geometry="{StaticResource faceTop}">
        <interactive3D:InteractiveVisual3D.Visual>
            <Button Content="Select File..."
              x:Name="buttonLoad" Click="OnSelectFile"/>
        </interactive3D:InteractiveVisual3D.Visual>
    </interactive3D:InteractiveVisual3D>

    <!-- Lights -->

    <ModelVisual3D>
        <ModelVisual3D.Content>
            <PointLight Position="5,10,5" Color="White"/>
        </ModelVisual3D.Content>
    </ModelVisual3D>

    <ModelVisual3D>
        <ModelVisual3D.Content>
            <AmbientLight Color="Gray"/>
        </ModelVisual3D.Content>
    </ModelVisual3D>

    <ModelVisual3D>
        <ModelVisual3D.Content>
            <SpotLight Color="White" Position="0,0,3"
              Direction="0,0,-1"/>
        </ModelVisual3D.Content>
    </ModelVisual3D>
</Viewport3D>
```

```
        </interactive3D:Interactive3DDecorator>
    </Grid>
</Window>
```

The code-behind provides the button functionality:

```
public partial class Window1 : Window
{
    public Window1()
    {
        InitializeComponent();
    }

    private void OnSelectFile(object sender, RoutedEventArgs e)
    {
        OpenFileDialog ofd = new OpenFileDialog();
        if (ofd.ShowDialog() == true)
        {
            mediaPlayer.Source = new Uri(ofd.FileName);
            //force the first frame to appear so we see a change
            mediaPlayer.Play();
            mediaPlayer.Pause();
        }
    }

    void OnPlay(object sender, RoutedEventArgs e)
    {
        mediaPlayer.Play();
    }

    void OnPause(object sender, RoutedEventArgs e)
    {
        mediaPlayer.Pause();
    }

    void OnStop(object sender, RoutedEventArgs e)
    {
        mediaPlayer.Stop();
    }
}
```

Use WPF in a WinForms App

Scenario/Problem: You want to take advantage of WPF, but can't afford to convert all your existing applications.

Solution: You can easily interoperate between Windows Forms and WPF with the ElementHost control.

```
public partial class Form1 : Form
{
    public Form1()
    {
        InitializeComponent();
        //create our WPF Control and add it to a hosting control

        //we can declare a WPF control directly--
        //after all, it's just .Net code
        MyWpfControl wpfControl = new MyWpfControl();
        //the WPF control declares this custom event
        wpfControl.ButtonClicked +=
           new EventHandler<EventArgs>(OnButtonClicked);
        ElementHost host = new ElementHost();
        host.Left = 5;
        host.Top = 100;
        host.Width = 160;
        host.Height = 66;
        host.Child = wpfControl;

        this.Controls.Add(host);
    }

    private void OnButtonClicked(object source, EventArgs e)
    {
        MessageBox.Show("WPF Button clicked");
    }
}
```

Figure 18.8 shows a Windows Forms application with a standard WinForms control and a WPF control. (It's a button with a Label and TextBox in it just to prove it's really WPF.)

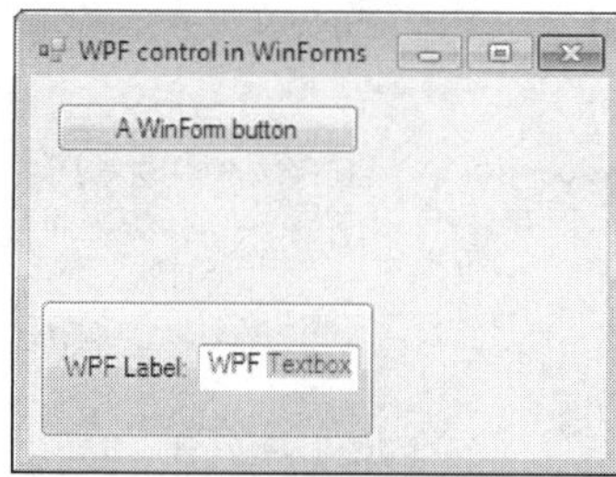

FIGURE 18.8
A provably WPF control inside a Windows Forms application.

Use WinForms in a WPF Application

Scenario/Problem: You want to start using WPF for new development but can't afford to reimplement all your existing controls and forms.

Solution: It's just as easy to go the other direction.

```
<Window x:Class="WinFormInWPF.Window1"
    xmlns="http://schemas.microsoft.com/winfx/2006/xaml/presentation"
    xmlns:x="http://schemas.microsoft.com/winfx/2006/xaml"
    xmlns:winforms="clr-namespace:System.Windows.Forms;
➥assembly=System.Windows.Forms"
    Title="WinForm control in WPF" Height="300" Width="300">
    <Grid>
        <!-- Yes, you can declare WinForms UI in XAML! -->
        <WindowsFormsHost Margin="12,41,66,12" Name="windowsFormsHost1">
            <winforms:NumericUpDown x:Name="numberPicker"/>
        </WindowsFormsHost>
        <Button Height="23" HorizontalAlignment="Left"
                Margin="12,12,0,0" Name="button1"
➥VerticalAlignment="Top" Width="75">WPF Button</Button>
    </Grid>
</Window>
```

Note that there is no NumericUpDown control in WPF (see Figure 18.9).

FIGURE 18.9
No NumericUpDown control in WPF. (Yet, we hope.)

CHAPTER 19

ASP.NET

IN THIS CHAPTER

- View Debug and Trace Information
- Determine Web Browser Capabilities
- Redirect to Another Page
- Use Forms Authentication for User Login
- Use Master Pages for a Consistent Look
- Add a Menu
- Bind Data to a GridView
- Create a User Control
- Create a Flexible UI with Web Parts
- Create a Simple AJAX Page
- Do Data Validation
- Maintain Application State
- Maintain UI State
- Maintain User Data in a Session
- Store Session State
- Use Cookies to Restore Session State
- Use ASP.NET Model-View-Controller (MVC)

Software is increasingly a web-based proposition, and ASP.NET is a wonderful platform for building advanced applications. With ASP.NET, you have access to the rich functionality of the entire .NET Framework. Although the topic of ASP.NET is large, this chapter gives you a jumpstart into the important topics.

View Debug and Trace Information

Scenario/Problem: You need to debug an ASP.NET application that is behaving badly, or you just want to add your own trace information to output.

Debugging ASP.NET applications can be a very different process from debugging native client applications. During development, Visual Studio's integrated debugger gives you a lot of power, but once an application is deployed, it's not always feasible to attach a debugger to a web app. Debug and trace information becomes vitally important.

Solution: ASP.NET has built-in support for dumping a lot of data to logs or even appending it to the bottom of the page you're looking at so you can easily view it. The following sections demonstrate a few different techniques you can use.

Enable Tracing for a Specific Page

To enable tracing for a specific page, add `Trace="true"` to the `@Page` element in the .aspx file:

```
<%@ Page Language="C#" AutoEventWireup="true"
    CodeBehind="Default.aspx.cs"
➥Inherits="BrowserCapsAndTracing._Default" Trace="true" %>
```

This will cause details of the web request to be dumped to the end of the web page (see Figure 19.1).

Enable Tracing for All Pages

If you cannot modify the pages themselves, or want to see trace info on every page, you can modify web.config to enable tracing on all pages:

```
<system.web>
    <trace enabled="true" localOnly="true" pageOutput="true"/>
    ...
```

Log Your Own Trace Messages

You can use the `Trace` class to write your own messages to the trace log:

```
protected void Page_Load(object sender, EventArgs e)
{
    if (!IsPostBack)
    {
        Trace.Write("Creating Capabilities Table");
        Table1.Rows.AddRange(
            new TableRow[]
            {
                CreateCapabilityRow("ActiveX",
                                    Request.Browser.ActiveXControls),
                ...
            });
    }
}
```

You can see the message “Creating Capabilities Table” in the trace output in Figure 19.1.

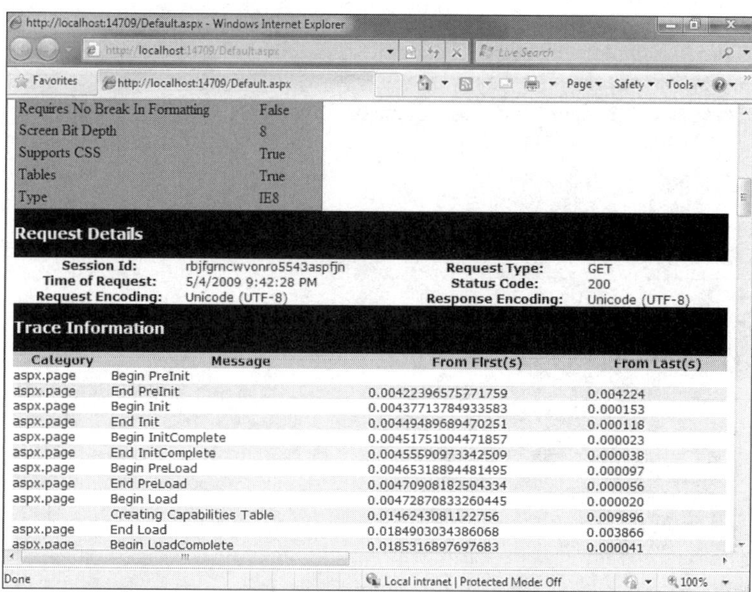

FIGURE 19.1
Tracing can dump detail of the request to the end of the produced page.

Determine Web Browser Capabilities

Scenario/Problem: You need to change your application's behavior based on the browser the user is using.

Given how many platforms websites must display on these days, including different browsers, operating systems, and mobile devices, it can seem amazing that the Web works at all. Each web browser has many differences in rendering, the ability to load add-ons such as ActiveX controls, JavaScript engines, and more.

Solution: .NET provides an easy way to discover many of these capabilities automatically, using the `Request.Browser` structure, which contains Boolean or string values for many important properties.

`CreateCapabilityRow` is just a helper method to create a table row to insert the results, as shown in Figure 19.2.

```
CreateCapabilityRow("ActiveX", Request.Browser.ActiveXControls),
CreateCapabilityRow("AOL", Request.Browser.AOL),
CreateCapabilityRow("Background Sounds",
➥Request.Browser.BackgroundSounds),
CreateCapabilityRow("Beta", Request.Browser.Beta),
CreateCapabilityRow("Browser",Request.Browser.Browser),
```

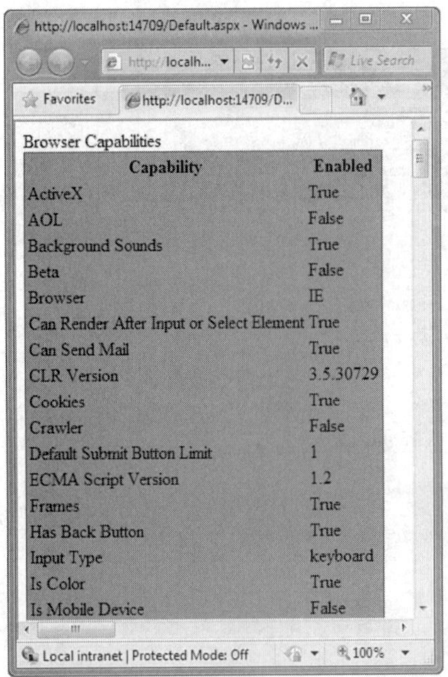

FIGURE 19.2
You can easily detect many differences in browsers that can affect your functionality.

Redirect to Another Page

Scenario/Problem: You need to redirect the user to another page for further processing.

Solution: There are two ways to send the user to another page. The first uses standard redirection:

```
protected void buttonRedirect_Click(object sender, EventArgs e)
{
    Response.Redirect("TargetPage.aspx");
}
```

This tells the user's browser to actually navigate to the target page.

If instead you want to actually transfer the processing of the current request to another page in the same directory without notifying the user (that is, the user's browser does not actually go to the other page), you can do the following:

```
protected void buttonSubmit_Click(object sender, EventArgs e)
{
    if (ProcessingChoice.SelectedValue == "Transfer")
    {
        Server.Transfer("TargetPage.aspx");
    }
}
```

From the user's perspective, the URL has not changed.

To see exactly how this works, look at the FormSubmitAndRedirect project in the included sample code.

Figure 19.3 shows the application running with a form allowing the user to select forms of transfer that should be done. Figure 19.4 shows the results if the second option is chosen.

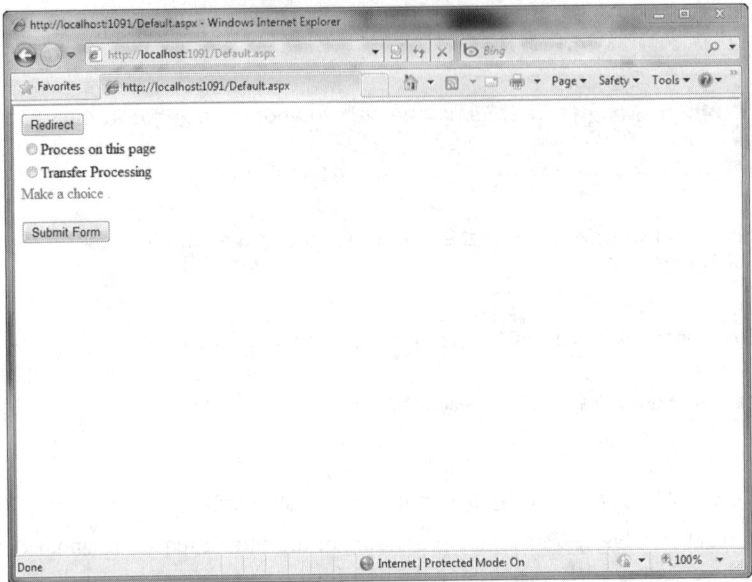

FIGURE 19.3
This simple app demonstrates how to process a form on the same page, redirect to another page, or transfer control to another page without notifying the user.

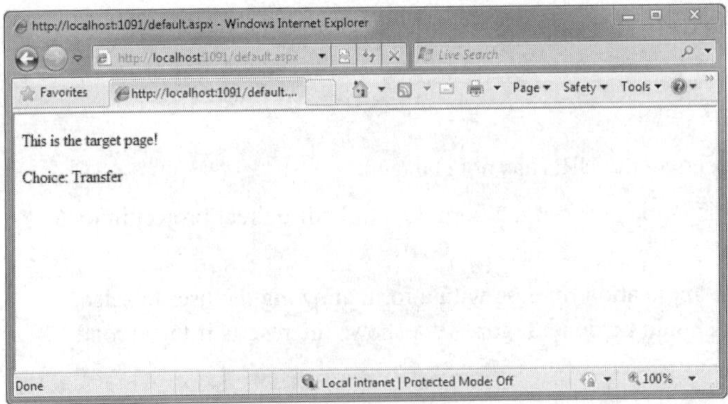

FIGURE 19.4
Notice how the output comes from the target page, but the URL still says default.aspx.

Use Forms Authentication for User Login

Scenario/Problem: You want to authenticate the user before allowing him to use part of the application.

Solution: A common workflow for user authentication on websites is to wait for a user to access a protected area, redirect him to a login form, then send him on to where he wanted to go. This is very easy to accomplish in ASP.NET.

First, you need to create your login page (see Listings 19.1 and 19.2).

LISTING 19.1 **LoginForm.aspx**

```
<%@ Page Language="C#" AutoEventWireup="true"
➥CodeBehind="LoginForm.aspx.cs"
➥Inherits="AuthDemo.LoginForm" %>
<!DOCTYPE html PUBLIC "-//W3C//DTD XHTML 1.0 Transitional//EN"
➥"http://www.w3.org/TR/xhtml1/DTD/xhtml1-transitional.dtd">
<html xmlns="http://www.w3.org/1999/xhtml" >
<head runat="server">
    <title>Login Form</title>
</head>
<body>
    <form id="form1" runat="server">
    <div>
        Username:
        <asp:TextBox ID="TextBoxUsername" runat="server" />
        <br />
        Password:<asp:TextBox ID="TextBoxPassword" runat="server" />
        <br />
        <asp:Button ID="ButtonStatus" runat="server" Text="Submit"
            onclick="ButtonStatus_Click" />
        <br />
        <asp:Label ID="LabelStatus" runat="server"
                   Text="Enter your login info" />
    </div>
    </form>
</body>
</html>
```

LISTING 19.2 **LoginForm.aspx.cs**

```
using System;
using System.Collections.Generic;
using System.Linq;
using System.Web;
using System.Web.UI;
using System.Web.UI.WebControls;
using System.Web.Security;
```

LISTING 19.2 **LoginForm.aspx.cs** (continued)

```
namespace AuthDemo
{
    public partial class LoginForm : System.Web.UI.Page
    {
        protected void Page_Load(object sender, EventArgs e)
        {
        }

        protected void ButtonStatus_Click(object sender, EventArgs e)
        {
            if (AuthenticateUser(TextBoxUsername.Text,
                                 TextBoxPassword.Text))
            {
                //want to keep user logged in? pass true instead
                FormsAuthentication.RedirectFromLoginPage(
                          TextBoxUsername.Text, false);
            }
            else
            {
                LabelStatus.Text = "Oops";
            }
        }

        private bool AuthenticateUser(string username, string password)
        {
            //you could authenticate against a database or a file here
            return username == "user" && password == "pass";
        }
    }
}
```

Then add the following configuration information to web.config under the `<system.web>` section:

```
<authentication mode="Forms" >
  <forms name=".ASPXAUTH" loginUrl="LoginForm.aspx" />
</authentication>
<!-- Require authentication for all pages in this folder-->
<authorization>
  <deny users="?" />
</authorization>
```

The only other page in this example is the default page, shown in Listing 19.3, which will automatically be protected by login.

LISTING 19.3 **Default.aspx**

```
<%@ Page Language="C#" AutoEventWireup="true"
         CodeBehind="Default.aspx.cs"
         Inherits="AuthDemo._Default" %>

<!DOCTYPE html PUBLIC "-//W3C//DTD XHTML 1.0 Transitional//EN"
➥"http://www.w3.org/TR/xhtml1/DTD/xhtml1-transitional.dtd">

<html xmlns="http://www.w3.org/1999/xhtml" >
<head runat="server">
    <title>Protected page</title>
</head>
<body>
    <form id="form1" runat="server">
    <div>
        Congratulations, you have been authenticated.</div>
    </form>
</body>
</html>
```

When the user tries to access Default.aspx, he is redirected to LoginForm.aspx first, shown in Figure 19.5, and then back to Default.aspx upon a successful authentication.

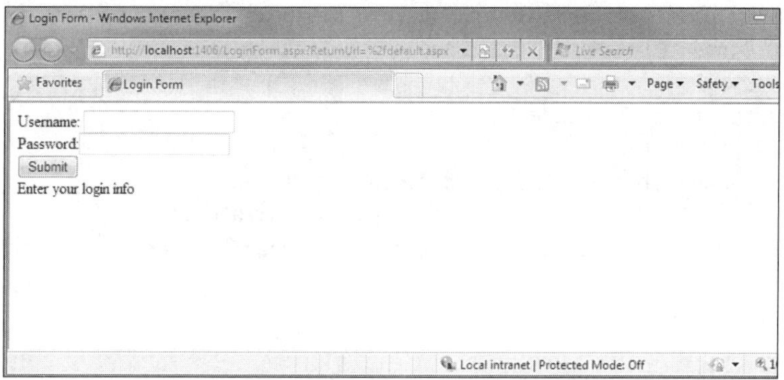

FIGURE 19.5
The login form LoginForm.aspx.

Use Master Pages for a Consistent Look

> **Scenario/Problem:** You want your pages to have a consistent, templated look and feel.

Solution: Master pages are essentially templates that define the overall structure of a page. They contain all the common elements for a set of pages as well as content placeholder objects that are filled in by content pages.

Listing 19.4 shows the master page for a book inventory application, which is the BooksApp sample application in the accompanying source code.

LISTING 19.4 **BooksApp—MasterPage.master**

```
<%@ Master Language="C#" AutoEventWireup="true"
         CodeBehind="MasterPage.master.cs"
➥Inherits="BooksApp.MasterPage" %>

<!DOCTYPE html PUBLIC "-//W3C//DTD XHTML 1.0 Transitional//EN"
➥"http://www.w3.org/TR/xhtml1/DTD/xhtml1-transitional.dtd">

<html xmlns="http://www.w3.org/1999/xhtml" >
<head runat="server">
    <asp:ContentPlaceHolder ID="head" runat="server">
    <title>Books App</title>
    </asp:ContentPlaceHolder>
</head>
<body>
    <form id="form1" runat="server">
    <div style="position:absolute;top:0px;width:800px;height:50px;">
        <asp:ContentPlaceHolder ID="Header" runat="server">

        </asp:ContentPlaceHolder>
    </div>
    <div style="position:absolute; top: 100px;
                                    left:110px; width:700px;">
        <asp:ContentPlaceHolder ID="MainContent" runat="server">

        </asp:ContentPlaceHolder>
    </div>
    </form>
</body>
</html>
```

As you can see, a master page is very similar to a normal .aspx page. Master pages can also have code-behind. This master page contains three `ContentPlaceHolder` objects for the <head> element, the body's header, and content sections. Notice that the <head> placeholder contains a default `<title>` tag. This will be used if the content page does not put its own content there.

Listing 19.5 shows a simple content page that fills in the `ContentPlaceHolder` objects.

LISTING 19.5 **Default.aspx**

```
<%@ Page Title="" Language="C#" MasterPageFile="~/MasterPage.Master"
➥AutoEventWireup="true" CodeBehind="Default.aspx.cs"
➥Inherits="BooksApp.WebForm1" %>
<asp:Content ID="Content1" ContentPlaceHolderID="head" runat="server">
    <title>Book Collection</title>
</asp:Content>
<asp:Content ID="Content2" ContentPlaceHolderID="Header" runat="server">
    <p align="center">
        Book Collection</p>
</asp:Content>
<asp:Content ID="Content3"
        ContentPlaceHolderID="MainContent" runat="server">
    <p>
        Use the menu to select pages</p>
</asp:Content>
```

This set of pages will be fleshed out in the following sections.

Add a Menu

Scenario/Problem: You want to provide a menu for site navigation.

Solution: Start by adding a Sitemap file called web.sitemap to your project. Give it this content:

```
<?xml version="1.0" encoding="utf-8" ?>
<siteMap xmlns="http://schemas.microsoft.com/AspNet/SiteMap-File-1.0" >
  <!-- there can only be one siteMapNode under siteMap,
       so we'll ignore it when we create the menu,
       and just use its children -->
  <siteMapNode url="" title=""  description="">
    <siteMapNode url="~/Default.aspx" title="Home"
                 description="Site default page" />
    <siteMapNode url="~/BookList.aspx" title="Book List"
                 description="List of all books"/>
    <siteMapNode url="~/BookDetail.aspx" title="Book Details"
                 description="Details of one book" />
  </siteMapNode>
</siteMap>
```

In the master page where you want the menu, add the following:

```
<div style="position:absolute; top:100px;
          width:100px; background-color:#DCDCFF;">
    <asp:Menu ID="MainMenu" runat="server"
              DataSourceID="SiteMapDataSource1">
    </asp:Menu>
    <asp:SiteMapDataSource ID="SiteMapDataSource1" runat="server"
        ShowStartingNode="False" />
</div>
```

This attaches the menu to a `SiteMapDataSource` object that automatically reads the web.sitemap file. Our simple menu is visible in Figure 19.6.

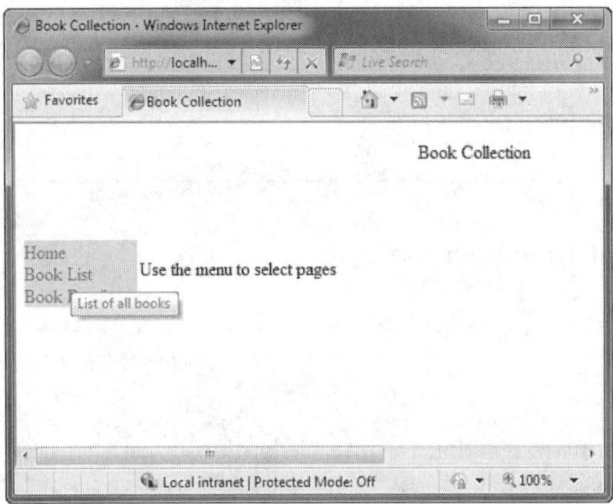

FIGURE 19.6
By adding to the web.sitemap file, you can immediately adjust the menu items.

Bind Data to a GridView

Scenario/Problem: You need to bind table data (such as from a database table) to a view on a web page.

Solution: Use the flexible GridView control. Listing 19.6 shows the BookList page that shows a grid of books.

LISTING 19.6 **BookList.aspx**

```
<%@ Page Title="" Language="C#" MasterPageFile="~/MasterPage.Master"
➥AutoEventWireup="true" CodeBehind="BookList.aspx.cs"
➥Inherits="BooksApp.WebForm2" %>
```

LISTING 19.6 **BookList.aspx** (continued)

```
<asp:Content ID="Content1" ContentPlaceHolderID="head" runat="server">
    <title>List of Books</title>
</asp:Content>
<asp:Content ID="Content2" ContentPlaceHolderID="Header" runat="server">
    List of Books
</asp:Content>
<asp:Content ID="Content3" ContentPlaceHolderID="MainContent"
         runat="server">
    <%-- disable column generation since we're
         specifying them below --%>
    <asp:GridView ID="BookListGrid" runat="server"
              AutoGenerateColumns="False">
        <Columns>
            <%-- Make the title into a link that
                 goes to a detail page --%>
            <asp:HyperLinkField HeaderText="Title"
                              DataNavigateUrlFields="ID"
➥DataNavigateUrlFormatString="BookDetail.aspx?id={0}"
            DataTextField="Title" />
            <asp:BoundField DataField="Author" HeaderText="Author" />
        </Columns>
    </asp:GridView>
</asp:Content>
```

To set up the databinding, the code-behind file for this page has the following:

```
public partial class WebForm2 : System.Web.UI.Page
{
    protected void Page_Load(object sender, EventArgs e)
    {
        if (!IsPostBack)
        {
            //BookDataSource.DataSet is our fake "database"
            BookListGrid.DataSource =
                BookDataSource.DataSet.Tables["Books"];
            BookListGrid.DataBind();
        }
    }
}
```

Figure 19.7 shows the grid with book data from our DataSet.

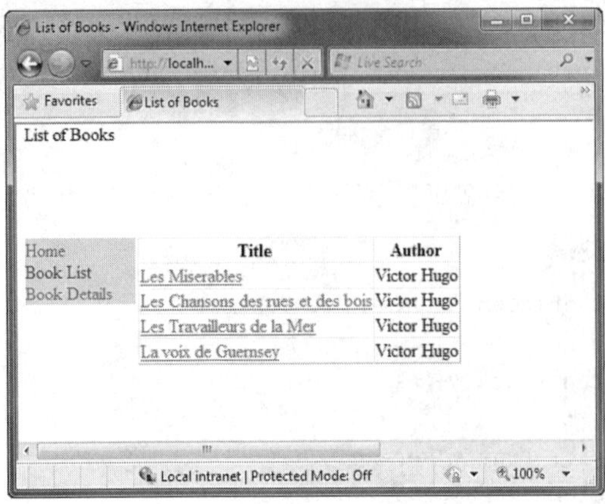

FIGURE 19.7
Binding a GridView to a data set automatically inserts rows of contents. You can configure it to sort and paginate the table as well.

Create a User Control

Scenario/Problem: You want to combine the basic ASP.NET controls into a coherent component that can be easily reused in multiple places (either on the same site or in different projects).

Solution: User controls in ASP.NET are similar to user controls in Windows Forms and WPF. They provide an easy way to encapsulate multiple controls into a unified interface.

Listing 19.7 shows the code for a control that binds a number of text fields together into a single book entry view. Listing 19.8 shows the code behind for this control.

LISTING 19.7 **BookEntrycontrol.ascx**

```
<%@ Control Language="C#" AutoEventWireup="true"
          CodeBehind="BookEntryControl.ascx.cs"
    Inherits="BooksApp.BookEntryControl" %>
<asp:Panel ID="Panel1" runat="server" BorderWidth="1px" Width="265px">
    <asp:Label ID="Label5" runat="server"
           Text="Book Entry" Font-Bold="True" />
    <asp:Table ID="Table1" runat="server">
        <asp:TableRow>
            <asp:TableCell>
```

LISTING 19.7 **BookEntrycontrol.ascx** (continued)

```
                <asp:Label ID="Label1" runat="server" Text="ID:" />
            </asp:TableCell>
            <asp:TableCell>
                    <asp:TextBox ID="TextBoxID" runat="server"
                                 ReadOnly="True"
➥Columns="5" />
            </asp:TableCell>
        </asp:TableRow>
        <asp:TableRow>
            <asp:TableCell>
                <asp:Label ID="Label6" runat="server" Text="Title:" />
            </asp:TableCell><asp:TableCell>
                    <asp:TextBox ID="TextBoxTitle" runat="server"
                                 Width="200px" />
            </asp:TableCell>
        </asp:TableRow>
        <asp:TableRow>
            <asp:TableCell>
                <asp:Label ID="Label2" runat="server" Text="Author:" />
            </asp:TableCell><asp:TableCell>
                    <asp:TextBox ID="TextBoxAuthor" runat="server"
                                 Width="200px" />
            </asp:TableCell>
        </asp:TableRow>
        <asp:TableRow>
            <asp:TableCell>
                <asp:Label ID="Label3" runat="server" Text="Year:" />
            </asp:TableCell><asp:TableCell>
                    <asp:TextBox ID="TextBoxPublishYear" runat="server"
                                 Width="75px" />
            </asp:TableCell>
        </asp:TableRow>
    </asp:Table>
</asp:Panel>
```

On the code side, it's possible to define properties that encapsulate the functionality of the control for those that use it.

LISTING 19.8 **BookEntryControl.ascx.cs**

```
using System;
using System.Collections.Generic;
using System.Linq;
using System.Web;
```

LISTING 19.8 **BookEntryControl.ascx.cs** (continued)

```
using System.Web.UI;
using System.Web.UI.WebControls;

namespace BooksApp
{
    public partial class BookEntryControl : System.Web.UI.UserControl
    {
        public int BookID
        {
            get { return int.Parse(TextBoxID.Text); }
            set { TextBoxID.Text = value.ToString(); }
        }

        public string Title
        {
            get { return TextBoxTitle.Text; }
            set { TextBoxTitle.Text = value; }
        }

        public string Author
        {
            get { return TextBoxAuthor.Text; }
            set { TextBoxAuthor.Text = value; }
        }

        public int PublishYear
        {
            get { return int.Parse(TextBoxPublishYear.Text); }
            set { TextBoxPublishYear.Text = value.ToString(); }
        }

        public bool IsEditable
        {
            get { return TextBoxID.ReadOnly; }
            set { TextBoxID.ReadOnly = TextBoxTitle.ReadOnly =
                    TextBoxAuthor.ReadOnly =
                       TextBoxPublishYear.ReadOnly = !value; }
        }

        protected void Page_Load(object sender, EventArgs e)
        {

        }
    }
}
```

To use this control in a page you must first register it and then place it in the markup like any other control, as shown in Listing 19.9.

LISTING 19.9 **BookDetail.aspx**

```
<%@ Page Title="" Language="C#" MasterPageFile="~/MasterPage.Master"
➥AutoEventWireup="true" CodeBehind="BookDetail.aspx.cs"
➥Inherits="BooksApp.BookDetailForm" %>
<%@ Register TagPrefix="how" TagName="BookEntry"
            Src="~/BookEntryControl.ascx" %>
<asp:Content ID="Content1" ContentPlaceHolderID="head" runat="server">
    <title>Book Detail</title>
</asp:Content>
<asp:Content ID="Content2" ContentPlaceHolderID="Header" runat="server">
    Book Detail
</asp:Content>
<asp:Content ID="Content3" ContentPlaceHolderID="MainContent"
            runat="server">
    <how:BookEntry runat="server" ID="bookEntry" IsEditable="false" />
</asp:Content>
```

The `<%@ Register >` tag defines how the control is referenced in the page. After that step, using it is the same as any built-in control.

The page's code-behind shows how to make use of the control's properties (see Listing 19.10).

LISTING 19.10 **BookDetail.aspx.cs**

```
using System;
using System.Collections.Generic;
using System.Linq;
using System.Web;
using System.Web.UI;
using System.Web.UI.WebControls;
using System.Data;

namespace BooksApp
{
    public partial class BookDetailForm : System.Web.UI.Page
    {
        protected void Page_Load(object sender, EventArgs e)
        {
            string idStr = Request.QueryString["id"];
            int id = 1;
            //parse the id to make sure it's a valid int
            if (int.TryParse(idStr, out id))
```

LISTING 19.10 **BookDetail.aspx.cs** (continued)

```
            {
                DataSet set = BookDataSource.DataSet;
                DataRow[] rows = set.Tables["Books"].Select(
                                     "ID=" + id.ToString());
                if (rows.Length == 1)
                {
                    bookEntry.BookID = id;
                    bookEntry.Title = rows[0]["Title"] as string;
                    bookEntry.Author = rows[0]["Author"] as string;
                    bookEntry.PublishYear = (int)rows[0]["PublishYear"];
                }
            }
        }
    }
}
```

Create a Flexible UI with Web Parts

Scenario/Problem: You want to create a website that features customizable, moveable widget-like components.

If you've ever been to websites such as www.msn.com and my.yahoo.com, you are familiar with websites that have componentized, moveable parts (see Figure 19.8).

Solution: Sites such as these have moveable, componentized layouts. It is quite easy to add this type of feature into your own application by using ASP.NET's web parts feature.

Define a `WebPartManager` and one or more `WebPartZones`. Into these zones you can place any standard or user-control object. In addition, there are prebuilt zones for editing the appearance and content of the web parts.

```
<%@ Page Language="C#" AutoEventWireup="true"
         CodeBehind="Default.aspx.cs"
➥Inherits="WebPartsDemo._Default" %>
<%@ Register TagPrefix="part" TagName="QuoteGenerator"
             Src="~/RandomQuoteControl.ascx"
➥%>
<%@ Register TagPrefix="part" TagName="TimeDisplay"
             Src="~/TimeDisplayControl.ascx" %>
```

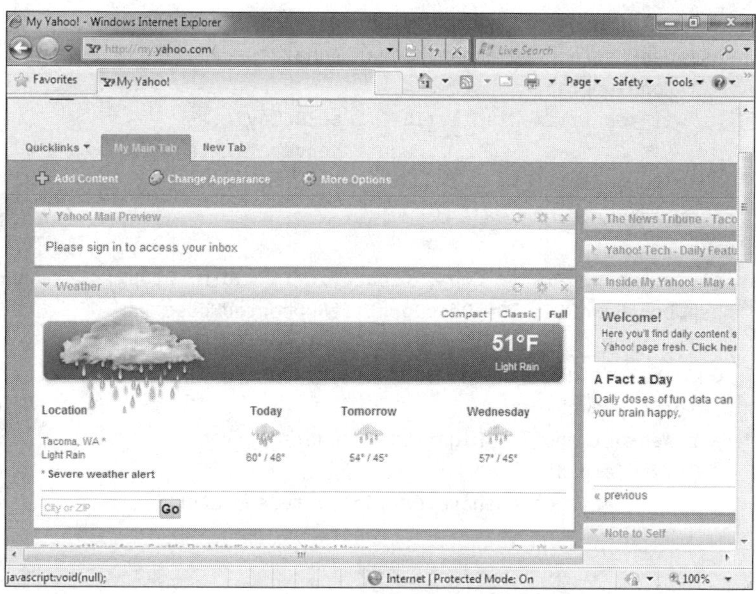

FIGURE 19.8
my.yahoo.com features movable, customizable widgets for news, movie times, images, and more.

```
<!DOCTYPE html PUBLIC "-//W3C//DTD XHTML 1.0 Transitional//EN"
➥"http://www.w3.org/TR/xhtml1/DTD/xhtml1-transitional.dtd">

<html xmlns="http://www.w3.org/1999/xhtml" >
<head runat="server">
    <title>Web Parts Demo</title>
</head>
<body>
    <form id="form1" runat="server">
    <asp:WebPartManager ID="WebPartManager1" runat="server"
                        Personalization- Enabled="true"/>
    <div>
        <div style="float: left; width: 250px;" >
            <asp:WebPartZone ID="LeftZone" runat="server">
                <ZoneTemplate>
                    <part:QuoteGenerator ID="QuoteGenerator1"
                                         runat="server"
➥title="Quotes"/>
                </ZoneTemplate>
            </asp:WebPartZone>
        </div>
```

```
        <div style="margin-left: 20px; float:left; width:250px;">
            <asp:WebPartZone ID="CenterZone" runat="server">
                <ZoneTemplate>
                    <part:TimeDisplay ID="TimeDisplay1"
                                          runat="server" title="Time"/>
                </ZoneTemplate>
            </asp:WebPartZone>
        </div>
        <div style="margin-left: 20px; float: left; width: 250px; ">
            <asp:DropDownList ID="DropDownListSupportedModes"
                              runat="server" AutoPostBack="true"
             OnSelectedIndexChanged="OnDisplayModeChanged">
            </asp:DropDownList>
            <asp:WebPartZone ID="Rightzone" runat="server">
                <ZoneTemplate>
                    <part:QuoteGenerator ID="QuoteGenerator2"
                                             runat="server"
                                  title="Quote"/>
                </ZoneTemplate>
            </asp:WebPartZone>
            <%-- These zones help manipulate the
                 look and content of the parts --%>
            <asp:EditorZone ID="EditorZone1" runat="server">
                <ZoneTemplate>
                    <asp:AppearanceEditorPart ID="AppearanceEditor1"
                                                    runat="server" />
                </ZoneTemplate>
            </asp:EditorZone>
            <asp:CatalogZone ID="CatalogZone1" runat="server">
                <ZoneTemplate>
                    <asp:PageCatalogPart ID="PageCatalogPart1"
                                             runat="server" />
                </ZoneTemplate>
            </asp:CatalogZone>
        </div>
    </div>
    </form>
</body>
</html>
```

The preceding code referenced two user controls. There is nothing special you need to do for these controls to work in a Web Part environment, as you can see in the following listings for one of those controls:

```
<!-- RandomQuoteControl.ascx -->
<%@ Control Language="C#" AutoEventWireup="true"
            CodeBehind="RandomQuoteControl.ascx.cs"
            Inherits="WebPartsDemo.RandomQuoteControl" %>
<asp:Table ID="Table2" runat="server">
    <asp:TableRow runat="server">
        <asp:TableCell ID="QuoteText"
                       runat="server">
        </asp:TableCell>
    </asp:TableRow>
    <asp:TableRow runat="server">
        <asp:TableCell ID="QuoteAuthor"
                       runat="server"
                       Font-Italic="True">
        </asp:TableCell>
    </asp:TableRow>
</asp:Table>
```

The code-behind just loads a random quote into the table cells:

```
using System;
using System.Collections.Generic;
using System.Linq;
using System.Web;
using System.Web.UI;
using System.Web.UI.WebControls;

namespace WebPartsDemo
{
    public partial class RandomQuoteControl : System.Web.UI.UserControl
    {
        private static Random rand = new Random();
        private static string[][] quotes = new string[][] {
            new string[]{"To be wicked does not insure prosperity.",
                          "Victor Hugo"},
            new string[]{"Not being heard is no reason for silence.",
                          "Victor Hugo"},
            new string[]{"Philosophy is the microscope of thought.",
                          "Victor Hugo"},
            //more quotes in the sample project
            };

        protected void Page_Load(object sender, EventArgs e)
        {
            string[] quote = quotes[rand.Next(0, quotes.Length)];
            QuoteText.Text = quote[0];
            QuoteAuthor.Text = quote[1];
```

```
        }
    }
}
```

You can find the source for the `TimeDisplayControl` in the WebPartsDemo sample application.

Note that the `title` attribute of the custom controls is not actually implemented on those controls, but the `WebPartManager` will use it to set the title bar text on the web parts.

By default, the `EditorZone` and `CatalogZone` are not visible. They can be made visible by setting the `DisplayMode` property on the `WebPartManager` object. In the code-behind, the available modes are put in a drop-down list, allowing the user to select one.

```
using System;
using System.Collections.Generic;
using System.Linq;
using System.Web;
using System.Web.UI;
using System.Web.UI.WebControls;
using System.Web.UI.WebControls.WebParts;

namespace WebPartsDemo
{
    public partial class _Default : System.Web.UI.Page
    {
        protected void Page_Load(object sender, EventArgs e)
        {
            if (!IsPostBack)
            {
                foreach (WebPartDisplayMode mode in
➥WebPartManager1.SupportedDisplayModes)
                {
                    DropDownListSupportedModes.Items.Add(mode.Name);
                }
            }
        }

        protected void OnDisplayModeChanged(object sender, EventArgs e)
        {
            WebPartManager1.DisplayMode =
➥WebPartManager1.DisplayModes[DropDownListSupportedModes.SelectedValue];
        }
    }
}
```

Create a Simple AJAX Page

Scenario/Problem: You want to allow rich interaction and send data to and from the web server without a full page refresh.

In the last few years, Asynchronous Javascript and XML (AJAX) has become the de facto standard for defining rich (well, richer than plain HTML) interaction on modern websites. AJAX allows you to update part of a web page without forcing a full refresh (and, incidentally, scrolling the page to the top).

Solution: Taking advantage of AJAX is easy with the built-in UpdatePanel control. Controls placed in an UpdatePanel automatically update themselves asynchronously using the same style of programming you're already used to.

The AJAX demo in Listings 19.11 and 19.12 shows two examples: a typical update in response to a button and a timer that causes a regular refresh of content. Figure 19.9 shows the demo in action.

LISTING 19.11 **AJAX Demo—Default.aspx**

```
<%@ Page Language="C#" AutoEventWireup="true"
         CodeBehind="Default.aspx.cs"
➥Inherits="AjaxDemo._Default" %>

<!DOCTYPE html PUBLIC "-//W3C//DTD XHTML 1.0 Transitional//EN"
➥"http://www.w3.org/TR/xhtml1/DTD/xhtml1-transitional.dtd">

<html xmlns="http://www.w3.org/1999/xhtml" >
<head runat="server">
    <title>AJAX Demo</title>
</head>
<body>
    <form id="form1" runat="server">
    <asp:ScriptManager ID="ScriptManager1" runat="server"/>
    <div>
        <asp:UpdatePanel ID="UpdatePanel1" runat="server">
            <ContentTemplate>
                <asp:TextBox ID="TextBoxValue" runat="server"
➥ReadOnly="True">0</asp:TextBox>
                <br />
                <asp:Button ID="ButtonIncrement" runat="server"
                            Text="Increment"
                    onclick="ButtonIncrement_Click" />
            </ContentTemplate>
```

LISTING 19.11 **AJAX Demo—Default.aspx** (continued)

```
        </asp:UpdatePanel>
        <asp:UpdatePanel ID="UpdatePanel2" runat="server">
            <ContentTemplate>
                <asp:Timer ID="Timer1" runat="server"
                           Interval="1000" ontick="OnTick" />
                <br />
                <asp:TextBox ID="TextBoxTime"
                             runat="server" ReadOnly="true"/>
            </ContentTemplate>
        </asp:UpdatePanel>
    </div>
    </form>
</body>
</html>
```

LISTING 19.12 **AJAX Demo—Default.aspx.cs**

```
using System;
using System.Collections.Generic;
using System.Linq;
using System.Web;
using System.Web.UI;
using System.Web.UI.WebControls;

namespace AjaxDemo
{
    public partial class _Default : System.Web.UI.Page
    {
        protected void Page_Load(object sender, EventArgs e)
        {
        }

        protected void ButtonIncrement_Click(object sender, EventArgs e)
        {
            int val = Int32.Parse(TextBoxValue.Text);
            ++val;
            TextBoxValue.Text = val.ToString();
        }

        protected void OnTick(object sender, EventArgs e)
        {
            TextBoxTime.Text = DateTime.Now.ToString("HH:mm:ss");
        }
    }
}
```

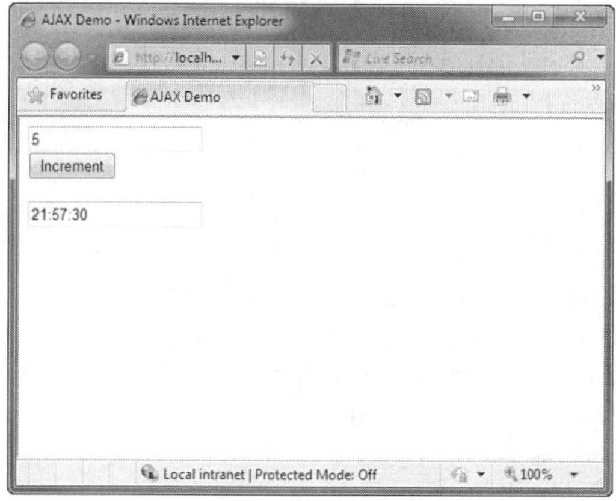

FIGURE 19.9
These two fields are updated independently of each other, without a page reload.

Do Data Validation

Scenario/Problem: You want to validate user input before sending it to the server.

Solution: In general, there are two places to do input and data validation: on the client and the server. On the client side, ASP.NET provides various controls for automatically checking that the input is in a certain range. On the server, ASP.NET runs these same rules automatically for you. If you have more complex validation methods, these can be run on the server.

The Validation demo in Listings 19.13 and 19.14 shows some of the built-in validators in action as well as a custom, server-side validator. Figure 19.10 shows a screenshot of the Validation demo.

LISTING 19.13 **Validation Demo—Default.aspx**

```
<%@ Page Language="C#" AutoEventWireup="true"
         CodeBehind="Default.aspx.cs"
➥Inherits="ClientSideValidation._Default" %>

<!DOCTYPE html PUBLIC "-//W3C//DTD XHTML 1.0 Transitional//EN"
➥"http://www.w3.org/TR/xhtml1/DTD/xhtml1-transitional.dtd">

<html xmlns="http://www.w3.org/1999/xhtml" >
<head runat="server">
    <title>Validation Demo</title>
```

LISTING 19.13 **Validation Demo—Default.aspx** (continued)

```
</head>
<body>
    <form id="form1" runat="server">
    <div>
        Name:
        <br />
        <asp:TextBox ID="TextBoxName" runat="server" />
        <asp:RequiredFieldValidator
            ID="RequiredFieldValidator1" runat="server"
            ErrorMessage="You must enter your name"
            ControlToValidate="TextBoxName" />
        <br />
        Date:
        <br />
        <asp:TextBox ID="TextBoxDate" runat="server" />
        <asp:RegularExpressionValidator
            ID="RegularExpressionValidator1" runat="server"
            ErrorMessage="Enter a date in the form MM/DD/YYYY"
            ControlToValidate="TextBoxDate"
             ValidationExpression="(0[1-9]|1[012])/
➥([1-9]|0[1-9]|[12][0-9]|3[01])/\d{4}"
            />
        <br />
        A Number from 1-10
        <br />
        <asp:TextBox ID="TextBoxNumber" runat="server" />
        <asp:RangeValidator ID="RangeValidator1" runat="server"
        ErrorMessage="Enter a value from 1 to 10"
        ControlToValidate="TextBoxNumber"
        MinimumValue="1" MaximumValue="10" />
        <br />
        A Prime Number < 1000:
        <br />
        <%-- Notice that you can have multiple validators per field --%>
        <asp:TextBox ID="TextBoxPrimeNumber" runat="server" />
        <asp:CompareValidator ID="CompareValidator1" runat="server"
            ErrorMessage="Number is not < 1000"
            ControlToValidate="TextBoxPrimeNumber"
            Operator="LessThan"
            ValueToCompare="1000" Type="Integer"
             />
        <%-- While the standard validators generate javascript,
```

LISTING 19.13 **Validation Demo—Default.aspx** (continued)

```
        a custom validator has to go back to the server to work--%>
        <asp:CustomValidator ID="CustomValidator1" runat="server"
            ErrorMessage="Number is not prime"
            ControlToValidate="TextBoxPrimeNumber"
            onservervalidate="OnValidatePrime" />
        <br />
        <asp:Button ID="buttonSubmit" runat="server" Text="Submit"
            onclick="buttonSubmit_Click"  />
    </div>
    </form>
</body>
</html>
```

LISTING 19.14 **Validation Demo—Default.aspx.cs**

```
using System;
using System.Collections.Generic;
using System.Linq;
using System.Web;
using System.Web.UI;
using System.Web.UI.WebControls;

namespace ClientSideValidation
{
    public partial class _Default : System.Web.UI.Page
    {
        protected void Page_Load(object sender, EventArgs e)
        {

        }

        protected void OnValidatePrime(object source,
                                       ServerValidateEventArgs args)
        {
            int val = 0;
            args.IsValid = false;
            if (int.TryParse(args.Value, out val))
            {
                args.IsValid = (val < 1000) && IsPrime(val);
            }
```

LISTING 19.14 **Validation Demo—Default.aspx.cs** (continued)

```
        }

        private bool IsPrime(int number)
        {
            //check for evenness
            if (number % 2 == 0)
            {
                if (number == 2)
                    return true;
                return false;
            }
            //don't need to check past the square root
            int max = (int)Math.Sqrt(number);
            for (int i = 3; i <= max; i += 2)
            {
                if ((number % i) == 0)
                {
                    return false;
                }
            }
            return true;
        }

        protected void buttonSubmit_Click(object sender, EventArgs e)
        {
            if (Page.IsValid)
            {
                /* Now that data is being submitted,
                   do your server-side validation
                 * here (or at some point before trusting it). */

                /*if (string.IsNullOrEmpty(TextBoxName.Text))
                {
                    Response.Redirect("MyErrorPage.aspx");
                }*/
            }
        }
    }
}
```

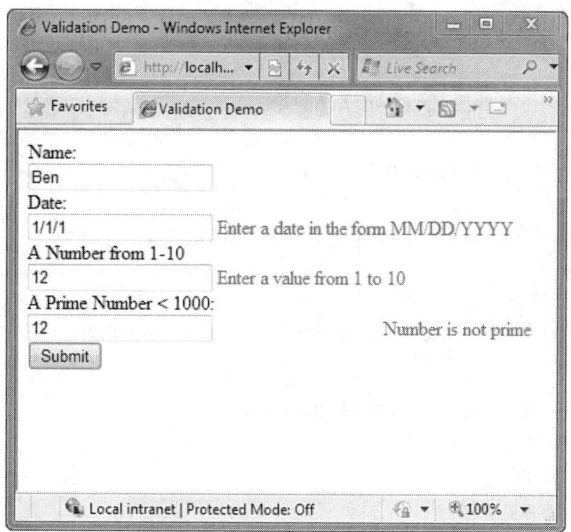

FIGURE 19.10

ASP.NET provides easy-to-use validation controls as well as a way to do custom validation, as in the prime number check in this example.

NOTE You should consider these data-validation controls to be for the *user's* benefit, *not yours*. Just because you use validation in the browser means nothing for your own integrity. For example, a user who disables JavaScript will not have his data validated on the client-side at all.

You should *always* validate data on the server side. Thankfully, ASP.NET does quite a bit of this for you automatically with the included validation controls. But always remember to add your own custom validation routines on the server when needed and include them in the .aspx code. When submitting, check the `Page.IsValid` property to ensure that all server-side validation succeeds before trusting the data.

A popular way to think about this is in terms of a boundary of trusted data. All user input has to pass through the trusted boundary, where it is inspected, sanitized, and normalized, before being given whatever (minimal) level of trust you give it.

Remember, never trust user input. Never.

Maintain Application State

Scenario/Problem: You need to store data on an application-wide basis.

Application data is exactly that: It is the same across the entire app, for all users in all sessions. It is the equivalent of a global variable.

Solution: The first way to store this is in the global Application static class, accessible from any page:

```
protected void Page_Load(object sender, EventArgs e)
{
    Application["LastPageLoad"] = DateTime.UtcNow;
    //...
    DateTime lastLoad = (DateTime)Application["LastPageLoad"];
}
```

If you have global data that you want to expire at some point, you can instead use the application cache:

```
protected void Page_Load(object sender, EventArgs e)
{
    //will not expire from cache
    Context.Cache["MyData"] = myDataSet;

    Context.Cache.Add(
        "MyExpiringData",
        myExpiringDataSet,
        // other cache objects that depend on this one
        null,
        // absolutely remove from cache in one hour
        DateTime.UtcNow.AddHours(1),
        // until then, remove 15 minutes after last access
        TimeSpan.FromMinutes(15),
        System.Web.Caching.CacheItemPriority.Normal,
        // delegate to call when an object is removed from cache
        null
        );
}
```

Maintain UI State

Scenario/Problem: You have state associated with a specific control that needs to be maintained across page loads.

Solution: The standard ASP.NET controls use something called View state to encode their values from one page load to another. View state is included as a hidden field in the request object. You can include your own information as well.

```
protected void buttonSubmit_Click(object sender, EventArgs e)
{
    ViewState["MyCustomData"] = 13;
    int val = (int)ViewState["MyCustomData"];
    //do something with it
}
```

Maintain User Data in a Session

Scenario/Problem: You need to store data associated with a specific user across page loads.

Solution: A user session generally starts when your user hits your site for the first time (and possibly logs in).

The Session State demo in Listings 19.15 and 19.16 shows how to store a user's name in the session and use that to change the UI.

LISTING 19.15 **Session State Demo—Default.aspx**

```
<%@ Page Language="C#" AutoEventWireup="true"
        CodeBehind="Default.aspx.cs"
➥Inherits="SessionDemo._Default" %>

<!DOCTYPE html PUBLIC "-//W3C//DTD XHTML 1.0 Transitional//EN"
➥"http://www.w3.org/TR/xhtml1/DTD/xhtml1-transitional.dtd">

<html xmlns="http://www.w3.org/1999/xhtml" >
<head runat="server">
    <title>Session state</title>
</head>
<body>
    <form id="form1" runat="server">
    <div>
        <asp:Label ID="LabelHello" runat="server" Text="Hello, "/>
        <asp:Label ID="LabelName" runat="server" Text=""/>
        <asp:Label ID="LabelEnterYourName" runat="server"
                Text="Enter your name: "/>
        <asp:TextBox ID="TextBoxName"
            runat="server"/>
        <asp:Button ID="ButtonSubmit" runat="server" Text="Submit"
```

LISTING 19.15 **Session State Demo—Default.aspx** (continued)

```
            onclick="ButtonSubmit_Click" />
    </div>
    </form>
</body>
</html>
```

LISTING 19.16 **Session State Demo—Default.aspx.cs**

```
using System;
using System.Collections.Generic;
using System.Linq;
using System.Web;
using System.Web.UI;
using System.Web.UI.WebControls;

namespace SessionDemo
{
    public partial class _Default : System.Web.UI.Page
    {
        protected void Page_Load(object sender, EventArgs e)
        {
            SetVisibility();
        }

        private void SetVisibility()
        {
            bool hasUser = !string.IsNullOrEmpty(
                                    Session["UserName"] as string);
            LabelHello.Visible = LabelName.Visible = hasUser;
            LabelEnterYourName.Visible
                    = TextBoxName.Visible
                    = ButtonSubmit.Visible
                    = !hasUser;
            if (hasUser)
            {
                LabelName.Text = Session["UserName"] as string;
            }
        }

        protected void ButtonSubmit_Click(object sender, EventArgs e)
        {
            Session["UserName"] = TextBoxName.Text;
```

LISTING 19.16 **Session State Demo—Default.aspx.cs** (continued)

```
            SetVisibility();
        }
    }
}
```

Store Session State

Scenario/Problem: You must decide where users' session information should be stored, especially if the default of in-process will not work for you.

This becomes a more important issue when your site is large enough to need multiple web servers or has enough users that their session information has significant memory requirements.

Solution: Session state is configured in the machine.config file, which is located in the Config directory under the .NET runtime installation folder. On my machine, this is C:\Windows\Microsoft.NET\Framework\v4.0.21006\Config. Each web server must have the machine.config file configured with the correct session state settings.

Store State in the Process

This is the default settings and does not need to be configured but to make it explicit:

```
<sessionState
    mode="InProc"
    cookieless="false"
    timeout="20"
/>
```

The cookieless setting applies to any type of session state server and tells .NET whether cookies should be used to identify clients.

The timeout setting is the number of minutes before a session is abandoned.

Store State on a State Server

A state server is a machine running the aspnet_state.exe service, which you can find in the Services applet in the Administrative Tools folder.

```
<sessionState
    mode="StateServer"
    stateConnectionString="tcpip=127.0.0.1:42626"
    cookieless="false"
    timeout="20" />
```

Just put the state machine's IP address in the `stateConnectionString` attribute.

Store State in a SQL Server Database

You can also store session information in a SQL Server database:

```
<sessionState
    mode="SQLServer"
    sqlConnectionString="data source=127.0.0.1;Trusted_Connection=yes"
    cookieless="false"
    timeout="20" />
```

You also need to configure SQL Server to have the right database. The .NET Framework comes with a SQL script (InstallSqlState.sql, located in the same directory as machine.config) to perform this installation on your SQL Server instance.

Use Cookies to Restore Session State

Scenario/Problem: You need to identify a user when he returns to your website.

Solution: Use a cookie. Cookies are merely bits of text that are included with a response and request. The browser will save the data locally and send it back the next time the user visits the site. This allows you to persist simple data (say, a user ID) on the user's system and use that to pull up his specific info when he logs back in the next time. Using them is quite easy.

Here, I've modified the previous session state example to look for a cookie with the username. The cookie expires in 30 seconds for easy retesting.

```
using System;
using System.Collections.Generic;
using System.Linq;
using System.Web;
using System.Web.UI;
using System.Web.UI.WebControls;

namespace SessionDemo
{
    public partial class _Default : System.Web.UI.Page
    {
        private const bool useCookie = true;

        protected void Page_Load(object sender, EventArgs e)
        {
            if (Session.IsNewSession && useCookie)
            {
```

```
            ReadCookie();
        }
        SetVisibility();
    }

    private void SetVisibility()
    {
        bool hasUser = !string.IsNullOrEmpty(
          Session["UserName"] as string);
        LabelHello.Visible = LabelName.Visible = hasUser;
        LabelEnterYourName.Visible
          = TextBoxName.Visible
          = ButtonSubmit.Visible
          = !hasUser;
        if (hasUser)
        {
            LabelName.Text = Session["UserName"] as string;
        }
    }

    protected void ButtonSubmit_Click(object sender, EventArgs e)
    {
        Session["UserName"] = TextBoxName.Text;

        SetVisibility();

        if (useCookie)
        {
            WriteCookie();
        }
    }

    private void ReadCookie()
    {
        foreach (string cookie in Request.Cookies)
        {
            if (cookie == "username")
            {
                Session["UserName"] = Request.Cookies[cookie].Value;
                return;
            }
        }
    }

    private void WriteCookie()
    {
```

```
            HttpCookie cookie = new HttpCookie(
➥"username", Session["UserName"] as string);
            //comment out if you want a session-cookie
            cookie.Expires = DateTime.Now.AddSeconds(30);
            Response.Cookies.Add(cookie);
        }
    }
}
```

Use ASP.NET Model-View-Controller (MVC)

Scenario/Problem: You want to use a framework to abstract away the data, view, and control parts of a web application, making it easier to build and easier to modify over time.

Solution: There are many frameworks out there that work on top of ASP.NET. Microsoft provides one called ASP.NET MVC (for Model-View-Controller), which ships with Visual Studio 2010.

In this section, we'll build a simple app to display our books database which was created in Chapter 13, "Databases."

Create the Application

In Visual Studio, create a new project and for the type select ASP.NET MVC 2 Web Application.

When it asks whether you want to create a unit test project, select No.

This creates a new project that contains a number of folders and files that are already generated for you, including folders for each of the types of components: controllers, models, and views.

Create the Model

For this, we'll use the Entity Framework, which was introduced in Chapter 13.

1. Right-click the Models folder and an ADO.NET Entity Data Model called Book.edmx.
2. In the Entity Data Model Wizard that comes up, select Generate from Database and click Next.
3. Choose the database we created in Visual Studio in Chapter 13, type `BooksDBEntities` for the connection settings, and click Next.

4. Expand the Tables tree and check the box next to the Books table. For Model Namespace, type `BooksDB.Models`, and click Finish.

You've now created an object model that maps the database data.

Create the Controller

Unlike in traditional ASP.NET where each URL maps to a specific page file in your source code, MVC maps URLs to controllers and methods. For example, the URL http://localhost:1000/Home/Index maps to a controller named HomeController, which must be in the Controllers folder of your project and named HomeController.cs. (The project creation wizard should have created this for you.)

In addition, the Index portion of the URL maps to a public method called `Index` that returns an ActionResult enumeration.

Modify the HomeController code to look like this:

```
using System;
using System.Collections.Generic;
using System.Linq;
using System.Web;
using System.Web.Mvc;

namespace MVCBooksApp.Controllers
{
    [HandleError]
    public class HomeController : Controller
    {
        MVCBooksApp.Models.BooksDBEntities _db =
              new Models.BooksDBEntities();

        public ActionResult Index()
        {
            //return a viewn named Index
            return View(_db.Books.ToList());
        }
    }
}
```

At this point, you should build the project.

Create the View

ASP.NET MVC looks for Views based on the name of the controller and the method being called.

NOTE If the Views\Home\Index.aspx file already exists, delete it. We'll recreate it here.

1. Right-click the `Index()` method in the HomeController and select Add View.
2. Give it the name `Index`.
3. Check the box Create a Strongly-Typed View.
4. In the View data class drop-down, select MVCBooksApp.Models.Book.
5. In the View content drop-down, select List.
6. Click Add.

You now have an application that will show a list of all the movies in the database, similar to what's shown in Figure 19.11.

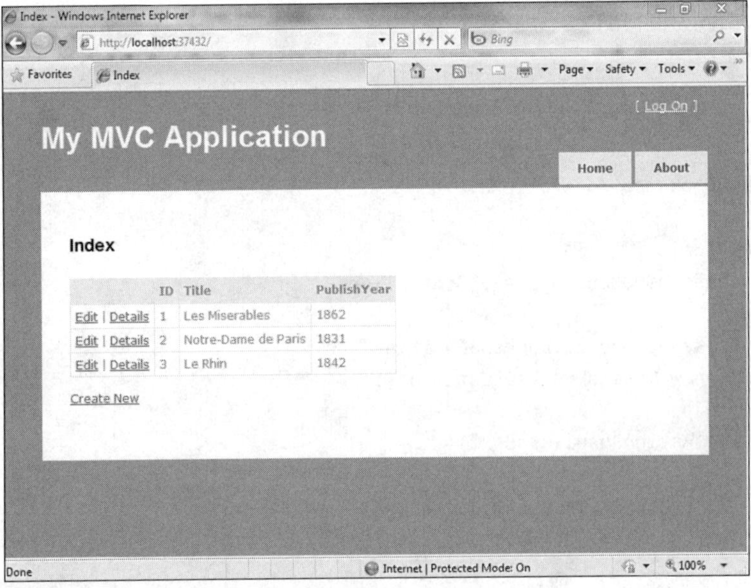

FIGURE 19.11
ASP.NET MVC does a lot of work behind the scenes to let you easily display data on a web page.

Enable Creation of New Records

The default version of the index page shows a Create New link. It's easy to add some functionality behind that.

To do this, we need to create a new action in the HomeController. Add two new methods to HomeController.cs:

```
//return the default Create view
public ActionResult Create()
{
    return View();
}

//called when the user submits the new book back to the server
[AcceptVerbs(HttpVerbs.Post)]
public ActionResult Create(
    [Bind(Exclude="Id")]
    MVCBooksApp.Models.Book newBook)
{
    if (!ModelState.IsValid)
        return View();
    _db.AddToBooks(newBook);
    _db.SaveChanges();
    //send us back to the Index
    return RedirectToAction("Index");
}
```

To create the view, follow the same steps for when you created the Index view, but for the View content drop-down, select Create.

From the generated HTML code in Create.aspx, you need to delete the field for ID, because it's an auto-generated field in the database:

```
<p>
    <label for="ID">ID:</label>
    <%= Html.TextBox("ID") %>
    <%= Html.ValidationMessage("ID", "*") %>
</p>
```

The finished page resembles Figure 19.12.

Edit Records

To edit existing records, we need to again add some methods to our controller, one that takes an ID parameter so that we know which record we're editing and the other to accept the POST request and send the updated record back to the database.

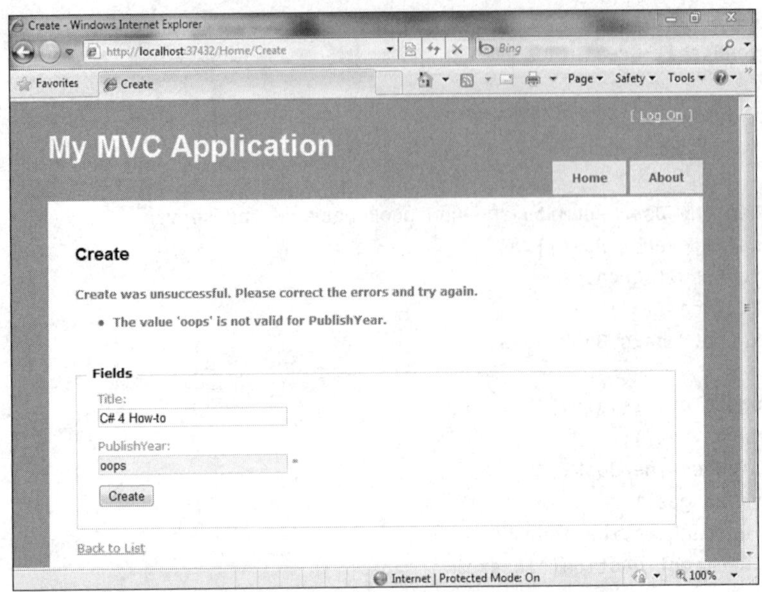

FIGURE 19.12
The Create page even has basic data validation already included.

Add these methods to HomeController.cs:

```
public ActionResult Edit(int id)
{
    //LINQ expression - see Chapter 21
    Models.Book book = (from b in _db.Books
                        where b.ID == id
                        select b).First();
    return View(book);
}

[AcceptVerbs(HttpVerbs.Post)]
public ActionResult Edit(Models.Book editBook)
{
    //get the original book from the database
    Models.Book book = (from b in _db.Books
                        where b.ID == editBook.ID
                        select b).First();
    if (!ModelState.IsValid)
        return View(book);
    //apply changes back to the original
    _db.ApplyCurrentValues(book.EntityKey.EntitySetName, editBook);
```

```
    _db.SaveChanges();
    return RedirectToAction("Index");
}
```

You can follow the same procedure as before to create the Edit View; for View content, choose Edit. You will also need to remove the ID fields from the generated HTML for this view.

NOTE To run the sample application MVCBooksApp, you need to modify the connection string for BooksDBEntities in the web.config file to point to your version of the database you created from Chapter 13.

NOTE To learn more about ASP.NET MVC and read quite a few tutorials, visit http://www.asp.net/learn/mvc.

CHAPTER 20

Silverlight

IN THIS CHAPTER

- Create a Silverlight Project
- Play a Video
- Build a Download and Playback Progress Bar
- Response to Timer Events on the UI Thread
- Put Content into a 3D Perspective
- Make Your Application Run out of the Browser
- Capture a Webcam
- Print a Document

In some ways, Silverlight is Microsoft's answer to Adobe Flash. More accurately, it's a way of getting .NET and WPF into users' browsers in an easily deployable format. Silverlight is essentially a web-deployed application platform that runs on the end user's computer.

Silverlight 1.0 was essentially a glorified media player. The only programming language it supported was JavaScript.

Silverlight 2 added a small version of the .NET Framework, more controls, a subset of WPF, and more data-access options. It was now programmable with any supported .NET language.

Silverlight 3 added yet more controls, more video and audio decoding options, more 3D support, more graphics hardware acceleration, and other improvements.

Silverlight 4 (in beta at the time of this writing) adds printing, even more controls, localization enhancements, web cam support, drag and drop, support for multitouch interfaces, and more.

This chapter demonstrates creating a simple Silverlight application and shows how to take advantage of new features in Silverlight 3 and 4.

Create a Silverlight Project

Scenario/Problem: Create a new Silverlight project.

Solution: As with all .NET code, you can use the SDKs alone with your text editor of choice to create Silverlight applications. For most of us, Visual Studio is usually the tool of choice. To use Visual Studio for Silverlight projects, you need to install the Silverlight 4 Beta Tools for Visual Studio, available from http://silverlight.net/getstarted/silverlight-4-beta/.

Once this is installed, you can follow these steps to create a basic Silverlight application:

1. In the Visual Studio menu, go to File, New, Project.
2. Find Silverlight in the project type tree.
3. Select Silverlight Application.
4. Select the appropriate options in the New Silverlight Application dialog box, shown in Figure 20.1. A Silverlight project must be hosted in a website, and this dialog box allows you to select which existing web project to associate it with (or you can create a new one).
5. Click OK, and Visual Studio generates two projects for you, named ApplicationName and ApplicationName.Web by default.

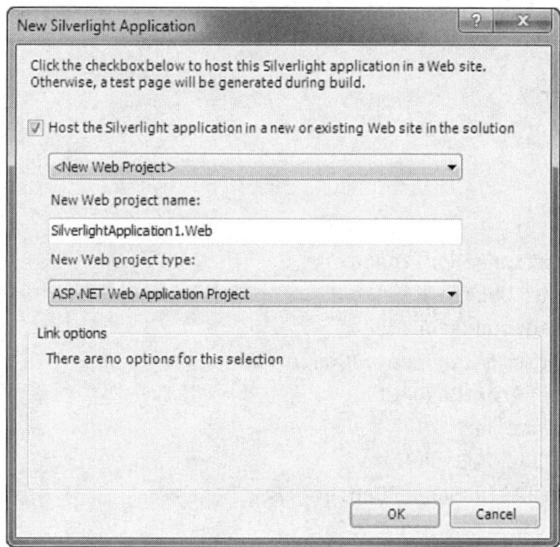

FIGURE 20.1
The New Silverlight Application dialog box allows you to specify basic settings for your application, such as which website to host it in.

Play a Video

Scenario/Problem: You want to play a video over the Web.

Solution: This seems to be a canonical example with Silverlight. After all, most of the early Silverlight apps were video players. However, we'll jazz up the example with more features through this chapter. Video content can be displayed with Silverlight's MediaElement control. We'll also add a few buttons to control the video and a TextBox to specify the URL of the video to play. Listing 20.1 shows the XAML for the main application page, and Listing 20.2 shows its code-behind.

LISTING 20.1 **MainPage.xaml**

```
<UserControl x:Class="VideoPlayer.MainPage"
    xmlns="http://schemas.microsoft.com/winfx/2006/xaml/presentation"
    xmlns:x="http://schemas.microsoft.com/winfx/2006/xaml"
    xmlns:local="clr-namespace:VideoPlayer"
    Width="400" Height="300">
    <Grid x:Name="LayoutRoot" Background="Black">
        <Grid.RowDefinitions>
            <RowDefinition Height="*"/>
            <RowDefinition Height="Auto"/>
        </Grid.RowDefinitions>
```

LISTING 20.1 **MainPage.xaml** (continued)

```
        <MediaElement Grid.Row="0"
            x:Name="videoPlayer"
            Stretch="Fill"
        >
        </MediaElement>
        <StackPanel Grid.Row="1">
            <StackPanel Orientation="Horizontal">
                <TextBlock Text="URL:"
                           Foreground="White"
                           VerticalAlignment="Center"/>
                <TextBox x:Name="textBoxURL"
➥Text="http://mschnlnine.vo.llnwd.net
➥/d1/ch9/8/7/1/6/6/4/MTSloobOnMac_2MB_ch9.wmv"
                        VerticalAlignment="Center" />
            </StackPanel>
            <StackPanel Orientation="Horizontal"
                        HorizontalAlignment="Center">
                <Button x:Name="buttonPlay" Content="Play" Margin="4"
➥Click="buttonPlay_Click" />
                <Button x:Name="buttonStop" Content="Stop" Margin="4"
➥Click="buttonStop_Click" />
            </StackPanel>
        </StackPanel>
    </Grid>
</UserControl>
```

LISTING 20.2 **MainPage.xaml.cs**

```
using System;
using System.Collections.Generic;
using System.Linq;
using System.Net;
using System.Windows;
using System.Windows.Controls;
using System.Windows.Documents;
using System.Windows.Input;
using System.Windows.Media;
using System.Windows.Media.Animation;
using System.Windows.Shapes;
using System.Threading;

namespace VideoPlayer
{
    public partial class MainPage : UserControl
```

LISTING 20.2 **MainPage.xaml.cs** (continued)

```
    {
        private static DependencyProperty IsPlayingProperty;

        static MainPage()
        {
            IsPlayingProperty = DependencyProperty.Register(
                  "IsPlaying", typeof(bool),
          typeof(MainPage),
                  new PropertyMetadata(false));
        }

        public bool IsPlaying
        {
            get
            {
                return (bool)GetValue(IsPlayingProperty);
            }
            set
            {
                SetValue(IsPlayingProperty, value);
            }
        }

        public MainPage()
        {
            InitializeComponent();
        }


        private void buttonPlay_Click(object sender, RoutedEventArgs e)
        {
            if (!IsPlaying)
            {
                //changing the source needlessly
                //causes the video to reset
                if (videoPlayer.Source == null ||
                    videoPlayer.Source.OriginalString
                      != textBoxURL.Text)
                {
                    videoPlayer.Source = new Uri(textBoxURL.Text);
                }
                videoPlayer.Play();
                IsPlaying = true;
                //it may be better to use a value converter
                //to set button text, but that would distract
                // from the essential part of this example
```

LISTING 20.2 **MainPage.xaml.cs** (continued)

```
                buttonPlay.Content = "Pause";
            }
            else if (videoPlayer.CanPause)
            {
                videoPlayer.Pause();
                IsPlaying = false;
                buttonPlay.Content = "Play";
            }
        }

        private void buttonStop_Click(object sender, RoutedEventArgs e)
        {
            videoPlayer.Stop();
            IsPlaying = false;
            buttonPlay.Content = "Play";
        }
    }
}
```

This is all the code you need to create your own media player on a website (see Figure 20.2). As you can see, it uses the familiar XAML and .NET code you are already used to.

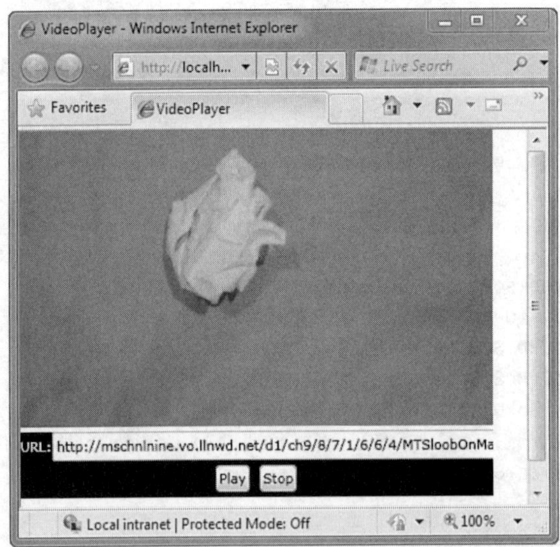

FIGURE 20.2
It requires very little effort to play most common types of media in a Silverlight application.

Build a Download and Playback Progress Bar

Scenario/Problem: You want to display a progress bar that shows how much of the video is buffered as well as the current playback position.

Solution: One thing every media content downloader needs is a bar that shows both download progress and playback position. Thankfully, Silverlight fully supports the concept of custom controls. Listing 20.3 shows the XAML, and Listing 20.4 shows the code-behind for this control.

LISTING 20.3 **PlayDownloadProgressControl.xaml**

```
<UserControl x:Class="VideoPlayer.PlayDownloadProgressControl"
    xmlns="http://schemas.microsoft.com/winfx/2006/xaml/presentation"
    xmlns:x="http://schemas.microsoft.com/winfx/2006/xaml"
    Width="400" Height="300">
    <Canvas x:Name="LayoutRoot" Background="White">
        <Line x:Name="DownloadProgress" X1="0" Y1="0"
              X2="0" Y2="0" Stroke="DarkGray"
              Canvas.Left="0" Canvas.Top="2" StrokeThickness="3"/>
        <Line x:Name="PlaybackProgress" X1="0" Y1="0"
              X2="0" Y2="0" Stroke="DarkGreen"
              Canvas.Left="0" Canvas.Top="2" StrokeThickness="3"/>
    </Canvas>
</UserControl>
```

LISTING 20.4 **PlayDownloadProgressControl.xaml.cs**

```
using System;
using System.Net;
using System.Windows;
using System.Windows.Controls;

namespace VideoPlayer
{
    public partial class PlayDownloadProgressControl : UserControl
    {
        public PlayDownloadProgressControl()
        {
            InitializeComponent();
        }
```

LISTING 20.4 **PlayDownloadProgressControl.xaml.cs** (continued)

```
        public void UpdatePlaybackProgress(double playbackPercent)
        {

            PlaybackProgress.X2 = PlaybackProgress.X1 +
              (playbackPercent * LayoutRoot.ActualWidth / 100.0);
        }

        public void UpdateDownloadProgress(double downloadPercent)
        {
            DownloadProgress.X2 = DownloadProgress.X1 +
             (downloadPercent * LayoutRoot.ActualWidth / 100.0);
        }
    }
}
```

To incorporate this into video player app, add the following bolded lines to the MainPage.xaml file from Listing 20.1:

```
...
<MediaElement Grid.Row="0"
    x:Name="videoPlayer"
    Stretch="Fill"
        DownloadProgressChanged="videoPlayer_DownloadProgressChanged"
>
</MediaElement>
<local:PlayDownloadProgressControl x:Name="progressBar"
            Height="4" Grid.Row="0"
      VerticalAlignment="Bottom"/>
<StackPanel Grid.Row="1">
...
```

The `DownloadProgressChanged` event notifies you when a new chunk has been downloaded so you can update the progress:

```
private void videoPlayer_DownloadProgressChanged(object sender,
                                                 RoutedEventArgs e)
{
    progressBar.UpdateDownloadProgress(
                    100.0 * videoPlayer.DownloadProgress);
}
```

However, there is no equivalent event for playback progress (which makes sense if you think about it: How often should an event like that fire anyway? Every millisecond? Every second? Every minute?) Because playback is application dependent, it is up to you to monitor the playing media and update your UI accordingly. This is the topic of the next section.

Response to Timer Events on the UI Thread

Scenario/Problem: You want a timer that fires events on the UI thread so you don't have to do the UI invoking yourself.

Solution: There are a few different timers you can use for triggering events at specific intervals, but recall that all UI updates must occur from the UI thread. You can always use `BeginInvoke` to marshal a delegate to the UI thread, but there's a simpler way. WPF and Silverlight provide the `DispatcherTimer` class in the `System.Windows.Threading` namespace, which always fires on the UI thread. You can use this timer for updating the playback progress.

```
private System.Windows.Threading.DispatcherTimer timer =
             new System.Windows.Threading.DispatcherTimer();

public MainPage()
{
    InitializeComponent();
    //one second
    timer.Interval = new TimeSpan(0,0,1);
    timer.Start();
    timer.Tick += new EventHandler(timer_Tick);
}

void timer_Tick(object sender, EventArgs e)
{
    switch (videoPlayer.CurrentState)
    {
        case MediaElementState.Playing:
        case MediaElementState.Buffering:
            if (videoPlayer.NaturalDuration.HasTimeSpan)
            {
                double total =
➥videoPlayer.NaturalDuration.TimeSpan.TotalMilliseconds;
                if (total > 0.0)
                {
                    double elapsed =
➥videoPlayer.Position.TotalMilliseconds;
                    progressBar.UpdatePlaybackProgress(
                                   100.0 * elapsed / total);
                }
            }
            break;
```

```
        default:
            //do nothing
            break;
    }
}
```

NOTE The `DispatcherTimer` is not Silverlight specific, and it can be used in any WPF app where you need a timer on the UI thread.

Figure 20.3 shows the video application with the progress bar in action.

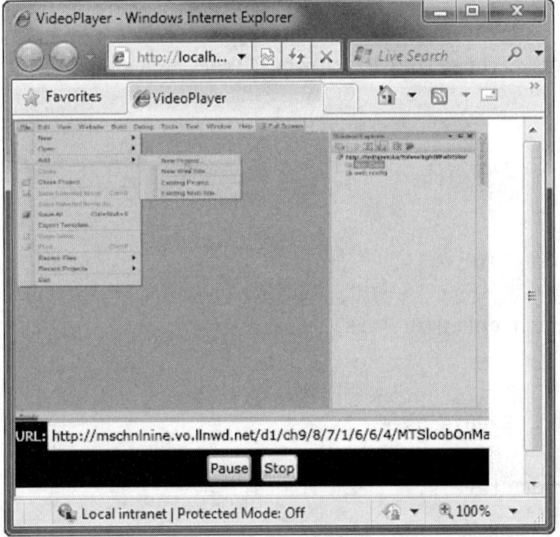

FIGURE 20.3
Silverlight allows many of the same features of WPF, such as user controls.

Put Content into a 3D Perspective

Scenario/Problem: You want to put controls onto a 3D surface in a Silverlight application.

Solution: You can use MediaElement.Projection to transform the MediaElement onto a 3D plane. Figure 20.4 shows the results.

```
<MediaElement Grid.Row="0"
    x:Name="videoPlayer"
    Stretch="Fill"
    DownloadProgressChanged="videoPlayer_DownloadProgressChanged">
    <MediaElement.Projection>
        <PlaneProjection RotationY="45" RotationX="-15"/>
    </MediaElement.Projection>
</MediaElement>
```

And like all other dependency properties, these can be animated.

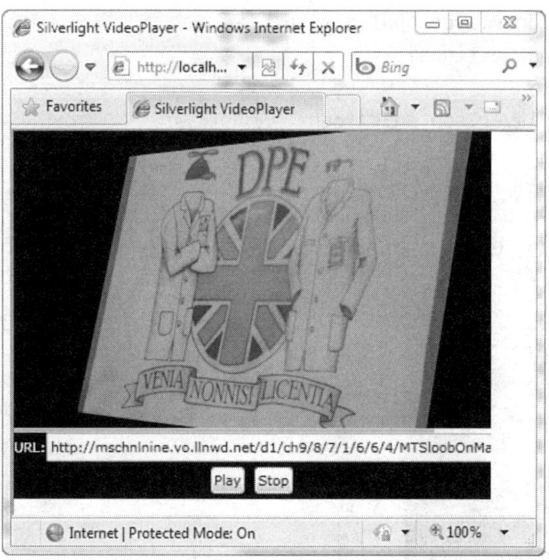

FIGURE 20.4
It's easy to add a 3D perspective to your Silverlight app with the Projection property.

Make Your Application Run out of the Browser

Scenario/Problem: You want the user to be able to download and run the application without being connected to the Internet.

Solution: When is a web application not a web application? When it's been enabled to run straight from the desktop. First, add a small (say, 48×48 pixels) PNG image file to your solution and set its `Build Action` to `Content`. In the Silverlight tab of your project's settings, there is a check box to enable running the application outside of the browser, in addition to a button that opens a dialog box enabling you to specify additional settings (such as the icon). Enabling this setting creates the file OutOfBrowserSettings.xml in the Properties folder of your project. It looks something like the following:

```
<OutOfBrowserSettings ShortName="VideoPlayer Application"
                      EnableGPUAcceleration="True"
                      ShowInstallMenuItem="True">
  <OutOfBrowserSettings.Blurb>
VideoPlayer Application on your desktop; at home,
➥at work or on the go.
</OutOfBrowserSettings.Blurb>
  <OutOfBrowserSettings.WindowSettings>
    <WindowSettings Title="VideoPlayer Application" />
  </OutOfBrowserSettings.WindowSettings>
  <OutOfBrowserSettings.Icons>
    <Icon Size="48,48">VideoPlayerIcon.png</Icon>
  </OutOfBrowserSettings.Icons>
</OutOfBrowserSettings>
```

When you right-click the application, you get an option to install it locally, as shown in Figure 20.5.

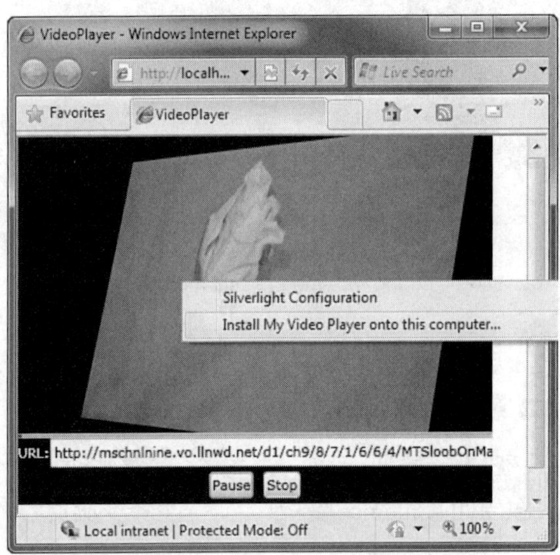

FIGURE 20.5
It's easy to make your Silverlight application available offline with some simple configuration settings.

Once the app is installed, right-clicking it gives you the option to remove it from the local machine.

Capture a Webcam

Scenario/Problem: You want to display video output from an attached web camera.

Solution: Use Silverlight 4's support for video capture devices.

To set this up, you need to first ask the user for permission to use the web cam. If granted, you can assign the device to a `CaptureSource` object and then assign that object to a `VideoBrush`. The `VideoBrush` can then be used as the `Fill` brush for the destination control (a `Rectangle` in this case).

This technique is demonstrated in Listings 20.5 and 20.6.

LISTING 20.5 **MainPage.xaml**

```
<UserControl x:Class="WebCam.MainPage"
    xmlns="http://schemas.microsoft.com/
➥winfx/2006/xaml/presentation"
    xmlns:x="http://schemas.microsoft.com/
➥winfx/2006/xaml"
    xmlns:d="http://schemas.microsoft.com/
➥expression/blend/2008"
    xmlns:mc="http://schemas.openxmlformats.org/
➥markup-compatibility/2006"
    mc:Ignorable="d"
    d:DesignHeight="300" d:DesignWidth="400">

    <Grid x:Name="LayoutRoot" Background="White">
        <Rectangle x:Name="videoRect" Fill="Bisque"
                   Width="640" Height="480"
                   VerticalAlignment="Top"
                   HorizontalAlignment="Left"/>
        <Button Content="Start Webcam"
                Name="buttonStartWebcam"
                Width="98"
                Height="23"
                HorizontalAlignment="Left"
                VerticalAlignment="Top"
                Click="buttonStartWebcam_Click" />
    </Grid>
</UserControl>
```

LISTING 20.6 **MainPage.xaml.cs**

```
using System;
using System.Windows;
using System.Windows.Controls;
using System.Windows.Documents;
using System.Windows.Input;
using System.Windows.Media;
using System.Windows.Media.Animation;
using System.Windows.Shapes;

namespace WebCam
{
    public partial class MainPage : UserControl
    {
        CaptureSource _captureSource = null;

        public MainPage()
        {
            InitializeComponent();

        }

        void StartWebcam()
        {
            if (_captureSource != null &&
                _captureSource.State != CaptureState.Started)
            {
                if (CaptureDeviceConfiguration.AllowedDeviceAccess
                 || CaptureDeviceConfiguration.RequestDeviceAccess())
                {
                    VideoCaptureDevice device =
➥CaptureDeviceConfiguration.GetDefaultVideoCaptureDevice();
                    if (device != null)
                    {
                        _captureSource = new CaptureSource();
                        _captureSource.VideoCaptureDevice = device;
                        _captureSource.Start();
                        VideoBrush brush = new VideoBrush();
                        brush.Stretch = Stretch.Uniform;
                        brush.SetSource(_captureSource);
                        videoRect.Fill = brush;
                    }
                }
            }
        }
```

LISTING 20.6 **MainPage.xaml.cs** (continued)

```
        private void buttonStartWebcam_Click(object sender,
                                             RoutedEventArgs e)
        {
            StartWebcam();
        }
    }
}
```

Print a Document

Scenario/Problem: You want to print from Silverlight to a printer attached to the user's computer.

Solution: Silverlight 4 now contains printer support which you can easily take advantage of.

Remember from Chapter 17, "Graphics with Windows Forms and GDI+," that printing in .NET is similar to drawing on the screen. In Silverlight, to print, all you need to do is generate any UIElement-derived object and pass it to the printing system, as this code demonstrates:

```
private void buttonPrint_Click(object sender, RoutedEventArgs e)
{
    PrintDocument doc = new PrintDocument();
    doc.PrintPage += new EventHandler<PrintPageEventArgs>(doc_PrintPage);
    doc.Print();
}

void doc_PrintPage(object sender, PrintPageEventArgs e)
{
    //simply set the PageVisual property to the UIElement
    //that you want to print
    e.PageVisual = canvas;
    e.HasMorePages = false;
}
```

The PrintPage event handler sets the PageVisual property to whatever control you want printed—it's as easy as that. Too see the full example, see the SketchPad sample project in the accompanying source code. This sample app lets you draw with the mouse and then print the results.

PART IV

Advanced C#

IN THIS PART

CHAPTER 21

LINQ

IN THIS CHAPTER

- Query an Object Collection
- Order the Results
- Filter a Collection
- Get a Collection of a Portion of Objects (Projection)
- Perform a Join
- Query XML
- Create XML
- Query the Entity Framework
- Query a Web Service (LINQ to Bing)
- Speed Up Queries with PLINQ (Parallel LINQ)

Language Integrated Query, or LINQ, is a flexible, SQL-like query language designed to give the programmer consistent syntax to query any data set, whether database, XML, or just plain objects. What's more, it's usable from the comfort and safety of your everyday C# file.

NOTE LINQ is a language that merely *looks* like SQL, and only superficially. If you're familiar with SQL, you'll notice that the various parts of the query appear in a different order than you're used to. LINQ is not directly related to actual database SQL languages and is *not* a way of embedding actual SQL queries in your code. It *is* a way of embedding generic queries in your code that may eventually turn into database queries, but LINQ can do so much more.

Query an Object Collection

Scenario/Problem: You want to query a collection for all objects meeting some criteria.

Solution: This and the following examples use some data objects to demonstrate how LINQ works.

```
class Book
{
    public string Title { get; set; }
    public int AuthorId { get; set; }
    public int PublishYear { get; set; }

    public Book(string title, int authorId, int year)
    {
        this.Title = title;
        this.AuthorId = authorId;
        this.PublishYear = year;
    }

    public override string ToString()
    {
        return string.Format("{0} - {1}", Title, PublishYear);
    }
}

class Author
{
    public int Id { get; set; }
    public string FirstName { get; set; }
```

```
    public string LastName { get; set; }
    public Author (int id, string firstName, string lastName)
    {
        this.Id = id;
        this.FirstName = firstName;
        this.LastName = lastName;
    }
}
//...
List<Book> books = new List<Book>{
    new Book("Le Rhin", 1, 1842),
    new Book("Les Burgraves",1, 1843),
    new Book("Napoléon le Petit",1, 1852),
    new Book("Les Châtiments",1, 1853),
    new Book("Les Contemplations", 1, 1856),
    new Book("Les Misérables", 1, 1862)  };

List<Author> authors = new List<Author>
{
    new Author(1, "Victor", "Hugo")
};
```

The most basic LINQ query just retrieves all the book information.

```
var allBooks = from book in books select book;
foreach (Book book in allBooks)
{
    Console.WriteLine(book.ToString());
}
```

The `var` keyword is often used with LINQ for reasons you'll see later. In this case, `allBooks` is a collection of `Book` objects. The output is as follows:

```
Le Rhin - 1842
Les Burgraves - 1843
Napoléon le Petit - 1852
Les Châtiments - 1853
Les Contemplations - 1856
Les Misérables – 1862
```

Order the Results

Scenario/Problem: You want to organize the results in some order.

Solution: Use the `orderby` statement.

Here's how to order the results in ascending order (the default):

```
var ordered = from book in books orderby book.Title select book;
```

Use the following for descending order:

```
var ordered = from book in books
              orderby book.Title descending
              select book;
```

And here's how to sort multiple columns:

```
var ordered = from book in books
              orderby book.PublishYear, book.Title descending
              select book;
```

Filter a Collection

Scenario/Problem: You want to select objects from a collection that satisfy a given condition.

Solution: Like SQL, LINQ has a `where` clause which can be used to filter the results according to the conditions you specify:

```
var before1850 = from book in books
                 where book.PublishYear < 1850
                 select book;
```

Here's the output:

```
Books before 1850:
Le Rhin - 1842
Les Burgraves - 1843
```

If you want to use multiple conditions, use the `&&` and `||` operators just as you would in an `if` statement:

```
var dateRange = from book in books
                where book.PublishYear >= 1850
                  &&  book.PublishYear <= 1855
                select book;
```

Get a Collection of a Portion of Objects (Projection)

Scenario/Problem: Given our Book object, you want to return a collection of objects that represent just the titles and publication years, dropping the author.

Solution: Before LINQ, this involved some usually trivial but clunky code to iterate over all the objects and insert the desired properties into a new collection. With LINQ, it's a single line (which is broken here due to the limited width of the page:

```
var justTitlesAfter1850 = from book in books
                          where book.PublishYear > 1850
                          select book.Title;
```

This line returns titles of books published after 1850:

```
Titles of books after 1850:
Napoléon le Petit
Les Châtiments
Les Contemplations
Les Misérables
```

The result, `justTitlesAfter1850`, is a collection of string objects, but what if you want to project out more than one field? See the next section.

Perform a Join

Scenario/Problem: You want to combine data from multiple tables.

Solution: Use the `join` keyword to combine tables on a common field.

This is where the true power of LINQ shines through. In this example, the `Author` collection will be combined with the `Book` collection, and only the author and title information will be projected out.

```
var withAuthors = from book in books
          join author in authors on book.AuthorId equals author.Id
          select new { Book = book.Title,
                       Author = author.FirstName + " "
                                + author.LastName };
Console.WriteLine("Join with authors:");
foreach (var bookAndAuthor in withAuthors)
{
    Console.WriteLine("{0}, {1}",
```

```
                        bookAndAuthor.Book,
                        bookAndAuthor.Author);
}
```

Here's the output:

```
Join with authors:
Le Rhin, Victor Hugo
Les Burgraves, Victor Hugo
Napoléon le Petit, Victor Hugo
Les Châtiments, Victor Hugo
Les Contemplations, Victor Hugo
Les Misérables, Victor Hugo
```

So what is the type of `withAuthors`? It is an anonymous type (see Chapter 1, "Type Fundamentals") generated for the purpose of just this LINQ query. Because there is no type name for it (at least, not in the code there isn't), `var` must be used to refer to both the collection and the collection's objects.

> **NOTE** LINQ can generates these anonymous objects as needed, but it can also set properties in an existing named object that you specify. See the LINQ to Bing example later in this chapter.

Query XML

> **Scenario/Problem:** You want to extract data from XML documents.

Solution: LINQ contains its own set of XML-manipulation classes that are optimized for LINQ queries. The syntax of the query itself is exactly the same as with plain objects:

```
XDocument doc = XDocument.Load("LesMis.xml");
var chaptersWithHe = from chapter in doc.Descendants("Chapter")
                     where chapter.Value.Contains(" he ")
                     select chapter.Value;

Console.WriteLine("Chapters with 'he':");
foreach (var title in chaptersWithHe)
{
    Console.WriteLine(title);
}
```

This example uses the same LesMis.xml file from Chapter 14's `XPath` discussion. The output is as follows:

```
Chapters with 'he':
What he believed
What he thought
```

Create XML

Scenario/Problem: You need to easily generate XML in a quick, hierarchical way.

Solution: Although LINQ can of course load and query XML generated from any source, it also provides very easy XML-creation mechanisms.

```
XElement xml = new XElement("Books",
                new XElement("Book",
                    new XAttribute("year",1856),
                    new XElement("Title", "Les Contemplations")),
                new XElement("Book",
                    new XAttribute("year", 1843),
                    new XElement("Title", "Les Burgraves"))
                    );
```

The preceding creates the following XML fragment:

```
<Books>
  <Book year="1856">
    <Title>Les Contemplations</Title>
  </Book>
  <Book year="1843">
    <Title>Les Burgraves</Title>
  </Book>
</Books>
```

Query the Entity Framework

Scenario/Problem: You need to query a database.

Solution: Although there is such a thing as LINQ to SQL, LINQ only works with SQL Server, and it has been more or less deprecated by Microsoft. The recommendation is to use LINQ to Entity Framework, so that is what will be discussed here.

Figure 21.1 shows the Entity Framework diagram of an Author and Book table, in addition to a Textbook table that is used later in this section.

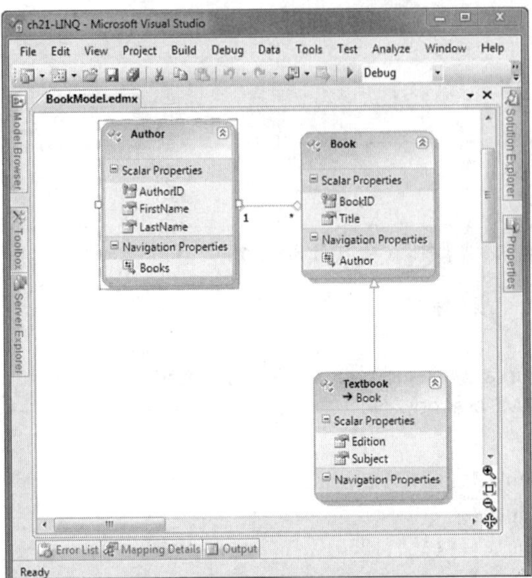

FIGURE 21.1
LINQ works very well with the Entity Framework, and you should use that rather than the deprecated LINQ to SQL when possible.

The LINQ code in this section is very similar to that in earlier sections:

```
//query all books
//See the LinqToEntities sample project for the definition of
//BooksEntities
BooksEntities bookContext = new BooksEntities();
var books = from book in bookContext.BookSet select book;
foreach (var book in books)
{
    //load the author info
    book.AuthorReference.Load();
    Console.WriteLine("{0}, {1} {2}", book.Title,
              book.Author.FirstName, book.Author.LastName);
}
```

The following output is produced:

```
Les Misérables, Victor Hugo
Les Contemplations, Victor Hugo
War and Peace, Leo Tolstoy
Notre-Dame de Paris, Victor Hugo
Biology: Visualizing Life, George Johnson
```

Use Entity Inheritance with LINQ

The Entity Framework allows you to specify inheritance relationships within the database tables. LINQ works seamlessly with this feature:

```
var textBooks = from book in bookContext.BookSet where book is Textbook
                select book as Textbook;
foreach (var textBook in textBooks)
{
    //load the author info
    textBook.AuthorReference.Load();
    Console.WriteLine("{0}, {1} {2} - {3}",
                    textBook.Title, textBook.Author.FirstName,
                    textBook.Author.LastName, textBook.Subject);
}
```

Query a Web Service (LINQ to Bing)

Scenario/Problem: You want to query a web service's public API with LINQ.

Solution: Out of the box, LINQ can query object collections, SQL, entities, and XML. To expand its capabilities, you have a choice: Implement a custom LINQ provider, or convert your target into one of the current implementations.

The latter option is generally much easier to implement and is shown in Listings 21.1 and 21.2. The Bing API is used to demonstrate using LINQ to convert the XML results to custom objects.

LISTING 21.1 **Bing.cs**

```
using System;
using System.Collections.Generic;
using System.Linq;
using System.Text;
using System.Xml.Linq;

namespace LinqToBing
{
    class SearchResult
    {
        public string Title { get; set; }
        public string Url { get; set; }
        public string Description { get; set; }
    }
```

LISTING 21.1 **Bing.cs** (continued)

```
    class Bing
    {
        public string AppId { get; set; }
        const string BingNameSpace =
➥ "http://schemas.microsoft.com/LiveSearch/2008/04/XML/web";

        public Bing(string appId)
        {
            this.AppId = appId;
        }

        public IEnumerable<SearchResult> QueryWeb(string query)
        {
            string escaped = Uri.EscapeUriString(query);
            string url = BuildUrl(escaped);
            XDocument doc = XDocument.Load(url);
            XNamespace ns = BingNameSpace;
            IEnumerable<SearchResult> results =
                from sr in doc.Descendants(ns + "WebResult")
                select new SearchResult
                {
                    Title = sr.Element(ns + "Title").Value,
                    Url = sr.Element(ns + "Url").Value,
                    Description = sr.Element(ns + "Description").Value
                };
            return results;
        }

        string BuildUrl(string query)
        {
            return "http://api.search.live.net/xml.aspx?"
                + "AppId=" + AppId
                + "&Query=" + query
                + "&Sources=Web"
                + "&Version=2.0"
                + "&Web.Count=10"
                + "&Web.Offset=0"
                ;
        }
    }
}
```

LISTING 21.2 **Program.cs**

```
using System;
using System.Collections.Generic;
using System.Linq;
using System.Text;
using System.Net;

namespace LinqToBing
{
    class Program
    {
        //#error Get your own AppId at http://www.bing.com/developers/
        const string AppId = "YOUR APPID HERE";

        static void Main(string[] args)
        {
            Bing search = new Bing(AppId);

            string query = "Visual Studio 2010";

            IEnumerable<SearchResult> results = search.QueryWeb(query);

            foreach (SearchResult result in results)
            {
                Console.WriteLine("{0}"
                    + Environment.NewLine + "\t{1}"
                    + Environment.NewLine + "\t{2}"
                    + Environment.NewLine,
                    result.Title, result.Url, result.Description);
            }

            Console.ReadKey();
        }
    }
}
```

NOTE To see an excellent example of how to create a custom LINQ provider (and gain an appreciation for how much work goes into creating a good one), see Fabrice Marguerie's LINQ to Amazon example at http://weblogs.asp.net/fmarguerie/archive/2006/06/26/Introducing-Linq-to-Amazon.aspx and in the book *LINQ in Action*.

Speed Up Queries with PLINQ (Parallel LINQ)

Scenario/Problem: You want to take advantage of multiple processor cores during LINQ queries.

Solution: Use the `AsParallel()` extension method.

If your original query is

```
var query = from val in data
            where (ComplexCriteria(val)==true)
            select val;
foreach (var q in query)
{
    //process result
}
```

where `ComplexCriteria()` is just an arbitrary Boolean function that examines the values in the data, then you can parallelize this with a simple addition:

```
var query = from val in data.AsParallel()
            where (ComplexCriteria(val)==true)
            select val;
foreach (var q in query)
{
    //process result
}
```

NOTE You are more likely to get elements returned out of order using PLINQ unless you specify that you want order preserved using the `AsOrdered()` or `OrderBy()` extension method, as shown here:

```
var query = from obj in data.AsParallel().AsOrdered() select obj;
var query = from obj in data.AsParallel().OrderBy(obj.Name)
            select obj;
```

Unfortunately, this might negate some of the benefits of using PLINQ.

NOTE PLINQ only works on LINQ to Objects and LINQ to XML.

CHAPTER 22

Memory Management

IN THIS CHAPTER

- Measure Memory Usage of Your Application
- Clean Up Unmanaged Resources Using Finalization
- Clean Up Managed Resources Using the Dispose Pattern
- Force a Garbage Collection
- Create a Cache That Still Allows Garbage Collection
- Use Pointers
- Speed Up Array Access
- Prevent Memory from Being Moved
- Allocate Unmanaged Memory

One of the greatest advantages to using a managed language such as C# in the Common Language Runtime (CLR) environment is that you don't have to worry about memory management as much as you did in languages such as C or C++.

That said, there are still memory-related topics that you need to understand as a C# developer. Furthermore, sometimes you just have to drop out of the world of managed code and get access to pointers. It's ugly, and you should try to avoid it, but it's there when you need it.

Measure Memory Usage of Your Application

Scenario/Problem: You need to find out how much memory your application is using.

Solution: The GC class contains many handy memory-related methods, including GetTotalMemory(), which is the amount of memory the garbage collector *thinks* is allocated to your application. The number may not be exactly right because of objects that haven't been garbage collected yet. However, this has the advantage of being able to tell you about how much memory a certain part of your program uses, rather than the entire process.

```
long available = GC.GetTotalMemory(false);
Console.WriteLine("Before allocations: {0:N0}", available);

int allocSize = 40000000;
byte[] bigArray = new byte[allocSize];

available = GC.GetTotalMemory(false);
Console.WriteLine("After allocations: {0:N0}", available);
```

This same code prints the following:

```
Before allocations: 651,064
After allocations: 40,690,080
```

Get the OS View of Your Application's Memory

You can also ask the operating system to give you information about your process:

```
//the Process class is in the System.Diagnostics namespace
Process proc = Process.GetCurrentProcess();
Console.WriteLine("Process Info: "+Environment.NewLine+
    "Private Memory Size: {0:N0}"+Environment.NewLine +
    "Virtual Memory Size: {1:N0}" + Environment.NewLine +
    "Working Set Size: {2:N0}" + Environment.NewLine +
```

```
    "Paged Memory Size: {3:N0}" + Environment.NewLine +
    "Paged System Memory Size: {4:N0}" + Environment.NewLine +
    "Non-paged System Memory Size: {5:N0}" + Environment.NewLine,
    proc.PrivateMemorySize64,
    proc.VirtualMemorySize64,
    proc.WorkingSet64,
    proc.PagedMemorySize64,
    proc.PagedSystemMemorySize64,
    proc.NonpagedSystemMemorySize64 );
```

Here's the output:

```
Process Info:
Private Memory Size: 75,935,744
Virtual Memory Size: 590,348,288
Working Set Size: 29,364,224
Paged Memory Size: 75,935,744
Paged System Memory Size: 317,152
Non-paged System Memory Size: 37,388
```

What each of those numbers mean is not necessarily intuitive, and you should consult a good operating system book, such as *Windows Internals* (Microsoft Press), to learn more about how virtual memory works.

> **NOTE** You can also use performance counters to track this and a lot of other information about your application or its environment. You can access these interactively from perfmon.exe, or see the MSDN documentation for the `PerformanceCounter` class to see how you can incorporate these into your own applications.

Clean Up Unmanaged Resources Using Finalization

> **Scenario/Problem:** You have a native resource (such as a kernel object) and need to ensure that it gets cleaned up by the garbage collector.

If for some reason you want to manage raw file handles, bitmaps, memory-mapped files, synchronization objects, or any other kernel object, you need to ensure that the resource is cleaned up. Each of these resources is represented by handles. To manipulate handles, you need to use native Windows functions via P/Invoke (see Chapter 26, "Interacting with the OS and Hardware").

Solution: Here's an example of a class that manages a file handle with help from the .NET classes:

```
using System;
using System.IO;
using System.Runtime.InteropServices;

namespace Finalizer
{
    public class MyWrappedResource
    {
        [DllImport("kernel32.dll", CharSet = CharSet.Auto,
            CallingConvention = CallingConvention.StdCall,
            SetLastError = true)]
        public static extern IntPtr CreateFile(
              string lpFileName,
              uint dwDesiredAccess,
              uint dwShareMode,
              IntPtr SecurityAttributes,
              uint dwCreationDisposition,
              uint dwFlagsAndAttributes,
              IntPtr hTemplateFile
              );

        [DllImport("kernel32.dll", SetLastError = true)]
        [return: MarshalAs(UnmanagedType.Bool)]
        static extern bool CloseHandle(IntPtr hObject);

        //IntPtr is used to represent OS handles
        IntPtr _handle = IntPtr.Zero;

        public MyWrappedResource(string filename)
        {
            _handle = CreateFile(filename,
                0x80000000, //access read-only
                1,          //share-read
                IntPtr.Zero,
                3,          //open existing
                0,
                IntPtr.Zero);
        }

        //Finalizers look like C++ destructors,
        //but they are NOT deterministic
        ~MyWrappedResource()
        {
```

```
            //note: in real apps, don't put anything
            //in finalizers that doesn't need to be there
            Console.WriteLine("In Finalizer");
            if (_handle != IntPtr.Zero)
            {
                CloseHandle(_handle);
            }
        }

        public void Close()
        {
            if (_handle != IntPtr.Zero)
            {
                //we're already closed, so this object
                //doesn't need to be finalized anymore
                GC.SuppressFinalize(this);
                CloseHandle(_handle);
            }
        }
    }
}
```

When .NET detects a finalizer in a class, it ensures that it is called at some point in garbage collection.

NOTE The finalization phase of the collection process can be quite expensive, so it's important to use finalizers only when necessary. They should almost never be used for managed resources—only unmanaged ones.

Clean Up Managed Resources Using the Dispose Pattern

Scenario/Problem: You need to ensure that managed resources (such as database connections) get cleaned up when needed.

Many types of resources are limited (files, database connections, bitmaps, and so on) but have .NET classes to manage them. Like unmanaged resources, you still need to control their lifetimes, but because they are wrapped in managed code, finalizers are not appropriate.

Solution: You need to use the dispose pattern. Let's look at a similar example as the last section, but with a managed resource. The `IDisposable` interface defines a Dispose method, but to use the pattern correctly you need to define a few more things yourself:

```
public class MyWrappedResource : IDisposable
{
    //our managed resource
    IDbConnection _conn = null;

    public MyWrappedResource(string filename)
    {
    }

    public void Close()
    {
        Dispose(true);
    }

    public void Dispose()
    {
        Dispose(true);
    }

    private bool _disposed = false;
    protected void Dispose(bool disposing)
    {
        //in a class hierarchy, don't forget to call the base class!
        //base.Dispose(disposing);
        if (!_disposed)
        {
            _disposed = true;
            if (disposing)
            {
                //cleanup managed resources
                if (_conn!=null)
                {
                    _conn.Dispose();
                }
            }
            //cleanup unmanaged resources here, if any
        }
    }
}
```

When using the dispose pattern, you call Dispose yourself when you're done with the resource:

```
//use try-finally to guarantee cleanup
MyWrappedResource res = null;
try
{
    res = new MyWrappedResource("TestFile.txt");
}
finally
{
    if (res != null)
    {
        res.Dispose(true);
    }
}
```

This pattern is so common that there is a shortcut syntax:

```
using (MyWrappedResource res = new MyWrappedResource("TestFile.txt"))
{
    //do something with res
}
```

NOTE You should not use the Dispose pattern with Windows Communication Framework objects. Unfortunately, they are not implemented according to this pattern. You can find more information on this problem by doing an Internet search for the numerous articles out there detailing this problem.

Use Dispose with Finalization

Whereas finalizers should not touch managed objects, `Dispose` can (and should) clean up unmanaged resources. Here's an example:

```
using System;
using System.IO;
using System.Runtime.InteropServices;
using System.Data;

namespace Dispose
{
    public class MyWrappedResource : IDisposable
    {
        [DllImport("kernel32.dll", CharSet = CharSet.Auto,
                CallingConvention = CallingConvention.StdCall,
                SetLastError = true)]
        public static extern IntPtr CreateFile(
              string lpFileName,
              uint dwDesiredAccess,
```

```
            uint dwShareMode,
            IntPtr SecurityAttributes,
            uint dwCreationDisposition,
            uint dwFlagsAndAttributes,
            IntPtr hTemplateFile
            );

        [DllImport("kernel32.dll", SetLastError = true)]
        [return: MarshalAs(UnmanagedType.Bool)]
        static extern bool CloseHandle(IntPtr hObject);

        //IntPtr is used to represent OS handles
        IntPtr _handle = IntPtr.Zero;

        //our managed resource
        IDbConnection _conn = null;

        public MyWrappedResource(string filename)
        {
            _handle = CreateFile(filename,
                0x80000000, //access read-only
                1,          //share-read
                IntPtr.Zero,
                3,          //open existing
                0,
                IntPtr.Zero);
        }

        ~MyWrappedResource()
        {
            //note: in real apps, don't put anything in
            //finalizers that doesn't need to be there
            Console.WriteLine("In Finalizer");
            Dispose(false);
        }

        public void Close()
        {
            Dispose(true);
        }

        public void Dispose()
        {
            Dispose(true);
        }
```

```
        private bool _disposed = false;
        protected void Dispose(bool disposing)
        {
            //in a class hierarchy, don't forget
            //to call the base class!
            //base.Dispose(disposing);

            Console.WriteLine("Dispose({0})", disposing);
            if (!_disposed)
            {
                _disposed = true;
                if (disposing)
                {
                    //cleanup managed resources
                    if (_conn!=null)
                    {
                        _conn.Dispose();
                    }
                    GC.SuppressFinalize(this);
                }

                //cleanup unmanaged resources, if any
                if (_handle!=IntPtr.Zero)
                {
                    CloseHandle(_handle);
                }
            }
        }
    }
}
```

Here's a little program to demonstrate what happens:

```
static void Main(string[] args)
{
    using (MyWrappedResource res = new MyWrappedResource("TestFile.txt"))
    {
        Console.WriteLine("Using resource...");
    }

    MyWrappedResource res2 = new MyWrappedResource("TestFile.txt");
    Console.WriteLine("Created a new resource, exiting");
    //don't cleanup--let finalizer get it!
}
```

It gives the following output:

```
Using resource...
Dispose(True)
Created a new resource, exiting
In Finalizer
Dispose(False)
```

See the Dispose project in the included source code.

Force a Garbage Collection

Scenario/Problem: You think you need to force a garbage collection.

Solution: The short answer is, don't. You are unlikely to outguess the garbage-collection system for efficiency. That said, if you really know what you're doing and you're going to measure the effects, here's how to do it:

```
GC.Collect();
```

One reason why people force a collection is that they're beginning a performance-sensitive operation that they don't want interrupted by garbage collection. However, the garbage collection system in .NET 4 has undergone major revision from previous versions and now does more collections in the background, so the need to do forced collections should be lessened.

Create a Cache That Still Allows Garbage Collection

Scenario/Problem: You want to cache objects (say, from a database) but still allow them to be garbage collected when necessary.

Solution: The problem is that just holding a reference to an object prevents it from being garbage collected. Enter `WeakReference`.

This simple Cache class uses `WeakReference` objects to store the actual values, allowing them to be garbage collected as needed.

```
public class Cache<TKey, TValue> where TValue:class
{
    //store WeakReference instead of TValue,
    //so they can be garbage collected
```

```
    private Dictionary<TKey, WeakReference> _cache =
            new Dictionary<TKey, WeakReference>();

    public void Add(TKey key, TValue value)
    {
        _cache[key] = new WeakReference(value);
    }

    public void Clear()
    {
        _cache.Clear();
    }

    //since dead WeakReference objects could accumulate,
    //you may want to clear them out occasionally
    public void ClearDeadReferences()
    {
        foreach (KeyValuePair<TKey, WeakReference> item in _cache)
        {
            if (!item.Value.IsAlive)
            {
                _cache.Remove(item.Key);
            }
        }
    }

    public TValue GetObject(TKey key)
    {
        WeakReference reference = null;
        if (_cache.TryGetValue(key, out reference))
        {
            /* Don't check IsAlive first because the
             * GC could kick in right after anyway.
             * Just retrieve the value and cast it. It will be null
             * if the object was already collected.
             * If you successfully get the Target value,
             * then you'll create a strong reference, and prevent
             * it from being garbage collected.
             */
            return reference.Target as TValue;
        }
        return null;
    }
}
```

NOTE Weak references should never be used for small items, and you should not rely on them as a crutch to solve memory problems for you. They are best used for items that can use a lot of memory, but are easily recreated as needed, such as in cache situations where it would be nice if the object were still around in memory, but you still want it to be garbage collected eventually.

This test program shows how it could be used:

```
class Program
{
    class Book
    {
        public int Id { get; set; }
        public string Title { get; set; }
        public string Author { get; set; }
    };

    static void Main(string[] args)
    {
        Cache<int, Book> bookCache = new Cache<int, Book>();
        Random rand = new Random();
        int numBooks = 100;

        //add books to cache
        for (int i=0;i<numBooks;++i)
        {
            bookCache.Add(i, GetBookFromDB(i));
        }

        //lookup random books and track cache misses
        Console.WriteLine("Looking up books...hit any key to stop");
        long lookups = 0, misses = 0;
        while (!Console.KeyAvailable)
        {
            ++lookups;
            int id = rand.Next(0, numBooks);
            Book book = bookCache.GetObject(id);
            if (book == null)
            {
                ++misses;
                book = GetBookFromDB(id);
            }
            else
            {
                //add a little memory pressure to increase
                //the chances of a GC
```

```
                GC.AddMemoryPressure(100);
            }
            bookCache.Add(id, book);
        }
        Console.ReadKey();
        Console.WriteLine("{0:N0} lookups, {1:N0} misses",
                          lookups, misses);
        Console.ReadLine();
    }

    static Book GetBookFromDB(int id)
    {
        //simulate some database access

        return new Book { Id = id,
                          Title = "Book" + id,
                          Author = "Author" + id };
    }
}
```

Use Pointers

Scenario/Problem: You need to directly access the memory of an object, either for efficiency or to interop with native code.

Solution: To use pointers in your code, you have to do a few things:

1. Mark the code block as `unsafe`.
2. Compile the project as `unsafe` using the `/unsafe` compiler switch (or in your project build settings).
3. Ensure that the target runtime environment has sufficient privilege to run unsafe code (it is a security risk after all).

Here's a simple example:

```
unsafe
{
    int x = 0;
    int* pX = &x;
    *pX = 13;
}
```

You can create pointers to any non-reference type (that also contains only non-reference types):

```
Point pt;
Point* pPt = &pt;
pPt->X = 13;
pPt->Y = 14;
pPt->Offset(1,2);

List<object> list = new List<object>();
//List<object>* pList = &list;//won't compile!
```

Entire methods and classes can be marked as unsafe:

```
unsafe class MyUnsafeClass {...}
unsafe void MyUnsafeMethod() {...}
```

Speed Up Array Access

Scenario/Problem: You want direct access to an array for performance reasons and are willing to forego .NET's array-bounds checking and take responsibility for safe behavior yourself.

Solution: By using pointers, you can speed up array lookups by an order of magnitude, but at the price of code safety and guarantees.

This code shows that by using pointers you can gain direct access to memory, potentially overwriting data you didn't mean to:

```
int size = 10;
int[] vals = new int[size];
try
{
    for (int i = 0; i < size+1; i++)
    {
        vals[i] = i;
    }
}
catch (IndexOutOfRangeException ex)
{
    Console.WriteLine("Caught exception: " + ex.Message);
}

Console.WriteLine("Going out of bounds");
//prevent vals from moving in memory
```

```
fixed (int* pI = &vals[0])
{
    //oops, going to far--overwriting memory we don't own!
    for (int i = 0; i < size+1; i++)
    {
        pI[i] = i;
    }
    Console.WriteLine("No exception thrown! We just overwrote memory we
➥shouldn't have!");
}
```

You can also use pointer arithmetic, just as you would in native languages:

```
fixed (int* pI = &vals[0])
{
    int* pA = pI;
    while (*pA < 8)
    {
        //increment 2 * sizeof(element)
        pA += 2;

        Console.WriteLine("*pA = {0}", *pA);
    }
}
```

Note that adding one to a pointer does not increase the memory address by 1 byte, but by 1 increment of the data type size, which in this example is an `int`, or 4 bytes.

NOTE Most programs do not need to use any of this pointer stuff, and it is quite dangerous to do so, as evidenced by the "unsafe" status you have to grant the code, in addition to the increased permissions required to run programs that do this. If at all possible, try to create programs that do not rely on these techniques.

Prevent Memory from Being Moved

Scenario/Problem: You need to force an object to remain in its memory location, especially for interop with native code.

When the garbage collector runs, it moves objects around in memory in a *compaction process*. This requires fixing up all the memory addresses for all the moved objects. Obviously, this is not possible for objects the GC does not know about—such as in a native code interop situation.

Solution: "Fix" the memory in place.

```
int[] vals = new int[10];
//the location of vals is fixed for the duration of the block
fixed (int* pI = &vals[0])
{
    pI[i] = 13;
}
```

NOTE You should keep memory fixed only as long as you absolutely need to. While memory is fixed in place, the GC is less efficient as it attempts to work around the unmovable block.

Allocate Unmanaged Memory

Scenario/Problem: You need a buffer of memory that unmanaged code can access and you don't want the GC involved at all.

Solution: Use the `Marshal.AllocHGlobal()` method and manually add some memory pressure:

```
unsafe class MyDataClass
{
    IntPtr _memory = IntPtr.Zero;

    public int NumObjects { get; private set; }
    public int MemorySize { get { return sizeof(Int32) * NumObjects; } }

    public MyDataClass(int numObjects)
    {
        this.NumObjects = numObjects;

        _memory = Marshal.AllocHGlobal(MemorySize);
        //we should tell the garbage collector that we are using more
        //memory so it can schedule collections better
        //(note--it still doesn't change the amount
        //that GC.GetTotalMemory returns)
        GC.AddMemoryPressure(MemorySize);

        Int32* pI = (Int32*)_memory;
        for (int i = 0; i < NumObjects; ++i)
        {
```

```
                pI[i] = i;
            }
        }

        //unmanaged resources need a finalizer to make
        //sure they're cleaned up!
        ~MyDataClass()
        {
            if (_memory != IntPtr.Zero)
            {
                Marshal.FreeHGlobal(_memory);
                //tell garbage collector memory is gone
                GC.RemoveMemoryPressure(MemorySize);
            }
        }
}
```

When you allocate memory in this way, .NET knows nothing about it, as this program snippet shows:

```
static void Main(string[] args)
{
    Console.WriteLine("Memory usage before unmanaged allocation: {0:N0}",
➥GC.GetTotalMemory(false));
    MyDataClass obj = new MyDataClass(10000000);

    //unmanaged memory is not counted!
    Console.WriteLine("Memory usage after unmanaged allocation: {0:N0}",
➥GC.GetTotalMemory(false));
}
```

The output is as follows:

```
Memory usage before unmanaged allocation: 665,456
Memory usage after unmanaged allocation: 706,416
```

The `AddMemoryPressure` method notifies the CLR that it should take this into account when scheduling garbage collection, but that is all the involvement it has. When your unmanaged memory is freed, you should release this pressure.

CHAPTER 23

Threads, Asynchronous, and Parallel Programming

IN THIS CHAPTER

- Easily Split Work Among Processors
- Use Data Structures in Multiple Threads
- Call a Method Asynchronously
- Use the Thread Pool
- Create a Thread
- Exchange Data with a Thread
- Protect Data Used in Multiple Threads
- Use Interlocked Methods Instead of Locks
- Protect Data in Multiple Processes
- Limit Applications to a Single Instance
- Limit the Number of Threads That Can Access a Resource
- Signal Threads with Events
- Use a Multithreaded Timer
- Use a Reader-Writer Lock
- Use the Asynchronous Programming Model

Using threads can give you great power, but as the old saying goes, with great power comes great responsibility. Using threads irresponsibly can easily lead to poor performance and unstable applications. However, using good techniques with threads can produce programs with higher efficiency and more responsive interfaces.

Thankfully, much research has been done in recent years in an attempt to simplify multithreading. In particular, the Task Parallel Library, now a part of .NET 4, allows you to easily split your code execution onto multiple processors without any messing around with threads or locks.

Easily Split Work Among Processors

Scenario/Problem: You have a task that is easily split into independent subtasks, or you have data that can be partitioned and computed separately.

Solution: Use the `Parallel` class in the `System.Threading` namespace to assign tasks to be automatically scheduled and wait for them to complete. The `Parallel` class automatically scales to the number of processors.

Process Data in Parallel

When you have a set of data that can be split over multiple processors and processed independently, you can use constructs such as Parallel.For(), as in this example with computing prime numbers:

```
using System;
using System.Collections.Generic;
using System.Linq;
using System.Text;
using System.Threading;
using System.Diagnostics;
using System.Threading.Tasks;

namespace TPLPrimes
{
    class Program
    {
        static void Main(string[] args)
        {
            int maxPrimes = 1000000;
            int maxNumber = 20000000;
            long primesFound = 0;
            Console.WriteLine("Iterative");
            Stopwatch watch = new Stopwatch();
            watch.Start();
```

```
    for (UInt32 i = 0; i < maxNumber; ++i)
    {
        if (IsPrime(i))
        {
            Interlocked.Increment(ref primesFound);
            if (primesFound > maxPrimes)
            {
                Console.WriteLine("Last prime found: {0:N0}",
                                   i);
                break;
            }
        }
    }
    watch.Stop();
    Console.WriteLine("Found {0:N0} primes in {1}",
                      primesFound, watch.Elapsed);

    watch.Reset();
    primesFound = 0;
    Console.WriteLine("Parallel");
    watch.Start();
    //in order to stop the loop, there is an
    //overload that takes Action<int, ParallelLoopState>
    Parallel.For(0, maxNumber, (i, loopState) =>
    {
        if (IsPrime((UInt32)i))
        {
            Interlocked.Increment(ref primesFound);
            if (primesFound > maxPrimes)
            {
                Console.WriteLine("Last prime found: {0:N0}",
                                   i);
                loopState.Stop();
            }
        }

    });
    watch.Stop();
    Console.WriteLine("Found {0:N0} primes in {1}",
                      primesFound, watch.Elapsed);

    Console.ReadKey();
}

public static bool IsPrime(UInt32 number)
{
```

```
            //check for evenness
            if (number % 2 == 0)
            {
                if (number == 2)
                    return true;
                return false;
            }
            //don't need to check past the square root
            UInt32 max = (UInt32)Math.Sqrt(number);
            for (UInt32 i = 3; i <= max; i += 2)
            {
                if ((number % i) == 0)
                {
                    return false;
                }
            }
            return true;
        }
    }
}
```

The output on my dual-core machine is shown here:

```
Iterative
Last prime found: 15,485,863
Found 1,000,001 primes in 00:00:15.7972400
Parallel
Last prime found: 15,485,867
Last prime found: 15,485,497
Found 1,000,002 primes in 00:00:08.8610525
```

Aside from the drastically reduced time, notice that the output results aren't necessarily in order and that the parallel version of the program doesn't come up with the same results as the iterative version. Rather than going through sequentially from 1 to 20,000,000 until a million primes are found, the input space is divided up; thus, it's possible to get results you otherwise wouldn't. It really depends on your problem and how you divide it up.

Run Tasks in Parallel

Rather than split up the data, you can split up the tasks to work on the data. Suppose you have iterative code that looks like this:

```
//see the TPLTextProcess sample project for these files
//The 6 parts of the History of the Decline and Fall of
//the Roman Empire by Edward Gibbon
string[] inputFiles =
```

```
{
    "decline1.txt", "decline2.txt", "decline3.txt",
    "decline4.txt", "decline5.txt", "decline6.txt"
};
foreach (string file in inputFiles)
{
    string content = File.ReadAllText(file);
    CountCharacters(content);
    CountWords(content);
}
```

You can use `Parallel` with some lambda expressions to parallelize the two calculation methods:

```
foreach(string file in inputFiles)
{
    string content = File.ReadAllText(file);
    Parallel.Invoke(
        () => CountCharacters(content),
        () => CountWords(content)
        );
}
```

On my system, the results are not as impressive as the previous example, but they are still significant:

```
Iterative
Elapsed: 00:00:08.5515745
Unique chars: 92
Unique words: 42976

Parallel
Elapsed: 00:00:06.4348502
Unique chars: 92
Unique words: 42976
```

Use Data Structures in Multiple Threads

Scenario/Problem: You have a data structure that needs to be accessed on multiple threads.

Solution: Before relying on thread-aware data structures, you should make sure that you need them. For example, if data doesn't really need to be accessed on multiple threads, then don't use them. Similarly, if data is read-only, then it doesn't need to be protected. Keep in mind that synchronizing thread access to a data structure, although it may be fast, is never as fast as no synchronization at all.

If every access to the data structure needs to be protected, use the concurrent collections described in the first section of Chapter 10, "Collections."

If only some access needs to be protected, consider using some of the synchronization objects (such as locks) described later in this chapter.

Call a Method Asynchronously

Scenario/Problem: You want to call a method and continue execution in the caller without waiting for the method to return.

Solution: This is one of the simplest ways of taking advantage of multithreading, as shown next:

```
using System;
using System.Threading;

namespace AsyncMethod
{
    class Program
    {
        // async method calls must be done through a delegate
        delegate double DoWorkDelegate(int maxValue);

        static void Main(string[] args)
        {
            DoWorkDelegate del = DoWork;

            //two ways to be notified of when method ends:
            // 1. callback method
            // 2. call EndInvoke
            IAsyncResult res =
                del.BeginInvoke(100000000, DoWorkDone, null);
            for (int i = 0; i < 5; i++)
            {
                Console.WriteLine("Doing other work...{0}", i);
                Thread.Sleep(1000);
            }

            //wait for end
            double sum = del.EndInvoke(res);
            Console.WriteLine("Sum: {0}", sum);
```

```
            Console.ReadKey();
        }

        static double DoWork(int maxValue)
        {
            Console.WriteLine("In DoWork");
            double sum = 0.0;
            for (int i = 1; i < maxValue; ++i)
            {
                sum += Math.Sqrt(i);
            }
            return sum;
        }

        static void DoWorkDone(object state)
        {
            //didn't pass in any state

            Console.WriteLine("Computation done");
        }
    }
}
```

This program produces the following output:

```
Doing other work...0
In DoWork
Doing other work...1
Doing other work...2
Doing other work...3
Computation done
Doing other work...4
Sum: 666666661666.567
```

You can call `EndInvoke` at any time to wait until the operation is done and get the results back.

Use the Thread Pool

Scenario/Problem: You have tasks that you want to assign to run in a separate thread, without the need to manage the threads yourself.

Solution: Using the thread pool is easier and more efficient than creating your own threads. All you have to do is pass it a method of your choosing.

```
private void OnPrintButton_Clicked()
{
    ThreadPool.QueueUserWorkItem(PrintDocument);
}

private void PrintDocument(object state)
{
    //do stuff to print in the background here
}
```

The BitmapSorter program in the included sample code uses the `ThreadPool` to do its sorting in a separate thread. Because the method it wants to call does not match the `WaitCallback` delegate signature, it uses an anonymous delegate to simplify the code:

```
ThreadPool.QueueUserWorkItem( () => {scrambledBitmap.Sort();} );
```

Create a Thread

Scenario/Problem: You need a thread for a long-running operation, perhaps for the entire lifetime of the application.

Solution: If your thread is going to stick around for a while, it's probably worth it for the application to own it rather than relying on the threadpool (which expects threads to eventually be returned to it).

```
static void Main(string[] args)
{
    Thread thread = new Thread(new ThreadStart(ThreadProc));
    thread.IsBackground = true;//so it ends when Main ends
    thread.Start();

    while (!Console.KeyAvailable)
    {
        Console.WriteLine("Thread ID: {0}, waiting for key press",
➥Thread.CurrentThread.ManagedThreadId);
        Thread.Sleep(1000);
    }
}

static void ThreadProc()
{
    //simulate work
    for (int i = 0; i < Int32.MaxValue; ++i)
```

```
    {
        if (i % 100000000 == 0)
        {
            Console.WriteLine("Thread ID: {0}, i: {1}",
➥Thread.CurrentThread.ManagedThreadId, i);
        }
    }
}
```

This program has the following partial output (it will keep running into you press a key):

```
Thread ID: 10, waiting for key press
Thread ID: 11, i: 0
Thread ID: 11, i: 100000000
Thread ID: 10, waiting for key press
Thread ID: 11, i: 200000000
Thread ID: 10, waiting for key press
Thread ID: 11, i: 300000000
Thread ID: 10, waiting for key press
Thread ID: 11, i: 400000000
```

NOTE You should try to use the thread pool as often as possible, especially if your threads are not long-lived. Thread creation is a relatively expensive process, and the pool maintains threads after you're done using them so that you don't have the overhead of creating and destroying them continually. The thread pool grows to adapt to your program's threading needs.

Exchange Data with a Thread

Scenario/Problem: You need to use data in more than one thread.

Solution: There are basically two ways of giving a thread access to shared data:

- Pass in `object` argument to the thread function.
- Use member fields in the same class.

For an example of the first option, here's a modified version of the previous code example, with the modified lines bolded:

```
static void Main(string[] args)
{
    Thread thread = new Thread(
```

```
                          new ParameterizedThreadStart(ThreadProc));
    thread.IsBackground = true;//so it ends when Main ends
    thread.Start(Int32.MaxValue);//argument to thread proc

    while (!Console.KeyAvailable)
    {
        Console.WriteLine("Thread ID: {0}, waiting for key press",
➥Thread.CurrentThread.ManagedThreadId);
        Thread.Sleep(1000);
    }
}

static void ThreadProc(object state)
{
    Int32 end = (Int32)state;
    //simulate work
    for (int i = 0; i < end; ++i)
    {
        if (i % 100000000 == 0)
        {
            Console.WriteLine("Thread ID: {0}, i: {1}",
➥Thread.CurrentThread.ManagedThreadId, i);
        }
    }
}
```

Because thread functions are just methods in classes, they also get access to all the fields and functionality in that same class (option 2). However, now you have to be careful. As soon as you talk about two threads potentially accessing the same data, you have to think about protecting the data. That's the topic of the next section.

Protect Data Used in Multiple Threads

Scenario/Problem: You need to ensure data integrity when data is accessed from more than one thread.

It is generally a good idea if two threads do not simultaneously try to write to the same area of memory, or even for one to read as the other writes—the results are understandably unpredictable.

Solution: .NET provides the `Monitor` class to protect data from access via multiple threads.

```
//volatile indicates the value should always be read from memory,
//never CPU cache
private volatile int value = 13;
// use a dummy object for the lock
private object valueLock = new object();
public void AddOne()
{
    Monitor.Enter(valueLock);
    ++value;
    Monitor.Exit(valueLock);
}

public void SubtractOne()
{
    Monitor.Enter(valueLock);
    --value;
    Monitor.Exit(valueLock);
}
```

NOTE Because `Monitor.Enter()` and `Monitor.Exit()` take any object for the lock, you might be tempted to just pass `this` to the methods. In a sense you're right—this is how it was originally intended. However, this ends up being a bad idea because you can't control who else locks on your object. Instead, the best practice is just to create a private dummy `object` in your class to serve as an explicit lock object.

There is a shortcoming to the preceding code. What if an exception is thrown between `Enter` and `Exit`? That value will be inaccessible until the process exits. The answer is to wrap it in a `try/finally` statement (see Chapter 4, "Exceptions"), and C# has a shorthand notation for this because it's so common:

```
//volatile indicates the value should always be read from memory,
//never CPU cache
private volatile int value = 13;
// use a dummy object for the lock
private object valueLock = new object();
public void AddOne()
{
    lock(valueLock)
    {
        ++value;
    }
}
```

```
public void SubtractOne()
{
    lock(valueLock)
    {
        --value;
    }
}
```

Attempt to Gain a Lock

Suppose you want to get a lock if possible, but if not, you want to do something else. This is possible, if you drop back to using the `Monitor` class explicitly:

```
bool protectedWorkComplete = false;
while (!protectedWorkComplete)
{
    if (Monitor.TryEnter(valueLock))
    {
        try
        {
            //do protected work
            protectedWorkComplete = true;
        }
        finally
        {
            Monitor.Exit(valueLock);
        }
    }
    else
    {
        //couldn't get a lock, so do something else meanwhile
    }
}
```

You can also pass a `TimeSpan` to `TryEnter` to tell it to try for that long before giving up.

> **NOTE** Locks are all well and good, but understand something: Having lots of threads contending for locks stops your program dead in its tracks. Performance-wise, locks can be expensive in many cases, and even when they're not, they can still be deadly when performance is critical. The real trick to building highly scalable applications is to avoid using locks as much as possible. This usually means being fiendishly clever in your design from the outset.

Use Interlocked Methods Instead of Locks

Scenario/Problem: You need to manipulate shared integer primitives and need to avoid the performance implications of using locks.

Solution: Looking at a preceding example,

```
public void AddOne()
{
    lock(valueLock)
    {
        ++value;
    }
}
```

you might wonder if a lock is really necessary just to increment a variable. After all, increment and decrement are extremely common operations and locks can be expensive.

Thankfully, there are a few functions to atomically perform some simple operations for you:

```
int value = 13;

private void ThreadProc()
{
    Interlocked.Increment(ref value);//adds one
    Interlocked.Decrement(ref value);//subtracts one
    Interlocked.Add(ref value, 13);//adds 13

    //set value to 99 and return the original value
    int originalValue = Interlocked.Exchange(ref value, 99);

    string s1 = "Hello";
    string sNew = "Bonjour";
    string sCompare = "Hello";

    // if (s1 == sCompare) s1 = sNew;
    string sOriginal = Interlocked.CompareExchange<string>(ref s1,
                                                            sNew,
                                                            sCompare);
}
```

This type of functionality is used to implement the rest of the synchronization objects, but you can use them yourself to do simple modifications of fields, or to exchange object references (perhaps you need to swap one data structure for a newer version of it).

Protect Data in Multiple Processes

Scenario/Problem: You need to protect memory, files or other resources that are shared across multiple processes.

Solution: You can use a mutex, which is like a `Monitor` object, but at an operating system level. Mutexes must be named so that both processes can open the same mutex object.

Here's a sample program that uses a mutex to protect a file from being written to by two instances of this same program (see Figure 23.1):

```
static void Main(string[] args)
{
    Mutex mutex = new Mutex(false, "MutexDemo");
    Process me = Process.GetCurrentProcess();
    string outputFile = "MutexDemoOutput.txt";

    while (!Console.KeyAvailable)
    {
        mutex.WaitOne();
        Console.WriteLine("Process {0} gained control", me.Id);
        using (FileStream fs = new FileStream(outputFile,
               FileMode.OpenOrCreate))
        using (TextWriter writer = new StreamWriter(fs))
        {
            fs.Seek(0, SeekOrigin.End);
            string output = string.Format("Process {0} writing timestamp
➥{1}", me.Id, DateTime.Now.ToLongTimeString());
            writer.WriteLine(output);
            Console.WriteLine(output);
        }
        Console.WriteLine("Process {0} releasing control", me.Id);
        mutex.ReleaseMutex();
        Thread.Sleep(1000);    }
}
```

As with monitors, you can attempt a wait on a mutex for a `TimeSpan` before giving up. In that case, if the mutex gives up, `WaitOne` will return `false`.

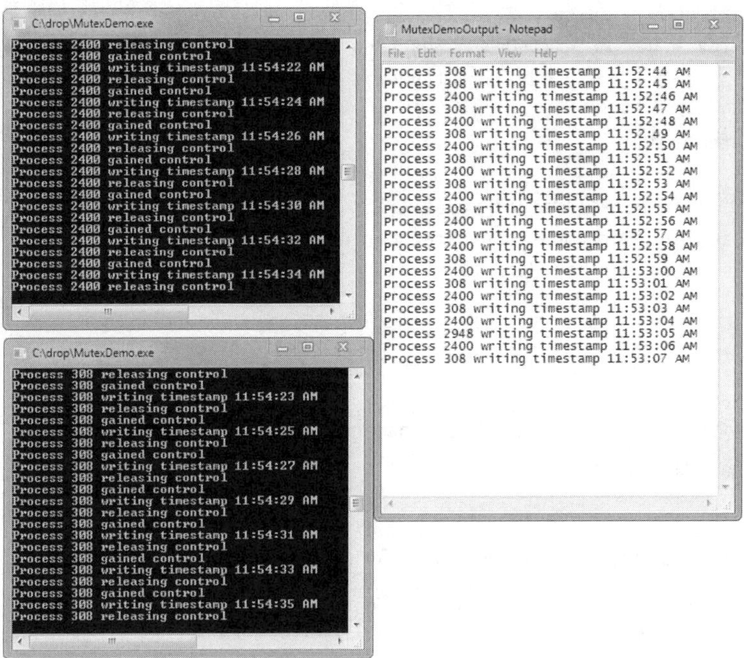

FIGURE 23.1
Each process locks the mutex before writing to the file.

> **NOTE** Make sure you choose good names for your mutexes. Either use a unique combination of your company, application, and mutex purpose, or use a globally unique identifier (GUID) to ensure no collisions with your own apps or others.

Limit Applications to a Single Instance

> **Scenario/Problem:** You want only one instance of your application running at a time.

Solution: Now that you have a way of creating a cross-process communication mechanism (simple, though it may be), you can use it to prevent users from running more than one instance of our program.

```
[STAThread]
static void Main()
{
    bool createdNew = false;
    Mutex mutex = new Mutex(true, "CSharpHowTo_SingleInstanceApp",
                            out createdNew);

    if (createdNew)
    {
        Application.EnableVisualStyles();
        Application.SetCompatibleTextRenderingDefault(false);
        Application.Run(new Form1());
    }
    else
    {
        MessageBox.Show(
           "You can only run a single instance of this app!");
    }
}
```

See the SingleInstanceApp demo in the projects for this chapter for the full source code.

NOTE If you want your mutex to prevent other users from starting your application, such as in a terminal service environment, prefix your mutex's names with "Global\". Otherwise, users in different sessions will be able to also run your application simultaneously (which is probably what you want).

Limit the Number of Threads That Can Access a Resource

Scenario/Problem: Some resources can have more than one simultaneous access, but you still want to limit it.

Solution: There are many instances where it's okay to have multiple threads access the same data, but you want to limit it to a certain number. For example, if your application downloads images from the Internet and you want to limit your bandwidth usage, it would be useful to limit the concurrent downloads to two or so. Semaphores can do this for you. In the following example, three progress bars are shown. Three threads are spun up to increment them. However, a Semaphore is created to limit the updating to only two progress bars at a time. This gives you a visual idea of what is happening (see Figure 23.2).

```
public partial class Form1 : Form
{
    //allow two concurrent entries (with a max of 2)
    //the two values allow you to start with some of them locked
    //if needed
    Semaphore _semaphore = new Semaphore(2, 2);
    private ProgressBar[] _progressBars = new ProgressBar[3];
    private Thread[] _threads = new Thread[3];

    const int MaxValue = 1000000;

    public Form1()
    {
        InitializeComponent();

        _progressBars[0] = progressBar1;
        _progressBars[1] = progressBar2;
        _progressBars[2] = progressBar3;

        for (int i = 0; i < 3; i++)
        {
            _progressBars[i].Minimum = 0;
            _progressBars[i].Maximum = MaxValue;
            _progressBars[i].Style = ProgressBarStyle.Continuous;
        }
    }

    private void buttonStart_Click(object sender, EventArgs e)
    {
        buttonStart.Enabled = false;
        for (int i = 0; i < 3; i++)
        {
            _threads[i] = new Thread(
                new ParameterizedThreadStart(IncrementThread));
            _threads[i].IsBackground = true;
            _threads[i].Start(i);
        }
    }

    private void IncrementThread(object state)
    {
        int threadNumber = (int)state;
        int value = 0;
        while (value < MaxValue)
        {
```

```
            //only two threads at a time will be
            //allowed to enter this section
            _semaphore.WaitOne();
            for (int i = 0; i < 100000; i++)
            {
                ++value;
                UpdateProgress(threadNumber, value);
            }
            _semaphore.Release();
        }
    }

    private void UpdateProgress(int thread, int value)
    {
        if (value <= MaxValue)
        {
            //must invoke because these must be updated on UI thread
            _progressBars[thread].Invoke(new MethodInvoker(delegate
            {
                _progressBars[thread].Value = value;
            }));
        }
    }
}
```

In this case, the resource being protected is GUI updates, but it could be a data structure as in the other examples. See the SemaphoreDemo in the sample projects to see the code in action.

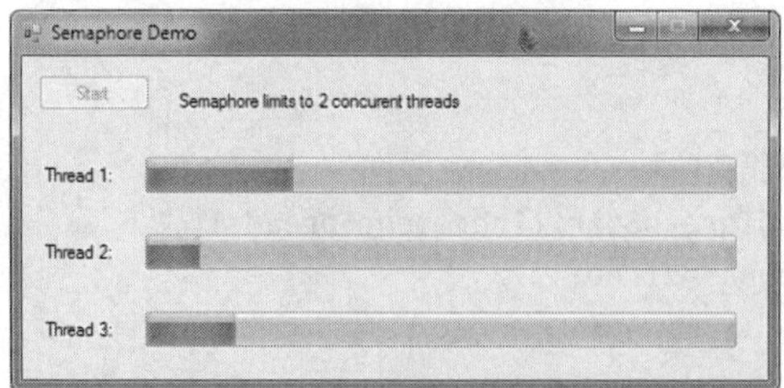

FIGURE 23.2
When you run this demo you'll notice that even though three tasks want to perform work, only two can run simultaneously because of the semaphore.

Signal Threads with Events

Scenario/Problem: Often, threads need to wait until something significant happens before continuing.

Solution: Events are some of the most useful signaling mechanisms available. There are two types of events: those with a manual reset, and those that automatically reset.

Setting an event is what causes other threads to wake up and continue with their work. When a `ManualResetEvent` is set, all waiting threads are woken up and the event remains set until you manually reset it.

Setting an `AutoResetEvent` causes only a single thread to be woken up (arbitrarily chosen, from the program's point of view) and the event is immediately reset.

See the EventDemo project in the accompanying source code for an example that effectively shows this difference. Like the Semaphore demo, the resource being protected is progress bar updating. Figure 23.3 shows this demo in action. Here is a portion of the main source code:

```
public partial class Form1 : Form
{
    ManualResetEvent _manualEvent = new ManualResetEvent(false);
    AutoResetEvent _autoEvent = new AutoResetEvent(false);

    private ProgressBar[] _progressBars = new ProgressBar[3];
    private Thread[] _threads = new Thread[3];

    const int MaxValue = 1000000;

    bool _manual = true;

    public Form1()
    {
        InitializeComponent();

        Init();
    }

    private void Init()
    {
        _manualEvent.Reset();
        _autoEvent.Reset();
```

```
        _progressBars[0] = progressBar1;
        _progressBars[1] = progressBar2;
        _progressBars[2] = progressBar3;

        for (int i = 0; i < 3; i++)
        {
            _progressBars[i].Minimum = 0;
            _progressBars[i].Maximum = MaxValue;
            _progressBars[i].Style = ProgressBarStyle.Continuous;
            _progressBars[i].Value = 0;
        }

        for (int i = 0; i < 3; i++)
        {
            if (_threads[i] != null)
            {
                _threads[i].Abort();
            }
            _threads[i] = new Thread(
               new ParameterizedThreadStart(ThreadProc));
            _threads[i].IsBackground = true;
            _threads[i].Start(i);
        }

    }

    private void buttonSet_Click(object sender, EventArgs e)
    {
        if (_manual)
        {
            _manualEvent.Set();
        }
        else
        {
            _autoEvent.Set();
        }
    }

    private void buttonReset_Click(object sender, EventArgs e)
    {
        if (_manual)
        {
            _manualEvent.Reset();
        }
        else
```

```
        {
            _autoEvent.Reset();
        }
    }

    private void ThreadProc(object state)
    {
        int threadNumber = (int)state;
        int value = 0;
        while (value < MaxValue)
        {
            if (_manual)
            {
                _manualEvent.WaitOne();
            }
            else
            {
                _autoEvent.WaitOne();
            }
            for (int i = 0; i < 100000; ++i)
            {
                ++value;
                UpdateProgress(threadNumber, value);
                //just so we don't peg the CPU at 100%
                Thread.Sleep(0);
            }
        }
    }

    private void UpdateProgress(int thread, int value)
    {
        //must invoke because these must be updated on UI thread
        _progressBars[thread].Invoke(new MethodInvoker(delegate
        {
            _progressBars[thread].Value = value;
        }));
    }

    private void OnEventTypeChanged(object sender, EventArgs e)
    {
        _manual = radioButtonManual.Checked;
        buttonReset.Enabled = _manual;
        Init();
    }
}
```

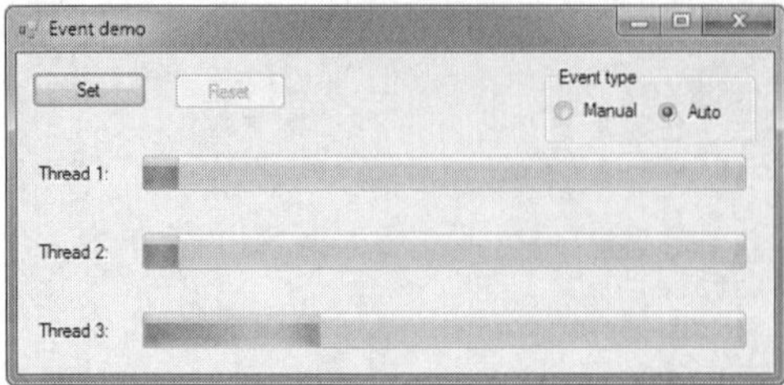

FIGURE 23.3
In manual mode, setting the event will cause all three threads to progress until you click the Reset button. In auto mode, setting the event will cause a single thread to go (until it checks for the event again).

Use a Multithreaded Timer

Scenario/Problem: You want a method to be called on its own thread at a specified interval.

Solution: You've seen a few uses for timers so far. Windows Forms has a timer that fires on the UI thread. WPF has the similar `DispatcherTimer`.

Another type of timer calls a method using the `ThreadPool` discussed earlier. This is good for things that need to happen periodically in your app that don't necessarily need UI.

```
static void Main(string[] args)
{
    //call TimerThreadProc in 1 second, then every 10 seconds
    //pass it the value 13
    System.Threading.Timer timer = new Timer(TimerThreadProc,
                                              13, 1 * 1000, 10 * 1000);
}

static private void TimerThreadProc(object state)
{
    int val = (int)state;
    //do thread work
}
```

Use a Reader-Writer Lock

Scenario/Problem: You need to protect access to a resource that is read often but written to less-often, on multiple threads.

Solution: It's safe to let multiple threads read the data at the same time, but when a thread needs to write, all other threads need to be blocked..NET originally provided the `ReaderWriterLock` for this situation, but it has performance problems that outweigh its usefulness in many situations. Thankfully, there is `ReaderWriterLockSlim`, which corrects many of its predecessor's shortcomings.

This program demonstrates using a `ReaderWriterLockSlim` on an array that's shared among a single writer and three readers:

```
class Program
{
    const int MaxValues = 25;
    static int[] _array = new int[MaxValues];
    static ReaderWriterLockSlim _lock = new ReaderWriterLockSlim();

    static void Main(string[] args)
    {
        ThreadPool.QueueUserWorkItem(WriteThread);

        for (int i = 0; i < 3; i++)
        {
            ThreadPool.QueueUserWorkItem(ReadThread);
        }

        Console.ReadKey();
    }

    static void WriteThread(object state)
    {
        int id = Thread.CurrentThread.ManagedThreadId;
        for (int i = 0; i < MaxValues; ++i)
        {
            _lock.EnterWriteLock();
            Console.WriteLine("Entered WriteLock on thread {0}", id);

            _array[i] = i*i;
            Console.WriteLine("Added {0} to array on thread {1}", _
                                  array[i], id);
```

```
            Console.WriteLine("Exiting WriteLock on thread {0}", id);
            _lock.ExitWriteLock();
            Thread.Sleep(1000);
        }
    }

    static void ReadThread(object state)
    {
        int id = Thread.CurrentThread.ManagedThreadId;
        for (int i = 0; i < MaxValues; ++i)
        {
            _lock.EnterReadLock();
            Console.WriteLine("Entered ReadLock on thread {0}", id);
            StringBuilder sb = new StringBuilder();
            for (int j = 0; j < i; j++)
            {
                if (sb.Length > 0) sb.Append(", ");
                sb.Append(_array[j]);

            }
            Console.WriteLine("Array: {0} on thread {1}", sb, id);
            Console.WriteLine("Exiting ReadLock on thread {0}", id);
            _lock.ExitReadLock();
            Thread.Sleep(1000);
        }
    }
}
```

Here's a portion of the output:

```
Entered WriteLock on thread 7
Added 25 to array on thread 7
Exiting WriteLock on thread 7
Entered ReadLock on thread 11
Entered ReadLock on thread 12
Array: 0, 1, 4, 9 on thread 12
Exiting ReadLock on thread 12
Array: 0, 1, 4, 9, 16 on thread 11
Exiting ReadLock on thread 11
Entered ReadLock on thread 13
Array: 0, 1, 4, 9 on thread 13
Exiting ReadLock on thread 13
```

Notice that threads 11 and 12 were able to get a read lock at the same time.

Use the Asynchronous Programming Model

Scenario/Problem: You have many actions in your application than can be accomplished in the background.

On many I/O classes, you will find a common set of methods. For example, on streams you can call `Read` or `BeginRead`. The first is a synchronous method that does not return until the data has been read. The second returns immediately, letting your program continue while the file is read from disk, the network, the Internet, or another data source.

Solution: The TextTokenizer sample app, shown in Figure 23.4, demonstrates how to use this method of programming. If only synchronous methods were used, it would be impossible to interact with the program (even just to close it!), but using asynchronous methods allows your program to respond to users and perform other tasks while the I/O is completing.

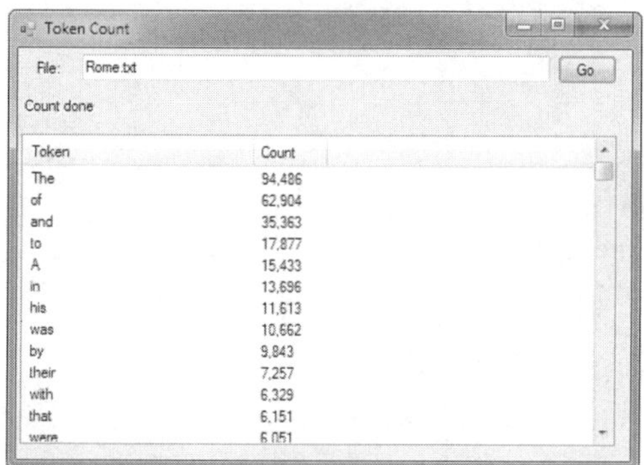

FIGURE 23.4

The TextTokenizer app demonstrates asynchronous file reading as well as implementing asynchronous `Begin`*XXX* methods on your own class.

```
private void buttonGo_Click(object sender, EventArgs e)
{
    UpdateProgress("Reading file");
    FileStream inputStream = new FileStream(textBoxUrl.Text,
                                            FileMode.Open);
    _buffer = new byte[inputStream.Length];
    //pass in the inputStream as the argument to the "Done" method
    IAsyncResult result = inputStream.BeginRead(buffer, 0,
                                                buffer.Length,
                                                FileReadDone,
                                                inputStream);
```

```
    //the IAsyncResult object can be used to track the progress
    //of the method while the file reading is going on,
    // we can do other work, like click buttons or exit the program
}

private void FileReadDone(IAsyncResult result)
{
    UpdateProgress("File read done");
    FileStream inputStream = result.AsyncState as FileStream;
    inputStream.Close();
//  ...
}
```

Although asynchronous programming is quite useful for I/O, you can implement it yourself for any type of operation, such as in the following class which performs the word counting:

```
using System;
using System.Collections.Generic;

namespace TextTokenizer
{
    struct WordCount
    {
        public string Word { get; set; }
        public int Count { get; set; }
    }

    class TokenCounter
    {
        delegate void CountDelegate();

        private string _data;
        private Dictionary<string, int> _tokens =
➥new Dictionary<string, int>(
➥StringComparer.CurrentCultureIgnoreCase);
        private List<WordCount> _wordCounts = new List<WordCount>();
        public IList<WordCount> WordCounts
        {
            get
            {
                return _wordCounts;
            }
        }

        public TokenCounter(string data)
```

```
{
    _data = data;
}

public void Count()
{
    //just split by standard word separators
    //to keep things simple


    char[] splitters = new char[]
                 {' ', '.', ',', ';',
                  ':','-','?','!','\t',
                  '\n','\r','(',')','[',
                  ']','{','}' };
    string[] words = _data.Split(splitters,
                      StringSplitOptions.RemoveEmptyEntries);
    foreach (string word in words)
    {
        int count;
        if (!_tokens.TryGetValue(word, out count))
        {
            _tokens[word] = 1;
        }
        else
        {
            _tokens[word] = count + 1;
        }
    }

    foreach (KeyValuePair<string, int> pair in _tokens)
    {
        _wordCounts.Add(new WordCount() {
                           Word = pair.Key,
                           Count = pair.Value });
    }
    _wordCounts.Sort(
    (Comparison<WordCount>)delegate(WordCount a, WordCount b)
    {
        return -a.Count.CompareTo(b.Count);
    });
}

public IAsyncResult BeginCount(AsyncCallback callback,
                               object state)
```

```
        {
            CountDelegate countDelegate = Count;
            return countDelegate.BeginInvoke(callback, state);
        }

        public void EndCount(IAsyncResult result)
        {
            //wait until operation finishes
            result.AsyncWaitHandle.WaitOne();
        }
    }
}
```

CHAPTER 24

Reflection and Creating Plugins

IN THIS CHAPTER

- Enumerate Types in an Assembly
- Add a Custom Attribute
- Instantiate a Class Dynamically
- Invoke a Method on a Dynamically Instantiated Class
- Implement a Plugin Architecture

Reflection is generally all about getting information about code. However, using the reflection APIs, you can dynamically execute code you load from an arbitrary assembly, giving you an easy way to implement a plugin architecture in your app.

Enumerate Types in an Assembly

Scenario/Problem: You want to dynamically discover the types present in a .NET assembly.

Solution: Reflection is most commonly used for discovery, and nearly everything in .NET is discoverable.

This snippet of code populates a System.Windows.Forms.TreeView control with classes, methods, properties, fields, and events from an assembly:

```
private void ReflectAssembly(string filename)
{
    treeView.Nodes.Clear();

    Assembly assembly = Assembly.LoadFrom(filename);
    foreach (Type t in assembly.GetTypes())
    {
        TreeNode typeNode = new TreeNode("(T) " + t.Name);
        treeView.Nodes.Add(typeNode);
        //get methods
        foreach (MethodInfo mi in t.GetMethods())
        {
            typeNode.Nodes.Add(new TreeNode("(M) "+mi.Name));
        }
        //get properties
        foreach (PropertyInfo pi in t.GetProperties())
        {
            typeNode.Nodes.Add(new TreeNode("(P) "+pi.Name));
        }
        //get fields
        foreach (FieldInfo fi in t.GetFields(BindingFlags.Instance |
➥BindingFlags.NonPublic | BindingFlags.Public))
        {
            typeNode.Nodes.Add(new TreeNode("(F) "+fi.Name));
        }
        //get events
        foreach (EventInfo ei in t.GetEvents())
        {
            typeNode.Nodes.Add(new TreeNode("(E) "+ei.Name));
        }
```

```
        //instead of all that, you could just use t.GetMembers to return
        //an array of MemberInfo (base class to all the above)
    }
}
```

See the EnumerateAssemblyTypes sample project for the full source code.

Add a Custom Attribute

Scenario/Problem: You want to attach metadata to a class, method, property, field, event, or method argument.

Solution: Define an attribute class. Attributes are used extensively in .NET. You've seen in Chapter 11, "Files and Serialization," that all you need to do to get basic serialization working on a class is to add the [Serializable] attribute above the class definition. In Chapter 12, "Networking and the Web," you saw that attributes on methods define service interfaces in WCF.

There is nothing magical about Attributes, however. All they do is attach metadata to another piece of code. It's up to your code to extract that metadata and do something with it.

The following example shows a simple attribute (which we used in Chapter 6, "Enumerations") that allows a developer to attach a culture string to any other program construct:

```
//attribute class name must end in "Attribute"
[AttributeUsage(AttributeTargets.All, AllowMultiple=true)]
class CultureAttribute : Attribute
{
    string _culture;

    public string Culture
    {
        get
        {
            return _culture;
        }
    }

    public CultureAttribute(string culture)
    {
        _culture = culture;
    }
}
```

The AttributeTargets enumeration allows you to decide what target are valid for this attribute. The valid values are Assembly, Module, Class, Struct, Enum, Constructor, Method, Property, Field, Event, Interface, Parameter, Delegate, ReturnValue, GenericParameter, and All. If you want to combine values you can use the | operator, like this: `AttributeTargets.Field | AttributeTargets.Property`.

You can also specify with AllowMultiple whether multiple instances of this attribute are valid on a single element.

To apply this attribute, you use the square brackets:

```
[CultureAttribute("en-CA")]
[Culture("en-US")]
class MyClass
{
    //...
}
```

Since every attribute ends in "Attribute," the compiler will allow you to just specify the first part of the class name when applying them.

In order to make use of the attribute, you must write code that is aware of the `CultureAttribute` class and look for it.

```
[Culture("en-US")]
[Culture("en-GB")]
class Program
{
    static void Main(string[] args)
    {
        CultureAttribute[] attributes =
         (CultureAttribute[])(typeof(Program)).GetCustomAttributes(
            typeof(CultureAttribute), true);
        //easy comma-separated list
        string list =
          attributes.Aggregate("",
                               (output, next) =>
                                (output.Length > 0)
                                ? (output + ", " + next.Culture)
                                : next.Culture);
        Console.WriteLine("Cultures of Program: {0}", list);

        Console.ReadKey();
    }
}
```

This example produces the output:

```
Cultures of Program: en-US, en-GB
```

Instantiate a Class Dynamically

Scenario/Problem: You want to instantiate a class from a dynamically loaded assembly.

Solution: Using reflection, it's possible to instantiate code from assemblies that are not referenced at build time. Suppose you have a class defined in DynamicInstantiateLib.dll:

```
public class TestClass
{
    public int Add(int a, int b)
    {
        return a + b;
    }

    public string CombineStrings<T>(T a, T b)
    {
        return a.ToString() + ", " + b.ToString();
    }
}
```

In a separate assembly that does not have a reference to DynamicInstantiateLib.dll, you can use this code to nevertheless create an instance of `TestClass`:

```
Assembly assembly = Assembly.LoadFrom("DynamicInstantiateLib.dll");

Type type = assembly.GetType("DynamicInstantiate.TestClass");
object obj = Activator.CreateInstance(type);
```

Because you don't have a reference, you can't use the actual type to refer to it. This would seem to make it hard to use, but there are a few ways around this, as seen in the next section.

Invoke a Method on a Dynamically Instantiated Class

Scenario/Problem: You need to execute code on a dynamically instantiated type.

Solution: Assuming the following code, you have a few options:

```
Assembly assembly = Assembly.LoadFrom("DynamicInstantiateLib.dll");

Type type = assembly.GetType("DynamicInstantiate.TestClass");
object obj = Activator.CreateInstance(type);
```

Method 1:

```
//invoke the Add method
int result = (int)type.InvokeMember("Add", BindingFlags.Instance |
                        BindingFlags.InvokeMethod | BindingFlags.Public,
                        null, obj,
                        new object[] { 1, 2 });
```

Note that we pass the `obj` because `Add` is an instance method, and `obj` is that instance.

Method 2:

`InvokeMember` does not work for generic methods, so here's another way (also valid for `Add`):

```
MethodInfo mi = type.GetMethod("CombineStrings");
MethodInfo genericMi = mi.MakeGenericMethod(typeof(double));
string combined = (string)genericMi.Invoke(obj, new object[]{2.5, 5.5});
```

Method 3:

New in C# 4.0, you can use dynamic types to have the method call resolved at runtime, as essentially a shortcut syntax for the previous methods:

```
//invoke the Add method using dynamic
dynamic testClass = Activator.CreateInstance(type);
result = testClass.Add(5, 6);

//invoke the CombineStrings<T> method using dynamic
combined = testClass.CombineStrings<double>(13.3, 14.4);
```

You won't get IntelliSense with dynamic types, but this definitely looks cleaner than using `MethodInfo` objects and `Invoke` calls.

> **NOTE** Beware: Putting off type checking until runtime has its costs, mostly in unforeseen errors. Take advantage of compiler-enforced static typing whenever possible and only use dynamic typing when absolutely necessary.

Implement a Plugin Architecture

Scenario/Problem: You want your application to be able to load optional modules dynamically, often provided by users.

Solution: By using all the principles of this chapter, plus a few more tidbits, it's extremely easy in .NET to create your own plugin system for your application (see Figure 24.1).

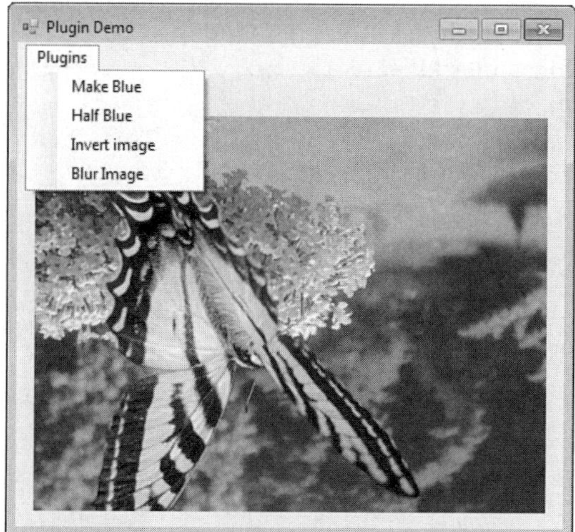

FIGURE 24.1
Implementing a plugin architecture is a snap with judicious use of interfaces and reflection.

Create a Shared Assembly

First, you need an assembly that both the plugins and the app can reference. This assembly defines the interfaces that plugins must implement and any common code you want to give them access to. For our simple example, there's just a single interface:

```
public interface IImagePlugin
{
    System.Drawing.Image RunPlugin(System.Drawing.Image image);
    string Name { get; }
}
```

Create a Plugin Assembly

Create a new assembly and add a reference to the previous assembly with the IImagePlugin interface. Then define this code:

```
//a simple plugin to make an image more blue
public class MakeBlue : IImagePlugin
{
    public System.Drawing.Image RunPlugin(System.Drawing.Image image)
    {
        Bitmap bitmap = new Bitmap(image);
        //make everything that has blue more blue
        for (int row=0; row < bitmap.Height; ++row)
        {
            for (int col=0;col<bitmap.Width; ++col)
            {
                //yes, using GetPixel and SetPixel is SLOW
                Color color = bitmap.GetPixel(col, row);
                if (color.B > 0)
                {
                    color = Color.FromArgb(color.A,
                                           color.R,
                                           color.G,
                                           255);
                }
                bitmap.SetPixel(col, row, color);
            }
        }
        return bitmap;
    }

    public string Name
    {
        get
        {
            return "Make Blue";
        }
    }
}
```

Search for and Load Plugins

The final step is discovery, which is just loading each DLL and checking to see if there are types that implement our interface. If so, create an instance of it and add it to the menu.

The following code is an excerpt from the PluginDemo sample project:

```
public partial class Form1 : Form
{
    private Dictionary<string, PluginInterfaces.IImagePlugin> _plugins =
            new Dictionary<string, PluginInterfaces.IImagePlugin>();
```

```
public Form1()
{
    InitializeComponent();

    Assembly assembly = Assembly.GetExecutingAssembly();
    string folder = Path.GetDirectoryName(assembly.Location);
    LoadPlugins(folder);
    CreatePluginMenu();
}

private void LoadPlugins(string folder)
{
    _plugins.Clear();

    //grab each dll
    foreach(string dll in Directory.GetFiles(folder, "*.dll"))
    {
        try
        {
            Assembly assembly = Assembly.LoadFrom(dll);
            //find every type in each assembly that
            //implements IImagePlugin
            foreach (Type type in assembly.GetTypes())
            {
                if (type.GetInterface("IImagePlugin") ==
➥typeof(PluginInterfaces.IImagePlugin))
                {
                    IImagePlugin plugin =
                      Activator.CreateInstance(type)
                                as IImagePlugin;
                    _plugins[plugin.Name] = plugin;
                }
            }
        }
        catch (BadImageFormatException )
        {
            //log--not one of ours!
        }
    }
}

private void CreatePluginMenu()
{
    pluginsToolStripMenuItem.DropDownItems.Clear();
    //dynamically create our menu from the plugin
    foreach (var pair in _plugins)
    {
```

```
            ToolStripMenuItem menuItem =
               new ToolStripMenuItem(pair.Key);
            menuItem.Click += new EventHandler(menuItem_Click);
            pluginsToolStripMenuItem.DropDownItems.Add(menuItem);
        }
    }

    void menuItem_Click(object sender, EventArgs e)
    {
        ToolStripMenuItem menuItem = sender as ToolStripMenuItem;
        PluginInterfaces.IImagePlugin plugin = _plugins[menuItem.Text];

        try
        {
            this.Cursor = Cursors.WaitCursor;
            pictureBox1.Image = plugin.RunPlugin(pictureBox1.Image);
        }
        catch (Exception ex)
        {
            //Never trust plugins!
            MessageBox.Show(ex.Message, "Plugin error");
        }
        finally
        {
            this.Cursor = Cursors.Default;
        }

    }

    private void buttonLoad_Click(object sender, EventArgs e)
    {
        OpenFileDialog ofd = new OpenFileDialog();
        ofd.Filter =
           "All images (*.bmp, *.png, *.jpg)|*.bmp;*.png;*.jpg";
        if (ofd.ShowDialog() == DialogResult.OK)
        {
            pictureBox1.Image = Image.FromFile(ofd.FileName);
        }
    }
}
```

NOTE Making a plugin work is really about defining a good set of interfaces. For example, you could allow communication the other way by defining an interface that your application implements and passing that to the plugin, allowing it to communicate and modify the application itself.

CHAPTER 25

Application Patterns and Tips

IN THIS CHAPTER

- Use a Stopwatch to Profile Your Code
- Mark Obsolete Code
- Combine Multiple Events into a Single Event
- Implement an Observer (aka Subscriber) Pattern
- Use an Event Broker
- Remember the Screen Location
- Implement Undo Using Command Objects
- Use Model-View-ViewModel in WPF
- Understand Localization
- Localize a Windows Form Application
- Localize an ASP.NET Application
- Localize a WPF Application
- Localize a Silverlight Application
- Deploy Applications Using ClickOnce

Although there is an infinite number of ways to build an application, over time a few reusable patterns emerge that are particularly helpful when designing complex programs. This chapter covers just a few particularly useful patterns.

As with all design patterns, there is no single way to implement these. In some cases, the overall design and idea are more important than the specific code used to implement them.

In addition to application patterns, there are some handy tips for building applications that didn't fit in anywhere else.

Use a Stopwatch to Profile Your Code

Scenario/Problem: You need to measure how long some code takes to run, especially for debugging and analysis.

Solution: Use the System.Diagnostics.Stopwatch class.

While there are many extensive profiling packages out there (there is a profiler included in some editions of Visual Studio), sometimes you just need to time a known block of code with a stopwatch.

```
System.Diagnostics.Stopwatch timer = new System.Diagnostics.Stopwatch();
timer.Start();
Decimal total = 0;
int limit = 1000000;
for (int i = 0; i < limit; ++i)
{
    total = total + (Decimal)Math.Sqrt(i);
}
timer.Stop();
Console.WriteLine("Sum of sqrts: {0}",total);
Console.WriteLine("Elapsed milliseconds: {0}",
timer.ElapsedMilliseconds);
Console.WriteLine("Elapsed time: {0}", timer.Elapsed);
```

This produces the output:

```
Sum of sqrts: 666666166.45882210823608
Elapsed milliseconds: 282
Elapsed time: 00:00:00.2828692
```

A useful trick when you need to use the Stopwatch for debugging purposes is to utilize the IDisposable interface to automate the use of the stopwatch:

```
class AutoStopwatch : System.Diagnostics.Stopwatch, IDisposable
{
    public AutoStopwatch()
    {
        Start();
    }

    public void Dispose()
    {
        Stop();
        Console.WriteLine("Elapsed: {0}", this.Elapsed);
    }
}
```

Now you can take advantage of the `using {}` syntax:

```
using (new AutoStopwatch())
{
    Decimal total2 = 0;
    int limit2 = 1000000;
    for (int i = 0; i < limit2; ++i)
    {
        total2 = total2 + (Decimal)Math.Sqrt(i);
    }
}
```

Besides `Start()` and `Stop()`, there are also `Reset()`, which stops and sets `Elapsed` to 0, and `Restart()`, which sets `Elapsed` to 0, but lets timer continue running.

Mark Obsolete Code

Scenario/Problem: You have "dead" code that should no longer be used, but you can't outright remove it because too many other parts use it. This is especially problematic when developing libraries.

Solution: Mark the method or class with the `[Obsolete]` attribute.

The compiler will warn anyone using an entity marked as obsolete with at least a warning. You can optionally supply a message for the compiler to present:

```
[Obsolete("Don't use this because...")]
class MyClass { }
```

You can also make it an error to use the obsolete code:

```
[Obsolete("Don't use this because...", true)]
class MyClass { }
```

Combine Multiple Events into a Single Event

Scenario/Problem: You have a class that can generate a lot of events in a short period of time. You don't want to waste overhead on just responding to events.

For example, if you have a UI that responds to updates from a data source, you need to take care that if the data source produces a lot of updates, your UI performance doesn't suffer.

Solution: Rather than notifying subscribers of each update, group them into a meta-event. For a starting example, assume you have a collection that notifies listeners when it has been updated:

```
class ItemAddedEventArgs<T> : EventArgs
{
    private T _item;
    public T Item {get;}

    public ItemAddedEventArgs(T item)
    {
        _items = item;
    }
}

class MyCollection<T>
{
    List<T> _data = new List<T>();

    public event EventHandler<ItemAddedEventArgs<T>> ItemsAdded;

    protected void OnItemsAdded(T item)
    {
        if (ItemsAdded != null)
        {
            ItemsAdded(this, new ItemAddedEventArgs<T>(item));
        }
    }
```

```
    public void Add(T item)
    {
        _data.Add(item);
        OnItemsAdded(item);
    }
}
```

The client of this collection happens to be a Windows Form. Here is part of its source code:

```
public partial class Form1 : Form
{
    MyCollection<int> _items = new MyCollection<int>();

    public Form1()
    {
        InitializeComponent();
    }

    void _items_ItemsAdded(object sender, ItemAddedEventArgs<int> e)
    {
        listViewOutput.Items.Add(e.Item.ToString());
    }

    private void buttonOneAtATime_Click(object sender, EventArgs e)
    {
        _items = new MyCollection<int>();
        _items.ItemsAdded += new
➥EventHandler<ItemAddedEventArgs<int>>(_items_ItemsAdded);

        GenerateItems();
    }

    private void GenerateItems()
    {
        listViewOutput.Items.Clear();

        for (int i = 0; i < 20000; i++)
        {
            _items.Add(i);
        }
    }
}
```

When the button is clicked, 20,000 items are added to the collection, which generates 20,000 event notifications, and 20,000 inserts and updates into the `ListView`.

The ListView has the ability to prevent UI updating during large inserts with the BeginUpdate and EndUpdate methods. This idea could also be used in your custom collection to batch updates.

The ItemAddedEventArgs<T> class must be updated to contain more than one item:

```
class ItemAddedEventArgs<T> : EventArgs
{
    private IList<T> _items = new List<T>();
    public IList<T> Items { get { return _items; } }

    public ItemAddedEventArgs()
    {
    }

    public ItemAddedEventArgs(T item)
    {
        _items.Add(item);
    }

    public void Add(T item)
    {
        _items.Add(item);
    }
}
```

Here's the updated MyCollection<T>:

```
class MyCollection<T>
{
    List<T> _data = new List<T>();
    int _updateCount = 0;

    public event EventHandler<ItemAddedEventArgs<T>> ItemsAdded;
    List<T> _updatedItems = new List<T>();

    protected void OnItemsAdded(T item)
    {
        if (!IsUpdating)
        {
            if (ItemsAdded != null)
            {
                ItemsAdded(this, new ItemAddedEventArgs<T>(item));
            }
        }
        else
        {
```

```
            _updatedItems.Add(item);
        }
    }

    protected void FireQueuedEvents()
    {
        if (!IsUpdating && _updatedItems.Count > 0)
        {
            //the event args have the ability to contain multiple items
            ItemAddedEventArgs<T> args = new ItemAddedEventArgs<T>();
            foreach (T item in _updatedItems)
            {
                args.Add(item);
            }
            _updatedItems.Clear();
            if (ItemsAdded != null)
            {
                ItemsAdded(this, args);
            }
        }
    }

    public bool IsUpdating
    {
        get
        {
            return _updateCount > 0;
        }
    }

    public void BeginUpdate()
    {
        //keep a count in case multiple clients call BeginUpdate,
        //or it's called recursively, though note that this
        //class is NOT thread safe.
        ++_updateCount;
    }

    public void EndUpdate()
    {
        --_updateCount;
        if (_updateCount == 0)
        {
            //only fire when we're done with all updates
            FireQueuedEvents();
```

```
        }
    }

    public void Add(T item)
    {
        _data.Add(item);
        OnItemsAdded(item);
    }
}
```

Now the client must call `BeginUpdate` before adding items to take advantage of this:

```
//in Form class

private void buttonUpdateBatch_Click(object sender, EventArgs e)
{
    _items = new MyCollection<int>();
    _items.ItemsAdded +=
      new EventHandler<ItemAddedEventArgs<int>>(_items_ItemsAdded);

    _items.BeginUpdate();
    GenerateItems();
    _items.EndUpdate();
}
void _items_ItemsAdded(object sender, ItemAddedEventArgs<int> e)
{
    listViewOutput.BeginUpdate();
    foreach (var i in e.Items)
    {
        listViewOutput.Items.Add(i.ToString());
    }
    listViewOutput.EndUpdate();
}
```

The time savings can be immense. Refer to the BatchEvents sample program in the included source code to see the difference. On my machine, the non-batched version took nearly 6 seconds, whereas the batched version took less than a second.

Implement an Observer (aka Subscriber) Pattern

Scenario/Problem: You want a component A to be notified of updates in another component B, without use of .Net events.

Solution: While most notification systems use .Net events to communicate, there are times when you want something a little more decoupled. For this, .Net 4 provides two interfaces to aid in implementing this common design pattern.

Use the `IObserver<T>` and `IObservable<T>` interfaces.

The `IObservable<T>` interface is implemented on the class that provides data for others to consume.

```
class DataGenerator : IObservable<int>
{
    private List<IObserver<int>> _observers = new List<IObserver<int>>();
    private int _lastPrime = -1;

    //inherited from IObservable<T>
    public IDisposable Subscribe(IObserver<int> observer)
    {
        _observers.Add(observer);
        observer.OnNext(_lastPrime);
        return observer as IDisposable;
    }

    //notifies all subscribers of the new data
    private void NotifyData(int n)
    {
        foreach (IObserver<int> observer in _observers)
        {
            observer.OnNext(n);
        }
    }

    //notifies all subscribers that no more data is coming
    private void NotifyComplete()
    {
        foreach (IObserver<int> observer in _observers)
        {
            observer.OnCompleted();
        }
    }

    private static Random rand = new Random();

    //let's just generate some aribtrary data
    public void Run()
    {
        for (int i=0;i<100;++i)
```

```
        {
            int n = rand.Next(1, Int32.MaxValue);
            if (IsPrime(n))
            {
                _lastPrime = n;
                NotifyData(n);
            }
        }
        NotifyComplete();
    }

    private static bool IsPrime(Int32 number)
    {
        //check for evenness
        if (number % 2 == 0)
        {
            if (number == 2)
                return true;
            return false;
        }
        //don't need to check past the square root
        Int32 max = (Int32)Math.Sqrt(number);
        for (Int32 i = 3; i <= max; i += 2)
        {
            if ((number % i) == 0)
            {
                return false;
            }
        }
        return true;
    }
}
```

The IObserver<T> is implemented on classes that want to know about the updates in the IObservable<T>-derived classes.

```
class DataObserver : IObserver<int>
{
    //give it a name so we can distinguish it in the output
    private string _name = "Observer";
    #region IObserver<int> Members

    public void OnCompleted()
    {
        Console.WriteLine(_name + ":Completed");
    }
```

```
    public void OnError(Exception error)
    {
        Console.WriteLine(_name + ": Error");
    }

    public void OnNext(int value)
    {
        Console.WriteLine(_name + ":Generated data {0}", value);
    }

    #endregion

    public DataObserver(string observerName)
    {
        _name = observerName;
    }
}
```

To tie them together, merely subscribe the observers to the data generator:

```
DataGenerator generator = new DataGenerator();

DataObserver observer1 = new DataObserver("01");
DataObserver observer2 = new DataObserver("02");

generator.Subscribe(observer1);
generator.Subscribe(observer2);

generator.Run();
```

The output is something like this:

```
01:Generated data -1
02:Generated data -1
01:Generated data 597759749
02:Generated data 597759749
01:Generated data 369128117
02:Generated data 369128117
01:Generated data 650236453
02:Generated data 650236453
01:Generated data 2143508953
02:Generated data 2143508953
01:Generated data 298906169
02:Generated data 298906169
01:Generated data 1296076711
02:Generated data 1296076711
01:Generated data 1970737339
```

```
02:Generated data 1970737339
01:Completed
02:Completed
Press any key to exit...
```

Use an Event Broker

Scenario/Problem: You have unrelated components that must respond to each others' events. You don't want to have them directly refer to each other.

Solution: An event broker is merely an object that acts as middleman for any number of events from any objects to any other object. In a way, this is taking the Observer Pattern (see previous section) even further.

Here's a simple event broker implementation:

```
public class EventBroker
{
    Dictionary<string, List<Delegate>> _subscriptions =
                           new Dictionary<string, List<Delegate>>();

    public void Register(string eventId, Delegate method)
    {
        //associate an event handler for an eventId
        List<Delegate> delegates = null;
        if (!_subscriptions.TryGetValue(eventId, out delegates))
        {
            delegates = new List<Delegate>();
            _subscriptions[eventId] = delegates;
        }
        delegates.Add(method);
    }

    public void Unregister(string eventId, Delegate method)
    {
        //unassociate a specific event handler method for the eventId
        List<Delegate> delegates = null;
        if (_subscriptions.TryGetValue(eventId, out delegates))
        {
            delegates.Remove(method);
            if (delegates.Count == 0)
            {
                _subscriptions.Remove(eventId);
```

```
            }
        }
    }

    public void OnEvent(string eventId, params object[] args)
    {
        //call all event handlers for the given eventId
        List<Delegate> delegates = null;
        if (_subscriptions.TryGetValue(eventId, out delegates))
        {
            foreach (Delegate del in delegates)
            {
                if (del.Method != null)
                {
                    if (del.Target != null)
                    {
                        del.DynamicInvoke(args);
                    }
                }
            }
        }
    }
}
```

Usage is very simple: Rather than raising normal .NET events, just call the appropriate methods on the `EventBroker`. The project contains three user controls: One of them raises the event and the other two listen for it. A form owns the event broker and ties everything together, as the following partial code example shows:

```
public partial class Form1 : Form
{
    //a single event broker to tie all controls together
    EventBroker _broker = new EventBroker();

    public Form1()
    {
        InitializeComponent();

        myControl11.SetEventBroker(_broker);
        myControl21.SetEventBroker(_broker);
        myControl31.SetEventBroker(_broker);
    }
}

public partial class MyControl1 : UserControl
{
```

```
    EventBroker _broker;

    public MyControl1()
    {
        InitializeComponent();
    }

    public void SetEventBroker(EventBroker broker)
    {
        _broker = broker;
    }

    //when user clicks button, fire the global event
    private void buttonTrigger_Click(object sender, EventArgs e)
    {
        if (_broker != null)
        {
            _broker.OnEvent("MyEvent");
        }
    }
}

public partial class MyControl2 : UserControl
{
    EventBroker _broker;

    public MyControl2()
    {
        InitializeComponent();
    }

    public void SetEventBroker(EventBroker broker)
    {
        _broker = broker;
        _broker.Register("MyEvent", new MethodInvoker(OnMyEvent));
    }

    private void OnMyEvent()
    {
        labelResult.Text = "Event triggered!";
    }
}
//MyControl3 is the same as MyControl2
```

See the EventBroker sample for the full source.

Using this method gives you a few advantages:

- Because strings are used, any component can publish or subscribe to any event without having to add a reference to a strongly typed object.
- Because no component knows anything about the origin or destination of events, it is trivial to add or remove components with breaking dependencies.

NOTE This method is most appropriate for global events that you need to communicate across the entire application, and passing objects around complicated code hierarchies just to listen for events is not worth the headache and maintenance problems that are entailed. For more local events, you should definitely just use the normal .NET event pattern.

Remember the Screen Location

Scenario/Problem: You want your application to remember its location on the screen and restore to that location the next time the app runs.

Solution: Although this task is easy, you need to take into account that when you restore an application, what used to be on the screen before might not be on the screen anymore. For example, a user might rearrange a multiple-monitor scenario, or merely change the resolution of his screen to something smaller.

The screen location should be a user-specific setting. For the following example, two user settings were created in the standard Settings.settings file (see Chapter 16, "Windows Forms").

```
public partial class Form1 : Form
{
    public Form1()
    {
        InitializeComponent();
    }

    protected override void OnLoad(EventArgs e)
    {
        base.OnLoad(e);
        RestoreLocation();
    }

    private void RestoreLocation()
    {
        Point location = Properties.Settings.Default.FormLocation;
```

```
        Size size = Properties.Settings.Default.FormSize;
        //make sure location is on a monitor
        bool isOnScreen = false;
        foreach (Screen screen in Screen.AllScreens)
        {
            if (screen.WorkingArea.Contains(location))
            {
                isOnScreen = true;
            }
        }
        //if our window isn't visible, put it on primary monitor
        if (!isOnScreen)
        {
            this.SetDesktopLocation(
                      Screen.PrimaryScreen.WorkingArea.Left,
                      Screen.PrimaryScreen.WorkingArea.Top);
        }

        //if too small, just reset to default
        if (size.Width < 10 || size.Height < 10)
        {
            Size = new Size(300, 300);
        }
    }

    private void SaveLocation()
    {
        //these are user settings I created in the
        //Properties\Settings.settings file
        Properties.Settings.Default.FormLocation = this.Location;
        Properties.Settings.Default.FormSize = this.Size;
        Properties.Settings.Default.Save();
    }

    protected override void OnClosing(CancelEventArgs e)
    {
        base.OnClosing(e);

        SaveLocation();
    }
}
```

Refer to the SaveScreenLocation project in the accompanying source code to see this code in practice.

Implement Undo Using Command Objects

Scenario/Problem: You want to be able to undo commands in your application.

Solution: Most programs that let the user edit content have the ability to let the user undo the previous action. This section demonstrates a simple widget application that allows undo functionality (see Figure 25.1).

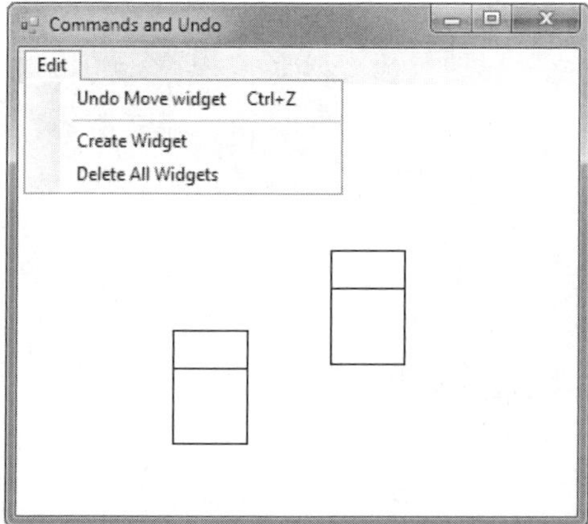

FIGURE 25.1
This simple application allows the user to undo moves, creations, and deletions.

The most popular way to implement this involves command objects that know how to undo themselves. Every possible action in the program is represented by a command object.

NOTE Not everything the user can do in your application needs to be a command. For example, moving the cursor and changing the current selection aren't usually considered actions. Generally, undoable commands should be those that change the user's data.

Define the Command Interface and History Buffer

Here's a possible interface:

```
interface ICommand
{
    void Execute();
    void Undo();
    string Name { get; }
}
```

We also need a way to track all our commands in the order they were issued:

```
class CommandHistory
{
    private Stack<ICommand> _stack = new Stack<ICommand>();

    public bool CanUndo
    {
        get
        {
            return _stack.Count > 0;
        }
    }

    public string MostRecentCommandName
    {
        get
        {
            if (CanUndo)
            {
                ICommand cmd = _stack.Peek();
                return cmd.Name;
            }
            return string.Empty;
        }
    }

    public void PushCommand(ICommand command)
    {
        _stack.Push(command);
    }

    public ICommand PopCommand()
    {
        return _stack.Pop();
    }
}
```

Given these two things, the specific implementations of commands depends on the data structures of the application.

In this case, we have an `IWidget` interface defining all our objects:

```
interface IWidget
{
    void Draw(Graphics graphics);
    bool HitTest(Point point);
```

```
    Point Location { get; set; }
    Size Size { get; set; }
    Rectangle BoundingBox { get; }
}
```

Define Command Functionality

One command we need is to be able to undo a drag/move operation. The command object needs only as much context to be able to do and undo the operation (in this case, the old location and the new location):

```
class MoveCommand : ICommand
{
    private Point _originalLocation;
    private Point _newLocation;
    private IWidget _widget;

    public MoveCommand(IWidget widget,
                       Point originalLocation,
                       Point newLocation)
    {
        this._widget = widget;
        this._originalLocation = originalLocation;
        this._newLocation = newLocation;
    }

    #region ICommand Members

    public void Execute()
    {
        _widget.Location = _newLocation;
    }

    public void Undo()
    {
        _widget.Location = _originalLocation;
    }

    public string Name
    {
        get { return "Move widget"; }
    }
    #endregion
}
```

Here's the `CreateWidgetCommand` object, which takes a different type of state:

```
class CreateWidgetCommand : ICommand
{
    private ICollection<IWidget> _collection;
    private IWidget _newWidget;

    public CreateWidgetCommand(ICollection<IWidget> collection,
➥IWidget newWidget)
    {
        _collection = collection;
        _newWidget = newWidget;
    }

    #region ICommand Members

    public void Execute()
    {
        _collection.Add(_newWidget);
    }

    public void Undo()
    {
        _collection.Remove(_newWidget);
    }

    public string Name
    {
        get { return "Create new widget"; }
    }

    #endregion
}
```

To use this functionality, you just have to create the command objects at the appropriate time. Here is the `Form` from the `CommandUndo` sample code. Look at the project in Visual Studio to see the full source.

```
public partial class Form1 : Form
{
    private CommandHistory _history = new CommandHistory();
    private List<IWidget> _widgets = new List<IWidget>();
    private bool _isDragging = false;
    private IWidget _dragWidget = null;
    private Point _prevMousePt;
    private Point _originalLocation;
    private Point _newLocation;
```

```
    public Form1()
    {
        InitializeComponent();

        panelSurface.MouseDoubleClick += new
➥MouseEventHandler(panelSurface_MouseDoubleClick);
        panelSurface.Paint += new PaintEventHandler(panelSurface_Paint);
        panelSurface.MouseMove +=
           new MouseEventHandler(panelSurface_MouseMove);
        panelSurface.MouseDown +=
           new MouseEventHandler(panelSurface_MouseDown);
        panelSurface.MouseUp +=
           new MouseEventHandler(panelSurface_MouseUp);

        editToolStripMenuItem.DropDownOpening += new
➥EventHandler(editToolStripMenuItem_DropDownOpening);
        undoToolStripMenuItem.Click +=
           new EventHandler(undoToolStripMenuItem_Click);
    }

    void panelSurface_MouseDown(object sender, MouseEventArgs e)
    {
        IWidget widget = GetWidgetUnderPoint(e.Location);
        if (widget != null)
        {
            _dragWidget = widget;
            _isDragging = true;
            _prevMousePt = e.Location;
            _newLocation = _originalLocation = _dragWidget.Location;
        }
    }

    void panelSurface_MouseMove(object sender, MouseEventArgs e)
    {
        if (!_isDragging)
        {
            IWidget widget = GetWidgetUnderPoint(e.Location);
            if (widget != null)
            {
                panelSurface.Cursor = Cursors.SizeAll;
            }
            else
            {
                panelSurface.Cursor = Cursors.Default;
            }
        }
```

```
        else if (_dragWidget != null)
        {
            Point offset = new Point(e.Location.X - _prevMousePt.X,
                e.Location.Y - _prevMousePt.Y);

            _prevMousePt = e.Location;

            _newLocation.Offset(offset);
            //update the widget temporarily as we move
            //-- not a command in this case
            //because we don't want to record every dragging operation
            _dragWidget.Location = _newLocation;

            Refresh();
        }
    }

    void panelSurface_MouseUp(object sender, MouseEventArgs e)
    {
        if (_isDragging)
        {
            //now perform the command so that Undo restores to location
            //before we started dragging
            RunCommand(new MoveCommand(_dragWidget,
                                        _originalLocation,
                                        _newLocation));
        }
        _isDragging = false;
        _dragWidget = null;
    }

    void panelSurface_MouseDoubleClick(object sender, MouseEventArgs e)
    {
        CreateNewWidget(e.Location);
    }

    private IWidget GetWidgetUnderPoint(Point point)
    {
        foreach (IWidget widget in _widgets)
        {
            if (widget.BoundingBox.Contains(point))
            {
                return widget;
            }
        }
```

```
    return null;
}

void panelSurface_Paint(object sender, PaintEventArgs e)
{
    foreach (IWidget widget in _widgets)
    {
        widget.Draw(e.Graphics);
    }
}

//menu handling
void editToolStripMenuItem_DropDownOpening(object sender,
                                            EventArgs e)
{
    undoToolStripMenuItem.Enabled = _history.CanUndo;
    if (_history.CanUndo)
    {
        undoToolStripMenuItem.Text = "&Undo "
                 + _history.MostRecentCommandName;
    }
    else
    {
        undoToolStripMenuItem.Text = "&Undo";
    }
}

void undoToolStripMenuItem_Click(object sender, EventArgs e)
{
    UndoMostRecentCommand();
}

private void createToolStripMenuItem_Click(object sender,
                                            EventArgs e)
{
    CreateNewWidget(new Point(0, 0));
}

private void clearToolStripMenuItem_Click(object sender,
                                           EventArgs e)
{
    RunCommand(new DeleteAllWidgetsCommand(_widgets));
    Refresh();
}
```

```
    private void CreateNewWidget(Point point)
    {
        RunCommand(new CreateWidgetCommand(_widgets,
                                           new Widget(point)));
        Refresh();
    }

    private void RunCommand(ICommand command)
    {
        _history.PushCommand(command);
        command.Execute();
    }

    private void UndoMostRecentCommand()
    {
        ICommand command = _history.PopCommand();
        command.Undo();
        Refresh();
    }
}
```

NOTE Although WPF has the notion of command objects already, they do not have the ability to undo themselves (which makes sense because undo is an application-dependent operation). The ideas in this section can be easily translated to WPF.

Use Model-View-ViewModel in WPF

Scenario/Problem: You want to separate UI from underlying data and behavior in WPF.

Solution: As WPF has increased in popularity, the Model-View-ViewModel pattern has emerged as a variation of Model-View-Presenter, which works very well with the WPF binding system.

The ViewModel solves the problem of trying to associate WPF controls with data objects that don't have any knowledge of UI. It maps plain data objects to data that WPF can bind to. For example, a color code in a database could be translated to a `Brush` for the view to use. The following sections tackle each part of this, piece by piece.

Figure 25.2 shows the final sample application which has two views of the data: a list of all widgets, and a view of a single widget.

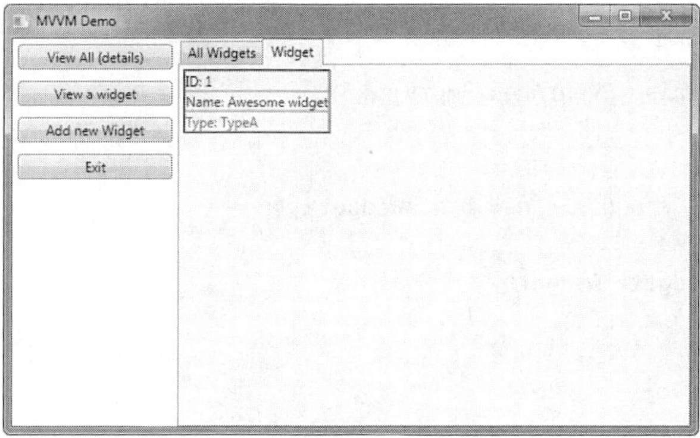

FIGURE 25.2
Very simple pieces can be combined to form elegant WPF applications that are easy to extend and maintain.

Define the Model

In this case, we'll just use objects in memory, but you could just as easily connect to a database, a web server, or a file.

```
enum WidgetType
{
    TypeA,
    TypeB
};

class Widget
{
    public int Id { get; set; }
    public string Name { get; set; }
    public WidgetType WidgetType { get; set; }

    public Widget(int id, string name, WidgetType type)
    {
        this.Id = id;
        this.Name = name;
        this.WidgetType = type;
    }
}

class WidgetRepository
{
    public event EventHandler<EventArgs> WidgetAdded;
    protected void OnWidgetAdded()
    {
```

```
        if (WidgetAdded != null)
        {
            WidgetAdded(this, EventArgs.Empty);
        }
    }
    private List<Widget> _widgets = new List<Widget>();

    public ICollection<Widget> Widgets
    {
        get
        {
            return _widgets;
        }
    }

    public Widget this[int index]
    {
        get
        {
            return _widgets[index];
        }
    }

    public WidgetRepository()
    {
        CreateDefaultWidgets();
    }

    public void AddWidget(Widget widget)
    {
        _widgets.Add(widget);
        OnWidgetAdded();
    }

    private void CreateDefaultWidgets()
    {
        AddWidget(new Widget(1, "Awesome widget", WidgetType.TypeA));
        AddWidget(new Widget(2, "Okay widget", WidgetType.TypeA));
        AddWidget(new Widget(3, "So-so widget", WidgetType.TypeB));
        AddWidget(new Widget(4, "Horrible widget", WidgetType.TypeB));
    }
}
```

As you can see, this data model has no notion of anything related to WPF.

Define the ViewModel

Because we'll have multiple ViewModel classes in this app, and they have some common functionality, let's define a base class:

```
abstract class BaseViewModel : INotifyPropertyChanged
{
    private string _displayName="Unknown";

    public string DisplayName
    {
        get
        {
            return _displayName;
        }
        set
        {
            _displayName = value;
            OnPropertyChanged("DisplayName");
        }
    }

    protected BaseViewModel(string displayName)
    {
        this.DisplayName = displayName;
    }

    #region INotifyPropertyChanged Members

    public event PropertyChangedEventHandler PropertyChanged;

    #endregion

    protected void OnPropertyChanged(string propertyName)
    {
        if (PropertyChanged != null)
        {
            PropertyChanged(this, new
➥PropertyChangedEventArgs(propertyName));
        }
    }
}
```

WPF uses the `INotifyPropertyChanged` interface to know when to update views that are bound to these ViewModel objects.

The first concrete ViewModel is the `WidgetViewModel`:

```
class WidgetViewModel : BaseViewModel
{
    private Widget _widget;

    public int Id { get { return _widget.Id; } }
    public string Name { get { return _widget.Name; } }
    public string WidgetType
    {
        get
        {
            return _widget.WidgetType.ToString();
        }
    }

    public WidgetViewModel(Widget widget)
        :base("Widget")
    {
        _widget = widget;
    }
}
```

The other ViewModel is for the view that will show a list of all `Widget` objects:

```
class AllWidgetsViewModel : BaseViewModel
{
    private WidgetRepository _widgets;
    //this collection of view models is available to
    //the view to display however it wants
    public ObservableCollection<WidgetViewModel>
                    WidgetViewModels { get; private set; }

    public AllWidgetsViewModel(WidgetRepository widgets)
        :base("All Widgets")
    {
        _widgets = widgets;
         //the ViewModel watches the model for changes and
         //uses OnPropertyChanged to notify the view of changes
        _widgets.WidgetAdded +=
           new EventHandler<EventArgs>(_widgets_WidgetAdded);

        CreateViewModels();
    }

    void _widgets_WidgetAdded(object sender, EventArgs e)
    {
```

```
        CreateViewModels();
    }

    private void CreateViewModels()
    {
        WidgetViewModels = new ObservableCollection<WidgetViewModel>();
        foreach (Widget w in _widgets.Widgets)
        {
            WidgetViewModels.Add(new WidgetViewModel(w));
        }
        OnPropertyChanged("WidgetViewModels");
    }
}
```

Define the View

The view involves mostly just setting up the UI and bindings to the ViewModel (see Listing 25.1). As you'll see in the next section, the `DataContext` property for this control will be set to the ViewModel.

LISTING 25.1 **AllWidgetsView.xaml**

```
<UserControl x:Class="MVVMDemo.AllWidgetsView"
             xmlns="http://schemas.microsoft.com/
➥winfx/2006/xaml/presentation"
             xmlns:x="http://schemas.microsoft.com/winfx/2006/xaml"
             xmlns:mc="http://schemas.openxmlformats.org/
➥markup-compatibility/2006"
             xmlns:d="http://schemas.microsoft.com/
➥expression/blend/2008"
             mc:Ignorable="d"
             d:DesignHeight="300" d:DesignWidth="300">
    <Grid>
        <ListView x:Name="ListViewWidgets"
                  ItemsSource="{Binding WidgetViewModels}"
                  >
            <ListView.View>
                <GridView>
                    <GridViewColumn Header="ID"
                                    DisplayMemberBinding="{Binding
                                            Path=Id}"/>
                    <GridViewColumn Header="Name"
                                    DisplayMemberBinding="{Binding
                                            Path=Name}" />
                    <GridViewColumn Header="Type"
                                    DisplayMemberBinding="{Binding
```

LISTING 25.1 **AllWidgetsView.xaml** (continued)

```
                                                                  Path=WidgetType}" />
                </GridView>
            </ListView.View>
        </ListView>
    </Grid>
</UserControl>
```

The Widget-specific view displays a single widget in a graphical way (see Listing 25.2).

LISTING 25.2 **WidgetGraphicView.xaml**

```
<UserControl x:Class="MVVMDemo.WidgetGraphicView"
             xmlns="http://schemas.microsoft.com/
➥winfx/2006/xaml/presentation"
             xmlns:x="http://schemas.microsoft.com/winfx/2006/xaml"
             xmlns:mc="http://schemas.openxmlformats.org/
➥markup-compatibility/2006"
             xmlns:d="http://schemas.microsoft.com/
➥expression/blend/2008"
             mc:Ignorable="d"
             d:DesignHeight="300" d:DesignWidth="300">
    <Grid>
        <Border BorderThickness="1" BorderBrush="Black"
                VerticalAlignment="Top" HorizontalAlignment="Left">
            <StackPanel HorizontalAlignment="Left"
                        VerticalAlignment="Top">
                <Border BorderThickness="1" BorderBrush="DarkGray">
                    <TextBlock>ID: <TextBlock Text="{Binding Path=Id}"/>
                    </TextBlock>
                </Border>
                <Border BorderThickness="1" BorderBrush="DarkGray">
                    <TextBlock Foreground="Blue">Name:
                      <TextBlock Text="{Binding Path=Name}"/>
                    </TextBlock>

                </Border>
                <Border BorderThickness="1" BorderBrush="DarkGray">
                    <TextBlock Foreground="Red">Type:
                       <TextBlock Text="{Binding Path=WidgetType}"/>
                    </TextBlock>                 </Border>
            </StackPanel>
        </Border>
    </Grid>
</UserControl>
```

Put Commands into the ViewModel

Now we just need to hook everything up with the MainWindow and MainWindowViewModel. The MainWindow needs to execute some commands, which should be done in the ViewModel. To do this, you can't use the standard WPF RoutedUIEvent, but you can easily develop your own command classes. A common way to do this is to create a command object that calls a delegate you specify:

```
//this is a common type of class, also known as RelayCommand
class DelegateCommand : ICommand
{
    //delegates to control command
    private Action<object> _execute;
    private Predicate<object> _canExecute;

    public DelegateCommand(Action<object> executeDelegate)
        :this(executeDelegate, null)
    {
    }
    public DelegateCommand(Action<object> executeDelegate,
➥Predicate<object> canExecuteDelegate)
    {
        _execute = executeDelegate;
        _canExecute = canExecuteDelegate;
    }
    #region ICommand Members

    public bool CanExecute(object parameter)
    {
        if (_canExecute == null)
        {
            return true;
        }
        return _canExecute(parameter);
    }

    public event EventHandler CanExecuteChanged;

    public void Execute(object parameter)
    {
        _execute(parameter);
    }

    #endregion
}
```

Now we can define the MainWindowViewModel:

```
class MainWindowViewModel : BaseViewModel
{
    private WidgetRepository _widgets = new WidgetRepository();
    private int _nextId = 5;

    //this is better than RoutedUICommand when using MVVM
    public DelegateCommand ExitCommand {get;private set;}
    public DelegateCommand OpenAllWidgetsListCommand
                                 { get; private set; }
    public DelegateCommand ViewWidgetCommand { get; private set; }
    public DelegateCommand AddWidgetCommand { get; private set; }

    public ObservableCollection<BaseViewModel> OpenViews
                                                { get; private set; }

    public MainWindowViewModel()
        :base("MVVM Demo")
    {
        ExitCommand = new DelegateCommand(executeDelegate => OnClose());
        OpenAllWidgetsListCommand =
                 new DelegateCommand(executeDelegate =>
➥OpenAllWidgetsList());
        ViewWidgetCommand =
           new DelegateCommand(executeDelegate => ViewWidget());
        AddWidgetCommand =
           new DelegateCommand(executeDelegate => AddNewWidget());

        OpenViews = new ObservableCollection<BaseViewModel>();
    }

    public event EventHandler<EventArgs> Close;

    protected void OnClose()
    {
        if (Close != null)
        {
            Close(this, EventArgs.Empty);
        }
    }

    private void OpenAllWidgetsList()
    {
        OpenViews.Add(new AllWidgetsViewModel(_widgets));
    }
```

```
    private void ViewWidget()
    {
        OpenViews.Add(new WidgetViewModel(_widgets[0]));
    }

    private void AddNewWidget()
    {
        _widgets.AddWidget(new Widget(_nextId++,
                                      "New Widget",
                                      WidgetType.TypeA));
    }
}
```

Now it's just a matter of binding the `MainView` parts to properties of the ViewModel (see Listing 25.3).

LISTING 25.3 **Mainwindow.xaml**

```
<Window x:Class="MVVMDemo.MainWindow"
        xmlns="http://schemas.microsoft.com/
➥winfx/2006/xaml/presentation"
        xmlns:x="http://schemas.microsoft.com/winfx/2006/xaml"
        xmlns:local="clr-namespace:MVVMDemo"
        Title="{Binding Path=DisplayName}" Height="377" Width="627">
    <Window.Resources>
        <DataTemplate x:Key="TabControlTemplate">
            <TextBlock Text="{Binding Path=DisplayName}"/>
        </DataTemplate>
        <!-- These templates tell WPF now to
             display our ViewModel classes-->
        <DataTemplate DataType="{x:Type local:AllWidgetsViewModel}">
            <local:AllWidgetsView/>
        </DataTemplate>
        <DataTemplate DataType="{x:Type local:WidgetViewModel}">
            <local:WidgetGraphicView/>
        </DataTemplate>
    </Window.Resources>
    <Grid>
        <Grid.ColumnDefinitions>
            <ColumnDefinition Width="150"/>
            <ColumnDefinition Width="*"/>
        </Grid.ColumnDefinitions>
        <StackPanel Grid.Column="0" >
            <Button x:Name="buttonViewAllGrid"
                    Margin="5" Command="{Binding
                Path=OpenAllWidgetsListCommand}">View All (details)
```

LISTING 25.3 **Mainwindow.xaml** (continued)

```
            </Button>
            <Button x:Name="buttonViewSingle"
                    Margin="5" Command="{Binding
               Path=ViewWidgetCommand}">View a widget</Button>
            <Button x:Name="buttonAddWidget"
                    Margin="5" Command="{Binding
               Path=AddWidgetCommand}">Add new Widget</Button>
            <Button x:Name="buttonExit" Margin="5" Command="{Binding
               Path=ExitCommand}">Exit</Button>
        </StackPanel>
        <TabControl HorizontalAlignment="Stretch"  Name="tabControl1"
➥VerticalAlignment="Stretch" Grid.Column="1"
                    ItemsSource="{Binding Path=OpenViews}"
                    ItemTemplate="{StaticResource TabControlTemplate}">
        </TabControl>
    </Grid>
</Window>
```

The line: `xmlns:local="clr-namespace:MVVMDemo"` brings the .NET namespace into the XML namespace `local` so that it can be used to refer to the controls in the XAML.

To see it all in action, look at the MVVMDemo project in the accompanying source code.

> **NOTE** The key point to MVVM is to make the view completely concerned with how data looks, never about behavior. Ideally, a view should be completely plug-and-play, with the only work being to hook up the bindings to the ViewModel.
>
> In addition, separating all the behavior from the GUI allows you to be far more complete in unit testing. The ViewModel doesn't care what type of view uses it—it could easily be a programmatic "view" that tests its functionality.

Understand Localization

> **Scenario/Problem:** You want your program to be translated into multiple languages.

Solution: The chapters on numbers and strings cover the display of those items in different cultures. To display your program's UI in a different culture requires a bit more work, and the process can be quite different, depending on the technology you use.

NOTE In .Net, culture applies to a thread. Each thread actually has two culture settings: culture and UI culture.

The culture is automatically determined from your region format. In Windows, this is set in Control Panel | Region and Language | Formats. This determines the default formats of numbers, times, and currencies in string formatting (see Chapter 5), but does not affect which localized resources are used.

The UI culture is automatically determined from the computer's native display language. To view the Windows UI in other languages, you need a localized copy of Windows, or you can install a language pack (only available with certain editions of Windows). Windows 7 lets you change display language in Control Panel | Region and Language | Keyboards and Languages | Display language.

To ease testing for the purposes of this section, the UI culture is manually set to be the same as the non-UI culture in configuration files or in the application startup code.

NOTE All .Net applications, regardless of platform, obey a hierarchy when looking for resource files. They look from most specific to least specific, until they get to the default resource repository (usually the application executable itself).

Cultures can be specified with either just the language (French: "fr"), or the language and a region (French-Canada: "fr-CA"). You must create all of your resource files using this standard naming scheme. If resources are stored in a file called Resources.dll, .Net will look for files in this order:

1. Resources.fr-CA.dll
2. Resources.fr.dll
3. Resources.dll
4. Application.exe

This general pattern holds true, even if resources are stored in separate folders.

Localize a Windows Forms Application

Windows Forms has the strongest support for localization in the Visual Studio IDE. To localize a form, follow these steps:

1. Change the form's `Localizable` property to `true`.
2. Change the form's `Language` property to each language you wish to localize. This will generate new language resource files for the form, such as Form1.en.resx, Form1.it.resx, and so on.
3. With the appropriate language selected, modify the text and other properties (such as location or size) of each element you wish to localize.
4. To add a new control, you must set the language back to Default.

Following these steps changes the form's `InitializeComponent` method to have a lot of code like this:

```
resources.ApplyResources(this.labelName, "labelName");
```

This will look in the resources for the appropriate values, including text, location, size, and other properties. Each culture will cause a new directory to be created in the output directory containing the appropriate resource DLL.

To have a global resource, not tied to a specific form, follow these steps:

1. (If one doesn't exist already) Right-click on the project, and select Add, then Add New Item…, then Resource file. Name it whatever you want, e.g. Resources.resx. Visual Studio will generate a class that automatically reads the resx file for the current culture and returns the right value with strongly typed properties. Only one class exists, regardless of how many cultures you want to translate the file into.
2. Add the desired strings and other resources (in the sample, it's just a string called `Message`).
3. Copy the resource file, or add a new one, called `Resources.it.resx`. Make sure it's in the same folder as the default file.
4. Make the necessary translations and changes.
5. Wherever you need to use the resource, use code similar to the following:

```
//my resources are in the Properties folder/namespace:
this.labelMessage.Text = Properties.Resources.Message;
```

Localize an ASP.NET Application

Localizing ASP.Net applications is conceptually similar to Windows Forms in many ways.

To localize a specific form, follow these steps:

1. Create the form in the default language (e.g., Default.aspx).
2. Go to the Tools menu and choose Generate Local Resource. Visual Studio will create the `App_LocalResources` folder, create the file Default.aspx.resx, and populate it with the keys and values from the ASPX file. It will also add `meta:resourceKey` properties to your ASPX file.

```
<asp:Label ID="LabelName" runat="server" Text="The Flag:"
                meta:resourcekey="LabelNameResource1"></asp:Label>
```

The name of the resource for this `Label's Text` property will be `LabelNameResource1.Text`.

3. Create additional resource files for each target culture, e.g. Default.aspx.it.resx, Default.aspx.fr-CA.resx. You can copy the original file and just rename it to prepopulate it with all the keys and values.
4. Translate each localized resource file.

To create a global resource file (not for a specific ASPX file), follow these steps:

1. Right-click the project, select Add ASP.Net Folder, then App_GlobalResources.
2. In the App_GlobalResources, add a new resource file (e.g., GlobalResources.resx)
3. Add appropriate values to the file (in this case, just a single string named Message).
4. Copy the file to localized versions, GlobalResources.it.resx, for example.
5. In your ASPX files, add code like this to reference the value Message:

```
<asp:TextBox ID="TextBox1" runat="server"
    Text="<%$ Resources:GlobalResources, Message %>"
    meta:resourceKey="TextBoxResource1" />
```

To test your web application, make sure that Culture and uiCulture values for the pages are set to Auto (the default):

```
<%@ Page Language="C#" AutoEventWireup="true" CodeFile="Default.aspx.cs"
Inherits="_Default" meta:resourcekey="PageResource1"
uiCulture="Auto" Culture="Auto" %>
```

Then set your web browser's language to the one you want to test and make sure it's at the top of the list. Most web browsers allow you to specify desired languages in order of preference.

In Internet Explorer 8, go to Tools | Internet Options | General | Languages.

In Firefox, go to Tools | Options | Content | Languages | Choose....

Localize a WPF Application

There are two methods of localizing a WPF application: using XAML and using resources and data binding. Unfortunately, either way, compared to Windows Forms applications, doing localization in WPF is currently a real chore. Table 25.1 highlights some of the pros and cons of the two approaches.

TABLE 25.1 **Pros and Cons of WPF Localization techniques**

	Pros	**Cons**
XAML	▶ Localization completely separate from development process ▶ More efficient than data binding ▶ Easy to modify CSV files	▶ No easy way to repeat process with UI updates, unless you are extremely good at version control ▶ The tool is unsupported ▶ Hard to integrate with resource files ▶ No Visual Studio support
Resources and data binding	▶ Data-binding is easy and well-understood by WPF developers ▶ Bindings are strongly typed and checked by the compiler ▶ Resources are relatively easy to manage, and are similar to the other .Net platforms	▶ No type conversion ▶ You must manually map each UI element to a resource ▶ Only works on dependency properties ▶ Some tools, such as Blend, do not load resources from satellite assemblies (yet)

XAML Localization

To localize your WPF application using the XAML method, follow these steps:

1. Manually edit the project file and add `<UICulture>en-US</UICulture>` under the `<PropertyGroup>` section.

2. Add this line to your `AssemblyInfo.cs` file:

```
[assembly: NeutralResourcesLanguageAttribute("en-US",
➥UltimateResourceFallbackLocation.Satellite)]
```

3. Open a command prompt and navigate to your project's directory. Run the command:

```
msbuild /t:updateuid
```

This will generate a UID for every WPF element, modifying your XAML files in the process. You should never manually edit these UIDs.

> **NOTE** msbuild is located with the .Net framework files, and the easiest way to run it is to start the command prompt with the shortcut that Visual Studio installs; this will initialize the correct environment settings to access the .NET Framework binaries.

4. Rebuild the project. A directory called en-US will appear in the output directory. This contains the resource DLL.

5. Obtain the LocBaml tool from the Windows SDK. On my computer, it was packaged in C:\Program Files\Microsoft SDKs\windows\v7.0\Samples\WPFSamples.zip. To get it to work in .Net 4, I had to recreate the project from

scratch and change the target framework to .Net 4.0. By the time you read this, the tool may work out of the box. However, the tool is not officially supported by Microsoft. (Are you starting to get nervous about this method yet?)

6. Copy `LocBaml.exe`, the generated resource DLL, and your application executable to the same folder and run this command from a prompt:

   ```
   locbaml.exe /parse myapp.resources.dll /out:translate_en-US.csv
   ```

7. Copy the file translate_en-US.csv to files with different names, depending on your target cultures, e.g., translate_it-IT.csv, translate_fr-CA.csv.
8. Open the csv files in a program that can edit them (such as any text editor or Excel) and translate the text into the target language. You can also modify things like file paths (in the case that you have different images for cultures, for example).

NOTE It's important to realize that other fields besides UI text will be present. When giving the files to translator, you may want to specify which fields need translating.

9. Create a new directory for the localized DLL, e.g. "it-IT."
10. Create a localized resource DLL by running:

    ```
    locbaml.exe /generate myapp.resources.dll
    ➥/trans: translate_it-IT.csv /out :.\it-IT /cul:it-IT
    ```

Copy the resource directory to the output directory, next to the existing `en-US` directory.

If you want to easily see the differences, you can add some code to the application startup that will set the UI culture to be to the region specified in Control Panel.

```
public App()
{
    //set UI to have whatever be same as non-UI,
    //which is what is in Control Panel
    Thread.CurrentThread.CurrentUICulture =
                    Thread.CurrentThread.CurrentCulture;
}
```

As you can see, this method is a little complex and tedious, especially if you need to make changes after localization has begun (make sure you have excellent version control practices). It's recommended that you build your own set of tools to manage this process, even if it's just a set of batch files.

Figures 25.3 and 25.4 show a localized WPF app running in English and Italian, with translated text and different resources.

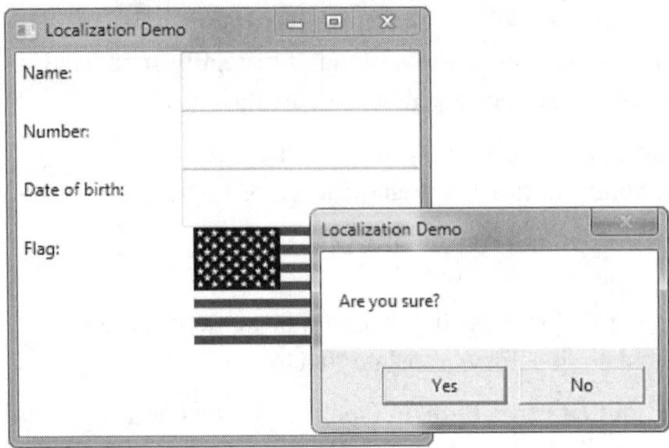

FIGURE 25.3
The localized app running in the default culture.

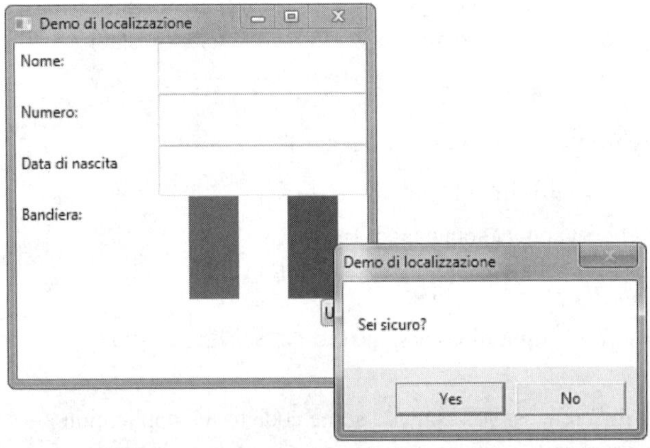

FIGURE 25.4
Changing the system's region to Italy causes the app to pick the localized DLL. If Windows were using the Italian language pack, then the Yes and No on the message box would also be in Italian.

See the LocWPFXAML project in the sample code for a full example.

Resource File Localization

Rather than go through all of that, you can use resource files just like with Windows Forms.

1. Create a global resource file and add strings, images, etc. to it.
2. Copy and rename it with the desired culture, e.g., Resources.it-IT.resx. (Make sure that this file is in the same directory as the original Resources.resx) Building the project should result in culture-specific directory being created under the output directory.

3. Create an XML namespace `Properties` in the `Window` where you want to use the localized resource:

   ```
   xmlns:props="clr-namespace:LocWPFResources.Properties"
   ```

4. Use data binding to attach the resources to XAML controls:

   ```
   <Label x:Name="labelName" Grid.Row="0" Grid.Column="0"
   Content="{x:Static props:Resources.labelName}" />
   ```

This is much simpler, but it does require more thought as you develop the UI of your application. Also, you can't directly bind very much other than strings.

For example, to use an image from resources in a XAML `Image` control, you can do something like this:

```
public MainWindow()
{
    InitializeComponent();

    //set the image
    imageFlag.BeginInit();
    imageFlag.Source = CreateImageSource(Properties.Resources.flag);
    imageFlag.EndInit();
}

private ImageSource CreateImageSource(System.Drawing.Bitmap bitmap)
{
    using (MemoryStream stream = new MemoryStream())
    {
        bitmap.Save(stream, System.Drawing.Imaging.ImageFormat.Jpeg);
        stream.Position = 0;
        //the OnLoad option uses the stream immediately
        //so that we can dispose it
        return BitmapFrame.Create(stream,BitmapCreateOptions.None,
                BitmapCacheOption.OnLoad);
    }
}
```

NOTE Given the complexities of localization, you should definitely give the topic a lot of thought before deciding on a strategy. I encourage you to read the whitepaper and look at the samples located at http://wpflocalization.codeplex.com/.

See the LocWPFResources project in the sample code for a full example.

Localize a Silverlight Application

Localized resources in Silverlight are very similar to the resource file methods just given.

1. After you create your Silverlight project, add a new resource file called, for example, `Resources.resx`. This is the default resource file. Visual Studio will also create a class to access these resources.
2. Add a resource file for each culture you will need, including the appropriate culture code in the filename, e.g., `Resources.it.resx` or `Resources.fr-CA.resx`.
3. In the project properties, go to the Sliverlight tab, and click the Assembly Information… button. Select the neutral language for your project (in my example, this is English, with no country).
4. Now edit the project file manually by right-clicking it in the Solution Explorer and selecting Unload Project. Right-click the project again and select Edit project.csproj.
5. Edit the `<SupportedCultures />` tag to include the non-default cultures you want. For example:

   ```
   <SupportedCultures>it;fr-CA</SupportedCultures>
   ```
6. Save and close the file.
7. Reload the project by right-clicking the project in Solution Explorer and selecting Reload Project.
8. Modify each resource file appropriately with translated versions of each resource. Make sure each resource file's access modifier is public.
9. Wrap the Visual Studio-generated wrapper class in another class:

   ```
   //for Silverlight to be able to bind to resources, we need to wrap
   //them in another class
   public class LocResources
   {
       public LocResources()
       {   }
       private static LocSilverlight.Resources resource = new
   ➥Resources();
       public LocSilverlight.Resources Resource
       { get { return resource; } }
   }
   ```
10. Add a reference to the wrapper class to the `Application.Resources` section of App.xaml:

    ```
    <Application xmlns="http://schemas.microsoft.com/winfx/2006/xaml/
                          presentation"
    ```

```
             xmlns:x="http://schemas.microsoft.com/winfx/2006/xaml"
             xmlns:local="clr-namespace:LocSilverlight"
             x:Class="LocSilverlight.App">
    <Application.Resources>
        <local:LocResources x:Key="LocResources"/>
    </Application.Resources>
</Application>
```

11. Bind UI elements to the resources:

```
<UserControl x:Class="LocSilverlight.MainPage"
    xmlns="http://schemas.microsoft.com/winfx/2006/xaml/
➥presentation"
    xmlns:x="http://schemas.microsoft.com/winfx/2006/xaml"
    xmlns:d="http://schemas.microsoft.com/expression/blend/2008"
    xmlns:mc="http://schemas.openxmlformats.org/
➥markup-compatibility/2006"
    xmlns:dataInput="clr-
➥namespace:System.Windows.Controls;assembly=
➥System.Windows.Controls.Data.Input"
    mc:Ignorable="d"
    d:DesignHeight="220" d:DesignWidth="243" >
    <Grid x:Name="LayoutRoot" Background="White"
          Height="181" Width="183">
        <dataInput:Label Name="labelMessage"
                         Height="50"
                         Width="100"
                         Margin="12,12,0,0"
                         HorizontalAlignment="Left"
                         VerticalAlignment="Top"
                         Content="{Binding Path=Resource.Message,
                                  Source={StaticResource
                                         LocResources}}"/>
        <Button Name="button1"
                Height="23"
                Width="75"
                Margin="37,76,0,0"
                HorizontalAlignment="Left"
                VerticalAlignment="Top"
                Content="{Binding Path=Resource.buttonExit,
                         Source={StaticResource
                                LocResources}}"/>
    </Grid>
</UserControl>
```

12. Test the application in different languages by editing the HTML or ASPX file in the accompanying web project with the following lines in the <object> tag:

```
<object ...>
  ...
  <param name="culture" value="it-it" />
  <param name="uiculture" value="it-it" />
  ...
</object>
```

NOTE Make sure you run the web project, not the Silverlight project, so you can use your edited HTML/ASPX file. Otherwise, Visual Studio will generate one for you, and it won't have the culture tags.

See the LocSilverlight project in the sample code for this project for a full example.

Deploy Applications Using ClickOnce

Scenario/Problem: You want to deploy your application via the Web, with a very simple process.

Solution: Use OneClick deployment. Here are the steps to follow:

1. Right-click the project in the Solution Explorer and select Properties.
2. Click the Security tab.
3. Check the Enable ClickOnce Security Settings box.
4. Select the appropriate trust level. Partial trust will cut off your application from most of the computer's resources, such as the file system.
5. Select the zone the application will be installed from.
6. Click the Publish tab (see Figure 25.3).
7. Select the folder to which you wish to publish the setup files.
8. Select whether the application should also be installed locally and available in the Start menu.
9. Click Options.
10. Select Deployment.
11. Enter a deployment web page, such as publish.htm.

Figure 25.5 shows the Publish settings in Visual Studio.

Once all of the options are set, you can right-click the project and select Publish.

To run the application, navigate to the generated HTML file and click Run. The .NET runtime will run your application under the restrictions you placed on it. To see the effect, the sample application lets you try to write a file both to the file system and to isolated storage. Only isolated storage is accessible.

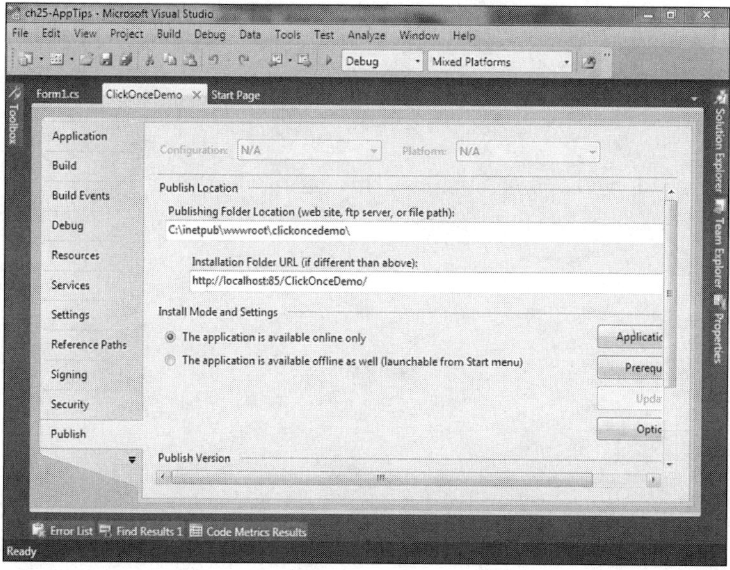

FIGURE 25.5

The Publish options allow you to specify where to put the setup files.

Figure 25.6 shows what happens when a locally-installed ClickOnce application with limited permissions tries to touch the file system.

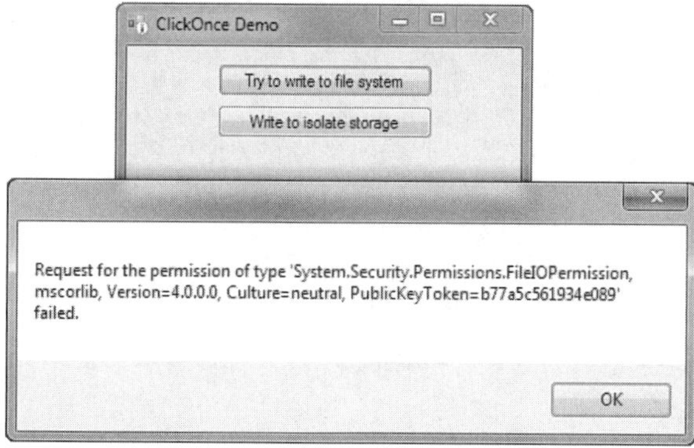

FIGURE 25.6

In a partial-trust application, trying to access local resources such as the file system will result in an exception.

NOTE You cannot create WPF windows in a partial-trust environment: You're limited to the browser window.

CHAPTER 26

Interacting with the OS and Hardware

IN THIS CHAPTER

- Get OS, Service Pack, and CLR Version
- Get CPU and Other Hardware Information
- Invoke UAC to Request Admin Privileges
- Write to the Event Log
- Access the Registry
- Manage Windows Services
- Create a Windows Service
- Call Native Windows Functions Using P/Invoke
- Call C Functions in a DLL from C#
- Use Memory-Mapped Files
- Ensure Your Application Works in Both 32-bit and 64-bit Environments
- Respond to System Configuration Changes
- Take Advantage of Windows 7 Features
- Retrieve Power State Information

Applications don't exist in a vacuum. They rely on the operating system to provide many vital services. Some of these, such as the location of important folders or the installed network adapters, are covered in earlier chapters (Chapters 11, "Files and Serialization," and 12, "Networking and the Web," respectively).

The OS can also present more information about itself and the hardware environment it's running on. This chapter talks mostly about the information you can obtain, as well as some Windows-specific technologies, such as the event log, Windows services, and memory-mapped files.

Get OS, Service Pack, and CLR Version

Scenario/Problem: You need to get version information for the current operating system.

Solution: Use the `System.Environment.OSVersion` class, as in this sample:

```
OperatingSystem os = System.Environment.OSVersion;
Console.WriteLine("Platform: {0}", os.Platform);
Console.WriteLine("Service Pack: {0}", os.ServicePack);
Console.WriteLine("Version: {0}", os.Version);
Console.WriteLine("VersionString: {0}", os.VersionString);
Console.WriteLine("CLR Version: {0}", System.Environment.Version);
```

This produces the following output (on my Windows 7 system):

```
Platform: Win32NT
Service Pack:
Version: 6.1.7600.0
VersionString: Microsoft Windows NT 6.1.7600.0
CLR Version: 4.0.21006.1
```

The version information is in a struct, so you can make decisions based on version or subversion values.

NOTE Notice that nowhere does it say "Windows 7" in the version information. "Windows 7" is really the brand, which has relatively little to do with version information. Your programs should make decisions based on version numbers, never names.

Get CPU and Other Hardware Information

Scenario/Problem: You need to get the number of CPUs, amount of memory, or other hardware information.

Solution: Although .NET does expose some basic hardware information, more can be retrieved using Windows Management Instrumentation (WMI) functionality.

```
using System;
using System.Management;
using System.Windows.Forms;

namespace HardwareInfo
{
    class Program
    {
        static void Main(string[] args)
        {
            /*There is a wealth of hardware information available in
             the WMI hardware classes.
             See http://msdn.microsoft.com/en-us/library/aa389273.aspx
             */
            Console.WriteLine("Machine: {0}", Environment.MachineName);
            Console.WriteLine("# of processors (logical): {0}",
                                  Environment.ProcessorCount);
            Console.WriteLine("# of processors (physical): {0}",
                                  CountPhysicalProcessors());
            Console.WriteLine("RAM installed: {0:N0} bytes",
                                  CountPhysicalMemory());
            Console.WriteLine("Is OS 64-bit? {0}",
                                  Environment.Is64BitOperatingSystem);
            Console.WriteLine("Is process 64-bit? {0}",
                                  Environment.Is64BitProcess);
            Console.WriteLine("Little-endian: {0}",
                                  BitConverter.IsLittleEndian);

            foreach (Screen screen in
               System.Windows.Forms.Screen.AllScreens)
            {
                Console.WriteLine("Screen {0}", screen.DeviceName);
                Console.WriteLine("\tPrimary {0}", screen.Primary);
                Console.WriteLine("\tBounds: {0}", screen.Bounds);
                Console.WriteLine("\tWorking Area: {0}",
                                      screen.WorkingArea);
                Console.WriteLine("\tBitsPerPixel: {0}",
                                      screen.BitsPerPixel);
            }

            Console.ReadKey();
        }
```

```
        private static UInt32 CountPhysicalProcessors()
        {
            //you must add a reference to the System.Management assembly
            ManagementObjectSearcher objects =
                new ManagementObjectSearcher(
                    "SELECT * FROM Win32_ComputerSystem");
            ManagementObjectCollection coll = objects.Get();
            foreach(ManagementObject obj in coll)
            {
                return (UInt32)obj["NumberOfProcessors"];
            }
            return 0;
        }

        private static UInt64 CountPhysicalMemory()
        {
            ManagementObjectSearcher objects =
                new ManagementObjectSearcher(
                  "SELECT * FROM Win32_PhysicalMemory");
            ManagementObjectCollection coll = objects.Get();
            UInt64 total = 0;
            foreach (ManagementObject obj in coll)
            {
                total += (UInt64)obj["Capacity"];
            }
            return total;
        }
    }
}
```

NOTE When you build a .NET application, you can specify the target platform: Any, x86, x64, or Itanium. When Any is selected, the same executable file will work on any OS and will be 64 bit on a 64-bit OS, and 32 bit on a 32-bit OS.

If you need your process to stay 32 bit even on a 64-bit OS, you need to specify x86 as the target. This is vital for interoperating with unmanaged code, or other managed libraries that were compiled with specific platform targets. See the section "Ensure Your Application Works in Both 32-bit and 64-bit Environments" later in this chapter to learn how to ensure your app works on all environments, as well as an example of calling a 32-bit unmanaged DLL from C#.

Invoke UAC to Request Admin Privileges

Scenario/Problem: You need to start your application with elevated privileges.

Solution: Starting with Windows Vista, applications are prohibited from running with administrative privileges by default. Attempting to do something that requires administrative access results in a system dialog box requesting confirmation and possibly a password for less-privileged users. This feature is implemented in two parts:

- A special icon indicating User Access Control (UAC) will be invoked.
- Performing the action in an elevated process.

The icon doesn't do anything in and of itself, and there is no direct support for it in .NET. You can turn it on by sending a message to the Button control. Here's a custom button class that implements this functionality:

```
public class UACButton : Button
{
    private bool _showShield = false;
    public bool ShowShield
    {
        get
        {
            return _showShield;
        }
        set
        {
            bool needToShow = value && !IsElevated();
            //pass in 1 for true in lParam
            if (this.Handle != IntPtr.Zero)
            {
                Win32.SendMessage(new HandleRef(this, this.Handle),
                                  Win32.BCM_SETSHIELD,
                    new IntPtr(0), new IntPtr(needToShow ? 1 : 0));
                _showShield = needToShow;
            }
        }
    }

    //don't need to elevate if we already are
    private bool IsElevated()
    {
        WindowsIdentity identity = WindowsIdentity.GetCurrent();
        WindowsPrincipal principal = new WindowsPrincipal(identity);
        return principal.IsInRole(WindowsBuiltInRole.Administrator);
    }

    public UACButton()
    {
```

```
        //very important--icon won't show up without this!
        this.FlatStyle = FlatStyle.System;
    }
}
```

The Win32 class is a simple wrapper for P/Invoked functionality (see the section "Call Native Windows Functions Using P/Invoke" later in this chapter):

```
class Win32
{
    [DllImport("User32.dll")]
    public static extern IntPtr SendMessage(HandleRef hWnd, UInt32 Msg,
➥IntPtr wParam, IntPtr lParam);

    //defined in CommCtrl.h
    public const UInt32 BCM_SETSHIELD = 0x0000160C;
}
```

It is impossible to elevate a process's privileges once the process has started, so the technique is to start your same process as an admin and pass it some command-line arguments (or otherwise communicate with it) to tell it what to do. That second process will do the required behavior, then exit. Leaving the second, elevated, process running and having the first exit is not recommended—your programs should always run with the least privilege possible.

Here is the button event handler (which has to do something requiring elevation):

```
private void buttonCreateSource_Click(object sender, EventArgs e)
{
    //you can't elevate the current process--you have to start a new one
    ProcessStartInfo startInfo = new ProcessStartInfo();
    startInfo.FileName = Application.ExecutablePath;
    startInfo.Arguments = "-createEventSource";
    //trigger the UAC prompt
    startInfo.Verb = "runas";
    try
    {
        Process proc = Process.Start(startInfo);
        proc.WaitForExit();
    }
    catch (Exception ex)
    {
        MessageBox.Show(
            "There was an error launching the elevated process: " +
                ex.Message);
    }
}
```

Then, when the program starts, you can look for the arguments:

```
[STAThread]
static void Main()
{
    string[] args = Environment.GetCommandLineArgs();
    foreach (string arg in args)
    {
        if (string.Compare("-createEventSource", arg)==0)
        {
            //we should be running as admin now, so
            //attempt the privileged operation
            CreateEventSource();
            //don't need to show UI--we're already running it,
            //so just exit
            return;
        }
    }
    Application.EnableVisualStyles();
    Application.SetCompatibleTextRenderingDefault(false);
    Application.Run(new Form1());
}
```

Write to the Event Log

Scenario/Problem: You want to write application events to the system event log so that administrators can use it.

Solution: Windows provides an API for any application, service, and driver to write to a common logging interface, managed by the OS. .NET wraps this API into the `EventLog` and related classes.

Before you can write to the event log, you need to do two things:

1. Create a log source. This is typically your application. This step requires administrative privileges and only needs to be done once, so it's typically done during application installation.
2. Decide which log your events should go to. By default, events are written to the Application event log, but you can create your own log as well.

The code to create a log source is as follows:

```
public const string LogName = "CSharpHowToLog";
//if you just want to put your messages in
```

```
//the system-wide Application Log, do this:
//public const string LogName = "Application";
public const string LogSource = "EventLogDemo";

private static void CreateEventSource()
{
    //this functionality requires admin privileges--
    //consider doing this during installation
    //of your app, rather than runtime
    if (!EventLog.SourceExists(LogSource))
    {
        //to log to the general application log, pass in
        //null for the application name
        EventSourceCreationData data =
            new EventSourceCreationData(LogSource, LogName);
        EventLog.CreateEventSource(data);
    }
}
```

NOTE In the EventLogDemo sample app, `CreateEventSource` is called after a UAC request because it requires admin privileges. See the previous section for how to accomplish this.

To do the actual logging, use the following:

```
using (EventLog log = new EventLog(Program.LogName, ".",
        Program.LogSource))
{
    int eventId = 13;//you define your own meaning for this
    log.WriteEntry(textBoxMessage.Text, EventLogEntryType.Information,
                   eventId);
}
```

You could, of course, save the `EventLog` object in your application to reuse it, rather than disposing of it right away.

Read from the Event Log

You can use the same set of objects to read existing log entries:

```
using (EventLog log = new EventLog(Program.LogName, ".",
                                   Program.LogSource))
{
    StringBuilder sb = new StringBuilder();
    foreach (EventLogEntry entry in log.Entries)
    {
```

```
        sb.AppendFormat("({0}, {1} {2}) {3}",
                        entry.TimeGenerated, entry.InstanceId,
                        entry.EntryType, entry.Message);
        sb.AppendLine();
    }
    MessageBox.Show(sb.ToString(),"Existing events");
}
```

Access the Registry

Scenario/Problem: You need to read and/or write settings in the registry.

Solution: Use the `Registry` and `RegistryKey` classes located in the `Microsoft.Win32` namespace:

```
//read from HKLM
using (RegistryKey hklm = Registry.LocalMachine)
using (RegistryKey keyRun =
     hklm.OpenSubKey(@"Software\Microsoft\Windows\CurrentVersion\Run"))
{
    foreach (string valueName in keyRun.GetValueNames())
    {
        Console.WriteLine("Name: {0}\tValue: {1}",
                 valueName, keyRun.GetValue(valueName));
    }
}
```

NOTE Registry keys are represented by handles, which are system resources that must be disposed of, hence the `using` statements.

```
//create our own registry key for the app
//true indicates we want to be able to write to the subkey
using (RegistryKey software =
           Registry.CurrentUser.OpenSubKey(@"Software", true))
//volatile indicates that this key should be deleted
//when the computer restarts
using (RegistryKey myKeyRoot =
       software.CreateSubKey(
           "CSharp4HowTo",
           RegistryKeyPermissionCheck.ReadWriteSubTree,
           RegistryOptions.Volatile))
```

```
{
    //automatically determine the type
    myKeyRoot.SetValue("NumberOfChapters", 28);

    //specify the type
    myKeyRoot.SetValue("Awesomeness",
                    Int64.MaxValue, RegistryValueKind.QWord);

    //display what we just created
    foreach (string valueName in myKeyRoot.GetValueNames())
    {
        Console.WriteLine("{0}, {1}, {2}", valueName,
                          myKeyRoot.GetValueKind(valueName),
                  myKeyRoot.GetValue(valueName));
    }

    //remove from registry (set a breakpoint
    //here to go look at it in regedit)
    software.DeleteSubKeyTree("CSharp4HowTo");
}
```

Here's the output from the preceding code:

```
Name: iTunesHelper      Value: "C:\Program Files (x86)\iTunes\
                                    iTunesHelper.exe "
Name: OpenDNS Update    Value: "C:\Program Files (x86)\OpenDNS
Name: LifeCam   Value: "C:\Program Files (x86)\Microsoft LifeCam\
                                LifeExp.exe "

NumberOfChapters, DWord, 28
Awesomeness, QWord, 9223372036854775807
```

NOTE In general, most .NET programs avoid the registry in favor of XML configuration files, but the access is there if you need it. Note that non-administrative programs don't have write permissions on HKLM in Windows Vista and later. If you try to write to it as a non-administrator, Windows will actually redirect you to a virtual HKLM for just that application. Better just to avoid it.

Manage Windows Services

Scenario/Problem: You want to start, pause, and stop services from your application.

Solution: You can control services (assuming you have the right privileges) with the System.ServiceProcess.ServiceController class:

```
ServiceController controller = new ServiceController("MyService");
controller.Start();
if (controller.CanPauseAndContinue)
{
    controller.Pause();
    controller.Continue();
}
controller.Stop();
```

Create a Windows Service

Scenario/Problem: You want to put your code in a service so that it is more easily manageable and can run when users are not logged in.

There is nothing inherently different about a Windows service compared to an application except the manageability interfaces it implements (to allow it to be remotely controlled, automatically started and stopped, failed over to different machines, and so on). Also, a Windows service has no user interface (and security settings generally prohibit services from attempting to invoke a UI). You can generally use all the same .NET code as in a regular application.

Solution: The heart of a service is a class that implements System.ServiceProcess.ServiceBase:

```
public partial class GenericService : ServiceBase
{
    Thread _programThread;

    bool _continueRunning = false;
    public GenericService()
    {
        InitializeComponent();
    }

    protected override void OnStart(string[] args)
    {
        _continueRunning = true;
        LogString("Service starting");
```

```
        _programThread = new Thread(new ThreadStart(ThreadProc));
        _programThread.Start();
    }

    protected override void OnStop()
    {
        _continueRunning = false;

        LogString("Service stopping");

    }

    private void LogString(string line)
    {
        using (FileStream fs = new FileStream(
              @"C:\GenericService_Output.log", FileMode.Append))
        using (StreamWriter writer = new StreamWriter(fs))
        {
            writer.WriteLine(line);
        }
    }

    private void ThreadProc()
    {
        while (_continueRunning)
        {
            Thread.Sleep(5000);
            LogString(string.Format("{0} - Service running.",
                                    DateTime.Now));
        }
    }
}
```

This service does nothing interesting—it just logs events to a file.

The `Main` function looks a little different:

```
static void Main()
{
    ServiceBase[] ServicesToRun;
    //yes, you can host multiple services in an executable file
    ServicesToRun = new ServiceBase[]
    {
        new GenericService()
    };
    ServiceBase.Run(ServicesToRun);
}
```

This is the basic functionality for a service, but to make it easier to install the service, you should implement a few more classes:

```
[RunInstaller(true)]
public partial class ProjectInstaller : Installer
{
    private System.ServiceProcess.ServiceProcessInstaller
        genericProcessInstaller;
    private System.ServiceProcess.ServiceInstaller
        genericServiceInstaller;

    public ProjectInstaller()
    {
        genericProcessInstaller =
           new System.ServiceProcess.ServiceProcessInstaller();

        genericProcessInstaller.Account =
         System.ServiceProcess.ServiceAccount.LocalSystem;
        genericProcessInstaller.Password = null;
        genericProcessInstaller.Username = null;

        genericServiceInstaller =
                new System.ServiceProcess.ServiceInstaller();
        genericServiceInstaller.ServiceName = "GenericService";
        genericServiceInstaller.StartType =
➥System.ServiceProcess.ServiceStartMode.Automatic;

        this.Installers.AddRange(
            new System.Configuration.Install.Installer[] {
                genericProcessInstaller,
                genericServiceInstaller});

    }
}
```

NOTE If you're using Visual Studio, much of this work is automated for you. For example, you can right-click the design view of the service object and then select Add Installer to create this for you.

With this installation class implemented, you can easily install the service into a system by using the .NET Framework tool InstallUtil.exe. To use this tool, start a Visual Studio command prompt with admin privileges and navigate to the directory containing the service executable and type:

```
InstallUtil /i GenericService.exe
```

To remove the service, type the following:

```
InstallUtil /u GenericService.exe
```

NOTE By default, services are not allowed to interact with the desktop. If you want a service to be able to do this, you need to modify the "Allow service to interact with desktop" setting in the service's properties in the service management snap-in.

Call Native Windows Functions Using P/Invoke

Scenario/Problem: You want to call native Win32 API functions from .NET.

Solution: Use P/Invoke, which is shorthand for Platform Invocation Services. It allows you to call native code directly from .NET. You've already seen some examples throughout the book where we needed to supplement .NET's functionality with that from the OS.

Using P/Invoke involves defining any structures you will need in .NET and then adding an import reference to the function you want to call, potentially mapping each argument to equivalent types.

Here's an example of the declaration for the SendMessage function:

```
[DllImport("User32.dll")]
public static extern IntPtr SendMessage(HandleRef hWnd,
                                        UInt32 Msg, IntPtr wParam,
                                        IntPtr lParam);
```

To call this, you would write the following:

```
SendMessage(new HandleRef(this, this.Handle), MESSAGE_NUMBER,
                       new IntPtr(0), new IntPtr(1));
```

A more sophisticated example is when you need the API function to fill in a structure:

```
[StructLayout(LayoutKind.Sequential)]
struct SYSTEM_INFO
{
    public ushort wProcessorArchitecture;
    public ushort wReserved;
    public uint dwPageSize;
    public IntPtr lpMinimumApplicationAddress;
    public IntPtr lpMaximumApplicationAddress;
    public UIntPtr dwActiveProcessorMask;
    public uint dwNumberOfProcessors;
```

```
    public uint dwProcessorType;
    public uint dwAllocationGranularity;
    public ushort wProcessorLevel;
    public ushort wProcessorRevision;
};

[DllImport("kernel32.dll")]
static extern void GetNativeSystemInfo(ref SYSTEM_INFO lpSystemInfo);

[DllImport("kernel32.dll")]
static extern void GetSystemInfo(ref SYSTEM_INFO lpSystemInfo);
```

A question that often arises is how to translate between various string representations. Windows natively uses C-style, NULL-terminated strings, whereas .NET uses the `String` object. The next section demonstrates how to do this.

Call C Functions in a DLL from C#

Scenario/Problem: You need to call a C-style function located in a DLL from C#.

Solution: P/Invoke is most commonly used for calling the native API, but you can also use it to call native code functions in any unmanaged DLL.

Listings 26.1–26.3 show the source code for a native code library that defines a C function that takes a `char*` argument.

LISTING 26.1 **MyCDll.h**

```
__declspec(dllexport) int SayHello(char* pszBuffer, int nLength);
```

LISTING 26.2 **MyCDll.cpp**

```
#include "stdafx.h"
#include "MyCDll.h"
#include <stdio.h>

__declspec(dllexport) int SayHello(char* pszBuffer, int nLength)
{
    ::strcpy_s(pszBuffer, nLength, "Hello, from C DLL");
    return strlen(pszBuffer);
}
```

LISTING 26.3 **MyCDll.def**

```
LIBRARY "MyCDll"
EXPORTS
    SayHello
```

See the MyCDll project in the examples for this chapter for the full source code.

On the C# side, using this function is quite easy. This code also demonstrates that to call a method that takes `char*`, you must first convert the string to bytes.

```
[DllImport("MyCDll.dll",  ExactSpelling=false,
    CallingConvention=CallingConvention.Cdecl, EntryPoint="SayHello")]
public static extern int SayHello(
    [MarshalAs(UnmanagedType.LPArray)] byte[] buffer,
    int length);

static void Main(string[] args)
{
    int size = 32;
    //we have to manually marshal the bytes to a String
    byte[] buffer = new byte[size];
    int returnVal = SayHello(buffer, size);
    string result = Encoding.ASCII.GetString(buffer,0, returnVal);
    Console.WriteLine("\"{0}\", return value: {1}", result, returnVal);
}
```

Use Memory-Mapped Files

Scenario/Problem: You want to access a file as if it were a memory buffer, or you need to access a file that is too large to put entirely in memory.

Solution: Memory-mapped files are not the most often used technology, but when you need them, they are very good at what they do. Memory-mapped files are exactly what they sound like: A portion of a file is put into memory. What's the difference between that and just reading the file in with a `FileStream`, you ask? Well, what if the file was 100GB in size?

As of this writing, loading a file that size into memory is out of the question for most computers. Memory-mapped files allow you to specify a portion of that file to load into memory, where you can then manipulate it much as any other in-memory structure, such as an array, and the changes are written back to the file automatically.

```
static void Main(string[] args)
{
    //these are small numbers for demo purposes,
    //but memory-mapped files really take off when you want to edit
    // files that are too large to fit in memory
    Int64 offset = 256;
    Int64 length = 64;

    using (FileStream fs = File.Open("DataFile.txt", FileMode.Open,
➥FileAccess.ReadWrite))
    using (MemoryMappedFile mmf = MemoryMappedFile.CreateFromFile(fs))
    using (MemoryMappedViewAccessor acc =
          mmf.CreateViewAccessor(offset, length,
➥MemoryMappedFileAccess.ReadWrite))
    {
        //now you can use the acc to treat the
       //file almost like an array
        for (Int64 i = 0; i < acc.Capacity; i++)
        {
            //convert char to byte because in .NET
            //chars are two bytes wide,
            acc.Write(i, (byte)(((i % 2) == 0) ? 'E' : 'O'));
        }
    }
}
```

Running this on a text file will result in a sequence of *E* and *O* characters being written in the middle.

Ensure Your Application Works in Both 32-bit and 64-bit Environments

Scenario/Problem: You want to ensure your application runs correctly on both 32-bit and 64-bit operating systems.

Solution: This is a simple configuration setting, with some caveats. In your project's build options, you can select the Platform target, which can be x86, x64, Itanium, or Any CPU. (Your list may vary, depending on what you've installed with Visual Studio; see Figure 26.1.)

Your default choice should be Any CPU. Because .NET assemblies consist of byte code that is just-in-time compiled (JIT compiled) to the current platform at runtime, your assemblies will work on any architecture without rebuilding from the source code.

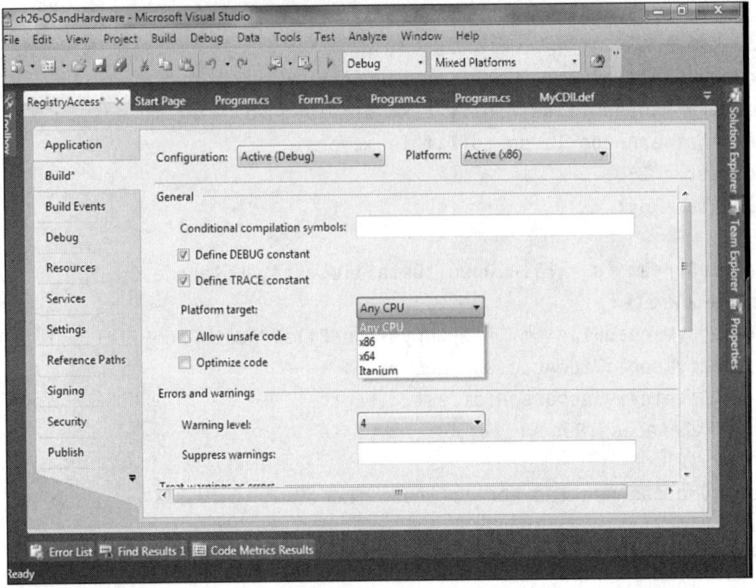

FIGURE 26.1
You can choose the target architecture of your assemblies.

However, there are times when it's not that simple. If your .NET assembly needs to reference or interop with another managed assembly or unmanaged DLL that was compiled with a specific architecture, then your assembly needs to match.

Let's look at an example. Suppose you have the following:

- .NET assembly: Any CPU
- 32-bit COM component

On a 32-bit operating system, this scenario will work because the .NET assembly will be just-in-time compiled as 32 bits.

However, on a 64-bit operating system, the .NET assembly will be 64 bits, and when it tries to call into the COM component, things will break.

In this case, it would be better to specify that your assembly should always be 32 bit. Keep in mind that x64 operating systems run 32-bit processes just fine.

Another consideration to keep in mind is that while .NET itself largely insulates you from platform architecture considerations, when you drop into unsafe code, use pointers, or rely on the size of `IntPtr`, you are asking for trouble when running on multiple architectures.

Respond to System Configuration Changes

Scenario/Problem: Your application needs to be aware of when the system's configuration changes, such as when screens change resolution (or get disconnected), when the power status changes, and so on.

Solution: The `Microsoft.Win32` namespace contains the `SystemEvents` class, which contains a number of static events your application can listen to, such as the following:

- `DisplaySettingsChanged` (and `-Changing`)
- `InstalledFontsChanged`
- `PaletteChanged`
- `PowerModeChanged`
- `SessionEnded` (the user is logging off; also `-Ending`)
- `SessionSwitch` (the current use has changed)
- `TimeChanged`
- `UserPreferenceChanged` (and `-Changing`)

For example, if your application listens for the `PowerModeChanged` event, you can detect if the computer is entering standby and you can shut down threads, stop computations, and so on.

NOTE You should always make sure your application detaches the event handlers when it ends; otherwise, you will leak memory in some cases.

Take Advantage of Windows 7 Features

Scenario/Problem: You want to access functionality specific to Windows 7, such as Libraries, common file dialogs, power managements APIs, application restart and recovery APIs, DirectX, and more.

Solution: Use the free Windows API Code Pack for Microsoft® .NET Framework, available at the MSDN code library. (The URL at the time of writing was http://code.msdn.microsoft.com/WindowsAPICodePack.)

Common File Dialogs

The Vista and Windows 7 file dialogs are shown when using the normal Windows Forms `OpenFileDialog` class, but using the `CommonOpenFileDialog` class from the API Pack provides a few more options, such the ability to add the file to the Most Recently Used list:

```
private void buttonWin7OFD_Click(object sender, EventArgs e)
{
    Microsoft.WindowsAPICodePack.Dialogs.CommonOpenFileDialog ofd = new
➥Microsoft.WindowsAPICodePack.Dialogs.CommonOpenFileDialog();
    ofd.AddToMostRecentlyUsedList = true;
    ofd.IsFolderPicker = true;
    ofd.AllowNonFileSystemItems = true;
    //there are other options as well
    ofd.ShowDialog();
}
```

Access Libraries

You can use the API Pack's `CommonOpenFileDialog` class to access non-filesystem objects, such as the Libraries introduced in Windows 7:

```
Microsoft.WindowsAPICodePack.Dialogs.CommonOpenFileDialog ofd = new
➥Microsoft.WindowsAPICodePack.Dialogs.CommonOpenFileDialog();
ofd.IsFolderPicker = true;
//allows you to pick things like Control Panel and libraries
ofd.AllowNonFileSystemItems = true;

if (ofd.ShowDialog() ==
      Microsoft.WindowsAPICodePack.Dialogs.CommonFileDialogResult.OK)
{
    ShellObject shellObj = ofd.FileAsShellObject;
    ShellLibrary library = shellObj as ShellLibrary;
    if (library != null)
    {
        textBoxInfo.AppendText(
            "You picked a library: " + library.Name + ", Type: "
            + library.LibraryType.ToString());
        foreach (ShellFileSystemFolder folder in (ShellLibrary)shellObj)
        {
            textBoxInfo.AppendText("\t" + folder.Path);
        }
    }
    textBoxInfo.AppendText(Environment.NewLine);
}
```

Retrieve Power State Information

Scenario/Problem: You want to retrieve information on the current power state of the system, such as whether it's using a battery, the current battery life, whether the monitor is on, if there's a UPS attached, and so on.

Solution: Use the API Code pack mentioned in the previous section. There is a `PowerManager` class with static properties to read power information.

```
bool isBatteryPresent = PowerManager.IsBatteryPresent;
string powerSource = PowerManager.PowerSource.ToString();
```

CHAPTER 27

Fun Stuff and Loose Ends

IN THIS CHAPTER

- Create a Nonrectangular Window
- Create a Notification Icon
- Create a Screen Saver in WPF
- Show a Splash Screen
- Play a Sound File
- Shuffle Cards

This chapter has a few topics that are slightly more frivolous than in the others. In it, you will learn some things that may be useful, but are more likely to lead to fun and games in some cases.

Create a Nonrectangular Window

Scenario/Problem: You want a window with a nonstandard shape, possibly including cutouts in the middle of the window.

Solution: Use a background image as a template and set a transparency key. When you do this, you are taking over all responsibility for painting and mouse interaction—the OS's windowing system can no longer help you with standard tasks, such as moving, maximizing, resizing, and more.

In Windows Forms

First, you need to create the background image. In this case, it's a simple black figure with a white background to represent transparency (see Figure 27.1).

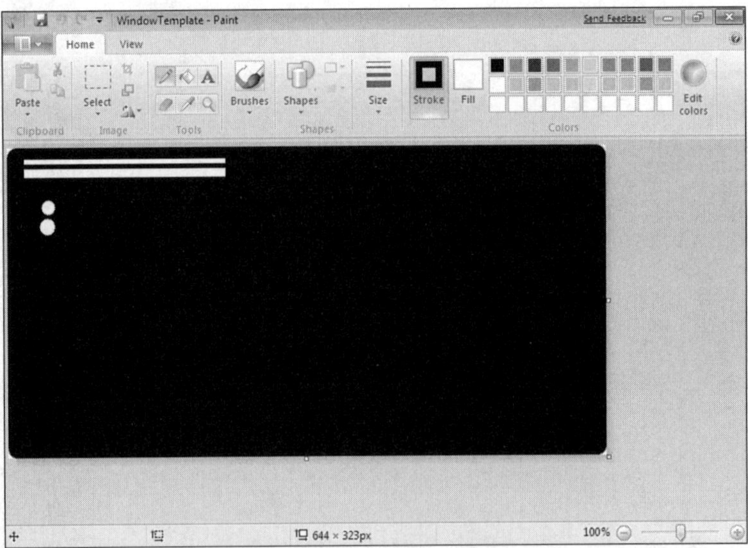

FIGURE 27.1

This image is added as a resource in the app. You can use any image to represent the window for your application—as long as you're willing to take responsibility for all interactions with it.

To allow the form to be moved, you need to handle the mouse messages yourself. In this case, to keep it simple, a mouse click anywhere on the form is translated into a simulated non-client mouse click to fool the OS into thinking the title bar has been clicked. The interop code is simple:

```
class Win32
{
     public const int WM_NCLBUTTONDOWN = 0xA1;
     public const int HTCAPTION = 0x2;

     [DllImportAttribute ("user32.dll")]
     public static extern int SendMessage(IntPtr hWnd, int Msg,
                                          int wParam, int lParam);
}
```

The form code intercepts the MouseDown event and sends a message to Windows telling it that we've clicked on the caption.

```
public Form1()
{
    InitializeComponent();

    //Turn off everything that the OS windowing system provides
    this.FormBorderStyle = FormBorderStyle.None;
    this.BackgroundImage = Properties.Resources.WindowTemplate;
    this.TransparencyKey = Color.White;

    this.Size = Properties.Resources.WindowTemplate.Size;

    this.MouseDown += new MouseEventHandler(Form1_MouseDown);
}

void Form1_MouseDown(object sender, MouseEventArgs e)
{
    //if we click anywhere on the form itself (not a child control),
    //then tell Windows we're clicking on the non-client area
    Win32.ReleaseCapture();
    Win32.SendMessage(this.Handle, Win32.WM_NCLBUTTONDOWN,
                      Win32.HTCAPTION, 0);
}

private void buttonClose_Click(object sender, EventArgs e)
{
    Application.Exit();
}
```

Figure 27.2 shows our custom window shape in action, complete with transparency.

FIGURE 27.2
Dragging on the black part will move the window, while clicking on the transparent holes goes through to the window behind it.

In WPF

The procedure is even simpler in WPF (see Listings 27.1 and 27.2). This code assumes the existence of an image in the project called WindowTemplate.png.

LISTING 27.1 **Window1.xaml**

```
<Window x:Class="TransparentFormWPF.Window1"
        xmlns="http://schemas.microsoft.com/
➥winfx/2006/xaml/presentation"
        xmlns:x="http://schemas.microsoft.com/winfx/2006/xaml"
        Title="Window1" Height="323" Width="644"
        Background="Transparent"
        WindowStyle="None"
        AllowsTransparency="True"
        >
    <Grid>
        <Image Source="images/WindowTemplate.png" >
            <Image.OpacityMask>
                <ImageBrush ImageSource="images/WindowTemplate.png" >
                </ImageBrush>
            </Image.OpacityMask>
```

LISTING 27.1 **Window1.xaml** (continued)

```
        </Image>
        <Button Content="Close" Height="23" HorizontalAlignment="Left"
           Margin="505,250,0,0" Name="buttonClose"
           VerticalAlignment="Top" Width="75"
           Click="buttonClose_Click" />
    </Grid>
</Window>
```

LISTING 27.2 **Window1.xaml.cs**

```
using System;
using System.Windows;
using System.Windows.Input;

namespace TransparentFormWPF
{
    /// <summary>
    /// Interaction logic for Window1.xaml
    /// </summary>
    public partial class Window1 : Window
    {
        public Window1()
        {
            InitializeComponent();
        }

        protected override void OnMouseDown(MouseButtonEventArgs e)
        {
            base.OnMouseDown(e);

            DragMove();
        }

        private void buttonClose_Click(object sender, RoutedEventArgs e)
        {
            this.Close();
        }
    }
}
```

Create a Notification Icon

Scenario/Problem: You want an icon to appear in the notification area of the system taskbar to notify users of the application's status.

Solution: Use the `NotifyIcon` class and attach a menu to it (see Figure 27.3).

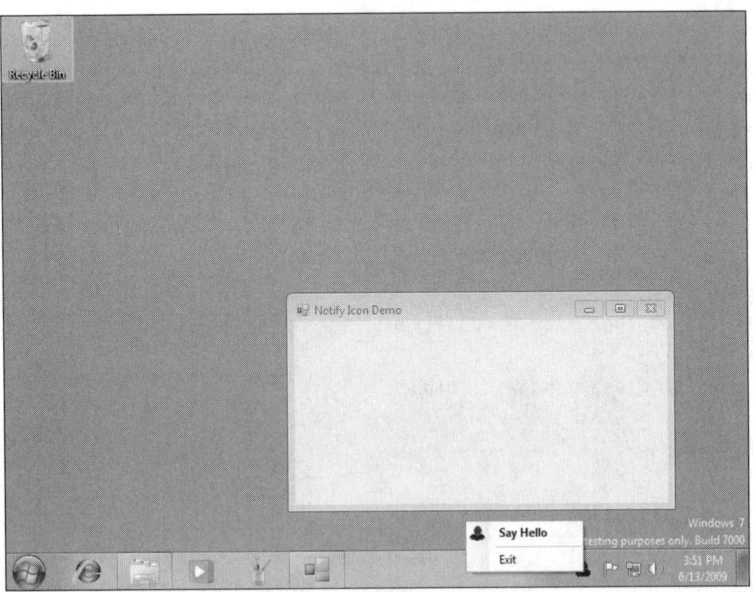

FIGURE 27.3
Use notification icons with care—many users get annoyed at them if they are seen as useless and ever-present.

This example shows a simple menu attached to an icon (called DemoIcon.ico, which you will need to add to your project's resources):

```
public partial class Form1 : Form
{
    private System.ComponentModel.IContainer components = null;

    private NotifyIcon notifyIcon;
    private ToolStripMenuItem sayHelloToolStripMenuItem;
    private ToolStripSeparator toolStripSeparator1;
    private ToolStripMenuItem exitToolStripMenuItem;
    private ContextMenuStrip menu;
```

```
    public Form1()
    {
        InitializeComponent();
    }

    private void sayHelloToolStripMenuItem_Click(object sender,
                                                  EventArgs e)
    {
        DoDefaultAction();
    }

    private void DoDefaultAction()
    {
        if (this.WindowState == FormWindowState.Minimized)
        {
            this.WindowState = FormWindowState.Normal;
        }
        MessageBox.Show("Hello");
    }

    private void exitToolStripMenuItem_Click(object sender, EventArgs e)
    {
        this.Close();
    }

    private void notifyIcon_MouseDoubleClick(object sender,
                                              MouseEventArgs e)
    {
        DoDefaultAction();
    }

    protected override void Dispose(bool disposing)
    {
        if (disposing && (components != null))
        {
            components.Dispose();
        }
        base.Dispose(disposing);
    }

    private void InitializeComponent()
    {
        this.components = new System.ComponentModel.Container();
        System.ComponentModel.ComponentResourceManager resources = new
➥System.ComponentModel.ComponentResourceManager(typeof(Form1));
```

```
        this.menu =
           new System.Windows.Forms.ContextMenuStrip(this.components);
        this.notifyIcon =
           new System.Windows.Forms.NotifyIcon(this.components);
        this.sayHelloToolStripMenuItem =
           new System.Windows.Forms.ToolStripMenuItem();
        this.exitToolStripMenuItem =
           new System.Windows.Forms.ToolStripMenuItem();
        this.toolStripSeparator1 =
           new System.Windows.Forms.ToolStripSeparator();
        this.menu.SuspendLayout();
        this.SuspendLayout();
        //
        // menu
        //
        this.menu.Items.AddRange(
           new System.Windows.Forms.ToolStripItem[] {
        this.sayHelloToolStripMenuItem,
        this.toolStripSeparator1,
        this.exitToolStripMenuItem});
        this.menu.Name = "menu";
        this.menu.Size = new System.Drawing.Size(153, 76);
        //
        // notifyIcon
        //
        this.notifyIcon.ContextMenuStrip = this.menu;
        this.notifyIcon.Icon =
           global::NotifyIconDemo.Properties.Resources.DemoIcon;
        this.notifyIcon.Visible = true;
        this.notifyIcon.MouseDoubleClick += new
➥System.Windows.Forms.MouseEventHandler(this.notifyIcon_MouseDoubleClick
);
        //
        // sayHelloToolStripMenuItem
        //
        this.sayHelloToolStripMenuItem.Font =
           new System.Drawing.Font("Segoe UI", 9F,
➥System.Drawing.FontStyle.Bold);
        this.sayHelloToolStripMenuItem.Image =
➥((System.Drawing.Image)(resources.GetObject("sayHelloToolStripMenuItem.
➥Image")));
        this.sayHelloToolStripMenuItem.Name =
           "sayHelloToolStripMenuItem";
        this.sayHelloToolStripMenuItem.Size =
           new System.Drawing.Size(152, 22);
        this.sayHelloToolStripMenuItem.Text = "&Say Hello";
```

```
        this.sayHelloToolStripMenuItem.Click += new
➥System.EventHandler(this.sayHelloToolStripMenuItem_Click);
        //
        // exitToolStripMenuItem
        //
        this.exitToolStripMenuItem.Name = "exitToolStripMenuItem";
        this.exitToolStripMenuItem.Size =
           new System.Drawing.Size(152, 22);
        this.exitToolStripMenuItem.Text = "E&xit";
        this.exitToolStripMenuItem.Click += new
➥System.EventHandler(this.exitToolStripMenuItem_Click);
        //
        // toolStripSeparator1
        //
        this.toolStripSeparator1.Name = "toolStripSeparator1";
        this.toolStripSeparator1.Size = new System.Drawing.Size(149, 6);
        //
        // Form1
        //
        this.AutoScaleDimensions = new System.Drawing.SizeF(6F, 13F);
        this.AutoScaleMode = System.Windows.Forms.AutoScaleMode.Font;
        this.ClientSize = new System.Drawing.Size(399, 191);
        this.Name = "Form1";
        this.Text = "Notify Icon Demo";
        this.menu.ResumeLayout(false);
        this.ResumeLayout(false);
    }
}
```

NOTE Do you really need an icon down there? Many users resent them, so take care. Consider well if you really need it. Perhaps you can create one temporarily to notify the user of events, but then remove it once they're acknowledged—much like the printer icon. At the very least, provide a way for the user to disable the icon.

You could also consider popping up a temporary window in a corner of the screen, like Outlook does with new mail notifications, or Windows Live Messenger does with various events. After a few seconds, these windows fade away.

Create a Screen Saver in WPF

Scenario/Problem: You want to develop your own screen saver.

Solution: There is nothing special about a screen saver, other than the following conventions:

- A single window that takes over the full screen.
- A configuration dialog box (optional).
- Responds to specific command-line arguments.
- File extension renamed from .exe to .scr.

The following sections detail the parts of a simple WPF screen saver that displays images from your pictures folder.

Options Dialog Box

When the /c option is passed, you should show an options form. Where you save your options is up to you (the registry, XML file, and so on).

In the case of this demo screen saver, it just shows a placeholder dialog box that says there are no options (see Listings 27.3 and 27.4).

LISTING 27.3 **OptionsWindow.xaml**

```
<Window x:Class="ScreenSaverWPF.OptionsWindow"
        xmlns="http://schemas.microsoft.com/
➥winfx/2006/xaml/presentation"
        xmlns:x="http://schemas.microsoft.com/winfx/2006/xaml"
        Title="Screen Saver Options" Height="300" Width="300"
        WindowStartupLocation="CenterScreen" ResizeMode="NoResize">
    <Grid>
        <TextBlock>No options available!</TextBlock>
        <Button Margin="203,234,0,0" IsDefault="True" IsCancel="True"
➥Click="Button_Click">Cancel</Button>
    </Grid>
</Window>
```

LISTING 27.4 **OptionsWindow.xaml.cs**

```
using System;
using System.Windows;

namespace ScreenSaverWPF
{
    public partial class OptionsWindow : Window
    {
        public OptionsWindow()
        {
            InitializeComponent();
        }
```

LISTING 27.4 **OptionsWindow.xaml.cs** (continued)

```
        private void Button_Click(object sender, RoutedEventArgs e)
        {
            this.Close();
        }
    }
}
```

Screen Saver Window

The main screen saver window sizes itself to fit the entire screen, and it cycles through the gathered images (see Listings 27.5 and 27.6).

LISTING 27.5 **ScreenSaverWindow.xaml**

```
<Window x:Class="ScreenSaverWPF.ScreenSaverWindow"
        xmlns="http://schemas.microsoft.com/
➥winfx/2006/xaml/presentation"
        xmlns:x="http://schemas.microsoft.com/winfx/2006/xaml"
        Title="Window1" Height="300" Width="300"
        WindowStyle="None"
        ResizeMode="NoResize"
        Background="Black" >
    <Canvas x:Name="canvas">
        <Image x:Name="imageFloating"
               Width="100" Height="100"
               Stretch="Fill" />
    </Canvas>
</Window>
```

LISTING 27.6 **ScreenSaverWindow.xaml.cs**

```
using System;
using System.Collections.Generic;
using System.Linq;
using System.Text;
using System.Windows;
using System.Windows.Controls;
using System.Windows.Input;
using System.Windows.Media;
using System.Windows.Media.Imaging;
using System.IO;
using System.Windows.Threading;

namespace ScreenSaverWPF
{
```

LISTING 27.6 **ScreenSaverWindow.xaml.cs** (continued)

```
public partial class ScreenSaverWindow : Window
 {
     FileInfo[] _images;
     int _imageIndex = 0;
     DispatcherTimer _timer;
     private Point _prevPt ;
     bool _trackingMouse = false;
     Random _rand = new Random();

     //full-screen constructor
     public ScreenSaverWindow()
     {
         InitializeComponent();

         SetFullScreen();

         Initialize();
     }

     //constructor for preview window
     public ScreenSaverWindow(Point point, Size size)
     {
         InitializeComponent();

         SetWindowSize(point, size);

         Initialize();
     }

     private void Initialize()
     {
         LoadImages();

         //timer to change image every 5 seconds
         _timer = new DispatcherTimer();
         _timer.Interval = new TimeSpan(0, 0, 5);
         _timer.Tick += new EventHandler(timer_Tick);
         _timer.Start();
     }

     private void LoadImages()
     {
         //if you have a lot of images, this could take a while...
         DirectoryInfo directoryInfo = new
            DirectoryInfo(
               Environment.GetFolderPath(
```

LISTING 27.6 **ScreenSaverWindow.xaml.cs** (continued)

```
                Environment.SpecialFolder.MyPictures));
            _images = directoryInfo.GetFiles("*.jpg",
                                            SearchOption.AllDirectories);
        }

        private void SetFullScreen()
        {
            //get a rectangle representing all the screens
            //alternatively, you could just have separate
            //windows for each monitor
            System.Drawing.Rectangle fullScreen =
              new System.Drawing.Rectangle(0,0,0,0);
            foreach (System.Windows.Forms.Screen screen in
➥System.Windows.Forms.Screen.AllScreens)
            {
                fullScreen =
                 System.Drawing.Rectangle.Union(fullScreen,
                                                screen.Bounds);
            }
            this.Left = fullScreen.Left;
            this.Top = fullScreen.Top;
            this.Width = fullScreen.Width;
            this.Height = fullScreen.Height;
        }

        private void SetWindowSize(Point point, Size size)
        {
            this.Left = point.X;
            this.Top = point.Y;
            this.Width = size.Width;
            this.Height = size.Height;
        }

        void timer_Tick(object sender, EventArgs e)
        {
            if (_images!=null && _images.Length > 0)
            {
                ++_imageIndex;
                _imageIndex = _imageIndex % _images.Length;

                this.imageFloating.Source = new BitmapImage(
                      new Uri(_images[_imageIndex].FullName));
                MoveToRandomLocation(imageFloating);
                Size size = GetImageSize(imageFloating);
                imageFloating.Width = size.Width;
                imageFloating.Height = size.Height;
```

LISTING 27.6 **ScreenSaverWindow.xaml.cs** (continued)

```
        }
    }

    private void MoveToRandomLocation(Image imageFloating)
    {
        double x = _rand.NextDouble() * canvas.ActualWidth / 2;
        double y = _rand.NextDouble() * canvas.ActualHeight / 2;

        Canvas.SetLeft(imageFloating, x);
        Canvas.SetTop(imageFloating, y);
    }

    private Size GetImageSize(Image image)
    {
        //this overly-simple algorithm won't
        //work for the preview window
        double ratio = image.Source.Width / image.Source.Height;
        double width = 0;
        double height = 0;
        if (ratio > 1.0)
        {
            //wider than is tall
            width = 1024;
            height = width / ratio;
        }
        else
        {
            height = 1024;
            width = height * ratio;
        }
        return new Size(width, height);
    }

    //end screen saver
    protected override void OnKeyDown(KeyEventArgs e)
    {
        base.OnKeyDown(e);

        Application.Current.Shutdown();
    }

    protected override void OnMouseMove(MouseEventArgs e)
    {
        base.OnMouseMove(e);
```

LISTING 27.6 **ScreenSaverWindow.xaml.cs** (continued)

```
            Point location = e.MouseDevice.GetPosition(this);
            //use _trackingMouse to know when we've
            //got a previous point to compare to
            if (_trackingMouse)
            {
                //only end if the mouse has moved enough
                if (Math.Abs(location.X - _prevPt.X) > 10
                    || Math.Abs(location.Y - _prevPt.Y) > 10)
                {
                    Application.Current.Shutdown();
                }
            }
            _trackingMouse = true;
            _prevPt = location;
        }
    }
}
```

The Application: Putting It All Together

The application XAML is mostly unremarkable, except for the fact that it does not specify a `Window` for the `StartupURI` property (see Listing 27.7).

LISTING 27.7 **App.xaml**

```
<Application x:Class="ScreenSaverWPF.App"
             xmlns="http://schemas.microsoft.com/
➥winfx/2006/xaml/presentation"
             xmlns:x="http://schemas.microsoft.com/winfx/2006/xaml">
</Application>
```

The code-behind file handles the various options and starts up the screen saver in the right mode (see Listing 27.8).

This screen saver handles three parameters:

Option	Description
`/s`	Start the screen saver in the normal mode.
`/p` *nnnn*	Start the screen saver inside the window with the handle of *nnnn*.
`/c`	Show the configuration window (if you have one).

If anything else is passed (or nothing at all), the screen saver should exit.

LISTING 27.8 App.xaml.cs

```
using System;
using System.Windows;

namespace ScreenSaverWPF
{
    public partial class App : Application
    {
        protected override void OnStartup(StartupEventArgs e)
        {
            if (e.Args.Length >= 1)
            {
                if (string.Compare("/c", e.Args[0], true) == 0)
                {
                    //show config
                    OptionsWindow window = new OptionsWindow();
                    window.ShowDialog();
                }
                else if (string.Compare("/p", e.Args[0], true) == 0
                         && e.Args.Length >=2)
                {
                    //preview screen saver inside an existing window

                    //next arg is a window handle
                    int handle = 0;
                    if (int.TryParse(e.Args[1], out handle))
                    {
                        IntPtr ptr = new IntPtr(handle);
                        Win32.RECT rect;
                        if (Win32.GetWindowRect(ptr, out rect))
                        {
                            //rather than inserting the WPF
                           //window into the existing window
                            // just put our window in
                            //the same place
                            ScreenSaverWindow previewWindow =
                              new ScreenSaverWindow(
                                      new Point(rect.Left, rect.Top),
                                      new Size(rect.Width,
                                               rect.Height));
                            previewWindow.ShowInTaskbar = false;
                            previewWindow.Show();

                            //important to stop preview
                            previewWindow.CaptureMouse();
                            return;
                        }
```

LISTING 27.8 **App.xaml.cs** (continued)

```
                }
            }
            else if (string.Compare("/s", e.Args[0], true) == 0)
            {
                //only run screen saver when /s is passed
                ScreenSaverWindow screenWindow =
                  new ScreenSaverWindow();
                screenWindow.Show();
                return;
            }
        }
        //shutdown on any errors and when config dialog is closed
        Application.Current.Shutdown();
    }
  }
}
```

The preceding code relies on a little bit of interop to get the bounds of a native window:

```
using System;
using System.Runtime.InteropServices;

namespace ScreenSaverWPF
{
    class Win32
    {
        [Serializable, StructLayout(LayoutKind.Sequential)]
        public struct RECT
        {
            public int Left;
            public int Top;
            public int Right;
            public int Bottom;

            public RECT(int left, int top, int right, int bottom)
            {
                Left = left;
                Top = top;
                Right = right;
                Bottom = bottom;
            }

            public int Height { get { return Bottom - Top; } }
            public int Width { get { return Right - Left; } }
        }
```

```
        [DllImport("user32.dll")]
        public static extern bool GetWindowRect(IntPtr hWnd,
                                                out RECT lpRect);

    }
}
```

Show a Splash Screen

Scenario/Problem: Your application needs to initialize data during startup and it takes a few moments.

Solution: Show a splash screen to display progress as you load the application.

In Windows Forms

If you want the splash screen to refresh itself correctly, you must run the initialization code on a separate thread so that the UI thread can refresh. Figure 27.4 shows the results with a simple splash screen with a progress bar and status label.

FIGURE 27.4
A splash screen can give the illusion your program is hard at work while the user waits for the app to be available.

The splash screen can be any form. In this case, it's a dialog box with no border, an image control that fills the entire form, and a progress and label control.

```
public partial class SplashScreen : Form
{
    public SplashScreen(Image image)
```

```
    {
        InitializeComponent();

        this.FormBorderStyle = FormBorderStyle.None;
        this.BackgroundImage = image;
        this.Size = image.Size;

        this.labelStatus.BackColor = Color.Transparent;
    }

    public void UpdateStatus(string status, int percent)
    {
        if (InvokeRequired)
        {
            Invoke(new MethodInvoker(delegate
            {
                UpdateStatus(status, percent);
            }));
        }
        else
        {
            progressBar.Value = percent;
            labelStatus.Text = status;
        }
    }
}
```

The application shows the splash form before starting the main form.

```
static class Program
{
    private static Thread _loadThread;
    private static SplashScreen _splash;

    [STAThread]
    static void Main()
    {
        Application.EnableVisualStyles();
        Application.SetCompatibleTextRenderingDefault(false);

        _splash = new SplashScreen(Properties.Resources.splash);

        _loadThread = new Thread((ThreadStart)delegate
            {
                //do loading tasks
                string[] fakeLoadingTasks = new string[]
                {
                    "Loading greebles",
```

```
                "Refactoring image levels",
                "Doodling",
                "Adding dogs and cats",
                "Catmulling curves",
                "Taking longer just because"
            };

            for (int i = 0; i < fakeLoadingTasks.Length; i++)
            {
                if (_splash != null)
                {
                    _splash.UpdateStatus(fakeLoadingTasks[i],
                                100 * i / fakeLoadingTasks.Length);
                }
                Thread.Sleep(2000);
            }
             //we're on a separate thread, so make
            //sure to call UI on its thread
            _splash.Invoke((MethodInvoker)delegate {
                                _splash.Close(); });
        });
        _loadThread.Start();

        _splash.TopLevel = true;
        _splash.ShowDialog();

        //now startup main form
        Application.Run(new Form1());
    }
}
```

In WPF

WPF actually has splash screen functionality built in, and if all you need is the image to show up while the main window loads, this will do it. To use it, set the build action for an image in your project to "SplashScreen" and the application will automatically show it during startup.

To get more functionality, like shown with the Windows Forms example, it's a fairly simple translation, as shown in Listing 27.9.

LISTING 27.9 **SplashScreen.xaml**

```
<Window x:Class="SplashScreenWPF.SplashScreen"
        xmlns="http://schemas.microsoft.com/
➥winfx/2006/xaml/presentation"
        xmlns:x="http://schemas.microsoft.com/winfx/2006/xaml"
        Title="SplashScreen" Height="384" Width="512"
```

LISTING 27.9 **SplashScreen.xaml** (continued)

```
        ResizeMode="NoResize"
        ShowInTaskbar="False"
        Topmost="True"
        WindowStyle="None" WindowStartupLocation="CenterScreen">
    <Grid>
        <Image HorizontalAlignment="Left" Name="image1" Stretch="Fill"
               VerticalAlignment="Top" Source="images/splash.png"  />
        <ProgressBar Name="progressBar" Minimum="0" Maximum="100"
                     VerticalAlignment="Bottom" Height="30"
                     Background="Transparent"/>
        <Label Name="statusLabel" VerticalAlignment="Bottom" Height="28"
               Background="Transparent"
               VerticalContentAlignment="Top">Loading
        </Label>
    </Grid>
</Window>
```

Here's the code-behind:

```
public partial class SplashScreen : Window
{
    private delegate void UpdateStatusDelegate(string status,
                                              int percent);
    private UpdateStatusDelegate _updateDelegate;

    public SplashScreen()
    {
        InitializeComponent();
        _updateDelegate = UpdateStatus;
    }

    public void UpdateStatus(string status, int percent)
    {
        if (Dispatcher.Thread.ManagedThreadId
            != Thread.CurrentThread.ManagedThreadId)
        {
            this.Dispatcher.Invoke(_updateDelegate, status, percent);
        }
        else
        {
            statusLabel.Content = status;
            progressBar.Value = percent;
        }
    }
}
```

The usage is similar to that in Windows Forms:

```
public partial class App : Application
{
    private static SplashScreen _splash = new SplashScreen();
    private delegate void WPFMethodInvoker();
    Thread _thread;
    protected override void OnStartup(StartupEventArgs e)
    {
        base.OnStartup(e);

        Thread thread = new Thread((ThreadStart)delegate
        {
            //do loading tasks
            string[] fakeLoadingTasks = new string[]
                {
                    "Loading greebles",
                    "Refactoring image levels",
                    "Doodling",
                    "Adding dogs and cats",
                    "Catmulling curves",
                    "Taking longer just because"
                };

            for (int i = 0; i < fakeLoadingTasks.Length; i++)
            {
                if (_splash != null)
                {
                    _splash.UpdateStatus(fakeLoadingTasks[i],
                             100 * i / fakeLoadingTasks.Length);
                }
                Thread.Sleep(2000);
            }

            _splash.Dispatcher.Invoke(
                (WPFMethodInvoker)delegate { _splash.Close(); });
        });
        thread.Start();
        //WinForms required a ShowDialog here, but this works in WPF
        _splash.Show();
    }
}
```

Figure 27.5 shows how we can take advantage of WPF's visual richness to create a neater splash screen than with Windows Forms.

FIGURE 27.5
With WPF, we can have a much richer experience, such as the transparency in this splash screen demonstrates.

Play a Sound File

Scenario/Problem: You want to play back a sound file.

Solution: Use the PlaySound API via P/Invoke.

```
class Win32
{
    [DllImport("winmm.dll", EntryPoint = "PlaySound",
               CharSet = CharSet.Auto)]
    public static extern int PlaySound(String pszSound,
                                       int hmod, int flags);

    [Flags]
    public enum Soundflags
    {
        SND_SYNC = 0x0000,
        SND_ASYNC = 0x0001,
        SND_NODEFAULT = 0x0002,
        SND_MEMORY = 0x0004,
        SND_LOOP = 0x0008,
        SND_NOSTOP = 0x0010,
        SND_NOWAIT = 0x00002000,
        SND_ALIAS = 0x00010000,
        SND_ALIAS_ID = 0x00110000,
```

```
        SND_FILENAME = 0x00020000,
        SND_RESOURCE = 0x00040004,
        SND_PURGE = 0x0040,
        SND_APPLICATION = 0x0080
    }
}
```

The first argument to `PlaySound` can be a filename, alias, or resource, depending on the flags you pass. The aliases are defined in the registry and the Sounds control panel applet.

```
Win32.PlaySound(".Default", 0, (int)(Win32.Soundflags.SND_ALIAS |
➥Win32.Soundflags.SND_ASYNC | Win32.Soundflags.SND_NOWAIT));
```

The `SND_ASYNC` flag tells the system to start playing the sound, but to return immediately, before it's done playing. This is usually what you want, to avoid hanging the UI while a sound plays.

Shuffle Cards

Scenario/Problem: You need to shuffle elements in a collection, such as cards in a deck.

Solution: Although simple, this solution is a very easy thing to get wrong, algorithmically. For more information, look at Wikipedia's entries on card-shuffling algorithms.

```
class Card { };
Random rand = new Random();
private static void ShuffleDeck(Card[] cards)
{
    int n = cards.Length;

    while (n > 1)
    {
        int k = rand.Next(n);
        --n;
        Card temp = cards[n];
        cards[n] = cards[k];
        cards[k] = temp;
    }
}
```

The accompanying source code wraps this algorithm into a test program that runs it millions of times and tracks the outcomes to see if the results are skewed in any way.

APPENDIX

Essential Tools

IN THIS APPENDIX

- Reflector
- NUnit
- NDepend
- FXCop
- Virtual PC
- Process Explorer and Process Monitor
- RegexBuddy
- LINQPad
- Where to Find More Tools

Over the years, every developer builds up an essential suite of tools for designing, debugging, building, analyzing, testing, and otherwise manipulating code. This chapter is about just a few that I have found most useful. Consider these a starting point.

Because URLs are prone to change over the years, I am omitting download links for these tools. You should be able to easily find them using your favorite search engine

Reflector

Purpose: To browse and decompile any .NET assembly into source code.

Originally developed by Lutz Roeder, Red Gate now maintains and furthers this handy little utility that distils .NET assemblies into source code (your choice of C#, VB, IL, and more).

I use this mostly as an educational tool for seeing what the .NET Framework library is doing internally. It's generally a bad idea to rely on implementation details, but sometimes it's nice to know what native API the Framework uses—as an instructive example. Reflector is shown in Figure A.1.

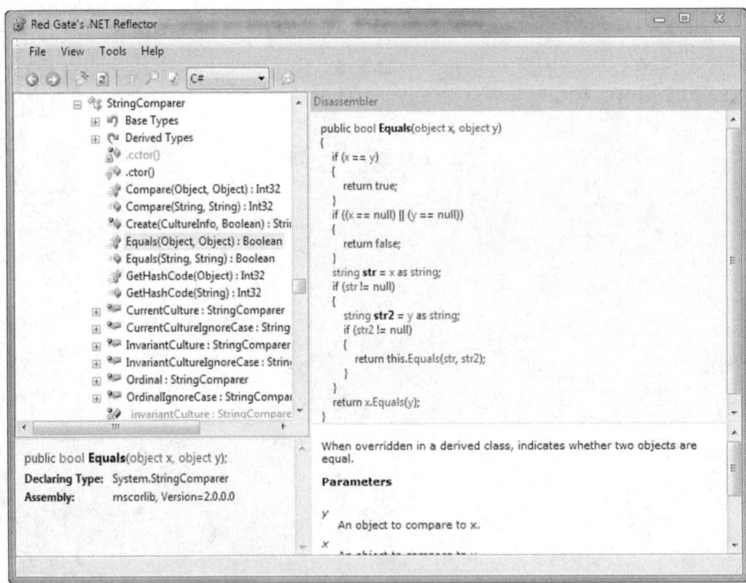

FIGURE A.1
Reflector is a great educational tool for seeing how the Framework classes work.

NUnit

Purpose: Unit-testing framework and harness.

Whether you use test-driven development or not, having a solid set of unit tests can give you a lot of assurances in code quality and the ability to refactor when necessary.

NUnit includes a library to annotate source code as tests, as well as a GUI and command-line harness to run the tests.

As an example, let's see some tests of an incomplete `ComplexNumber` class:

```
using System;

namespace MathLib
{
    public struct ComplexNumber
    {
        private double _real;
        private double _imaginary;

        public double RealPart
        {
            get { return _real; }
            set { _real = value; }
        }
        public double ImaginaryPart
        {
            get { return _imaginary; }
            set { _imaginary = value; }
        }

        public ComplexNumber(double real, double imaginary)
        {
            _real = real;
            _imaginary = imaginary;
        }

        public static ComplexNumber operator*(ComplexNumber a,
                                              ComplexNumber b)
        {
            return new ComplexNumber((a.RealPart * b.RealPart)
                                    - (a.ImaginaryPart *
                                       b.ImaginaryPart),
                (a.RealPart * b.ImaginaryPart)
                + (b.RealPart * a.ImaginaryPart));
```

```
        }
    }
}
```

In a separate assembly, you then define the test class:

```
using System;
using NUnit.Framework;//add a reference to nunit.framework.dll

namespace MathLib.Test
{
    [TestFixture]
    public class ComplexNumberText
    {
        //setup/teardown for entire fixture
        [TestFixtureSetUp]
        public void FixtureSetup()
        {
        }

        [TestFixtureTearDown]
        public void FixtureTeardown()
        {
        }

        //setup/teardown for every test in the fixture
        [SetUp]
        public void Setup()
        {
        }

        [TearDown]
        public void TearDown()
        {
        }

        //the actual test cases
        [TestCase]
        public void MultiplyTest_RealsOnly()
        {
            ComplexNumber a = new ComplexNumber(2,0);
            ComplexNumber b = new ComplexNumber(3,0);
            ComplexNumber c = a * b;
            Assert.That(c.RealPart, Is.EqualTo(6.0));
            Assert.That(c.ImaginaryPart, Is.EqualTo(0.0));
        }
```

```
        [TestCase]
        public void MultiplyTest_RealAndImaginary()
        {
            ComplexNumber a = new ComplexNumber(2, 4);
            ComplexNumber b = new ComplexNumber(3, 5);
            ComplexNumber c = a * b;
            Assert.That(c.RealPart, Is.EqualTo(-14.0));
            Assert.That(c.ImaginaryPart, Is.EqualTo(22.0));
        }
    }
}
```

The test runners load the assembly and discover each test, allowing you to run them. Green means good! NUnit is shown in Figure A.2.

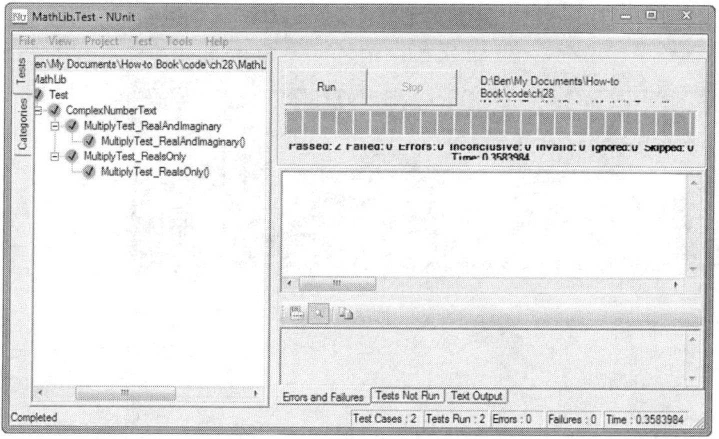

FIGURE A.2

NUnit's GUI is a great way to see at a glance which tests are passing or failing.

NOTE Although you can and should install NUnit into your local system, you should also copy the main NUnit binaries into a subfolder in your project, especially if you are using a source code control system and/or automated tests. This ensures that other developers (or your future self) don't need to install additional tools once they retrieve the source code: It's all a self-contained package.

NOTE All editions of Visual Studio now include built-in unit testing tools with the classes in `Microsoft.VisualStudio.TestTools.UnitTesting` namespace. It does not have all the feature of NUnit or other competing products, but it does have the advantage of being fully integrated with Visual Studio. In addition, some editions of Visual Studio include other analysis tools like code coverage that can use the built-in unit testing.

NDepend

Purpose: To analyze the codebase as well as show statistics, dependencies, and areas for improvement.

NDepend is such a powerful program that it's hard to describe everything it can do. It can show at a glance where the largest or most complex parts of your program are. It can show you dependencies among classes or assemblies. You can give and even create custom queries to report on—for example, all methods starting with "Do" that have more than 15 parameters and a cyclomatic complexity greater than 2.6. NDepend is shown in Figure A.3.

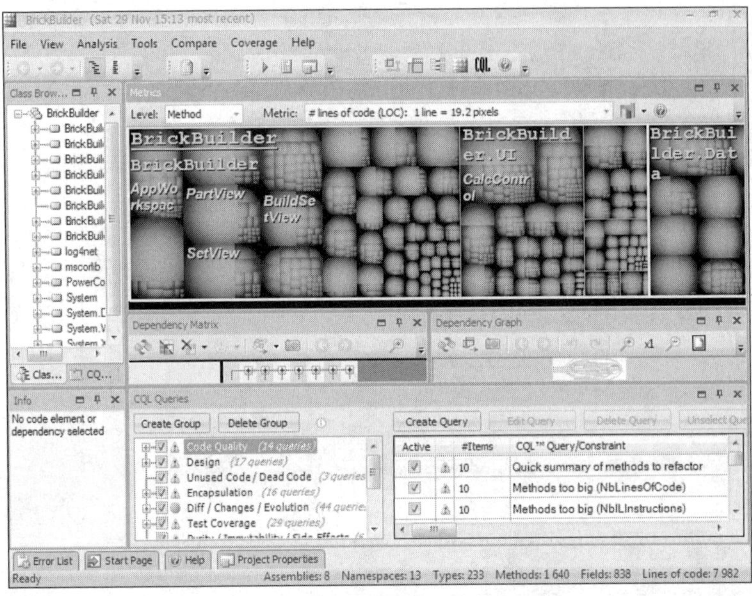

FIGURE A.3
The default view of NDepend shows some of its many capabilities, and hints at some others.

NOTE Some editions of Visual Studio also contains analysis and code metrics tools, but they are not as extensive as NDepend.

FXCop

Purpose: To analyze your source code for design, globalization, performance, and other problems.

This tool is a good sanity check on your code to ensure you're following best practices wherever feasible. It can analyze your code, recommend changes, tell you if the recommended change is breaking, and point you to more information about why the change was recommended.

There is also an SDK where you can create your own sets of rules particular to your company or project.

I ran the tool on the `ComplexNumber` class mentioned earlier in this chapter. As you can see in Figure A.4, it had a few recommendations.

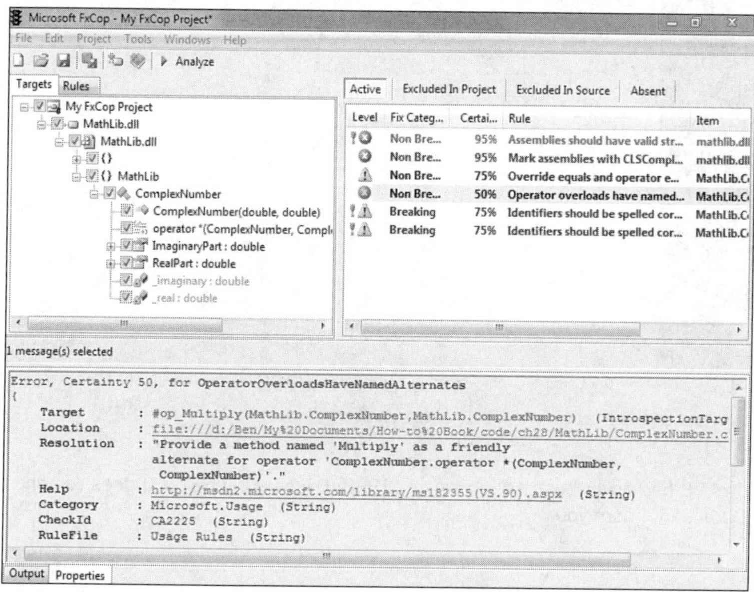

FIGURE A.4

FXCop is a valuable check that you're using .NET according to recommended patterns and practices.

Virtual PC

Purpose: To run virtualized operating systems for testing.

It is very difficult to maintain computers with all possible operating systems on which your application must run. Rather, install them all in virtual machines. This is far more convenient for testing software because you can do it all on your desktop.

Virtual PC is free (as of this writing), but you must have licenses for the operating systems you install (see Figure A.5). If you have Windows 7, you can get Windows Virtual PC, instead.

NOTE For best results in a virtual machine, have a *lot* of memory available. I have 8GB of RAM in my development desktop, which means I can dedicate fully 2GB to a virtual installation of Windows 7, for example. To take advantage of this much memory, you must be running a 64-bit version of Windows.

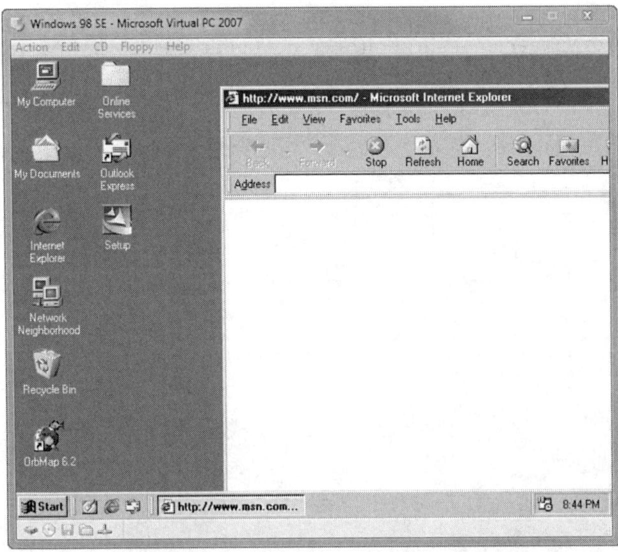

FIGURE A.5
Running Windows 98 has never been so fun since...1998. By the way, .NET 2.0 does run on Windows 98. Go ahead, I dare you.

Process Explorer and Process Monitor

Purpose: To analyze running programs for process, thread, file, network and registry information.

SysInternals (now owned by Microsoft) produced some gems of utilities, and the two I use most are Process Explorer and Process Monitor.

Process Explorer, shown in Figure A.6, is sort of like a super version of the Windows Task Manager. In addition to processes, it can show you threads, which process has open handles on a file, performance information, and for .NET processes, numerous CLR counters.

Process Monitor, shown in Figure A.7, is a real-time trace of file, registry, network, and process information. You can use it to see how a process is using the file system, for example, or where in the registry it is writing.

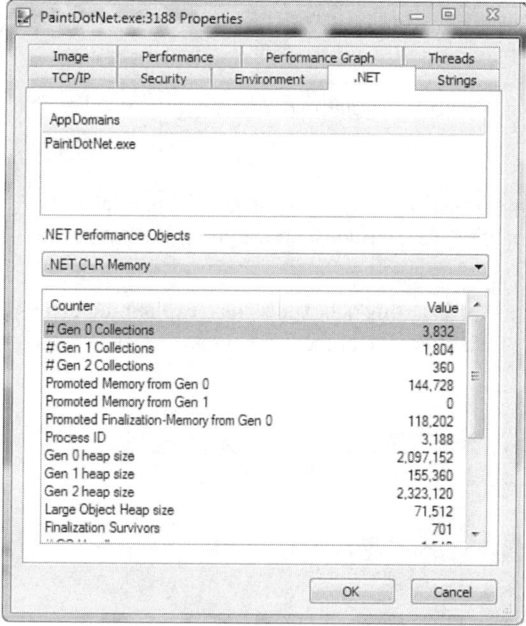

FIGURE A.6

Process Explorer can delve deep into all sorts of details about a running process—very useful for debugging.

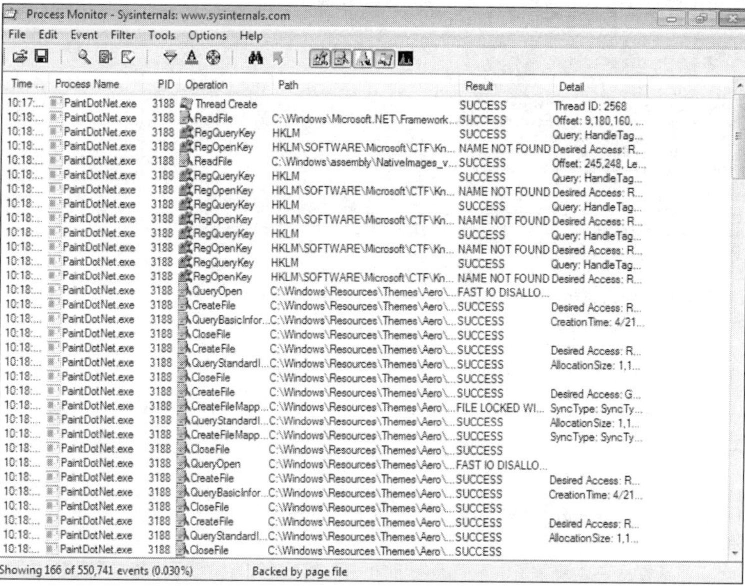

FIGURE A.7

Process Monitor can answer all sorts of questions about what a program is doing right now.

RegexBuddy

Purpose: To interactively construct and test regular expressions.

Yes, you *could* easily build a regular expression tester yourself, but the ones already out there offer some not-so-trivial features. RegexBuddy, shown in Figure A.8, is one of the best, but there are others.

Among other things, they offer menus for inserting subexpressions, explain the expressions in English (or close to it), give instant graphical feedback, provide syntax highlighting, and more.

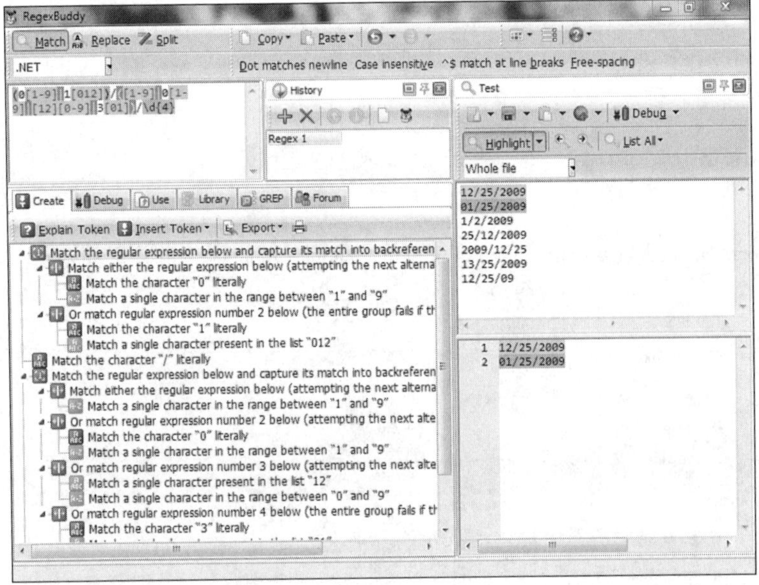

FIGURE A.8
RegexBuddy (and its many cousins) offer vast tools for analyzing and creating regular expressions.

LINQPad

Purpose: Builds queries with LINQ, primarily for LINQ to SQL.

This application is kind of like RegexBuddy for LINQ. It has a tight interface that lets you quickly test out LINQ queries against databases.

LINQPad also lets you just test out quick code snippets to see the results, without having to create dummy test project. Figure A.9 shows the tool in action against our Books database from Chapter 13, "Databases."

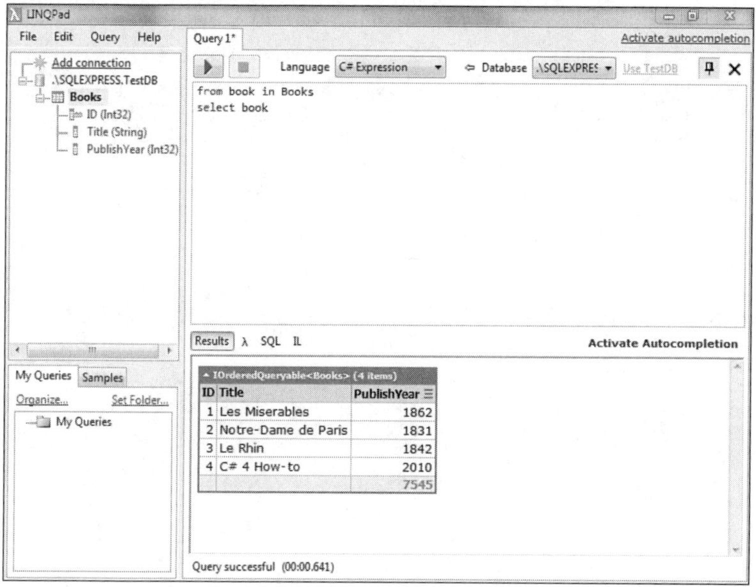

FIGURE A.9
LINQPad offers an easy way to construct and test LINQ queries against databases.

Where to Find More Tools

There are many "ultimate tool lists" on the Internet, but probably one of the most famous is Scott Hanselman's Ultimate Developer and Power Users Tool List for Windows. Updated at least every year, I encourage you to check it out at www.hanselman.com/tools.

Symbols

A

E

F

M

O

P

Q

R

S

T

X–Z

The **How-To series** publishes titles with informative "how-to" information for each of its respective topic areas. The titles focus on detailing each step necessary to accomplish a goal for a given scenario.

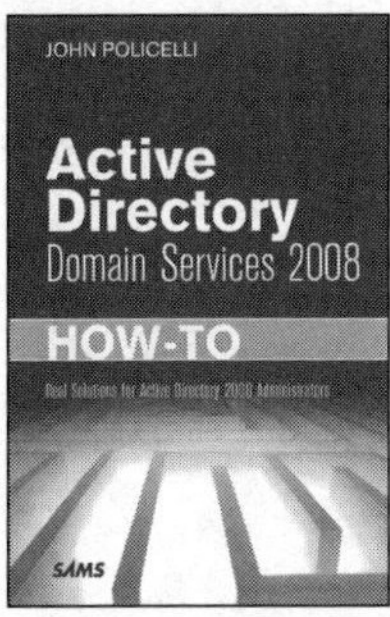

Active Directory Domain Services 2008 How-To
ISBN-13: 9780672330452

Coming Soon

Microsoft Office Communications Server 2007 R2 How-To
ISBN-13: 9780672330933

Exchange Server 2007 How-To
ISBN-13: 9780672330483

Coming Soon

Silverlight 4 How-To
ISBN-13: 9780672330629

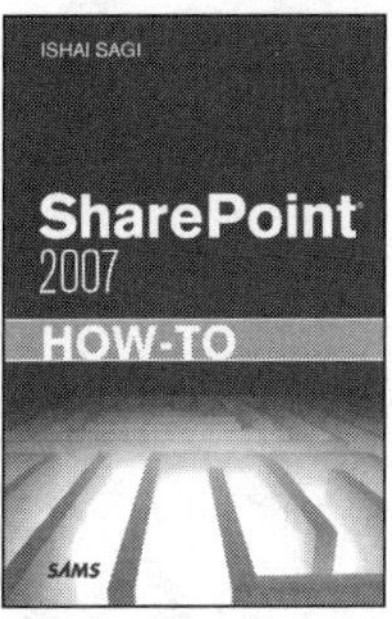

SharePoint 2007 How-To
ISBN-13: 9780672330506

Windows Server 2008 How-To
ISBN-13: 9780672330759

How-To series books are available at most retail and online bookstores. For more information or to order direct, visit our online bookstore at **informit.com/store**

Online editions of all How-To series titles are available by subscription from Safari Books Online at **safari.informit.com**